Disability Discrimination:
The Law and Practice

Declan O'Dempsey MA (Cantab), Dip Law
of the Middle Temple, Barrister

and

Andrew Short LLB (Hons) (Bristol)
of Gray's Inn, Barrister

Consulting Editor
David Ruebain
David Levene & Co, Solicitors

LAW & TAX

© Pearson Professional Limited 1996

ISBN 075200 2813

Published by
FT Law & Tax
21–27 Lamb's Conduit Street, London WC1N 3NJ

A Division of Pearson Professional Limited

Associated Offices
Australia, Belgium, Canada, Hong Kong,
India, Japan, Luxembourg,
Singapore, Spain, USA

A CIP catalogue record for this book is available from the
British Library.

Printed by Bell & Bain Ltd.
Typeset by Tradespools Ltd, Frome, Somerset

Contents

Preface

Combatting discrimination can be expensive. The Disability Discrimination Act 1995 is intended to prohibit discrimination against disabled people, but without placing an undue financial burden on the businesses and others that are subject to its provision. Setting the point at which prohibiting discrimination creates an 'undue financial burden' is a political question. All but the ignorant wish to reduce or eliminate discrimination, but how much is society willing to spend to do so? Many of the criticisms of the DDA result from a perception that the government was more diligent in seeking to limit the financial consequences of the legislation than it was in seeking to prevent discrimination. In particular, the exclusion of small employers from Pt II, the absence of an enforcement body, the delayed implementation of some of the central provisions and the power to place a financial cap upon the duties to adjust can be seen as triumphs of the desire to avoid cost over the desire to prevent discrimination. Nonetheless, the DDA has the potential to have a significant impact upon the treatment of people with disabilities in the fields of employment, transportation and the provision of goods, services and premises. In particular, in placing a duty to make reasonable adjustments upon employers, trade organisations and service providers, the DDA recognises that discrimination can result from environmental and organisational barriers that exclude disabled people from jobs and services as well as from the overt or covert prejudice of individuals.

It remains to be seen if the DDA in practice will have the successes, failures and flaws of the Americans with Disabilities Act 1990. We derived assistance from the Americans with Disabilities Act Documentation Centre (at http://janweb.icdi.wvu.edu/kinder/) and the volume and quality of materials available at that website will be of substantial assistance to those seeking to interpret, enforce and comply with the DDA. A vast number of people have assisted us in writing this book in a more traditional fashion. Our colleagues at 4 Brick Court, particularly Martin Seaward, Nick O'Brien, Mark Mullins, Susan Belgrave, Jill Brown and Rajeev Thacker, commented helpfully on drafts at various stages. David Ruebain was the consulting editor, though the width and depth of his knowledge and understanding of this field are not properly reflected in this book. Susan Marshall and Paul Crick from FT Law & Tax have been encouraging, helpful, supportive and menacing as appropriate. Further thanks go to Andrew Bano, Barbara Calvert QC, Clare Cozens,

Charlie George, Katie Ghose, Jonathan Glasson, Lord Lowry, Neil Johnson, Robert McGeachy, Mary Stacey, Susie Schofield, Charles Mullaney, Dr Mark Tanner, Toucan Employment and Frances Tomlinson have all helped at various stages and in various ways. All of the above have contributed to the production of this book, although we are entirely responsible for the views expressed and the mistakes made.

This book is dedicated to the memory of John Bedford and John Schofield.

Table of Cases

Table of Statutes

Table of Statutory Instruments

Disability Discrimination: Introduction and Institutions

> But to think the battle for full civil rights for Britain's 6.5 million disabled people is now won is like regarding Brighton Pier as a viable route to France.
> Rt Hon Alf Morris MP *The Guardian*, February 21, 1996

The Conservative government of John Major introduced the Disability Discrimination Act 1995 (DDA 1995) as a direct response to the cross party support shown for the Civil Rights (Disabled Persons) Bill which in 1994 became the 17th attempt to bring in full anti-discrimination legislation. It was introduced as a private member's Bill. The government succumbed to pressure from all parties, including government backbenchers, and the unfavourable publicity given to the government's tactics which halted the Bill's progress.

Marred by an unfortunate parliamentary history, in which government amendments were tabled late and at short notice, the DDA 1995 bears all the hallmarks of policy made on the hoof. Many of the concepts are left vague, and much of the new law is contained in regulations and codes. There are 38 regulation making powers in the Act. Practitioners will find themselves having to struggle with the resultant fudge for a few years to come. There is an interesting discussion of the 'unfortunate' parliamentary history at pp 78-80 of Cooper and Vernons, *Disability and the Law* (Jessica Kingsley Publishers, 1996).

William Hague, the then Minister for Disabled People, introduced the Bill for the government. He gave the following outline of the Bill as it stood at that time:

> Part I defines disability for the purposes of the new law. Opposition Members have implied in their reasoned amendment that we have defined the concept too narrowly. But a wider definition that stretched the concept of disability too far would lack credibility and be open to abuse. Our definition is the right one because employers and service providers will understand it and it will therefore make the Act operable.
>
> Part II concerns the employment right. The new employment right is broadly on the lines of present anti-discrimination provision for women and ethnic minorities, but with the additional requirements on employers to make reasonable adjustment to overcome any practical constraints imposed by a person's disability. The right covers all aspects of employment: when disabled people apply for work or take up employment and when people become disabled during their working lives. It will

replace the outdated and unworkable quota scheme. Like that scheme it will cover a broad range of physical and mental disabilities.

The Bill provides for codes of practice to be issued which will help employers in deciding whether an adjustment is reasonable in a particular case. They will need to take account of the cost of the adjustment and its usefulness in overcoming the practical effect of the disability . . . The new right will apply to employers with 20 or more employees . . . and include 83% of all employees. (*Hansard* 24 January 1995, Vol 253, No 36, col 148–149)

He continued:

Part III contains the access provisions. Service providers will be required to change policies, practices and procedures that make it impossible or unreasonably difficult for disabled people to make use of goods. They will also be required to provide auxilliary aids or services—such as induction loops—or remove physical barriers to help disabled people gain access to goods facilities and services. (*ibid*, col. 150)

Education and public transport are also dealt with in the Act, but these receive either a wholly cursory treatment or place the introduction of the provisions into force very far into the future.

The Minister stated that the Bill was drafted in such a way that indirect as well as direct discrimination can be dealt with (col 150). Finally, the Minister dealt with Pt IV of the Bill, which then dealt with the National Disability Council. Rejecting Opposition amendments which would have had the effect of establishing a body with similar powers to the Equal Opportunities Commission or the Council for Racial Equality, the Minister stated:

As for the much vaunted test cases [supported by the EOC], we believe that there is a better way of reviewing and keeping the law up to date without the horrific legal costs that such cases can accumulate. We recognise that the effects of the Disability Discrimination Bill, when enacted, will need to be sustained and reviewed to ensure that it is having the intended effect and that changes in society's attitude and behaviour towards disabled people need to be kept under review so that discrimination can be countered effectively, now and in the future.

That is why we need the National Disability Council. It will work closely with existing organisations representing the interests of disabled people. Its primary duties will be to advise the government on measures relating to the elimination of discrimination and the drawing up of codes of practice to help with the interpretation of the Bill.

. . . The Bill makes provision for the establishment of an advice and support service to help disabled people secure their rights and to promote the settlement of disputes arising under the right of access to goods and services. (*Hansard* col. 154)

The Bill changed significantly as it went through its parliamentary stages as a result of the concessions made by the government. Thus, for example, changes were introduced to the concepts of justification of discrimination in the employment provisions, and even during the opening speech of the second reading debate the Minister made a concession that the Bill should cover the letting of property and its sale (col 155), and provision was made for disability statements in education (see Chap 14) only after further debates in parliament.

Use of Parliamentary materials

In general, reference to parliamentary materials is not permitted as an aid to the construction of statutes, but there are exceptions to this rule. The reports of Commissions and White Papers may be used in order solely to ascertain the mischief which a provision is intended to cure (*Assam Railways & Trading Co Ltd* v *Commissioners of Inland Revenue* [1935] AC 445, at 457–8). In *R* v *Secretary of State for Transport, ex p Factortame Ltd* [1990] 2 AC 85, the House of Lords looked at a Law Commission Report for the purpose of drawing an inference as to the intention of Parliament from the fact that Parliament had not implemented one of its recommendations. The House of Lords in *Pickstone* v *Freemans plc* [1989] AC 66 departed from the general rule when construing a statutory instrument. In *Pepper* v *Hart* [1993] AC 593, the House of Lords held that the use of clear ministerial statements by the courts as a guide to the construction of ambiguous legislation would not infringe Art 8 of the Bill of Rights 1689. However reference to parliamentary materials will only be permitted where such material clearly discloses the mischief aimed at or the legislative intent behind the ambiguous or obscure words. It is unlikely that any statement other than the statement of the Minister or other promoter of a Bill would meet these criteria.

Hansard may be referred to in the following circumstances:

(1) where the legislative provision is ambiguous or obscure or leads to absurdity;

(2) where the materials which are relied upon consist of one or more statements by Ministers or other promoters of a Bill;

(3) where other parliamentary materials are needed to understand the statements of the Ministers and their effects.

Where words in a statute are capable of bearing more than one meaning, and Parliament considered what interpretation should be placed upon those words, the court should look at parliamentary materials in appropriate cases, regardless of the practical difficulties that may be created by such a practice. Where the interpretation previously given to ambiguous words by a court conflicts with that expressed by the Minister at the time of the promotion of a Bill, the Minister's interpretation should in the future prevail.

The following practice should be followed if a passage from parliamentary debates is to be referred to under the principles in *Pepper* v *Hart* [1993] AC 593, and *Pickstone* v *Freemans plc* [1989] AC 66 or otherwise (see *Practice Direction: Hansard Extracts* [1995] 1 WLR 192; [1995] 1 All ER 234). The practice direction applies to both final and interlocutory hearings. Unless the judge directs otherwise, the party that intends to refer to any extract from *Hansard*, must serve upon all parties and the court:

(a) copies of the extract; together with

(b) a brief summary of the argument intended to be based upon such report.

Service of the extract and summary of arguments must be effected, not less than five clear working days before the first day of the hearing, whether or not there is a fixed date. Service on the court is effected by sending (in the Crown Office) two copies to the Head of the Crown Office, Room C312, Royal Courts of Justice. In the county court, service is effected by sending two copies to the chief clerk of the relevant county court.

If a party fails to comply with the Practice Direction the court may make such order, relating to costs and otherwise, as was in all the circumstances appropriate. No such practice direction applies to proceedings in the Industrial Tribunals in which the employment provisions will be enforced. However the practice direction is designed to save adjournments as a result of such references, and if a party simply produces such materials in the course of argument it may be that a tribunal would grant an adjournment so that the argument could properly be considered by the other party. In such circumstances the tribunal may impose a costs sanction on the party producing the *Hansard* materials without warning.

Throughout the text references will be made by name to Lord Mackay of Ardbrecknish, Minister of State at the Department of Social Security, and William Hague MP, Minister for Social Security and Disabled People.

The National Disability Council

The DDA establishes two Disability Councils, appointed by the Secretary of State to advise him on disability issues. There is first a National Disability Council (NDC) and second a Northern Ireland Disability Council. A member of the latter sits on the former and they are charged with advising the Secretary of State on the reduction and elimination of discrimination against disabled people and the operation of the Act, with the exception of its employment provisions.

Sections 50 to 52 of the DDA establish the National Disability Council. The duty of the NDC set out in s 50(2) is to advise the Secretary of State, either on its own initiative or when asked to do so by the Secretary of State:

(a) on matters relevant to the elimination of discrimination against disabled persons and persons who have had a disability;

(b) on measures which are likely to reduce or eliminate such discrimination; and

(c) on matters related to the operation of the DDA or of provisions made under that Act.

By s 50(3) the Secretary of State may confer additional powers on the NDC but that does not include power to confer on the Council any functions with respect to the investigation of any complaint which may be the subject of proceedings under the DDA (s 50(4)).

In discharging its duties under s 50, the NDC must have, in particular, regard to the following:

(a) the extent and nature of the benefits which would be likely to result from the implementation of any recommendation which it makes; and

(b) the likely cost of implementing any such recommendation.

By s 50(6) if the NDC makes any recommendation in the discharge of any of its functions it must, if it is reasonably practicable to do so, make an assessment of the following:
  (a) the likely cost of implementing the recommendation; and
  (b) the likely financial benefits which would result from implementing it.
If the NDC proposes to give the Secretary of State advice on a matter, it must, before giving the advice, consult any body which was established by any enactment or by a Minister of the Crown for the purpose of giving advice in relation to disability, or any aspect of disability. In addition it must consult any body that has functions in relation to the matter to which the advice relates. It must also consult such other persons as it considers appropriate and have regard to any representations made to it as a result of any such consultations.

The NDC may have no fewer than ten members, and it may not have more than 20 members (Sched 5, paras 3(1) and (3)). By Sched 5, para 5 the members must either have knowledge or experience of the needs of disabled persons, or of a particular group of disabled persons. Alternatively members may be persons who have been disabled, or be members of professional bodies or bodies representing business interests or industry. The Secretary of State has a duty to attempt to secure that at least half of the members of the NDC are either disabled persons or persons who have had a disability or the parents or guardians of a person with a disability (Sched 5, para 7). At least 60 per cent of the current NDC are reported to satisfy that condition. The term of office of a member is five years (Sched 5, para 4).

The power conferred on the Council to give advice on its own initiative does not include power to give advice in respect of any matter which relates to the operation of any provision of or arrangements made under one of the following Acts:
  (a) the Disabled Persons (Employment) Acts 1944 and 1958;
  (b) the Employment and Training Act 1973;
  (c) the Employment Rights Act 1996; or
  (d) s 2(3) of the Enterprise and New Towns (Scotland) Act 1990.
Further it may not give advice as a result of its duty to give advice on matters related to the operation of the DDA in respect of any matter arising under the employment provisions, or in relation to codes of practice under ss 53 and 54, or in relation to s 56 (help for persons suffering discrimination) or s 61 (which relates to the Secretary of State's power to make arrangements for the provision of supported employment under s 15 of the Disabled Persons (Employment) Act 1944). However, when there is no national advisory council established under s 17(1)(a) of the Disabled Persons (Employment) Act 1944 or a person appointed to act generally under s 60(1) of the DDA, the NDC may give advice in relation to these matters.

The National Advisory Council on the Employment of People with Disabilities (NACEPD) will continue to advise the Secretary for Education and Employment on employment issues. However there is a power in s 56(10) for the Secretary of State to abolish the NACEPD, which may in future be exercised.

The NDC is responsible for preparing Codes of Practice on the new rights of access to goods, facilities, services and premises and is required to produce an annual report which is laid before Parliament. In the first year of its establishment it set itself three tasks:

(1) proposals for a Code of Practice on the rights of access to goods, facilities, services and premises. Once established the NDC will monitor the effectiveness of these codes;

(2) giving advice to the government on the implementation of the Act (in particular on the rights of access to goods, facilities, services and premises, and on setting up the mechanisms to monitor the operation of the DDA); and

(3) working with disability organisations, and public and private service providers to identify practical ways in which discrimination against disabled people can be removed and advising the government accordingly.

The National Disability Council Regulations 1996 (SI No 11) came into force on 29 January 1996 and make provision for membership of the NDC. The regulations are made under powers conferred by s 67 and s 68 of, and paras 4(4) and 7 of Sched 5 to, the DDA. Regulation 2 provides for the circumstances in which the Secretary of State may remove a member of the Council from office. These are:

(a) that he has, throughout a continuous period of six months ending not earlier than three months before the date on which the removal takes effect, failed, without the consent of the NDC, to attend meetings of the NDC;

(b) that he is an undischarged bankrupt or is otherwise unable to pay his debts; and

(c) that he is incapable of discharging the functions of his office or has been guilty of misbehaviour.

The Secretary of State may, with the approval of the Treasury, pay expenses of the Council which he is satisfied were reasonably incurred (reg 3). The regulations setting up the NDC in Northern Ireland are the Disabled Persons (SI Rules of Northern Ireland 1996 No 13)

Provision is made for the NDC to receive expert advice, have research commissioned, and to appoint advisers by The National Disability Council (No 2) Regulations 1996 (SI No 1410) made under s 50(8), 67(3) and 68(1) of, and para 7 of Sched 5 to, the DDA. By reg 2 the Secretary of State may, at the request of the NDC, commission research to be undertaken on the NDC's behalf to assist it in the fulfilment of its statutory duties. The NDC may appoint a person to act as an adviser to it if the Secretary of State is satisfied that:

(a) the person to be appointed has a specialist skill or knowledge which is neccessary to assist the NDC in the fulfilment of its statutory duties;

(b) none of the members of the NDC has the specialist skill or knowledge in question; and

(c) it is not part of the function of the members of the NDC to provide the advice which the NDC requires from the person to be appointed, and the advice is not required to be provided to the NDC under any of the provisions of Sched 5 of the Act.

In addition the following conditions must be fulfilled to the Secretary of State's satisfaction:

(a) save in exceptional circumstances where a longer period of appointment is necessary, the appointment is not to exceed 12 months; and

(b) the appointment is made in accordance with procedures agreed between the NDC and the Secretary of State.

EU legislation

The United Kingdom is a signatory to the Treaty of Rome which established the European Economic Communities. Section 2 of the European Communities Act 1972 provides that European Community law is part of domestic law. EU law takes precedence over domestic law where there is a conflict between them (European Communities Act 1972, s 2 and *Van Duyn* v *Home Office (No 2)* [1975] 3 All ER 190). The Treaty of Economic Union (TEU), signed at Maastricht, created the European Union which covers social as well as economic matters. The Member States have committed themselves to co-operation in the fields of justice and home affairs. There is no provision under the Treaty which relates specifically to equality of treatment for disabled persons. However where there is a Treaty provision which has application and which is sufficiently clear and precise it may found an individual right which may be maintained against other individuals. In addition there are regulations which are binding in their entirety on Member States and take precedence over all domestic law. These are directly applicable and also permit an individual to rely upon them in domestic courts. By contrast Directives, such as the Workplace Directive, are expressed in terms of policy aims and leave the Member State with a discretion as to how the objective is to be implemented into domestic law. Nevertheless, where the directive is unambiguous, an individual can rely upon it in a domestic court against the state or an emanation of the state, and may, in appropriate cases, obtain damages against a Member State for a failure to implement its provisions (*Francovitch* v *Italian Republic* [1995] ICR 722). Decisions are issued by the Council or Commission, and are fully binding on the specific legal entities, either individuals or corporations, as well as Member States to which they are addressed. They do not found general rights. The Council may also make recommendations. Recommendations do not have binding force. The Court of Justice, in *Grimaldi* v *Fonds des Maladies Professionelles* [1990] IRLR 400, recognised that recommendations do not confer directly enforceable rights upon individuals (see Art 189(5) of the Treaty). The court nevertheless held that recommendations are to be taken into account by domestic courts. Recommendations should, it should be stated, be taken into account in order to clarify provisions of national or EC law.

One such recommendation is the EC Recommendations on the Employment of Disabled Persons adopted by the EC Council. Recommendation 86/376 is addressed to the Member States. It obliges the Member States to take all appropriate measures 'to promote fair opportunities for disabled people in the field of employment and vocational training' in respect of access to employment and training, retention in employment or training, protection from unfair dismissal, and opportunities for promotion and in-service training. They are to take steps to eliminate negative discrimination and to provide for positive action. Although the DDA was not a provision of national law implementing a specific provision of community law, it must be assumed to be consistent with the obligations of the UK under EU law. It may be that in a case of obscurity in the provisions of the DDA the recommendation could be referred to in order to indicate the true interpretation of the provision.

Article 26 of the Charter of the Fundamental Social Rights of Workers sets out the principle that disabled persons are to have access to additional concrete measures aimed at improving their social and professional intergration. Particular attention is to be paid to vocational training, ergonomics, accessibility and mobility. These rights will be the subject of further directives.

The legislative context

It is unnecessary for the practitioner to know the full details of anti-discrimination measures before the DDA. In the main, provision for the rights of disabled persons proceeded by way of special provision for disabled persons rather than a prohibition on discrimination against them. However, in outline, before the DDA's introduction there were statutory and non-statutory provisions, particularly in relation to employment. Legislation made provision for special assistance to be given to disabled persons in the fields of income benefits, housing adaptations, parking, and under the criminal law. The legislative context of the rights under the DDA is set out below. Many services are provided in connection with these rights, and these will be affected by the provisions relating to goods and services (see Part 3).

Local Authorities

Local authorities are the largest group of service providers having pre-existing statutory duties. In the context of these rights, in certain situations, the duty on a local authority service provider may be higher than that on a non-local governmental service provider. Rights for disabled persons were created under the National Assistance Act 1948, the Health Service and Public Health Act 1968, the National Health Service Act 1977, the Mental Health Act 1983, the Disabled Persons (Services, Consultation and Representation) Act 1986, the Children Act 1989, the National Health Service and Community Care Act

1990, and the Carers (Recognition and Services) Act 1995. Duties were given to Housing Authorities in respect of disabled persons under s 3 of the Chronically Sick and Disabled Persons Act 1970. Under the Local Authority (Miscellaneous Provisions) Act 1976 provision was made for sanitary appliances at places of entertainment.

Under s 1 of the Chronically Sick and Disabled Persons Act 1970 (CSDPA) the authority has a duty to inform itself of the number of disabled persons living in its area. The definition of disabled person used in this provision is 'suffering with a permanent and substantial handicap'. Clearly the duties owed by a local authority in respect of disabled persons under the DDA will be owed to a wider group whose impairments would not qualify them for assistance under this Act. A person may apply to be registered with the local authority as a disabled person in this narrow sense and his need of any of the following services will then be assessed by it: home help; the provision of a television or radio or help using the library or of a telephone together with special equipment to operate it; assistance to attend educational, sporting and other facilities; home adaptations (access), and equipment designed to achieve increased security, safety, comfort or convenience for the disabled person living there (see 29 of the National Assistance Act 1948, CSDPA 1970, s 2 and Sched 8, para 3(1) of the NHS Act 1977; and for further services see s 21 of and Sched 8 to the NHS Act 1977).

Once satisfied that the person has a need for one of these services which is not being met, the authority must inform the disabled person of any welfare services provided by it capable of meeting that need. It must inform the disabled person of all relevant welfare services of which it has knowledge and from which the disabled person may benefit (Disabled Persons (Services, Consultation and Representation) Act 1986, s 9). It must make arrangements for the service to be provided if necessary through an agency or otherwise indirectly (such as by assisting the disabled person to make an application for a relevant grant). Whether something is a need may be determined in the light of the resources of the authority, and it may levy a reasonable charge having regard to the ability of the disabled person to make any payment.

Information must be obtained from any person giving a substantial degree of care to the disabled person who is living at home. His willingness to continue in this role should be ascertained in order to take account of it in assessing future needs (see the Disabled Persons (Services, Consultation and Representation) Act 1986, s 8) The authority may be ordered to assess the disabled person's needs for these services as there is a duty to do so under ss 3 and 4 of the Disabled Persons (Services, Consultation and Representation) Act 1986.

Local authorities also have duties under the National Health Service and Community Care Act 1990. The full details of these duties are outside the scope of this work, but many of the services to be supplied by a local authority will be affected by the goods, services and facilities provisions under the DDA. The existence of the 1990 Act duties arguably also effects the scope of the defence open to a local authority in terms of its knowledge of financial and other sources of help in considering whether to make an adjustment to a policy or practice. The authority must produce a plan which it must publish relating to community care services provided directly (or purchased by it from another body—(the majority) in its area. The services covered are defined in s 46(3) of the National Health Service and Community Care Act 1990. The local authority may, during its assessment of the person's need for services, ask the District Health Authority or the local Housing Authority to participate in the assessment and to assist in meeting any needs which are established by the assessment (NHSCA 1990, s 47(3)).

Children
The Children Act 1989 imposes duties on local authorities in relation to 'disabled children' who are defined as a child who is 'blind, deaf or suffers from mental disorder of any kind or is substantially and permanently handicapped by illness, injury or deformity or such other disability as may be prescribed' (s 17(11)). The duties are set out in ss 17(5), 18, 20, 23, and 24. The local authority must provide services constructed to minimise the effect of the disability on the disabled child in addition to the services listed above.

Non-local authority goods, services and motor transport

Before the introduction of the DDA there was already some specific legislation dealing with the rights of disabled persons in respect of facilities, goods and services. The Chronically Sick and Disabled Persons Act 1970 made provision for sanitary conveniences both public (s 5) and at various premises open to the public (s 6), for signs at buildings (s 7), and access to and facilities at offices and other premises (s 8). The Trading Representations (Disabled Persons) Act 1958 made provision for the registration of sellers of goods which are advertised as made by or sold for the benefit of blind or otherwise disabled persons. Under the Highways Act 1980, s 175A there is a duty to have regard to the needs of disabled and blind persons in executing works.

There were various provisions in relation to transport. The Chronically Sick and Disabled Persons Act 1970 made provision for the use of badges on motor cars used by disabled persons (s 21), and invalid carriages (eg 20). Similarly the Transport Act 1982 made provision in relation to the refusal or withdrawal of a disabled person's badge (s 68).

Housing

The duties of local authorities in respect of adaptations to the home of a disabled person have been referred to already (see p xxxvii). Consideration could be given to the guidance in Appendix 1 of the (now obsolete) DoE Circular 59/78 as to alterations which might benefit a disabled person. Assistance for disabled persons in relation to their homes may be obtained from the local authority by means of a Disabled Facilities Grant (see Local

Government and Housing Act 1989, Pt VIII). The maximum grant is £20,000. In addition the disabled person may be entitled to Home Repair Assistance in respect of minor repairs.

A disabled person will also fall into a priority need category for the purposes of s 59 of the Housing Act 1985, dealing with the housing of homeless persons. Such persons are vulnerable (see Code of Guidance to the 1985 Act, para 2.12(c)).

Education

Section 41 of the 1944 Education Act made provision for the functions of local education authorities in respect of further education including that of disabled persons. The Chronically Sick and Disabled Persons Act 1970 made provision for access to and facilities at university and school buildings (s 8). Under the Disabled Persons (Services, Consultation and Representation) Act 1986, ss 5 and 6 duties are placed on local authorities to assess a disabled person who is leaving school. For the effect of the DDA see Chap 14.

Employment

DDA 1995: Advisers

Under s 60 of the DDA the Secretary of State may appoint such persons as he thinks fit to advise or assist him in connection with matters relating to the employment (or self-employment) of disabled persons who have had a disability (s 60(1) and (5)). Such persons may be appointed by the Secretary of State to act generally or in relation to a particular area or locality (s 60(2)). The Secretary of State may (with Treasury approval) pay to any person so appointed allowances and compensation for loss of earnings.

Section 17 of, and Sched 2 to, the Disabled Persons (Employment) Act 1944 make provision for national advisory council and district advisory committees. By order the Secretary of State may repeal s 17 of the 1944 Act or provide for its provision to cease to have effect so far as it concerns either the council or the committees. However before such an order repeals s 17, it shall have effect so as to reflect the definition of disabled person for the purposes of the DDA (see p 3). This includes disabled persons currently having a disability, and those who had a disability in the past. Until such an order is made the definition of 'disabled person' in s 16 of the Chronically Sick and Disabled Persons Act 1970 (which extends the functions of the national advisory council) will be read as if it were the same as under the DDA.

Local Authorities

Section 7 of the Local Government and Housing Act 1989 requires that every appointment of a person to a paid office or employment by a local authority or parish or community must be on merit. This prevents a local authority recruiting only disabled persons to advertised vacancies. Merit may be ignored as an appointment criterion only in respect of registered disabled persons (under the 1944 Act) so long as the employer remains below the statutory quota. However with the introduction of the DDA a requirement of merit will apply to all appointments.

Employment before the DDA

Before the DDA under the Disabled Persons (Employment) Act 1944 disabled persons (as defined under that Act) could register as disabled. The Department of Employment maintained a register of disabled persons under s 6 of the 1944 Act. A disabled person could apply at a jobcentre to be entered upon the register. However his disability had to be likely to last for at least 12 months (s 7(2)) and he had to have attained school leaving age, and want to engage in remunerative work. He also was required to have a reasonable prospect of obtaining and keeping work. A registered disabled person was issued with a certificate of registration, known as a 'green card', which an employer or prospective employer, who was subject to the 1944 Act, could demand to see.

The Disabled Persons (Registration) Regulations 1945 (SR&O No 938, as amended by the Disabled Persons (Registration) (Amendment) Regulations 1946 (SR&O No 262) and the Disabled Persons (Registration) (Amendment) Regulations (1959) (SI No 1510) provided for persons to be disqualified from the register. A refusal without reasonable cause to attend or to complete vocational training, if so required by the Department of Employment, can result in the disabled person being removed from the register. A persistent refusal without reasonable cause to undertake suitable work could also result in removal from the register.

The register was divided into two parts. It may be that in future under the employment provisions of the DDA, which part a person was registered under will make a difference to the way in which treatment of him may be justified. The first part of the register was of those capable of non-sheltered employment. The second part was of those only suitable for sheltered employment. A person would be eligible for sheltered employment if he could do a job, but was very slow at it. Under the Sheltered Placement Scheme an employer would employ such a person, and be subsidised by the Employment Service for employing him even though productivity was lost.

Those employing more than 20 had to employ a quota (3 per cent of the workforce (Disabled Persons (Standard Percentage) Order 1946 (SR&O No 1258)) of registered disabled persons unless the employer obtained a permit of exemption. This was normally readily granted, and although being below quota was a criminal offence it was not enforced. The quota percentage could be lowered for up to a year on an application of an employer whose particular circumstances suggested that 3 per cent is too great (see the Disabled Persons (General) Regulations 1945). Records of registered disabled persons employed had to be kept. The 1944 Act designated certain occupations as reserved for registered disabled persons (s 12(1)). These were supposed to afford specially suitable opportunities for disabled employment. The Disabled Persons (Designated Employments) Order 1946 (SR&O No 1257) identified employment as a passenger electric lift attendant and as a car park attendant as designated employments.

There was a special percentage of 0.1 per cent in respect of employment in the capacity of master or crew member of a British ship (Disabled Persons (Special Percentage) (No 1) Order 1946 (SR&O No 236)).

Employment: company duties

Where the average weekly size of the workforce during the previous year has exceeded 250 persons, the directors of a registered company must provide a directors' report for each financial year, by virtue of s 234 of the Companies Act 1985 (as substituted). The report (together with the accounts and the auditors' report) is sent to the shareholders and debenture holders, is laid before the shareholders in general meeting and delivered to the Registrar of Companies (although a private company may elect to dispense with the laying of accounts and reports in general meeting). The directors' report must disclose, among other things, information concerning the employment, training and advancement of disabled persons (as defined by the 1944 Act). Such disclosure need be made only where the average number of employees employed by the company within the UK in each week of the financial year exceeds 250 (CA 1985, Sched 9). A failure to comply with this requirement is a criminal offence and any director of the company at the relevant time may be liable to a fine (CA 1985, s 234(5)). It is a defence, however, to show that all reasonable steps were taken to comply with the requirement (CA 1985, s 234(6)).

The statement in the directors' report must describe the policy that has been employed to give full and fair consideration to applications for employment made to the company by disabled persons. Regard must be had to their aptitudes and abilities (CA 1985, Sched 9).

The company's practice in continuing the employment of, and for arranging appropriate training for, employees who have become disabled during the period of their employment with the company must be outlined. This applies as much to disabilities whose causation is unrelated to employment as to work-related disabilities. Information must also be given about company policy on the training, career development and promotion of disabled employees in the company.

Dismissal of a disabled person before the DDA 1995

Section 9(5) of the 1944 Act permitted the dismissal of registered disabled persons. However, covered employers could not dismiss a registered disabled person without reasonable cause if, as a result of that dismissal, the number of registered disabled persons employed by them would be less than the specified quota. The dismissal was legally valid (s 13(5)), but the dismissal was a criminal offence (s 9(6) and (7)).

Non-statutory measures and sources of assistance

There is a voluntary *Code of Good Practice on the Employment of Disabled People* issued by the Department of Employment which set out 'best practice' for employing disabled employees. Placing, Assessment and Counselling Teams (PACTs) now issue this Code. The Code of Good Practice gives employers guidance concerning recruitment and selection of disabled employees (paras 5.1–5.21). Emphasis is placed upon good job descriptions and job requirements, methods of recruitment, selection procedures, interviewing and health screening. Reference may be made when considering drafting a questionnaire or replying to one under the enforcement provisions. In addition a number of statutory and extra-statutory schemes and measures existed in this area.

Sheltered employment

Facilities to enable registered disabled persons with severe disabilities, who are unable to obtain employment in the open labour market or to compete on comparable terms with able-bodied persons, to be trained and to work or be employed under special conditions were provided under s 15 of the 1944 Act.

PACTs and ADCs

Placing, Assessment and Counselling Teams are local teams of people who have experience or skill in maintaining disabled persons in work. ADCs are regional Ability Development Centres. They are available to evolve new techniques for providing employment for disabled persons. Until they are abolished the PACTs will maintain the Register of Disabled Persons. They work with disabled persons on vocational training and rehabilitation. They issue the Code of Good Practice referred to above and encourage good practice by the award of the disability symbol to employers wishing to demonstrate that they have taken proactive measures to facilitate disabled persons' employment. PACTs subsumed the work of the Disablement Advisory Service.

Access to work

The Access to Work Scheme assists disabled persons with the practical difficulties they may encounter in seeking work. The scheme can assist with payment for communications (persons or equipment) for hearing impaired or deaf persons. This can include the use of a communicator at interview, part time readers or assistance at work for visually impaired or blind persons, practical help for persons to get to work or help at work including support workers, and adaptations of existing equipment or the provision of new equipment for the disabled person's needs. Equipment may be loaned to the employer, and alterations to premises or the working enviroment may be made to enable the disabled person to work in the environment. This includes grant aid to assist in adapting premises, and help with transport costs.

The above list simply gives examples. If some other form of practical or personal help could make it possible for a disabled person to do a job effectively it may be possible for the Access to Work Scheme to assist and from 1 June 1996 80 per cent of approved costs are available to persons who are unemployed and disabled. From 1 June 1996 the Scheme also meets up to 80 per cent of the approved costs of all other approved assistance. In addition 100 per cent of approved costs which are in excess of £10,000 over three years may be paid. There is a threshold of £300 per year below which support is not available. Funding may be approved for three years or less. At the end of that period any renewed application will be considered in the light of the rules then applicable.

The concept of 'approved costs' needs some explanation. These are costs of alterations, travel, or equipment which are agreed between the employer and the Employment Service (ES). There is internal guidance for PACTs on approved costs, and this is normally available on request. However advisers should be aware that whether a cost is approved will be a matter for negotiation between the employment service and the employer. Thus if the ES agrees to fund part of the cost of installing electric sliding doors in a shop so that disabled person may work there (the approved assistance), the shop's other customers will benefit from this installation. In such circumstances it may be that the ES would only approve funding for half the cost, and suggest that the benefit to the business warrants the employer paying the other half. Similarly the quality of an improvement may be taken into account. Thus if a disabled person specified the highest specification of a piece of equipment the ES might only agree to fund equipment of an adequate specification. Clearly the internal policy guidance of PACT' may be taken into account to determine whether a decision on a particular request for funding is rational or not. Decisions of PACTs may in theory be open to judicial review. However, as the scheme is essentially discretionary, the number of cases in which the decision not to fund an alteration is sufficiently irrational will be limited.

The Job Introduction Scheme, Special Aids to Employment Scheme, Adaptations to Premises and Equipment Scheme, Assistance with Fares to Work Scheme, Personal Reader Service Scheme, and Business on Own Account Scheme provided financial or practical help and encourage employers to make reasonable arrangements for accommodating disabled workers. Most of these have now been subsumed in the Access to Work Scheme. The Employment Service may make a grant under the Job Introduction Scheme to an employer partially covering the cost of employing a disabled person so that the disabled person may demonstrate his capabilities to the new employer. If the position is expected to last more than six months after the trial period, during the trial period of six weeks the employer may reclaim the money he pays to the employee for travel, lunch and expenses.

The Major Organisations Development Unit also provides large employers with advice on good practice in relation to the employment of disabled persons. In addition the Employers' Forum on Disability may provide the employer with advice on the employment of a disabled person and the adjustments that may need to be made. Some of its guidance leaflets are also relevant to the provisions on goods and services (see eg *Welcoming Disabled Customers*).

The availability of such advice is significant in determining whether an employer who has failed to make an adjustment can justify his failure.

Records

Section 14 of the 1944 Act and the Disabled Persons (General) Regulations 1945 required employers to maintain certain employment records which had to be kept for two years from the date to which they relate, and were open to inspection by the Department of Employment. There were criminal sanctions for failure to observe the requirements of record keeping. The records thus generated will be discoverable documents within an application under the DDA. Such documentation may go to demonstrate the employer's commitment or lack of it to the employment of (registered) disabled persons.
The records must show the following:
  (a) the total number of employees, and their names;
  (b) the names of those employees employed for not more than 30 hours per week (distinguishing those who are employed for less than 10 hours);
  (c) the date of engagement of every employee;
  (d) the date of termination of employment of any employee;
  (e) the number, and names, of registered disabled persons employed;
  (f) the names of persons employed in employment where a special percentage quota applies;
  (g) the name of every reinstated employee and of every person employed under a permit;
  (h) the name, and date of engagement, of every person employed in a designated employment (identifying separately such employees who are registered disabled persons, reinstated persons or employed under a permit); and
  (i) the date on which any existing employee has been moved to designated employment.

Repeals of earlier legislation

The DDA 1995 repeals the statutory disabled workers' quota scheme and the reserved occupations of the Disabled Persons (Employment) Acts 1944 and 1958. Section 61(7) of the DDA repeals the duty of employers employing 20 or more employees to maintain a statutory 3 per cent quota of registered disabled persons. The designated employment scheme is also abolished. The Disabled Persons (Employment) Acts 1944 definition of 'disabled person' and the register of disabled persons will disappear as the relevant provisions of the DP(E)A 1944 is repealed (DDA 1995, s 61(7)).

Criticisms of the DDA

The most hotly contested issues in the parliamentary debates were the role of the NDC and the exemption offered to employers to employ fewer than 20 people. Although the details of these debates are of little interest to the practitioner, both the role of the NDC and the small employer's exemption run counter to the spirit of the Act in its final form. For example, discrimination against a disabled employee may be justified (among other grounds) on the financial and organisational disruption that a proposed adjustment would give rise to. The smaller the employer the easier it is likely to be justify discrimination. There would seem therefore to be no justification for excluding employers employing less than a particular number. The National Disability Council can merely advise the Minister. In the Minister's words during the opening speech, the government was 'trying to frame our legislation in such a way as to require people to do things differently and also to change attitudes in the country without creating a backlash against the objectives that we are trying to secure.' (col 155). It is difficult to see how this is to be achieved if the only effective enforcement available is by individual actions rather than test cases which at least have been through the vetting procedures adopted by both the EOC and CRE for cases given their support. Without such a body a disproportionate burden of enforcement will fall to trades unions (in the case of employment rights) and organisations of and for disabled persons (in those and cases of other rights).

Leading organisations for and of disabled persons have levelled many criticisms at the DDA. Chief among these were the following. The definition of disability used is based on a medical model rather than a social model. Further a person will not be able to claim redress where he is perceived to be disabled but is not actually disabled. The international rules relating to equal opportunities for disabled persons, the United Nations Standard Rules on the Equalisation of Opportunities for Persons with Disabilities (Gen Ass Res 48/96 of December 1993) (The UN Standard Rules) contemplates the use of a social model in legislation to be introduced in its wake. A social model of disability signifies the intimate link between 'the limitation experienced by individuals with disabilities, the design and structure of their enviroments and the attitude of the general population' (Introduction, para 5). Rather than rendering discrimination unlawful, unless it is unreasonable not to discriminate, the DDA introduces categories in which it is lawful to discriminate against disabled persons. Thus it can be said that the DDA regulates discrimination rather than preventing it.

Employers employing fewer than 20 employees may discriminate in relation to employment in a way which would be unjustifiable in all other respects. Blatant and abusive discrimination could not be remedied, contrary to the preamble to r 7 of the UN Standard Rules. Similarly private clubs and societies may unjustifiably discriminate against prospective members and members. Equal access to education is not provided for. Education is excluded from the part of the Act dealing with of the Act. The DDA does not require schools to have clear signs and it does not require lecturers to provide lecture notes in an accessible format. The requirements of reasonable adjustment are not comprehensive, allowing many forms of discrimination to continue.

Buildings will not be required to be fully accessible until the year 2005. Providers of goods and services have to change policies and procedures by 1998. However they are only required to provide auxiliary aids and services by the year 2000. Finally service providers will have to remove 'physical barriers' by 2005. It is likely that this will simply defer any attempt to comply with these provisions, rather than permitting service providers to incorporate the adjustments in advance of these dates. Groups of disabled persons are not specifically recognised for the purposes of representation or consultation in the DDA (cf United Nations Standard Rules, r 18). Stations are covered by Pt III and the duty to make reasonable adjustments. However vehicles are, for the most part, excluded (see Part 4).

International Context

Whilst it should be noted that the international instruments mentioned below do not form part of UK law they represent international standards and norms which may assist in cases where the intent of a piece of legislation is to be considered, and the national legislation is not clear. Where the legislation is clear it prevails even if inconsistent with the international convention (*Brind* v *Secretary of State for the Home Department* [1991] AC 696). The one exception to this principle is certain principles of EU law which prevail over national provisions. However in the area of disability there is (at the moment) little material which will be of use to the practitioner. Groundwork for the rights of disabled persons may be found in the following Treaties and Declarations:

- The International Covenant on Economic Social and Cultural Rights;
- The international Convention on Civil and Political Rights, in particular Art 26;
- Art 11(c) of the Declaration on Social Progress and Development;
- Declaration of the Rights of Mentally Retarded Persons; and
- Declaration on the Rights of Disabled Persons.

The last of these affirms the right of respect for the disabled person's human dignity, defined as the right to enjoy a decent life as normal and as full as possible. Under the Declaration disabled persons are to have the right to secure and maintain, according to their capabilities, employment or to engage in useful productive and remunerative occupation and to join trade unions. No disabled person is to be subjected as far as his residence is concerned to differential treatment other than that required by his condition or by the improvement that his condition may derive therefrom. Most significantly the DDA should be seen in the context of the declaration that disabled persons are to be protected from all exploitation, all regulations and all treatment that are of a discriminatory abusive, or degrading nature.

The United Nations' Commission for Social Development has the job of monitoring the UN Standard Rules on the Equalisation of Opportunities for Persons with Disabilities (see above). The rules identify the following target areas for equal participation by disabled persons in society:

(1) Accessibility: programmes of action to make the physical environment and information accessible should be undertaken (r 5);

(2) Education: there should be equal primary, secondary and tertiary educational opportunities as an integral part of the education system (r 6);

(3) Employment: persons with disabilities must be empowered to exercise their human rights particularly in the field of employment. Both in rural and urban areas they must have equal opportunities for productive and gainful occupation in the labour market;

(4) Culture (r 10); and

(5) Recreation and Sports (r 11).

In addition the International Labour Organisation has agreed Convention 142 Concerning Vocational Guidance and Vocational Training in the Development of Human Resources (1975). Open, flexible and complementary systems of vocational education, training and guidance must be introduced (Art 2).

The European Convention on Human Rights requires that the rights enjoyed under it are to be enjoyed without discrimination of any kind. Thus the right to fair administration of justice must be observed with due regard to the prevention of discrimination. Similarly the right to freedom from degrading treatment must be enjoyed without such discrimination. Where a person has exhausted his remedies under a national legal system, and he considers that one of his rights under the ECHR has been violated he may apply to the European Commission on Human Rights. Should that Commission rule the complaint admissible, the European Court of Human Rights will consider it.

List of abbreviations

ACAS	Advisory, Conciliation and Arbitration Service
ADA	Americans With Disabilities Act 1990
CRE	Commission for Racial Equality
CCR	County Court Rules 1981
DDA	Disability Discrimination Act 1995
DP(E)A	Disabled Persons (Employment) Act 1944
EA	Education Act 1996
EOC	Equal Opportunities Commission
FHEA	Further and Higher Education Act 1992
LEA	Local Education Authority
LTA	Landlord and Tenant Acts
MHA	Mental Health Act 1983
NDC	National Disability Council
PACTs	Placement Assessment and Counselling Teams
PSV	Public service vehicle
RRA	Race Relations Act 1976
RSC	Rules of the Supreme Court 1965
SDA	Sex Discrimination Act 1975
DD(C No 3) Order	Disability Discrimination (Commencement No 3 and Savings and Transitional Provisions) Order 1996
DD(E) Regs	Disability Discrimination (Employment) Regs 1996
DD(MoD) Regs	Disability Discrimination (Meaning of Disability) Regs 1996
DD(SP) Regs	Disability Discrimination (Services and Premises) Regs 1996
DD(SS) Regs	Disability Discrimination (Sub-leases and Sub-tenancies) Regs 1996

Further information

Promoters of the Disability Discrimination Act 1995 in Parliament

James Paice, Parliamentary Under Secretary of State for Employment
William Hague, Minister of State (Minister for Social Security and Disabled People)
Lord Mackay of Ardbrecknish, Minister of State, the Department of Social Security
Lord Henly, Minister of State, the Department of Education and Employment
Lord Inglewood, government spokesperson on Education and Employment (promoted DDA at certain stages)

Various disability resource sites

1 DisabilityNet
www.globalnet.co.uk/~pmatthews/DisabilityNet/DisabilityInfo.html
http://www.globalnet.co.uk/~pmatthews/DisabilityNet/index.html

2 Sites sorted by disability
http://www.indie.ca/et/21.htm

3 UK Online Disability service
http://www.odis.org.uk/

4 RNIB
http://www.rnib.org.uk/

5 Deaf Education Database
http://call-centre.cogsci.ed.c.uk/SSC/DEDbPages/2/DEDb2857

6 Deaf–Blind resources
http:/www.deafworldweb.org/dww/int/uk/deafblind.html

7 Disability resources
http:/www.disability.com/cool.html

8   National Disability Council
http:/www.open.gov.uk/ndc/ndchome.html

9   Americans with Disabilities Act Document Centre
http://janweb.icdi.wvu.edu/kinder/

Part 1

Disability

Chapter 1

The Concept of Disability

Introduction

The Disability Discrimination Act 1995 (DDA) only prohibits discrimination against some of those who are (or in some cases were) disabled persons. It does not prevent discrimination against non-disabled persons or in favour of disabled persons. Anyone seeking to rely upon the DDA must first show that they come within the DDA's definition of 'disabled person'. The only exception is for the anti victimisation provisions in s 55 (see p 251 below).

The primary definition and associated provisions

The DDA defines disability as follows:

1(1) Subject to the provisions of Schedule 1, a person has a disability for the purposes of this Act if he has a physical or mental impairment which has a substantial and long-term adverse effect on his ability to carry out normal day-to-day activities.

(2) In this Act 'disabled person' means a person who has a disability. These concepts of disability and disabled person are central to the DDA. The government intended the provisions to be interpreted widely so as to include everyone who is generally regarded as disabled. The primary definitions of s 1 are supplemented by the provisions of Sched 1 and by the Disability Discrimination (Meaning of Disability) Regulations 1996 (SI No 1455) (DDMOD Regs). Furthermore, the Secretary of State has issued Ministerial Guidance under s 3 of the DDA to provide practical advice as to whether or not an impairment has a substantial and long term effect upon a person's ability to carry out normal day-to-day activities. A tribunal or court faced with these issues must take into account any of the guidance which appears to it to be relevant.

Part II (employment) and Pt III (goods, facilities, services and premises) of the DDA also apply to a person who had, but no longer has, a disability (s 2 and Sched 2, discussed at p 22 below). Finally, there are transitional provisions which deem *some* of those registered as disabled under the *Disabled Persons (Employment) Act 1944* to be disabled persons (Sched 1, para 7, and see p 23 below).

3

The primary definition can be broken down into the following elements which will be considered in turn. There must be

(1) a physical or mental impairment;
(2) which has an adverse effect upon a person's ability to carry out normal day-to-day activities;
(3) the effect must be substantial; and
(4) the effect must be long term.

Physical or mental impairment

Impairment

The DDA does not provide a definition of 'impairment', although Sched 1, para 1(2) enables regulations to be made prescribing conditions that are or are not to be treated as amounting to impairments (see pp 9 and 10). The concept is best viewed as a clinical one, in accordance with the medical model of disability adopted in the legislation. What must be considered is the physical, mental and psychological state of the individual in comparison with a hypothetical norm. Some assistance may be taken from the World Health Organisation (WHO) definition of 'impairment' as:

> any loss or abnormality of psychological, physiological or anatomical structure or function. *International Classification of Impairments, Disabilities and Handicaps: A Manual of Classification relating to the Consequences of Disease* (WHO 1980, p 2).

The minister stated that:

> the terms physical and mental are intended to be seen in their widest sense and should comprehensively cover all forms of impairment (*Hansard*, Report SC E, 2 February 1995, col 71, Hague).

'Physical or mental impairment' is intended to be an all embracing term (*Hansard*, Report SC E, 7 February 1995, col 101, Hague). It includes sensory impairment, learning, psychiatric and psychological disability (*Hansard*, Report SC E, 2 February 1995, col 71/2, Hague). It also includes conditions such as cancer or HIV infection.

Both physical and mental impairments attract equal protection under the DDA. They are not separately defined. In many cases there may be a physical element to a mental impairment and vice versa. For example, senile dementia is a psychosis with an organic cause. No medical definition can adequately specify precise boundaries between mental and physical impairments in all cases. However, there are special provisions about some (but not all) forms of mental impairment which make it convenient to consider mental impairments first.

Mental impairment

Schedule 1, para 1(1) of the DDA provides that 'mental impairment includes an impairment resulting from or consisting of a mental illness only if it is "a clinically well recognised illness" '. It is essential to note that only some mental impairments result from or consist of a mental illness. Many mental impairments, such as learning disabilities, are not mental illnesses and are not subject to the 'clinically well recognised' provision. However, in order to decide if the provision applies in a particular case, it will be crucial to establish:

(a) whether or not an impairment is a 'mental impairment';

(b) whether or not a mental impairment 'consists of or results from a mental illness'; and

(c) whether or not such a mental illness is 'clinically well recognised'.

Meaning of 'mental impairment'

There is no definition of mental impairment in the DDA. Section 68(1) of the DDA provides that the term 'mental impairment' does not have the same meaning as in s 1(2) of the Mental Health Act 1983 (MHA), although the fact that an impairment would be a mental impairment for the purposes of the MHA does not prevent it from being a mental impairment for the purposes of the DDA. It is submitted that s 68(1) simply makes it clear that mental impairment has a much wider meaning in the DDA than in the MHA. A mental impairment within the meaning of s 1(2) of the MHA almost certainly will amount to an impairment for the purposes of the DDA. The MHA defines mental impairment as 'a state of arrested or incomplete development of mind ... which includes significant impairment of intelligence and social functioning and is associated with abnormally aggressive or seriously irresponsible behaviour...' ie a learning disability (formerly 'mental handicap') which is associated with such behaviour.

This forms only one category of mental disorder which s 1(2) of the MHA defines as 'mental illness, arrested or incomplete development of mind, psychopathic disorder and any other disorder or disability of mind'. Such conditions would also be mental impairments according to the ordinary meaning of those words. Each one of them would also be an impairment as defined by the WHO (see also the definition of mental disorder at p xxi of the American Psychiatric Association's DSM-IV). They would amount to impairments for the purposes of the DDA, subject to certain statutory exclusions.

The government said that 'the area of difference [between the DDA and MHA definitions] lies in alleged mental illnesses which have not achieved adequate clinical recognition' (*Hansard*, HL, 13 June 1995, Vol 564, col 1663, Mackay). This explanation is mistaken because it assumes that all mental impairments are a form of mental illness. This is not the case under either piece of legislation. Section 1(2) of the MHA and medical opinion recognises that only some 'mental disorders' are mental illnesses. Only mental illness needs to be 'clinically well recognised' to be an impairment for the purposes of the DDA (see below). Other forms of mental impairment do not.

Meaning of mental illness
A mental impairment resulting from or consisting of a mental illness only comes within the Act if it is 'a clinically well recognised illness', (Sched 1, para 1). However, although 'mental illness' is a familiar term, its meaning is far from clear.

There is no universal medical definition of 'mental illness' and the term is used with little precision in psychiatric practice (*Oxford Textbook of Psychiatry*, 3rd edn, Oxford University Press 1996, p 56). Furthermore, in common with most of the Mental Health legislation (see the Mental Health (Northern Ireland) Order 1986 (SI No 595) for an exception) there is no legal definition of 'mental illness' in the DDA. There has been a number of attempts to provide a definition of the term 'mental illness' to which regard could be had. Consideration was given to incorporating a closed definition into the MHA (see eg *A Review of the Mental Health Act 1959*, App II (DHSS 1976)). This was rejected as being overly restrictive and unlikely to last the test of time whilst the absence of definition was thought not to have caused any problems in practice (1975 Cmnd 7320, para 1.16/1).

A lay view of 'mental illness' was adopted by Lawton LJ in *W* v *L* [1974] QB 711. After noting that they were ordinary words of the English language, without particular legal or medical significance, he said, at p 719, that they should be construed

> in the way that ordinary sensible people would construe them ... what would the ordinary sensible person have said about the patient's condition in this case if he had been informed of his behaviour ...? In my judgement such a person would have said 'Well, the fellow is obviously mentally ill'.

This approach, characterised as the 'man-must-be-mad' test by Hoggett *Mental Health Law*, 4th edn, Sweet & Maxwell, 1996, p 32) has been criticised as preferring any common but misinformed view of non-normative behaviour to clinical assessment and analysis of behavioural evidence (*Mental Health Services: Law and Practice*, Gostin, Shaw & Sons' para 9.02).

At first glance such a test appears inconsistent with the requirement that the condition be 'clinically well recognised'. Nonetheless, a broad definition of mental illness would allow the equally broad application of the 'clinically well recognised' proviso. Conversely, the scope of the proviso shrinks in parallel to any restriction in the definition of mental illness. If the definition were to include only the major forms of psychoses (eg schizophrenia, organic psychotic conditions such as senile dementia, and affective psychoses such as manic depressive psychoses) the proviso would have no practical effect.

Nonetheless, it is suggested that this lay approach to mental illness should not be followed under the DDA. Firstly, legislation which is intended to combat commonly held stereotypes and misinformed prejudice against perceived differences or 'otherness' should not depend upon those attitudes for its definitions. In addition, the lay approach to the concept of mental illness is only concerned with whether and the extent to which the person's *behaviour* departs from a hypothetical norm. It is not concerned with the *cause* of that behaviour nor with whether the behaviour is usual for that individual. As such it makes no distinction between mental illness and other forms of mental impairment which may involve extreme variations in personality from a hypothetical norm, such as psychopathic and other personality disorders and, in some circumstances, mental handicap, none of which comprise mental illness.

The Butler Report (*Report of the Committee on Mentally Disordered Offenders 1975* Cmnd 6244, para 1.13) adopted a narrower, quasi-medical definition of mental illness as a 'disorder which has not always existed in the patient but has developed as a condition overlying the sufferer's usual personality'. This would encompass psychoses. It would also include neuroses (such as some forms of depression, hysteria, phobias and obsessions) which also result in a change to the sufferer's usual personality, even though these conditions are more akin to personality disorders in the view of many psychiatrists.

In the absence of any guidance as to the meaning of mental illness the Butler Committee's approach, whilst not perfect, is to be preferred. It retains a role for clinical analysis. It does not rely upon common attitudes and, potentially, prejudice. It would exclude mental handicap, psychopathic disorders and other personality disorders. Finally, it is sufficiently broad to retain a significant role for the 'clinically well recognised' proviso.

Clinically well recognised

This requirement was intended to bring people with conditions like 'schizophrenia, manic depression, and severe and extended depressive psychoses' within the protection of the DDA whilst preventing claims 'based on obscure conditions unrecognised by reputable clinicians ... [and] moods and mild eccentricities' (*Hansard*, Report SC E, 7 February 1995, col 104, Hague).

Although no definition is provided of 'clinically well recognised', the government stated that 'a reference is needed to a reasonably substantial body of practitioners who accept that a condition exists' (*Hansard*, Report SC E, 7 February 1995, col 100, Hague). The guidance states that it requires recognition by a respected body of medical opinion (para 14).

Parallels can probably be drawn with the field of medical negligence. McNair J said, in *Bolam v Friern Hospital Management Committee* [1957] 1 WLR 582 at 587, that a doctor was not negligent 'if he acted in accordance with a practice accepted as proper by a responsible body of medical men'. The concept of a substantial body of medical opinion was used in *Hillis v Potter* [1984] 1 WLR 641 at 643, where Hirst J stated:

In every case the court must be satisfied that the standard contended for on their behalf accords with that upheld by a substantial body of medical opinion, and that this body of medical opinion is both respectable and responsible, and experienced in this particular field of medicine.

In *Defreitas* v *O'Brien* [1995] PIQR p281 at p290, the Court of Appeal stated that a responsible body of medical opinion was not a quantitative concept to be established by 'counting heads'. Instead, it was open to a judge to find as a fact that a small number of specialists was sufficient to constitute a body of responsible opinion.

It is submitted that an illness recognised by a respectable and responsible body of medical opinion experienced in the particular field would satisfy the definition, even if an equally weighty (or weightier) body did not. The provision does not require that a majority or any other numerical threshold of medical opinion be established. Any such approach would almost certainly be inoperable and would also be contrary to the expressed parliamentary intention. However, ultimately it will still be a question of fact and degree for the tribunal or judge.

In practical terms, a finding that a condition is or is not 'clinically well recognised' will depend upon the quality of the expert evidence adduced. This includes the quality of the expert, as the more eminent the people recognising the illness (in the eyes of the court or tribunal), the fewer of them will be required. It may be that courts and tribunals will more readily accept that an illness is well recognised if it has a recognised name with pathology and symptomology, (see, albeit in a different context, *Mughal* v *Reuters Ltd* [1993] IRLR 571). Conditions which are specifically mentioned in the major systems of classification, such as DSM-IV or the *International Classification of Diseases 10th edn Classification of Mental and Behavioural Disorders: Clinical Descriptions and Diagnostic Guidelines* (ICD-10) (WHO 1992) are very likely to be clinically well recognised (guidance, para 14). Alternatively, identifying a body of literature affirming the existence of an illness may assist. It is essential that great care is taken in setting the letter of instructions to any expert witness (see below, p26).

Specified personality disorders excluded from the DDA

Any tendency to set fires, to steal, to physical or sexual abuse of other persons, to exhibitionism or to voyeurism are to treated as not amounting to impairments for the purposes of the DDA (DDMOD Regs 1996, reg 4(1)).

Other disorders or disability of the mind

Various other conditions which are neither a mental illness not a personality disorder will comprise an impairment for the purposes of the DDA. Most obviously, a learning disability is a mental impairment for the purposes of the DDA (guidance, para 13) whether or not it is associated with the abnormally aggressive or irresponsible required under the MHA. Neuroses (if they are not a form of mental illness) will also fall under the broad umbrella of mental impairment. In addition, the effects of head or other injuries, illnesses such as encephalitis, or other degeneration of the mind may amount to impairments even if they do not cause a mental illness.

Physical impairments

In contrast to a mental impairment (which results from or consists of a mental illness) there is no provision requiring a physical impairment to be 'clinically well recognised'. In the case of a physical impairment, the only dispute is likely to be whether the person has the impairment at all. Therefore, where there is doubt as to whether a mental illness is 'clinically well recognised', but a physiological or organic basis could be established for the condition, the complainant would be best advised to argue that the organic base itself constitutes a physical impairment in that it is a loss or abnormality of structure or function.

In addition, certain personality disorders are deemed not to comprise impairments within the DDA and a person suffering from such a personality disorder is not a disabled person (DDMOD Regs 1996, reg 4(1)), and see p 254). However, where the specified personality disorder has been caused by brain damage or disease, the complainant may be able to rely upon the brain damage or disease itself as a physical impairment rather than the consequent personality disorder in order to come within the definition of a disabled person.

Exclusions and inclusions

Regulations made under Sched 1, para 1(2) have provided that certain conditions do not amount to impairments for the purposes of the DDA.

Addictions

Addictions to (or dependency upon) alcohol, tobacco or any other substance will not amount to an impairment (DDMOD Regs 1996, reg 3(1)) unless the addiction was originally the result of the administration of medically prescribed drugs or other medical treatment (DDMOD Regs 1996, reg 3(2)). This only excludes the addition itself and an impairment caused by the addiction or the substance, such as cirrhosis, cancer or delirium tremens, will be covered by the DDA (guidance, para 11).

Hayfever

Seasonal allergic rhinitis (hayfever) is deemed not to be an impairment (DDMOD Regs 1996, reg 4(2)). However, this does not prevent the condition from being taken into account for the purposes of the Act where it aggravates the effect of another condition (DDMOD Regs 1996, reg 4(3)).

Deemed inclusions

To date no regulations have been made under Sched 1, para 1(2) deeming any particular conditions to amount to an impairment.

Adverse effect upon normal day-to-day activities

In order to satisfy the definition of disability, the impairment must have a 'substantial and long term adverse effect' upon someone's 'ability to carry out normal day-to-day activities' (s 1).

Adverse effect

This part of the provision is self explanatory and unlikely to cause much difficulty in practice. There is an adverse effect where the impairment limits, prevents, restricts or otherwise hampers the individual's ability to carry out normal day-to-day activities.

Normal day-to-day activities

An impairment is only taken to affect the ability to carry out normal day-to-day activities if it affects one or more of the following:
  (a) mobility;
  (b) manual dexterity;
  (c) physical co-ordination;
  (d) continence;
  (e) ability to lift carry or otherwise move everyday objects;
  (f) speech, hearing or eyesight;
  (g) memory or ability to concentrate, learn or understand; or
  (h) perception of the risk of physical danger.
  (See Sched 1, para 4).
This general list is intended to be broad and all embracing. It is exhaustive, and at least one of the activities must be adversely affected for the person to fall within the definition. The requirement is still satisfied if the impairment only has an indirect effect on the ability to carry out one of the listed activities. For example, the guidance suggests that account should be taken of:
  (1) *medical advice*—where a person has been professionally advised to change, limit or refrain from a normal day-to-day activity on account of an impairment (Guidance para C6);
  (2) *pain or fatigue*—where an impairment causes pain or fatigue limiting the person's ability to perform relevant activities over a sustained period (Guidance, para C6) and
  (3) *mental illness* (eg depression)—whether a person is in practice unable to sustain an activity over a reasonable period despite a physical ability to perform a task (Guidance, para C7).

The intended breadth of the list was made clear by the government after Lord Carter moved an amendment (*Hansard*, HL, 13 June 1995, Vol 564, col 1667) to insert express references to the following activities:

(1) standing;
(2) sitting and rising from sitting;
(3) reaching;
(4) remaining conscious;
(5) breathing;
(6) sleeping;
(7) ability to communicate with other people;
(8) stability of mood;
(9) ability to go, or confidence in going, outside the home;
(10) ability to cope with unfamiliar environments; and
(11) ability to care for oneself.

The government's position was that the amendment was not necessary as 'the points are covered clearly in paragraph 4(1)' (*Hansard*, HL, 13 June 1995, Vol 564, col 1671). Lord Mackay explained this in greater detail at col 1672:

> Perhaps I may now turn to the amendment itself and the little list which the noble Lord wishes to add to my little list. There are a number of elements in it which all relate to mobility which is the first matter dealt with on my list. Paragraph 4(1) (*a*) refers specifically to mobility ... The ability to stand, to sit, to rise from sitting, to breathe, to move confidently outside the home and to cope with unfamiliar environments as listed in the amendment are all essential to normal mobility. 'Mobility' is the first item in my list in Schedule 1 and it is a broad category of activity which, I believe, includes all the matters in the noble Lord's list. The ability to reach is also referred to in the amendment. That is clearly related to 'physical coordination' and to the 'ability to lift, carry or otherwise move everyday objects' both of which are actually listed in the Bill. The ability to remain conscious, which also appears in the amendment, will affect all normal day-to-day activities—even including attending this place—[*sic*] while the ability to breath will affect 'mobility', 'ability to lift' and 'speech' as set out in the schedule. The amendment also includes 'ability to communicate with other people'. Turning to the categories already in the Bill, that is covered in large part by 'speech, hearing or eyesight'. However it also introduces the concept of language as a barrier which may be an important factor in some cases. But I believe it would be irrelevant to the purposes of the Bill. I recognise that some people will have difficulty in communicating because of some severe learning disabilities, but they are covered by the phrase, 'memory or ability to concentrate, learn or understand' which is contained in the bill.
>
> 'Stability of mood' is also suggested by the noble Lord in his amendment. I believe that this is a very difficult concept; indeed we have discussed it once or twice this afternoon. I believe that the normal boundaries would be almost impossible to set. Where someone has a clinically diagnosed depression, that will affect memory, ability to learn, concentrate or understand. The Bill, rightly, does not encompass the concepts of unhappiness, lack of self-confidence or lack of self-worth as disabilities in their own right.
>
> Finally, there is the suggestion in the amendment of the ability to sleep and the 'ability to care for oneself'. The first category is very difficult to define because there are people who sleep very little but who perform all their day-to-day

activities prodigiously well. Each of us seems to have quite different sleep needs. If someone has severe insomnia in connection with another condition—such as for example manic depression—and is unable to concentrate as a result, that will clearly have an effect on his normal day-to-day activities. The difficulty with the phrase 'ability to care for oneself' is that it does not explain the nature of the problem. People who need help in caring for themselves do so because of a physical or mental disability which effects areas of activity already within the list; for example, mobility, co-ordination, or the ability to concentrate, learn or understand, or indeed continence. There I believe that that is covered in the schedule. I hope that I have been able to give the desired reassurances. Although it is not included in the list, the noble Lord, Lord Carter, mentioned the question of cerebral palsy, as regards hand movments and the list. That would be covered by 'physical co-ordination' in sub-paragraph (c) of the schedule. I understand why the noble Lord tabled the amendment. Indeed I thank him for doing so because it has given me the opportunity actually to show what we mean by the list that we have provided. I hope that I have been able to reassure the noble Lord and other Members of the Committee who took part in the debate that the list of 'normal day-to-day activities' in Schedule 1 is sufficiently comprehensive and is appropriate to the purposes of the Bill.

As a result of the reassurances given, the amendment was withdrawn (col 1673). Note that in all cases, whether the activity was covered or not depended on the effect on the activities which were already in the Bill.

Although the phrase 'normal day-to-day activies' (s 1(1)) suggests that more than one activity must be affected before a person can qualify as a disabled person, Sched 1, para 4 makes it clear that it is enough if only one of the activities is so affected (see also, Guidance, para C5).

Guidance on the meaning of normal day-to-day activities

The Guidance states that

> [T]he term 'normal day-to-day activities' is not intended to include activities which are normal only for a particular person or group of people. Therefore in deciding whether an activity is a 'normal day-to-day activity' account should be taken of how far it is normal for most people and carried out by most people on a daily or frequent and fairly regular basis (Guidance, para C2)

It gives examples of restricted activities such as playing a musical instrument or sport or performing a highly skilled task. Impairments which affect only such an activity are not meant to be covered. (Guidance, para C3).

In addition to identifying factors to be taken into account in deciding whether an affect on a day-to-day activity is a substantial adverse affect, the Guidance illustrates the breadth of the categories of normal day-to-day activity.

Mobility

This covers moving or changing position in a wide sense, in accordance with the reassurance given by the Minister (see p 11 above). Account is to be taken of the extent to which a person can engage in activities such as:

(1) getting around unaided or using a normal means of transport;
(2) leaving home with or without assistance;
(3) walking a short distance;
(4) climbing stairs;
(5) travelling in a car or completing a journey on public transport;
(6) sitting or standing;
(7) bending or reaching, or
(8) getting around in an unfamiliar place. (Guidance, para C14)

Manual dexterity
This covers the ability to use hands and fingers with precision. Account is to be taken of the extent to which the person can:
(1) manipulate the fingers on each hand; or
(2) co-ordinate the use of both hands together to do a task; or
(3) pick up or manipulate small objects, communicate through writing or typing on standard machinery.
The Guidance suggests that loss of function in the dominant hand would be expected to have a greater effect than equivalent loss in the non-dominant hand (para C15). However if the impairment to the non-dominant hand has the requisite adverse effect, it is irrelevant that the manual dexterity of the dominant hand is unaffected.

Physical co-ordination
This covers balanced and effective interaction of body movement, including hand and eye co-ordination and the ability to carry out 'composite' activities such as walking and using hands at the same time. In the case of a child, it is necessary to take account of the level of achievement which would be normal for a person of the particular age (Guidance, para C16 and see p 14 below).

Continence
This covers the ability to control urination and/or defecation. Account should be taken of the frequency and extent of the loss of control and the age of the individual (Guidance, para C17).

Ability to lift, carry or otherwise move everyday objects
Account should be taken of a person's ability to repeat the lifting, carrying or otherwise moving of everyday objects, or their ability to bear weights over a reasonable period of time. Everyday objects might include such items as books, a kettle of water, bags of shopping, a briefcase, an overnight bag, a chair or other piece of light furniture (Guidance, para C18).

Speech hearing or eyesight
This involves the ability to speak, hear or see and includes face-to-face, telephone and written communication.

Speech   Account should be taken of how far a person is able to speak clearly at a normal pace and rhythm and to understand someone else speaking normally in his native language. Any effects on speech patterns or which impede the acquisition or processing of one's native language (for example by someone who has had a stroke) should be considered (Guidance, para C19(*i*)).

Hearing   The issue is the extent to which a person can hear against a level of background noise of a range and type that most people would be able to hear adequately. If a person uses a hearing aid or similar device, what needs to be considered is the effect experienced if the person is not using the hearing aid or device (Guidance, para C19(*ii*) and Sched 1, para 6(1), and see p 264).

Eyesight   What needs to be considered is the eyesight in light of a level and type normally acceptable to most people for normal day-to-day activities. If a person's sight is corrected by spectacles or contact lenses, or could be corrected by them, it is the corrected eyesight that is to be taken into account (Guidance, para C19(*iii*) and Sched 1, para 6(3), and see p 264).

Memory and ability to concentrate, learn or understand
The Guidance suggests that account be taken of the person's ability to:
  (1)   remember;
  (2)   organise his thoughts;
  (3)   plan a course of action and execute it;
  (4)   take in new knowledge;
  (5)   understand spoken or written instructions;
  (6)   read text in standard English or straightforward numbers; and
  (7)   remain conscious.
This includes considering whether the person learns to do things significantly more slowly than is normal. (Guidance, para C20 at p 265).

Perception of the risks of physical danger
This includes both the underestimation and overestimation of physical danger, including danger to the person's well being. Account should be taken, for example, of whether the person is inclined to neglect basic functions such as eating, drinking, sleeping, keeping warm and personal hygiene. Account should also be taken of reckless behaviour which puts the person at risk, or excessive avoidance behaviour without a good cause (Guidance, para C21).

Babies and young children

Where a child under six years of age has an impairment which does not have an effect on normal day-to-day activities, the impairment is deemed to have a substantial and long-term adverse effect on the ability of the child to carry out normal day-to-day activities if it would normally have such an effect on the ability of a person aged six years or over (DDMOD Regs 1996, reg 6).

Regulations

Regulations may make further provision for matters which are and are not to be treated as affecting the ability of the person to carry out normal day-to-day activities. The DDMOD Regs 1996 have made such provision regarding babies and young children (see above) and tattoos and body piercing (see p 19 below).

Substantial ... adverse effect

The adverse effect must be 'substantial'. An adverse effect is substantial if it is more than minor or trivial, going beyond the usual differences in ability that exist between people (Guidance, para A1). This follows the legislative intention expressed by Mr Hague at *Hansard*, Report SC E, 2 February 1995, col 76; ' "substantial" is commonly understood to be more than minor', and at *Hansard*, Report SC E, 7 February 1995 col 82;

> It is necessary to include [the word substantial in the Bill] otherwise quite minor conditions might be covered ... [There is a need] to refer to a substantial impairment so that we do not bring quite trivial matters within the scope of the legislation.

Provided an impairment is shown to have a substantial adverse effect, it satisfies the definition. There is no further gradation of disability within the DDA. Everyone who falls within the definition is, formally at least, equally protected by its provisions. The effect of the definition is that some disabled people will have to emphasise the effects of the impairment on their lives in a way which they might be extremely reluctant to do. For example, they may have to stress how difficult things are when their instincts are to do the opposite.

In the Australian decision *Tillmanns Butcheries Pty Ltd* v *Australasian Meat Industry Employees Union* (1979) 42 FLR 331 at 348, Deane J said 'the word "substantial" is not only susceptible of ambiguity; it is a word calculated to conceal a lack of precision'. Not only does this illustrate the ambiguity which justifies the reference to *Hansard*, but it also recognises that the question will often be one of fact and degree for the tribunal. The Guidance and the legislative intention demonstrates that a very low threshold was envisaged for an impairment to be substantial. This demonstrates that the more onerous meaning of 'substantial' adopted by the House of Lords in a case under the Rent Acts as equivalent to 'considerable, solid, or big' should not be applied under s 1 of the DDA (*Palser* v *Grinling* [1948] AC 291 at 361). In another case under the same legislation the Court of Appeal purported to follow *Pasler* v *Grinling* but treated a finding by a judge that something was 'by no means minimal' as being in effect a finding that it was substantial (*Marchant* v *Charters* [1977] 1 WLR 1181 at 1186).

There are special rules for people with progressive conditions and where the effects of an impairment are corrected or controlled by medical treatment, prosthesis or other aid (see Sched 1, paras 6 and 8 and pp 19 and 20).

Guidance on substantial adverse effects

The Guidance gives numerous examples of functional limitations which it would and would not be reasonable to regard as showing a substantial adverse effect on each category of normal day-to-day activity concerning whether an adverse affect is substantial (Guidance, Pt II(C), and see pp 260 to 266). The Guidance points out that those examples are simply indicators or illustrations. They are not exhaustive and are not tests to be applied in each case. Therefore, a person who is able to perform some or all of the activities given as examples in the Guidance may still experience a substantial adverse effect on his ability to perform normal day-to-day activities. The test is whether the impairment has a substantial adverse effect (in whatever way) on any of the normal day-to-day activities. In the examples of effects which should not be regarded as substantial, the Guidance proceeds on the basis that the effect described is the only effect of the impairment. If there are no other substantial adverse effects it will not be reasonable to regard the impairment as having a substantial effect. However, the person may be inhibited in other activities, and this instead may indicate a substantial adverse effect on normal day-to-day activities (Guidance, paras C9–C12). The examples given in the Guidance for each category of day-to-day activity are summarised below.

Mobility
It would be reasonable to regard the inability to travel a short journey as a passenger in a vehicle, the inability to walk other than at a slow pace or with unsteady or jerky movements, difficulty in going up or down steps, stairs or gradients, inability to use one or more forms of public transport, or the inability to go out of doors unaccompanied as being substantial adverse effects. It would not be reasonable to regard the inability to travel in a car for a journey lasting more than two hours without discomfort, difficulty walking unaided a distance of about 1.5 km or a mile (depending upon the age of the person and the type of terrain) without discomfort, or having to stop the following as substantial adverse effects.

Manual dexterity
It would be reasonable to regard a loss of function in one or both hands such that the person cannot use the hand or hands, an ability to handle a knife and fork at the same time, or the ability to press the buttons on keyboards or keypads but only much more slowly than is normal for most people as substantial adverse effects. It would not be reasonable to regard an inability to undertake activities requiring delicate hand movements, such as threading a small needle, an inability to reach typing speeds standardised for secretarial work, or an inability to pick up a single small item, such as a pin as substantial adverse effects.

Physical co-ordination
It would be reasonable to regard an ability to pour liquid into another vessel only with unusual slowness or concentration, or an inability to place food into one's own mouth with fork or spoon without unusual concentration or assistance as substantial adverse effects. It would not be reasonable to regard mere clumsiness or an inability to catch a tennis ball as substantial adverse effects.

Continence
It would be reasonable to regard even infrequent loss of control of the bowels, loss of control of the bladder while asleep at least once a month, or frequent minor faecal incontinence or frequent minor leakage from the bladder as substantial adverse effects. It would not be reasonable to regard an infrequent loss or control of the bladder while asleep or infrequent minor leakage from the bladder as substantial adverse effects.

Ability to lift, carry or otherwise move everyday objects
It would be reasonable to regard an inability to pick up objects of moderate weight with one hand or to carry a moderately loaded tray steadily as substantial adverse effects. It would not be reasonable to regard an inability to carry heavy luggage without assistance or to move heavy objects without a mechanical aid as substantial adverse effects.

Speech
It would be reasonable to regard an inability to give clear basic instructions orally to colleagues or providers of a service, an inability to ask specific questions to clarify instructions or taking significantly longer than average to say things as substantial adverse effects. It would not be reasonable to regard an inability to articulate fluently due to a minor stutter, lisp or speech impediment, an inability to speak in front of an audience, having a strong regional or foreign accent or an inability to converse in a language which is not the speaker's native language as substantial adverse effects.

Hearing
It would be reasonable to regard an inability to hold a conversation with someone talking in a normal voice in a moderately noisy environment or to hear and understand another person speaking clearly over the telephone as substantial adverse effects. It would not be reasonable to regard an inability to hold a conversation in a very noisy place such as a factory floor, or to to sing in tune as substantial adverse effects.

Eyesight
It would be reasonable to regard an inability to see to pass the eyesight test for a standard driving test, an inability to recognise by sight a known person across a moderately-sized room, a total inability to distinguish colours, an

inability to read ordinary newsprint, or an inability to walk safely without bumping into things as substantial adverse effects. It would not be reasonable to regard an inability to read very small or indistinct print without the aid of a magnifying glass, an inability to distinguish a known person across a substantial distance (eg a playing field) or an inability to distinguish between red and green as substantial adverse effects.

Memory or ability to concentrate, learn or understand
It would be reasonable to regard an intermittent loss of consciousness and associated confused behaviour, a persistent inability to remember the names of familar people such as family or friends, an inability to adapt after a reasonable period to minor change in a work routine, an inability to write a cheque without assistance or considerable difficulty in following a short sequence such as a simple recipe or a brief list of domestic tasks as substantial adverse effects. It would not be reasonable to regard occasionally forgetting the name of a familiar person, such as a colleague, an inability to concentrate on a task requiring application over several hours, an inability to fill in a long, detailed technical document without assistance, an inability to read at faster than normal speed or minor problems with writing or spelling as substantial adverse effects.

Perception of the risk of physical danger
It would be reasonable to regard an inability to operate safely properly-maintained equipment, a persistent inability to cross a road safely, an inability to nourish oneself (assuming nourishment is available) or an inability to tell by touch that an object is very hot or cold as substantial adverse effects. It would not be reasonable to regard a fear of significant heights, underestimating the risk associated with dangerous hobbies, such as mountain climbing or underestimating risk (other than obvious ones) in unfamiliar workplaces as substantial adverse effects.

Cumulative effects

The Guidance states that an impairment which does not have a substantial adverse effect on any one category of day-to-day activity may nevertheless have a substantial adverse effect on the person's ability to carry out normal day-to-day activities if its effects on several categories are taken together. It gives the examples of breathing difficulties or manic depression (Guidance, paras A4–A5 at p 256).

In addition a person may have more than one impairment, none of which is sufficient alone to have a substantial effect. In such a case, account should be taken of whether there is a substantial effect overall on one or more categories. For example, a minor impairment which affects physical coordination and an irreversible but minor injury to a leg, taken together, may have a substantial effect on mobility even though neither impairment had such an effect in itself (Guidance, para A6).

Account should be taken of how far a person can reasonably be expected to manage the effects of an impairment to prevent or reduce its effects on normal day-to-day activities, although the possibility of coping strategies breaking down must be taken into account when assessing the effects of the impairment (Guidance, paras A7–A8). However, the effects of some measures taken to treat or correct an impairment will have to be disregarded under the special rules relating to medical treatment (Guidance, para A9; Sched 1, para 6, and see p 20 below).

Severe disfigurement

A severe disfigurement is deemed to have a substantial adverse affect upon a person's ability to carry out normal day-to-day activities, except in circumstances that may be prescribed by regulations (Sched 1, para 3(1) and (2)). 'Disfigurement' is not defined, but the Guidance gives the examples of scars, birthmarks, limb or postural deformation or skin diseases. Whether a disfigurement is severe is a matter of degree, but it may be necessary to take account of where the feature in question is, eg on the back as opposed to the face (Guidance, para A17).

Deliberately acquired disfigurements

A severe disfigurement consisting of a tattoo which has not been removed or a piercing of the body (including any object attached through the piercing) for decorative or other non-medical reasons is deemed not to have a substantial adverse affect upon normal day-to-day activities (DDMOD Regs 1996, reg 5 and Sched 1, paras 3(2) and (3) and Guidance, para 8).

Progressive conditions

A person who has a progressive condition is deemed to have an impairment with a substantial adverse effect upon his ability to carry out normal day-to-day activities if the following three conditions are satisfied.

A progressive condition
Firstly, someone seeking to take advantage of this provision must prove that they have a 'progressive condition'. Although 'progressive condition' is not defined, examples such as cancer, multiple sclerosis, muscular dystrophy or HIV infection are provided (Sched 1, para 8(1)(a)).

An effect
Secondly, the condition must result in an impairment which has (or had) an effect upon the person's ability to carry out normal day-to-day activities, but it need not have (or have had) a substantial adverse effect upon that ability (Sched 1, para 8(1)(b) and (c)). In other words, the condition must have become symptomatic and begun to have an effect upon the normal day-to-day

activities. People with (currently) asymptomatic or latent conditions or with a predisposition to develop disabling conditions in the future will not be covered by this provision if it has not begun to have such an effect. The reference to an impairment which 'had' an effect ensures that people whose symptoms have gone into remission or have been corrected or removed by medical treatment etc are still covered by the provision. However, if the medical treatment etc prevents the impairment from having an effect at all, the person will fall outside of this provision. Although Sched 1, para 6 provides that the impact of medical treatment and other measures to correct the effect of an impairment is to be ignored where the impairment would otherwise have a substantial adverse effect upon normal day-to-day activities (see p 257 below), this appears not to apply where the effect is less than substantial.

Likely future effect
Thirdly, the condition must be likely to result in the person having an impairment which does have a substantial adverse effect upon his ability to carry out normal day-to-day activities in the future (Sched 1, para 8(1)). There is no time limit within which the substantial adverse effect is to become manifest. The Guidance suggests that 'likely' means more likely than not, ie on a balance of probabilities (para B7, but see *Davies* v *Taylor* [1974] QB 207 at 222, and *Re H and R* [1996] 1 All ER 1).

HIV infection
Symptomatic HIV infection is within the definition if it has any adverse effect upon the individual's normal day-to-day activities, but asymptomatic HIV infection is not (*Hansard*, Report SC E, 7 February 1995, col 85, Hague). It may be that people diagnosed as HIV positive will qualify as disabled persons as a result of having concomitant conditions such as depression which do have an effect upon their ability to carry out normal day-to-day activities (see also p 260).

Medical treatment and other corrective measures

Where 'an impairment would be likely to have a substantial adverse effect upon the person's abilities to carry out normal day-to-day activities, but for the fact that measures are being taken to treat or correct it', it is treated as continuing to have that substantial adverse effect (Sched 1, para 6(1)). 'Measures' is defined as 'including, in particular, medical treatment and the use of a prosthesis or other aid' but that list is not exhaustive (Sched 1, para 6(2)). The Guidance suggests that it may include any behaviour suggested by a medical practitioner (para A9). It is not clear what activities engaged in, or other aids used, by a person to treat or correct an impairment would not be included within the term 'measures'.

The only current exception to this provision is where an impairment to eyesight is or could be corrected by spectacles, contact lenses or in another prescribed manner. In such a case, the impairment will only constitute a disability if the eyesight as corrected (or correctable) still has or would have a substantial adverse effect upon normal day-to-day activities (Sched 1, para 6(3)(a)). Regulations may be made to increase the scope of this exception (Sched 1, para 6(3)(b)).

The provision does not apply if the impairment has been 'removed' by the treatment, for example if a cancer is cured or full hearing restored by an operation. In such a case there will be no impairment. Furthermore, there would be no ongoing effect upon a person's abilities, even in the absence of ongoing treatment or use of prosthesis or aid (Guidance, para B6). However, the person may still be entitled to the protection of parts of the DDA as a person who has had a disability (see s 2 and p 22 below). Although it will often be obvious whether or not this provision applies, it will not always be so. For example, the application of this provision to a hip replacement or a course of exercise or diet adopted on medical advice is uncertain.

Babies and young children

See p 14 above.

Long term adverse effect

An adverse effect is long term if it:
 (1) has lasted at least 12 months [Sched 1, para 2(1)(a)]; or
 (2) is likely to last at least 12 months [Sched 1, para 2(1)(b)]; or
 (3) is likely to last for the rest of the life of the person affected [Sched 1, para 2(1)(c)].

Again, 'likely' appears to mean more likely than not (Guidance, para B7 but see Davies v Taylor [1974] QB 207 at 222 and Re H and R [1996] 1 All ER 1).

In deciding if this part of the definition is satisfied, the duration of any adverse effect before and after the date of the act complained of must be taken into account. The typical duration of the particular impairment must also be taken into account, together with any relevant factors specific to the individual, such as their age and general state of health (Guidance, para B8). However, if, at the date of the act complained of, an impairment had not had and was not likely to have a substantial adverse effect upon normal day-to-day activities for at least 12 months, or for the rest of the person's life, that person would not have been a disabled person at that time. As such, they would not be entitled to bring proceedings under the DDA in relation to that act, even if the impairment did, unexpectedly or against the balance of probability, last for 12 months or for the rest of their lives.

Recurring conditions

The DDA makes express provision for recurring or fluctuating conditions (Sched 1, para 2(2)). An impairment which ceases to have a substantial adverse effect on normal day-to-day activities is deemed to continue to have such an effect if it 'is likely to recur'. Again, 'likely' seems to mean more likely than not, ie on a balance of probability (Guidance, para B7 but see *Davies* v *Taylor* [1974] QB 207 at 222 and *Re H and R* [1996] 1 All ER 1).

Although the effect must have recurred or be likely to recur in a period beyond 12 months from when it was first experienced in order to satisfy the long term requirement, there is no outer limit upon the period during which the effect must recur or be likely to recur.

At para B5 the Guidance says that the behaviour of the person should be taken into account in assessing the likelihood of recurrence. For example, if avoidance action could fairly readily be taken it may mean that there will be no further recurrence, although any possibility that the management may break down should be taken into account. Provided this is limited to an assessment of likelihood, it is unobjectionable. It should not be interpreted as excluding an impairment where avoidance action could readily and reasonably be taken but, for whatever reason, is unlikely to be taken as there is no general exclusion of self inflicted disability (cf the provisions on addiciton at p 9 above and on deliberately acquired disfigurement at p 19 below). Furthermore, in so far as the future behaviour referred to consists of taking measures to treat or correct (but not cure) the impairment, it is the untreated or uncorrected effect of the impairment which is to be considered (Sched 1, para 6 and see p 20 above and p 258 below).

Past impairments

Section 2(1) provides that Pt II (employment) and Pt III (goods, facilities and services) of the DDA apply to a person who had but no longer has a disability within the meaning of s 1(1). This includes people who had such a disability at any time before or after the DDA came into force (s 2(4)). Whether such a person had a disability at a particular time is to be determined in accordance with the provisions of and made under the DDA in force when the act complained of took place (s 2(5)).

Substantial . . . adverse effects

The criteria for establishing a substantial adverse effect in relation to a current impairment apply equally in the context of a past impairment.

Long term adverse effects

A past impairment is treated as having had a long term effect if it lasted for at least 12 months (Sched 2, para 5 and see Guidance, para B9).

Recurring conditions

An impairment which ceased to have a substantial adverse effect on a person's ability to carry out normal day-to-day activities is treated as continuing if it recurred or recurs (Sched 2, para 5). Therefore, if the effects of the impairment recurred at least 12 months after the first occurrence, they were long term for the purposes of the DDA (Guidance, para B9).

Registered disabled persons

Any person who was registered disabled under s 6 of the Disabled Persons (Employment) Act 1944 on 12 January 1995 and 2 December 1996 (the date when Sched 1, para 7 came into force) will be deemed to be a disabled person for a period of three years from the date when the paragraph comes into force. Thereafter they will be regarded as persons who have had a disability (Sched 1, para 7(2)(b). Regulations may prescribe circumstances in which persons are no longer to be deemed to be disabled persons (Sched 1, para 7(6)).

Persons not within the definition

Someone who does not fall within the definition of 'disabled person' under s 1 is not protected by the DDA. In particular it does not include people who are wrongly perceived to have or to have had a disability. This is one major difference between the DDA and both the UK Civil Rights (Disabled Persons) Bill and the US legislation under the Rehabilitation Act 1973 and Americans with Disabilities Act 1990. In addition those who have an association with a disabled person, such as a partner, parent or carer, are not protected by the DDA.

Organisations

The definition does not include organisations of or for people with disabilities, and discrimination against such organisations is not in itself within the DDA. For example, if a landlord refuses to lease premises to such an organisation that wishes to provide residential or other services for disabled people on the grounds that it would upset the neighbours, there is no discrimination actionable under the DDA. However, where there is sufficient nexus between the person to establish the relationship of agency, such as purchasing a ticket to the theatre for a disabled person, the disabled person may have a cause of action. In addition, in the limited areas in which judicial review is possible, such organisations arguably have *locus standi* (see eg *R* v *Gloucester County Council, ex p RADAR* (1995) unreported, QBD, 21 December).

Chapter 2

The Concept of Disability: Practice and Procedure

Introduction

In most cases under the DDA there will be little doubt as to whether a person has a disability and the matter will not often be in dispute. In difficult cases the approach set out in the checklist at the end of this chapter could usefully be adopted to help identify possible issues. The practice and procedure involved in bringing and resisting claims under the employment provisions of Pt II of the DDA is dealt with in Chap 8 below. Chapter 13 considers the practice and procedure in claims relating to goods, services and premises claims under Pt III. As establishing or denying that a person is or was a disabled person as defined in ss 1 and 2 raises the same issues under either Pt II or Pt III, they will be dealt with together in the remainder of this chapter.

Establishing whether a person is or is not disabled

Narrowing the issues

Once the claim has been issued and the Defence or Notice of Appearance (IT3) received, it should be apparent if, and to what extent, there is a dispute about the applicant/plaintiff's right to bring a claim under the DDA. However, advisers should consider whether it is possible to narrow the issues further. This can save both parties from wasted expenditure on matters that are not going to be at issue. Further and better particulars and interrogatories can be used in both the county court and Industrial Tribunal (CCR Ord 13, r 2 and Ord 15, r 11; IT (Rules of Procedure) Regulations 1993 r 4(1) and (3); see pp 111 to 114 below). In County Court proceedings a party should consider serving a notice to admit facts under CCR Ord 20, r 2 so as to put the other party under pressure as to costs. In the Industrial Tribunal, it may be possible to require the respondent to identify the areas in dispute at a directions hearing.

Collecting the evidence

The principal witness on the issue of disability will usually be the applicant/ plaintiff. Evidence will be needed to provide the court or tribunal with details of the impairment, its effects and duration, paying particular attention to any matters identified as being or likely to be in dispute. In addition, friends, family, colleagues, carers and health care professionals may be able to give evidence as to the effect of any impairment upon the individual's ability to carry out normal day-to-day activities.

Bear in mind that clear examples of the impact of the impairment upon particular activities, whether or not found in the Guidance, will be much easier to understand than abstract statements. For example, evidence that someone always makes a cup of tea (rather than a pot) because he cannot lift a full kettle will have more impact than a bland statement that he has difficulty in lifting objects. Finally, be aware of coping strategies developed by the applicant/plaintiff which may disguise the impact which an impairment has upon day-to-day abilities or of any tendancy to minimise problems (see p 15).

Evidence of benefits received by the applicant/plaintiff or their carer will often be useful. Find out if Severe Disablement Allowance, Disability Working Allowance, Disability Living Allowance, Incapacity Benefit, Industrial Injuries Disablement Benefit, Reduced Earnings Allowance, or Invalid Care Allowance are or have been paid. Although the test for the various benefits do not depend upon the definition of disabled person in the DDA and the award of a benefit will not bind either a court or a tribunal, this will be persuasive. However, bear in mind that difficulties may arise with claims under the employment provisions if a condition of payment is that the person is incapable of any work, as with Severe Disablement Allowance or Incapacity Benefit. Evidence of the provision of assistance or home adaptations by Social Services, the NHS or the Independent Living Funds will assist someone to prove they are a disabled person. Similarly, the fact that a child has a statement of special education needs or that an adult is in receipt of services under the Access to Work Scheme may also assist here.

If the applicant/plaintiff was registered as disabled under the Disabled Persons (Employment) Act 1944, certificates of registration should be obtained which will conclusively prove the matters certified (Sched 1, para 7(3)).

Expert evidence

In most cases expert evidence of disability will not be needed. The steps referred to above under the heading 'narrowing the issues' should be taken to ensure that it is necessary before costs are incurred. In many cases, there will not be sufficient resources to allow evidence to be obtained from an independent expert even if it is desirable. However, Community Nurses and other health care workers already involved with the applicant/plaintiff may be willing to provide evidence if asked. In addition there may already be reports on the condition of the disabled person from such health care workers which could be requested.

Where it needs to (and can) be obtained, the adviser should always give considerable thought to the questions to be asked of the expert to ensure that the report addresses the correct issues. An expert should not be expected to be knowledgeable about the terms of the DDA. Clear instructions will have to be given to familiarise the expert with the terms of the DDA, for example:

(1) a clear statement of the purpose of the instruction should be given;

(2) if the effect of the impairment on the ability of the person to carry out normal day-to-day activities is in issue, the expert should be made aware of the full extent of the concept of 'normal day-to-day activities', and what is meant by the concept of a 'substantial adverse effect'. A clear statement of the legal test should be set out at the beginning of the letter in language that an intelligent non-lawyer could understand;

(3) the expert should have access to the relevant medical and psychiatric records;

(4) experts preparing a report to an industrial tribunal should be reminded that the tribunal will not necessarily be familiar with medical concepts and, so far as possible, the report should be readily understandable by the members of the tribunal;

(5) the expert should be asked to provide a distinct paragraph dealing with the consequences of the impairment. This should deal with the consequences that have occurred and those which would normally be expected from the impairment. These should be related to the expanded list of normal day-to-day activities given in the Act. There should be a wholly separate set of paragraphs dealing with the diagnosis of the condition;

(6) if the issue is whether an impairment is physical or a mental illness (and subject to the clinically well recognised proviso) the expert should be asked to identify or deny any physiological basis;

(7) if the issue is whether a mental impairment is a well recognised mental illness, the expert should be asked to express an opinion in terms of one of the recognised and accepted international systems of classification, such as the WHO's ICD10 or the American Psychiatric Association's DSM-IV. The relevant medical literature should be reviewed;

(8) if the effect of the provisions regarding medical treatment or other measures is in issue, the expert should be asked to identify the measures being taken and set out the likely effect of the impairment if those measures were not taken;

(9) if the issue is the likely duration of the adverse effect, the expert should be asked to express an opinion on the balance of probabilities.

The letter should make it very clear that the expert should contact the adviser for further information if there is any aspect on which he is not clear.

Care should be taken to choose the correct expert for the subject matter. For example, if the issue is whether a mental illness is clinically well-recognised, the evidence of a consultant will carry far more weight than that of the person's own doctor. Conversely, if the issue is whether the impairment has a substantial and long term adverse effect on the person's ability to carry out normal day-to-day activities, the doctor treating the individual may be of more use. Consider which speciality is most appropriate to the issue or if more than one expert is necessary. A clinical psychologist may be able to give an assessment of whether there is cognitive dysfunction but not be qualified to identify a clinically well recognised mental illness. An occupational therapist may be able to assess the ability to carry out normal day-to-day activities. (See the guidance in *National Justice Compania Naviera SA* v *Prudential Assurance Co (The Ikarian Reefer)* [1993] 2 Lloyd's Rep 68 on the duties of an expert.)

Obtaining medical records

For the applicant or plaintiff
If medical evidence is necessary, the applicant/plaintiff's advisers will often be required to obtain the medical records. These may be needed as evidence in their own right or for the benefit of an expert providing a report. Letters requesting copies of the records should be accompanied by the written authority of the applicant/plaintiff for their release to the adviser or nominated expert. It will assist the process if the letter confirms that the reasonable copying charges and postal fees will be met and that the adviser has no instructions to take any proceedings against the authority releasing the records, assuming that to be the case. If necessary, applications can be made under the Access to Health Records Act 1990. Many hospitals prefer to send the records required for the purposes of a report directly to the expert rather than releasing them to the individual or his solicitor.

If an employer (or potential employer) obtained a medical report on the applicant/plaintiff, he may be entitled to obtain a copy of that report from the medical practitioner under the Access to Medical Reports Act 1988.

For the respondent or defendant
The respondents/defendants may wish to have access to the applicant/plaintiff's medical records. If so, they can seek access under r 4(1)(*b*) of the Industrial Tribunal (Constitution and Rules of Procedure) Regulations 1993 (SI No 2687) and/or CCR Ord 14. Disclosure should be ordered if necessary for disposing fairly of the action (CCR Ord 14, r 8).

Requiring the applicant/plaintiff to submit to an examination

In some cases, the respondent/defendant may wish to have its own expert examine the plaintiff. The county court has jurisdiction to stay proceedings where an applicant/plaintiff refuses to submit to a medical examination (see CCR Ord 13, r 1 and *Edmeades* v *Thames Board Mills Ltd* [1969] 2 QB 67) and ultimately strike out the claim for want of prosecution. Presumably, the Industrial Tribunals have the general power to give directions under r 16(1) of the Rules of Procedure Regulations 1993 (and see pp 111 to 115). In deciding whether or not to grant a stay, the court or tribunal must balance the individual's right of privacy with the respondent/defendant's right to defend himself and choose his own expert witness (*Starr* v *NCB* [1977] 1 All ER 243 at 250). Each right is equally important (*Prescott* v *Bulldog Tools Ltd* [1981] 3 All ER 869 at 875. There is a three stage test.

Firstly, is the request reasonable from the defendant's point of view? The defendant must show that they reasonably require an examination in order properly to prepare the defence (*Starr* v *NCB* [1977] 1 All ER 243 at 249d). If they do not, a stay will not be granted.

Secondly, is the refusal reasonable from the applicant/plaintiff's point of view? The fact that the applicant/plaintiff is confused by the effects of a brain injury (or other impairment) are to be taken into consideration in deciding if the refusal is reasonable (see *Hall* v *Avon Area Health Authority (Teaching)* [1980] 1 All ER 516). If the refusal is not subjectively reasonable, the stay will be granted.

If both request and refusal are reasonable, the court or tribunal is to weigh the objective reasonableness of the request against reasonableness of the refusal and use its discretion to reach as just a determination as possible between the parties. For example, it may be reasonable to require an examination but to allow a third party to be present at the examination where the applicant/plaintiff is in a confused or nervous state because of a disability (*Hall* v *Avon* above) although this will not always be so (see *Whitehead* v *Avon CC* (1995) *The Times*, 3 May). The more intrusive the proposed procedure the more weight is to be given to the refusal, and it will be likely to be reasonable to refuse to undergo a procedure where there is a real though minimal real risk of serious injury (*Aspinall* v *Sterling Mansell Ltd* [1981] 3 All ER 866). However, a stay will not be refused simply because the procedure is unpleasant (*Prescott* v *Bulldog Tools* [1981] 3 All ER 869). In common with the practice in personal injury litigation, it is likely that the defendant/respondent will have to pay the applicant/plaintiff's reasonable expenses and loss of earnings.

Checklist

Registered as disabled

—Was the person registered as disabled:
- on 12 January 1995?
- on 2 December 1996?

If so, he is deemed to be a disabled person.

Impairment

—Is there an impairment?
—What functional or physiological feature indicates impairment/abnormality?
—Is the impairment excluded from the DDA (ie is it an addiction, hayfever, or specified personality disorder)?
—Is the impairment physical or mental?
—If the impairment is mental, does it consist of or result from a mental illness?
—If the impairment consists of or results from a mental illness, is it a clinically well recognised mental illness?

Adverse effect upon normal day-to-day activities

—Does the impairment have a direct or indirect adverse effect upon one or more of the specified normal day-to-day activities?
—If so, which ones?
—Would it have such an effect in the absence of medical treatment or other measures (except glasses or contact lenses)?
—If the person is a child under six years old, would the impairment have a substantial adverse effect on a person aged six or over?

Substantial effect

—Is the effect substantial?
—Is the cumulative effect upon two or more of the specified activities substantial?
—Is there a substantial indirect effect from pain or fatigue etc arising from the impairment?
—Is the cumulative effect of two or more impairments upon the specified day-to-day activities substantial?
—Does the person have a severe disfigurement?
—If so, does it consist of a tattoo that has not been removed or of a body piercing?
—Does the person have a progressive condition?

—Does the condition have an effect (albeit not a substantial one) upon day-to-day activities?

—Is it likely to have a substantial effect in the future?

—Would the effect be substantial in the absence of medical treatment or other measures (except glasses or contact lenses)?

Long term effect

—Has the effect lasted for 12 months or more?

—Is the effect likely to last for 12 months?

—Is the effect likely to last for the rest of the person's life?

—Is the effect recurrent?

—If so, is it likely to recur more than 12 months after it first had that effect?

Part 2

Employment

Chapter 3

Employment: an Overview

Introduction: Part II and the employment code

Part II of the DDA deals with discrimination against disabled persons in the field of employment. The provisions are designed to make overt or covert discrimination related to the disability unlawful and, in certain circumstances, to require employers to modify workplaces and work practices that exclude or disadvantage people with disabilities. There are three forms of discrimination under the DDA. Firstly, s 5(1) provides that an employer discriminates against a disabled employee or applicant if he treats him less favourably than others for a reason which relates to the person's disability, unless he can show that the treatment is justified. Secondly, s 6 places a duty on the employer to make reasonable adjustments to workplaces and practices which put the disabled person at a substantial disadvantage in comparison with those who are not disabled. Section 5(2) of the DDA provides that an employer discriminates against the disabled person if he fails to make a reasonable adjustment, unless he can show that the failure is justified. Finally, s 55 of the DDA provides that an employer discriminates against a person (who need not be disabled) if he treats him or her less favourably because they have or are believed to have brought or assisted proceedings under the DDA or asserted that the employer has contravened the DDA. As the victimisation provisions apply equally to some other parts of the DDA, they are dealt with separately at p 251 below.

The duty to make reasonable adjustments is entirely new to British discrimination law. There are substantial differences between the other forms of discrimination as applied by the DDA and the sex and race discrimination legislation, particularly less favourable treatment. As a result, caution must be exercised when using case law under the Sex Discrimination Act 1975 (SDA) and the Race Relations Act 1976 (RRA) in interpreting the DDA. However, there are many similarities and some assistance may be taken from the existing authorities.

Section 4 of the DDA makes it unlawful for an employer to discriminate against employees and applicants for employment in the ways set out in that section. In common with the equivalent provisions in the SDA and RRA, this is widely drawn and covers most aspects of the employment relationship. Nonetheless, express provision is made for advertisements (s 11),

33

Occupational Pension Schemes (s 17) and Insurance Services (s 18). However, the DDA will only apply to certain forms of employment. These are established by ss 4, 64 (Application to Crown etc) and s 68 (interpretation). In addition, there is a general exemption for small employers with less than 20 employees (s 7) and limited exemptions for certain charitable and similar organisations (s 10). However, the DDA will protect contract workers (s 12).

Sections 13 to 15 will, when brought into force, make it unlawful for trade organisations to discriminate against disabled members or applicants for membership.

The enforcement provisions are contained in s 8, Sched 3 and Sched 4, pt I. Section 9 restricts the circumstances in which any person can contract out of their rights under the DDA, including any right to present a claim to an Industrial Tribunal.

There are associated provisions under which an employer is made vicariously liable for the discriminatory acts of his employees and agents (s 58) and whereby the employee or agent is made liable for assisting unlawful discrimination (s 57). Section 16 facilitates alterations required by the duty to adjust to premises occupied under a lease. As these provisions are common to or identical to equivalent provisions in other parts of the DDA, they are dealt with in Chap 16.

Regulations

Further provision regarding performance-related pay, occupational pension schemes, agricultural wages, contract workers and the duty to adjust by making alterations to buildings are made in the Disability Discrimination (Employment) Regulations 1996 (SI No 1456) (DD(E) Regs 1996). Section 16 (alterations to premises held under a lease) is supplemented by the DD(E) Regs 1996 and the Disability Discrimination (Sub-leases and Sub-tenancies) Regulations 1996 (SI No 1333) (DD(SS) Regs 1996).

Employment Code

The employment provisions of the DDA are supplemented by the provisions of the *Code of Practice for the Elimination of Discrimination in the Field of Employment against Disabled Persons, or Persons who have had a Disability* (the Employment Code) issued under s 53(1)(*a*). It is similar in status and effect to the Codes issued by the Equal Opportunities Commission and Commission for Racial Equality under the sex and race discrimination legislation. It gives practical guidance to employers and others in eliminating discrimination and should assist in avoiding complaints to industrial tribunals. The Employment Code is admissible in evidence in any proceedings under the Act before an Industrial Tribunal, county court or sheriff court (s 53(5)) who must take into account such parts of the Codes as they consider relevant to any question arising in proceedings under the DDA (s 53(6)). Although a breach of the Code is not automatically unlawful (s 53(4)), such a failure may assist a tribunal to determine that there has been unlawful discrimination in contravention of the DDA, particularly where that depends upon determining whether something is reasonable, practicable, substantial or material.

Commencement

The DDA employment provisions came into effect on 2 December 1996 (Disability Discrimination Act (Commencement No 3 and Saving and Transitional Provisions) Order 1996 (SI No 1474) (DDA (No 3) Order 1996).

Chapter 4

Less Favourable Treatment

Establishing discrimination

In order to establish discrimination by less favourable treatment, a disabled person has to show that (1) for a reason which relates to his disability (2) he was treated by the employer less favourably than the employer treats or would treat others to whom that reason does not or would not apply. Even if a disabled person can prove those two things, there will still be no discrimination if the employer can show that the treatment was justified. Section 5(1) provides as follows:

> 5(1) For the purposes of this Part, an employer discriminates against a disabled person if—
>
> > (a) for a reason which relates to the disabled person's disability, he treats him less favourably than he treats or would treat others to whom that reason does not or would not apply; and
> >
> > (b) he cannot show that the treatment is justified.

'For a reason which relates to his disability'

The use of the phrase 'for a reason which relates to his disability' instead of 'on the grounds of his disability' marks an important departure from the less favourable treatment provisions of sex and race discrimination legislation. The earlier legislation referred to less favourable treatment 'on the grounds of ... sex' or 'on racial grounds' (SDA 1975, s 1(1)(*a*) and RRA 1976, s 1(1)(*a*) respectively). Section 5(1) of the DDA has a potentially much wider application than those provisions. It will encompass some acts which would amount to 'indirect discrimination' or would not amount to discrimination at all under the sex and race legislation.

'for'

The reason which relates to the disabled person's disability need not be the only reason for the less favourable treatment. It is enough if it was a substantial or important reason for the treatment (see *Owen & Briggs* v *James* [1982] ICR 618, CA under the RRA 1976) or the substantial and effective reason for the treatment (see *R* v *CRE, ex p Westminster CC* [1984] ICR 770) or 'the factor which determines' the treatment (*Stockton-on-Tees BC* v *Brown* [1988] ICR 410).

'a reason'

The wording of the DDA and the focus on the 'reason' for the treatment is akin to the provisions relating to unfair dismissal in the Employment Rights Act 1996 (ERA 1996) (see s 98, unfair dismissal, and s 100, health and safety dismissals). Perhaps the closest analogy is with ERA 1996, s 99 which deals with dismissal 'for a reason connected with pregnancy'. The authorities on those provisions may be of some guidance to the operation of the DDA, at least until a body of caselaw is built up under the new Act.

In *Abernethy* v *Mott Hay and Anderson* [1974] ICR 323, a case on unfair dismissal, 'the reason for' dismissal was said to be the 'set of facts known to the employer, or it may be of beliefs held by him, which cause him to dismiss the employee', *per* Cairns LJ at 330b. It is arguable that the word 'reason' should be given the same meaning under the DDA.

'which relates to his disability'

The provisions obviously cover less favourable treatment based on straightforward prejudice, such as a decision not to employ someone simply because they have a history of mental health problems. The provisions will also apply where the reason 'relates to' the disability but goes beyond the mere fact of the disability, such as a refusal to employ someone because she uses a wheelchair (see the example given in the Employment Code, para 4.2) or has a guide dog. This would still be the case even if an applicant with the same disability would have been appointed if, for example, she had used crutches or a white stick.

In many cases the reason for the treatment may be overt. The employer will admit that the reason for the less favourable treatment related to the applicant's disability and seek to prove that the treatment was justified. However, in other cases, especially those involving simple prejudice, the employer may advance a potentially valid reason for the treatment. An applicant will then have to show that the reason proffered by the employer was not in fact the true reason for the less favourable treatment. Subject to the defence of justification, these cases are comparable to those involving direct discrimination under the sex and race legislation. Although direct evidence of prejudice will rarely be available, it may be possible to infer the reason for the less favourable treatment from the circumstances, (see *Noone* v *North West Thames Regional Health Authority* [1988] IRLR 195, CA; *Baker* v *Cornwall CC* [1990] IRLR 194, CA; and *King* v *The Great Britain–China Centre* [1991] IRLR 513, CA).

The extent to which s 5(1)(a) encompasses what is termed indirect discrimination under the race and sex legislation is uncertain. There is little doubt that s 5(1)(a) would be satisfied where the less favourable treatment results from the application of a health-related policy or rule that is applied to all disabled and non-disabled persons where the rule is closely related to the disability and its direct effects. For example, less favourable treatment resulting from the application of the following rules would satisfy s 5(1)(a):

(1) a refusal to employ a person with diabetes because of a rule that all employees have a controlled blood sugar level (as in the US case of *Bentivegna* v *US Department of Labour* (1982) 694 F.2d 619); or

(2) a dismissal in pursuance of a policy of dismissing everyone with an absence record of more than 15 per cent for two consecutive years where the absences were caused by a disability.

Some assistance may be obtained from the caselaw on what is now s 99 of the ERA 1996. In *Stockton-on-Tees BC* v *Brown* [1988] ICR 410 at 416d Lord Griffiths said that:

> Mrs Brown was selected for dismissal on the ground of redundancy because she needed maternity leave to give birth, and if that is not a reason connected with her pregnancy I do not know what is. I certainly cannot agree with Croom-Johnson LJ that the pregnancy was only a remote cause of her dismissal. Her pregnancy was the reason why she was selected for dismissal on the ground of redundancy rather than one of the other applicants

However, other cases may be less obvious and depend upon the application of requirements that appear, *prima facie*, to be disability neutral. An employer may refuse to employ someone because they do not have a driving licence. The applicant may not have a driving licence or be able to drive because of a disability. For example they may have had a licence which had been revoked because they no longer met the minimum eyesight standards or had developed epilepsy. In such a case, the 'reason' for the less favourable treatment is the fact that the applicant does not have a driving licence. That 'reason' is a 'reason which relates to the disabled person's disability'. The employer would treat others to whom that reason does not apply (ie an applicant with a driving licence) differently.

During a debate on the Bill, Lord Henley on behalf of the government gave the example of an applicant for a job who cannot type because of arthritis. He said that what is now s 5(1)(a):

> ... correctly reflects the need to show that the treatment was for a reason relating to the disability, and not the mere fact of disability. Thus, if the employer is rejecting people who cannot type, he will be treating more favourably those who can. The person with arthritis who did not get the job can show that he or she was treated less favourably than the person with typing abilities who did. The employer may well be able to justify that treatment—for example, if a disabled person was not adequately able to do the job, even taking account of any reasonable adjustment. But at least the disabled person would have to be given due consideration under the Bill (*Hansard*, HL, 18 July 1995, Vol 566, col 120).

It is not clear how closely related the 'reason' must be to the disability for it to satisfy the section. In the example given above, the employee may have a physical disability which made it more difficult (in practice) to obtain a licence without acting as an absolute bar to doing so. This is probably a question of fact and degree. However, it is submitted that the words 'ought to be read widely in order to give full effect to the mischief at which the statute was aimed', see *Clayton* v *Vigers* [1989] ICR 713, EAT.

An employer may be required to modify or adjust a rule or criterion which has an adverse impact on a disabled applicant or employee in order to comply with the duty to make reasonable adjustments (DDA 1995, s 6, discussed at p 49 below). If it is not, discrimination consisting of a failure to make a reasonable adjustment under s 5(2) may be established *in addition* to a finding of less favourable treatment for a reason which relates to the person's disability. An act of discrimination will not be rendered lawful merely because the employer acted out of a benign motive, (see *James* v *Eastleigh BC* [1990] ICR 554, HL. The motive will only prevent less favourable treatment from comprising unlawful discrimination if it justifies the treatment (see p 42).

Knowledge

If the less favourable treatment is alleged to have consisted of simple prejudice directly related to the disability, such as a refusal to employ someone because of his mental health problems or because he uses a wheelchair, it will be necessary to prove that the employer knew that the applicant suffered from mental health problems or used a wheelchair. As a matter of logic, an employer cannot have acted for those reasons without knowing of the relevant disability.

The position is less straightforward where the less favourable treatment results from a reason which relates to the disability but is not the disability itself. It is not clear whether s 5(1) can be satisfied if the employer does not know of the existence of the disability or that the 'reason ... relates' to the disability. Does the provision require the employer to know that the applicant has epilepsy or arthritis and/or that the lack of a driving licence or the inability to type was caused by those disabilities? The case law on what is now s 99 of the ERA 1996 suggests that the answer is yes. In *Del Monte Ltd* v *Mundon* [1980] ICR 694, the EAT held that:

> .... if [s 99] is relied on, it seems to us essential that it be shown that the employers knew or believed that the woman was pregnant or that they were dismissing her for a reason connected with her pregnancy. If they do not know of her pregnancy, or do not believe that the pregnancy exists, it does not seem to us that it is possible for the employers to have as their reason for the dismissal that the woman was pregnant. In a case where it is said that the reason for the dismissal is another reason connected with her pregnancy, not the pregnancy itself, it seems to us that the employers have to know the facts alleged by the employee as grounding the reason and also to know that those facts relied upon are connected with the pregnancy.

However, there is no express requirement for knowledge in s 5. This contrasts with the provisions on reasonable adjustment, in which s 6(6) expressly provides that the duty does not arise if the employer does not know and could not reasonably be expected to know that the person has a disability and is placed at a substantial disadvantage by an arrangement or physical feature (see p 51 below). It may be that the absence of an express requirement in relation to less favourable treatment indicates that such knowledge is not a prerequisite. This, it can be argued, would not place an undue burden on employers, because, where they do not know and could not reasonably be expected to know of the disability, it will usually be easier to justify the decision as there will be no duty to make reasonable adjustments (see p 51). Even if knowledge is required under s 5(1), it is also not clear whether constructive knowledge is sufficient as it is in relation to the duty to adjust (DDA 1995 s 6(6), Employment Code, paras 4.57 and 4.62, and see pp 289–90). In the absence of binding authority these points remain open.

Less favourable treatment, direct and indirect discrimination

During its passage through parliament, the promoters of the Bill stated that 'the Bill makes clear that indirect discrimination ... would be illegal. ... The Bill addresses the overall problems of indirect discrimination' (Paice, Standing Committee E, 7 February 1995, col 143). Despite this, there has been much debate as to the extent to which the DDA covers indirect discrimination in the absence of a section modelled directly on s 1(1)(*b*) of the SDA 1975 and s 1(1)(*b*) of the RRA 1976. In that debate, the less favourable treatment provisions of s 5 have often been seen as the direct equivalent of the direct discrimination provisions of those Acts. Indirect discrimination was said to be covered, if at all, by the duty to make reasonable adjustments in s 6.

It is submitted that it is wrong to categorise the less favourable treatment provisions of the DDA as concerning only what would be direct discrimination under the earlier legislation. Although s 5(1) does include direct discrimination, it also encompasses some things that are more akin to indirect discrimination as defined in those Acts. See the examples set out at p 38 above, where the requirement or rule would be applied to all applications. Although there may be a duty to adjust in those examples, there would still be less favourable treatment for a reason relating to the person's disability. As noted above (at p 39) there are likely to be many cases where discrimination will be established under both s 5(1) and s 5(2) on the same facts.

Furthermore, in the driving licence example (at p 38), s 5(1) discrimination could still be established even if the applicant would have got the job without a driving licence had they obtained maximum points on all other selection criteria, provided the absence of a licence was the substantial and effective reason for their rejection. In this respect, s 5 has a potentially wider application than the indirect discrimination provisions of the sex and race legislation, where the 'requirement or condition' must be an 'absolute bar' to the applicant's success to satisfy the provisions (see *Perera* v *Civil Service Commission* [1983] ICR 428, CA and *Meer* v *Tower Hamlets LB* [1988] IRLR 399, CA).

Furthermore, unlike the SDA 1975 or the RRA 1976, the DDA does not require a disabled person to show that disabled people (or people with a particular disability) are disproportionately affected by a rule, requirement or criteria. Both the less favourable treatment and the reasonable adjustment provisions focus on effect upon the individual with a disability. They are not concerned with the potential impact of treatment, arrangements or physical features upon disabled persons as a group.

'Treats him less favourably than he treats or would treat others to whom that reason does not or would not apply'

This part of the section is broadly similar to the equivalent provisions in the race and sex discrimination legislation and the authorities under those Acts are of substantial assistance here.

'Treats him less favourably'

There is no need to show that the treatment of others was objectively better in order to establish less favourable treatment. A denial of a choice or option which is valued by the disabled person is enough (see *R* v *Birmingham City Council, ex p Equal Opportunities Commission* [1989] 1 All ER 769, HL). Words of discouragement could amount to less favourable treatment, in appropriate circumstances (*Simon* v *Brimham Associates* [1987] ICR 569, CA). It is likely that differences of treatment so minor as to be *de minimis* will be ignored (*Jeremiah* v *Ministry of Defence* [1980] ICR 13, CA). And see pp 37 above.

'Than he treats or would treat others to whom that reason does not or would not apply'

The treatment must be less favourable than the treatment that was (or would have been) given to others to whom the reason for the less favourable treatment did not or would not apply. The comparator used for this purpose may be:

(1) someone without a disability treated more favourably by the employer; or

(2) someone with a different disability treated more favourably by the employer (where an employer treats someone with a physical disability more favourably than someone with a mental illness); or

(3) someone with the same disability but to whom the 'reason' does not apply treated more favourably by the employer (where an employer treats a blind applicant who uses a white stick more favourably than a blind applicant with a guide dog).

In addition, in each of the examples given above a hypothetical comparator can be used where the employer 'would' have treated such a person more favourably. (See generally the Employment Code at para 4.3 and *Leeds Private Hospital* v *Parkin* [1992] ICR 571.)

And the employer 'cannot show that the treatment in question is justified'

If it is established that the employer treated a disabled person less favourably 'for a reason which relates to the disabled person's disability', discrimination will be made out unless the employer shows that the treatment was 'justified' under s 5(1)(*b*). Section 5(3) provides that treatment can only be justified 'if the reason for it is both material to the circumstances of the particular case and substantial'. Section 5(5) provides that:

(1)   where the employer is under a duty to make a reasonable adjustment under s 6 in relation to the disabled person;

(2)   but fails without justification to make that adjustment;

(3)   the employer can only justify the less favourable treatment if the less favourable treatment would have been justified even if he had complied with the duty to make a reasonable adjustment.

The burden of proving justification is on the employer, and is on a balance of probabilities (see *National Vulcan Engineering Insurance Group* v *Wade* [1978] IRLR 225). It is not entirely clear whether the test is objective or subjective.

The argument in support of the subjective approach is as follows. Section 5(3) provides that less favourable treatment is justified if *'the reason for it* is both material and substantial' (emphasis added). The word 'reason' should be given the same meaning as in s 5(1)(*a*) and in the unfair dismissal legislation, namely the 'set of facts known to the employer, or *it may be of beliefs held by him*, which cause him to' treat the disabled person less favourably (emphasis added) (see *Abernethy* v *Mott Hay and Anderson* [1974] ICR 323 and above at p 37). On this basis, it is argued, justification is made out if the employer's belief is substantial and material even though the belief may be wrong.

However, although the point may require determination by the appeal courts, the better view seems to be that an objective test for justification should be adopted in relation to the employment provisions. There is no reference to the 'belief' or 'opinion' of the employer in the subsection. An earlier version of the justification provision, which depended upon the employer's reasonable opinion, was abandoned in favour of the current provision at the report stage. In contrast, the justification provisions in relation to goods and services in s 20(1)(*b*) and s 20(3) and premises in s 24(2) are based around the reasonable opinion of the service provider, landlord or manager. The legislative history indicates that the primary motivation for abandoning a test which depended upon the employer reasonably holding a particular opinion was to provide a wider and more flexible concept. In addition, it shows that the government intended to distinguish between the concept of justification in relation to the employment provisions and the 'opinion-based' approach used in the goods, services and premises part of the DDA. Lord Henley said that what is now s 5(3):

> ... substitutes for a fixed list of specific justifications a principle that can be applied much more easily in the wide and varied range of circumstances that can arise in the

field of employment . . . The approach that we now propose for the right of access [to goods and services] differs from that proposed for the employment right. Amendments Nos 67, for goods and services, and 78, for premises, retain the concept of a reasonably held opinion and fixed list of justification. We are satisfied that this continues to be right and relevant in the very different context. Service providers often have to take very quick and perhaps less informed decisions when serving someone. So an opinion-based approach remains appropriate. Nevertheless, the proper degree of objectivity is imposed because the opinion must be reasonably held (*Hansard*, HL 18 July 1995, col 119).

This supports the view that justification will not be established by matters reasonably but wrongly believed by the employer. If this is right, the employer will have to establish that the treatment was, in fact, justified. An employer will not be able to show that less favourable treatment was justified simply because he reasonably believed that it was. Further support for this 'objective' interpretation of justification can be found in the authorities on 'justifiable' requirements under SDA 1975, ss 1(1)(*b*)(ii) and 3(1)(*b*)(ii) and RRA 1976, s 1(1)(*b*)(ii), although particular caution must be exercised when considering these authorities as a guide to the DDA because of the influence of European sex discrimination legislation and case law. The statutory provisions on justifiable requirements allow an employer to resist an indirect discrimination claim if he can show that a requirement or condition would be 'justifiable' irrespective of the sex, marital status, colour, race, nationality or ethnic or national origins of the person to whom it is applied. In *Hampson* v *Department of Education and Science* [1989] IRLR 69 the Court of Appeal stated that the test in relation to the justifiable 'is an objective one. It is not sufficient for the employer to establish that he considered his reasons adequate. . . . 'justifiable' requires an objective balance between the discriminatory effect of the condition and the reasonable needs of the party who applies the condition', *per* Balcombe LJ at para 33/4. See also *Cobb* v *Secretary of State for Employment and Manpower Services Commission* [1989] IRLR 464, EAT and *Board of Governors of St Matthias Church of England School* v *Crizzle* [1993] IRLR 472, EAT. The Employment Code makes clear that the factors which justify less favourable treatment under the DDA are not limited to the economic or other reasonable needs of the employer.

'Material to the circumstances of the particular case'
The justification must relate to the circumstances of the individual case. An employer will not be able to rely upon stereotypes, generalised assumptions or blanket exclusions of people with certain disabilities which do not examine or take the particular circumstances into account. Therefore, an employer should not refuse to shortlist a blind person for a job involving computers because they think that blind people cannot use them. A general assumption that blind people cannot use computers would not be a material reason becasue it is not related to the particular circumstances (Employment Code, para 4.6). It will usually be relevant to consider the individual's abilities, the type of job and its particular requirements and the employers' needs.

'substantial'

Paragraph 4.6 of the Employment Code suggests that something is 'substantial' if it is 'not just trivial or minor', giving the word substantial the same meaning as in the definition of disability (s 1(1)) and see p 15 above). This interpretation is supported by the rebuttable presumption that a word has the same meaning throughout a statute (*Cramas Properties Ltd* v *Connaught Fur Trimmings Ltd* [1965] 1 WLR 892). It has been suggested that the word should be given a more onerous meaning of 'considerable, solid, or big' as adopted in the Rent Acts (see *Palser* v *Grinling* [1948] AC 291, HC at 361 and p 15 above). In support of this argument, it can be noted that the Ministers' statements that 'substantial' simply meant 'more than minor' etc (see p 15 above) were made before the word 'substantial' was introduced into the provisions on justifying less favourable treatment on 18 July 1995 on Report in the House of Lords. However, given the contents of the Employment Code and the presumption referred to above, the word 'substantial' in s 5(3) is likely to be interpreted to mean more than minor or trivial. This would establish a low test.

Examples

The Employment Code gives the examples of matters which are or are not likely to be substantial and to justify less favourable treatment (para 4.6).

> A factory worker with a mental illness is sometimes away from work due to his disability. Because of that he is dismissed. However the amount of time off is very little more than the employer accepts as sick leave for other employees and so is very unlikely to be a substantial reason.
>
> ... Someone who has psoriasis (a skin condition) is rejected for a job involving modelling cosmetics on a part of the body which in his case is severely disfigured by the condition. That would be lawful if his appearance would be incompatible with the purpose of the work. This is a substantial reason which is clearly related—material—to the individual circumstances.

See also the examples under Employment Code, para 4.7.

Justification and the duty to make adjustments

Discrimination by less favourable treatment cannot be justified where the employer is under a duty to make a reasonable adjustment but fails (without justification) to make it *unless* the less favourable treatment would have been justified even after that adjustment (DDA 1995, s 5(5) and Employment Code, para 4.7). The duty to make reasonable adjustments is discussed in detail at p 48 below. This is best illustrated by way of the examples given in the Employment Code, para 4.7.

> An employee who uses a wheelchair is not promoted, solely because the workstation for the more senior post is inaccessible to wheelchairs—although it could readily be made accessible by rearrangement of the furniture. [It is therefore very likely that the employer was under a duty to adjust by rearranging the

furniture. The example proceeds on the basis that the employer has failed, without justification, to comply with the duty by rearranging the furniture.] If the furniture had been rearranged, the reason for refusing promotion would not have applied. The refusal of promotion would therefore not be justified

The other example given by the Employment Code concerns an applicant for a typing job who is not the best applicant because her typing speed is too slow due to arthritis in her hands. It may be that a reasonable adjustment, such as an adapted keyboard, would overcome this problem, so that the employer was under a duty to make that adjustment. If the adjustment was made the typing speed would no longer be a 'substantial' reason for refusing to employ her and would not justify the less favourable treatment under s 5(3). In these circumstances, if the adjustment was not made, in breach of the duty to adjust *and* without justification, the employer would not be able to justify the less favourable treatment because of s 5(5).

However, it may be that providing an adapted keyboard would improve the applicant's typing speed but still leave her slower than the successful candidate. Provided this difference in speed was both substantial and of practical importance to the job (ie material) the less favourable treatment would still be justified under s 5(3) after the adapted keyboard was provided. Therefore, even if the employer failed without justification to provide the keyboard, the less favourable treatment would still be justified under s 5(5).

A difficult case

In some limited circumstances it may be arguable that a minor or trivial difference in ability justifies treating a disabled person less favourably for a reason relating to the disabled person's disability. For example, in the example given above, the two applicants may have had identical qualifications and similar experience and aptitudes, save that, even after a reasonable adjustment had been made, one applicant's typing speed was very marginally slower because of arthritis. This marginal difference in speed would have no significant impact on their ability to do the job. If there was nothing else whatsoever to separate the two applicants, would an employer be justified in selecting the other applicant because of that insubstantial difference in typing speeds? The marginal relative slowness would not be sufficiently substantial to refuse the applicant with arthritis if there were no other applicants. However, it may be that the need to make a selection on some rational grounds where there is nothing else to choose between candidates will render the minor difference in speed sufficiently substantial in the particular circumstances.

Deemed justification

Regulations may prescribe circumstances in which less favourable treatment is and is not justified (s 5(6)(*a*) and (*c*)). The DD(E) Regs 1996 deem less favourable treatment relating to performance related pay (p 79), agricultural wages (p 80) and occupational pension schemes (p 77) to be justified in certain circumstances. No regulations have yet been made to prescribe any circumstances in which less favourable treatment is not justified.

Checklist on less favourable treatment

Was there less favourable treatment for a reason related to the disability?

—What is the less favourable treatment alleged?
—Did the employer treat someone else more favourably:
  - someone without a disability?
  - someone with a different disability?
  - someone with the same disability to whom the reason for the treatment did not apply?
—If not, would the employer have treated others more favourably in the same circumstances?
—What was the reason for the less favourable treatment?
—Was the reason for the less favourable treatment
  - the fact of the disability?
  - related to the disability?
—Did the employer know of the disability?
—Did the employer know that the reason related to the disability?

Was the treatment justified?

—Is the less favourable treatment deemed to be justified? (see checklist on unlawful acts)
  - treatment relating to performance related pay
  - agricultural wages
  - occupational pension schemes
—Was the reason for the treatment substantial?
—Was the reason for the treatment material to the particular case?
—Was the employer under a duty to adjust?
—Had the employer complied with the duty to adjust?
—If not, was the failure to comply with the duty justified? (see checklist on the duty to adjust)
—If not, would the treatment have been justified if the employer had complied with the duty to adjust?

Chapter 5

The Duty to Adjust

Introduction

The introduction of the duty to adjust is, potentially, one of the most far reaching provisions of the new law. It tacitly accepts that the physical design of work places and the nature of working practices can produce greater obstacles to the employment of someone with a disability than any physical or other limitations caused by the disability itself. To this extent, there is recognition of the social model of disability. The provision does not require an employer to treat a disabled person more favourably than he would treat others (s 6(7)). It only requires an employer, in certain circumstances, to take reasonable steps to remove or reduce disadvantages to a disabled person that result from the arrangements made or premises occupied by the employer.

Discrimination and the duty to adjust

The definition of discrimination in cases involving the duty to adjust is set out in s 5(2):

> 5(2) For the purposes of this Part, an employer also discriminates against a disabled person if—
> (a) he fails to comply with a section 6 duty imposed on him in relation to the disabled person; and
> (b) he cannot show that his failure to comply with that duty is justified.

In order to establish discrimination by a failure to comply with the s 6 duty to make a reasonable adjustment, a disabled person has to show both that the employer was under a duty to adjust, and that the employer failed to comply with that duty. Even if a disabled person can prove those two things, there will still be no discrimination under the DDA if the employer can show that the failure to comply was justified. The duty is imposed only for the purposes of determining if an employer has discriminated against a disabled person within the meaning of s 5(2). A breach of the duty does not give rise to an independent right of action (s 6(12)).

The duty

The employer's duty to adjust is set out in s 6 of the DDA.

Duty of employer to make adjustments

6(1) Where
    (a) any arrangements made by or on behalf of an employer, or
    (b) any physical feature of premises occupied by the employer, place the disabled person concerned at a substantial disadvantage in comparison with persons who are not disabled, it is the duty of the employer to take such steps as it is reasonable, in all the circumstances of the case, for him to have to take in order to prevent the arrangements or feature having that effect.

The duty to adjust arrangements in s 6(1)(a) only applies in relation to arrangements for determining to whom employment should be offered (s 6(2)(a)) or to any term, condition or arrangements on which employment, promotion, a transfer, training or any other benefit is offered or afforded (s 6(2)(b)).

'Arrangements for determining to whom employment should be offered'

The word 'arrangements' is not defined, but is intended to be widely construed (Employment Code, para 5.2). This was the parliamentary intention:

> The broad term 'arrangements' has been deliberately used ... to cover anything done by or for an employer as part of his recruitment process or in making available opportunities in employment. It would not only include work practices and procedures so far as such procedures have any bearing on determining who is offered employment or to whom such opportunities are to be made available: it would go wider than that. (*Hansard*, Report SC E, 7 February 1995, col 142, Paice)

It is far wider than the 'requirement or condition' in the indirect discrimination provisions of the sex and race legislation (SDA 1975, s 1(1)(b); RRA s 1(1)(b), (see p 70 below). The tribunal will have to decide the purpose of the activity described as an arrangement. It will consitute an arrangement if its purpose was to determine who should be offered employment.

The Employment Code makes clear that the job specification, advertisements (and see the provisions about adverts in s 11 discussed at p 70 below), the selection process, including the location and timing of interviews, assessment techniques, interviewing and selection criteria all form part of the 'arrangements' for the purposes of the sub-section (para 5.2). It would also cover such matters as the form in which information is provided about a vacancy and the form in which applications are to be made (eg handwritten, typed etc). As the provision covers arrangements made 'on behalf of' as well as those made 'by' the employer, the employer's duty will extend to arrangements made by an external recruitment agency or other outside body as well as those made by its own managers and personnel staff.

It will probably not include arrangements specified by or under a statutory procedure, as such arrangements are not made by the employer (see *Ealing, Hammersmith & Hounslow Family Health Services Authority* v *Shukla* [1993] ICR 710 at 719). In any event, there may be a statutory enactment defence in such a case (see p 250).

'Any term, condition or arrangements on which employment, promotion, a transfer, training or any other benefit is offered or afforded'

This provision expressly encompasses the terms and conditions of employment. In addition, 'arrangements' again has a wide meaning. It includes practical matters such as working conditions, practices and methods as well as selection processes and criteria (Employment Code, para 4.16).

> [Sub-section 1] is intentionally drafted in general terms which we believe employers will understand. 'Arrangements' is widely defined and will cover a wide range of working conditions including what I might describe as the telecommunications environment in which the person works. [The government understood Lord Ashley's] concern that the duty on employers to make reasonable adjustment should cover adjustments such as preventing new (digital) telephones from interfering with hearing aids and making adjustments to a telephone, or providing a telephone which is compatible for use with a hearing aid. ... I can assure the noble Lord that the duty of reasonable adjustment already covers such areas (*Hansard*, HL 13 June 1995, col 1766, Inglewood).

It is not clear what this provision does not cover, although it would appear to exclude the terms of the dismissal. It would include the procedures or arrangements by which the decision to dismiss is reached. For example, it would apply to disciplinary proceedings leading to dismissal or arrangements or procedures for redundancy selection.

'Any physical feature of premises occupied by the employer'

Regulation 9 of the DD(E) Regs 1996 provides that:

> the following are to be treated as physical features (whether permanent or temporary—
>
> (a)   any feature arising from the design or construction of a building on the premises;
> (b)   any feature on the premises of any approach to, exit from or access to such a building;
> (c)   any fixtures, fittings, furnishings, furniture, equipment or materials in or on the premises;
> (d)   any other physical element or quality of any land comprised in the premises.

It is unclear whether this list is intended to be exhaustive, although sub-para (d) is intended to be very widely construed. 'Premises' includes land of any description (s 68). The duty to adjust in relation to premises held under a lease is discussed in detail at p 233 below.

'Place the disabled person concerned' and the question of knowledge

The duty under s 6 is a specific and individualised duty. It only requires an employer to make adaptations in relation 'to the disabled person concerned'. It does not require an employer to make general adaptations to make work places and practices accessible to disabled people in general (Employment Code, para 5.19).

In cases involving arrangements for determining to whom employment should be offered, 'the disabled person concerned' is any person who is an applicant for that employment or has notified the employer that he may be an applicant for that employment (s 6(5)(a)). In any other case, this means either an applicant for the relevant employment or an employee of the employer concerned (s 6(5)(b)).

Furthermore, the duty to adjust does not arise if the employer does not know and could not reasonably be expected to know:

(a) that the disabled applicant or potential applicant may be an applicant for employment; or

(b) in any case that the person has a disability and is likely to be placed at a substantial disadvantage (s 6(6)).

The Employment Code deals with this issue at paras 4.57, 4.61/2 and 5.12 but gives little guidance as to when an employer could reasonably be expected to know that a particular disabled person is or may be an applicant. The disabled applicant will usually have to make his disability known from the outset in order to be protected, which many people will not wish to do. Knowledge of an employee or agent is imputed to the employer but not that of an independent contractor (Employment Code, para 4.62/3).

'at a substantial disadvantage in comparison with persons who are not disabled'

A disadvantage is substantial if it is more than minor or trivial (see p 15 above). For example, an employer is unlikely to be required to widen a particular doorway for a wheelchair when there is an easy alternative route to the same destination (Employment Code, para 4.17, and see eg *Reeves* v *TGWU* [1980] ICR 728). The comparison can be made with a non-disabled person who is or was not disadvantaged by the arrangement, term or condition or with a hypothetical comparator who would not be or have been so disadvantaged (Employment Code, para 4.13).

Provided the disabled person concerned can show that he was placed at a substantial disadvantage, there is no need to show that a substantial proportion of disabled people or disabled people in general are or would be similarly disadvantaged (see p 40).

Regulations

Regulations may prescribe circumstances in which arrangements or features are or are not to be taken to have such an effect (s 6(7)(*a*) and (*b*)). Regulation 4(2) of the DD(E) Regs 1996 provides that terms or practices establishing performance-related pay are deemed not to place a disabled person at a substantial disadvantage (see p 79).

'it is the duty of the employer to take such steps as it is reasonable, in all the circumstances of the case, for him to have to take in order to prevent the arrangements or feature having that effect'

The DDA sets out examples (not an exhaustive list) of some of the steps which an employer may have to take in fulfilment of the duty (s 6(3)). They are only examples and an employer will only be required to make such adjustments in so far as is reasonable. They will not have to be taken in every case. In addition, an employer may have to take a step that is not listed (Employment Code, para 4.20) or more than one step (Employment Code, para 4.33). The statutory examples are set out in italics at 1 to 7 below. More detailed examples are given in the Employment Code at para 4.20. These are summarised below and set out in full in Appendix 2 at p 276 below.

1   Making adjustments to premises
This may include structural or other physical adjustments such as widening a doorway, providing a ramp or moving furniture for a wheelchair user; relocating light switches, door handles or shelves for someone who has difficulty in reaching; or providing appropriate contrast in decor for a visually impaired person. (Employment Code, para 4.20). Adjustments to premises are considered in detail in Chap 16 below.

2   Allocating some of the disabled person's duties to another person
Minor or subsidiary duties may be reallocated to another employee. For example, a duty requiring someone occasionally to work on the open roof of a building might be transferred away from an employee with severe vertigo (Employment Code, para 4.20). Similarly, subsidiary duties which require a driving licence could be reallocated from a disabled person who does not have a licence because of his disability. An employer is unlikely to be required to reallocate duties that are essential to the job done or to be done by the disabled person. This is a question of fact and degree. The amount of time usually spent performing the particular duties will often be an indicator of whether they are essential. However, a rarely performed duty may still be essential in particular circumstances. For example, a security guard may not be regularly required to carry an unconscious adult to safety, but the consequences of him or her not being able to do so when required could be extremely serious.

3   Transfering an employee to fill an existing vacancy
If an employee cannot continue to do the same job because of a disability, and
no reasonable adjustment could be made to enable them to continue with the
current job, then they might have to be considered for any suitable alternative
posts which are available, with reasonable retraining if necessary
(Employment Code, para 4.20).

4   Altering an employee's working hours
A disabled person could be allowed to work flexible hours with additional
breaks to overcome fatigue arising from the disability or to fit with the
availability of a carer (Employment Code, para 4.20). Similarly, a late start
and late finish may be introduced to allow someone with mobility difficulties
to use public transport outside the rush hour (Employment Code, para 5.27).

5   Assigning an employee to a different place of work
A wheelchair user's work station could be transferred from an inaccessible
third floor office to an accessible one on the ground floor or to other premises if
the first building is inaccessible (Employment Code, para 4.20). In appropriate
circumstances it could mean allowing the employee to work from home.

*6   Allowing an employee to be absent during working hours for rehabilita-
tion, assessment or treatment*
An employer might have to allow a disabled person more time off during work
than would be allowed to non-disabled employees, to enable them to receive
physiotherapy or psychoanalysis or undertake employment rehabilitation.
(Employment Code, para 4.20)

7   Giving an employee, or arranging for them to be given, training
This may involve training in the use of pieces of equipment used only by the
disabled person, such as training a visually impaired person so that they can
use a computer with speech output. It may also involve adapting training given
to other employees so as to take account of the disabled person's disability
(Employment Code, para 4.20).

8   Acquiring or modifying equipment
An employer might have to provide special equipment (such as an adapted
keyboard for a visually impaired person or someone with arthritis) or an
adapted telephone for someone with a hearing impairment or modified
equipment (such as longer handles on a machine). There is no requirement to
provide or modify equipment for personal purposes unconnected with work,
such as providing a wheelchair if a person needs but does not have one
(Employment Code, para 4.20).

9   Modifying instructions or reference manuals
The format of instructions or manuals may need to be modified (eg produced
in braille or on audio tape) and instructions for people with learning
disabilities may need to be conveyed orally with individual demonstration
(Employment Code, para 4.20).

10   Modifying procedures for testing or assessment
Employers may need to ensure that particular tests do not adversely affect
people with particular types of disability. A person with restricted manual
dexterity who would be disadvantaged by a written test might have to be given
an oral test (Employment Code, para 4.20). Alternatively, it may be reasonable
to allow them longer to complete a written test. Similarly, it may be necessary
to give a person with learning disabilities an oral test if they are unable to read.

11   Providing a reader or interpreter
This could involve a colleague reading mail to a person with a visual
impairment at set times during the day or, in appropriate circumstances, the
hiring of a reader or sign language interpreter (Employment Code, para.
4.20)).

12   Providing supervision
This may involve providing a support worker or help from a colleague for
someone whose disability leads to uncertainty or lack of confidence
(Employment Code, para 4.20).
    Further examples of practical steps that may be taken in particular cases are
set out at pp 70 below.

The extent of the duty

The employer is only under a duty to make the reasonable adjustment if it is
reasonable for it to have to do so. A list of some of the matters to be taken into
account is provided in s 6(4) of the DDA. Certain steps may require very little
of the employer, such as providing limited supervision from a colleague, or
giving the person training in house, or allowing the employee occasionally to
be absent during working hours for rehabilitation, assessment or treatment.
These are activities most employers are engaged in regularly, requiring
usually only slight modifications. Others require alterations to the premises,
providing equipment, or reallocating duties. These may be rather less
practicable in certain situations. Although one of the factors may be
determinative (for example if the step would be entirely ineffective or
wholly impracticable), in most cases the various factors will have to be
considered and balanced against each other.
    It is important to note that the provision refers to 'such steps as *it is*
reasonable' for the employer to take (emphasis added). The question is
whether or not it was, in fact, reasonable for the employer to take that step.
There are no grounds for putting a gloss on the words to introduce the concept

of a range of reasonable beliefs. An employer will not be able to show that he was not under a duty to make an adjustment simply because his belief that it was not reasonable for him to take a step was within a range of reasonable beliefs (see *Cross International* v *Reid* [1985] IRLR 387 at para 23).

The extent to which taking the step would prevent the effect in question (s 6(4)(*a*))

The tribunal must consider whether and to what extent taking the step would prevent the feature or arrangement placing the disabled person at a substantial disadvantage in comparison with persons who are not disabled. It is unlikely to be reasonable for an employer to have to take a step that is of little benefit to the disabled employee (Employment Code, para 4.22) although it may be reasonable if there is no or minimal cost to the employer:

> '[I]f the only adjustment possible could make no more than a small improvement to the output of someone who was significantly under-productive, then [the adjustments] might not be reasonable if they were costly or disruptive.' (*Hansard*, HL, 18 July 1995, Vol 566, col 184, Henley).

The extent to which it is practicable for the employer to take that step (s 6(4)(*b*))

It is more likely to be reasonable for an employer to take a step which is easy to take than one which is difficult (Employment Code, para 4.23). For example, it may not be reasonable for an employer to have to wait for an adjustment to be made to an entrance if it needs to appoint an employee urgently. However, it may still be reasonable for the employer to make a temporary adjustment in the meantime if it is possible to do so, such as using a different entrance (Employment Code, para 4.23) or even different workplace until the adjustment can be made. This will depend upon all the circumstances, including the size of the undertaking, the work pattern, the degree of urgency and the feasibility and cost of temporary arrangements. Where the proposed adjustment would involve reallocating duties to other employees, it will be necessary to consider whether the other employees are willing to take on those other duties and/or whether they can be required to do so under their own contracts of employment.

If a job applicant has not informed an employer, and the employer could not reasonably be expected to know of his disability prior to the interview, no duty to adjust will arise (s 6(6) and p 51 above). Nonetheless, once the applicant arrives for interview the employer may be under a duty to make a reasonable adjustment from the time that he first learns of the disability and disadvantage. However, what the employer has to do in such circumstances might be less extensive than if advanced notice had been given (Employment Code, para 5.16) as it may not be practicable to make any or as extensive adjustments at such short notice.

The financial and other costs which would be incurred by the employer in taking the step and the extent to which taking it would disrupt any of his activities (s 6(4)(c))

If an adjustment costs little or nothing and is not disruptive, it is likely to be reasonable unless some other factor (such as practicability or effectiveness) made it unreasonable. Costs include staff and oither resource costs. The significance of the cost may depend upon what the employer might otherwise have to spend in the circumstances.

> It would be reasonable for an employer to have to spend at least as much on an adjustment to enable the retention of a disabled person—including any retraining—as might be spent on recruiting and training a replacment
> (Employment Code, para 4.24).

Similarly the savings that will be made by not having to purchase, maintain and replace chairs may be set off against the cost of adapting a workstation for an applicant who uses a wheelchair.

In considering the financial cost of a measure involving the acquisition of machinery or other equipment, regard should be had to the tax implications of a purchase for the employer. Many of the reasonable adjustments likely to be made by employers under s 6 will qualify for allowances or for deductions under the normal rules of taxation (*Hansard*, HL, 13 June 1995, Vol 564, col 1775, Lord Inglewood).

> So for example a firm that employs a reader for a visually impaired employee could write off the cost of employing the reader for tax purposes. (Col 1776).

The value of the employee's experience and expertise to the employer may also be relevant, as will factors such as the resources (including training) invested in the employee, the employee's length of service, skill, knowledge, relationship with clients and pay (Employment Code, para 4.25). 'It is more likely to be reasonable to make an adjustment with significant costs if the employee is going to be in the job for some time' (Employment Code, para 4.26). The less inconvenience an adjustment will cause to other employees or the employer, the more likely it is to be reasonable for the employer to take that step (Employment Code, para 4.27).

The extent of the employer's financial and other resources (s 6(4)(d))

> It is more likely to be reasonable for an employer with substantial financial resources to have to make an adjustment with a significant cost than for an employer with fewer resources. The resources in practice available to the employer as a whole should be taken into account, as well as other calls on those resources. ...
> (Employment Code, para 4.28).

Where the resources of the employer are spread across more than one 'business unit' or 'profit centre' the whole of the resources available and the competing calls on those resources should also be taken into account in assessing reasonableness (Employment Code, para 4.29).

It is more likely to be reasonable for an employer with a large number of staff to make some adjustments (such as reallocating duties, transferring the employee to an alternative post, or providing supervision from existing staff) than an employer with few employees. However, an employer with fewer employees may still need to make those adjustments if it was reasonable to do so in the circumstances (Employment Code, para 4.30).

The nature of the employer's resources should also be considered. For example, it may be more reasonable to expect a construction company to carry out physical modifications to a building than a restaurant.

The availability of financial and other assistance to the employer with respect to taking that step (s 6(4)(*e*))

Outside assistance available to an employer for taking any step will be relevant (Employment Code, para 4.31). This may involve financial support or grants, the modification of existing equipment, the provision of specialised equipment, training, support or supervision from government programmes or voluntary bodies. One example of such a scheme is the Access to Work Scheme which assists disabled persons with the practical difficulties they may encounter in seeking work. A number of schemes such as the Job Introduction Scheme, the Special Aids to Employment Scheme, Adaptations to Premises and Equipment Scheme, Assistance with Fares to Work Scheme, Remote Working Scheme and Business on Own Account Scheme, have for the most part been subsumed into the Access to Work scheme. If some other form of practical or personal help could make it possible for a disabled person to do a job effectively it may be possible for the Access to Work Scheme to assist.

In addition the Major Organisations Development Unit provides large employers with advice on good practice in relation to the employment of disabled persons. Employers' Forum on Disability may provide the employer with advice on the employment of a disabled person and the adjustments that may need to be made. The Department for Education and Employment also runs employment and training programmes, which must be made available to disabled persons on the same terms as they are available to non-disabled persons.

Alternatively, it may be that the disabled applicant or employee already has a particular piece of adapted equipment, such as an adapted car or keyboard, which he is willing to use for work. In such a case it would not be reasonable for the employer to state that the cost of an adapted car or keyboard made it unreasonable for him to make the adjustment (Employment Code, para 4.31).

Regulations (s 6(8))

Regulations may make provisions as to circumstances in which it is or is not reasonable for employers to have to take steps of a prescribed description (s 6(8)(c) and (e)) and as to steps which it is always or never reasonable for an employer to have to take (s 6(8)(d) and (f)). To date, the only regulations made under this power concern contract work (DD(E) Regs 1996, reg 7, and see p 67) and alterations of premises.

Premises

It is deemed never to be reasonable for an employer to take a step to alter a physical characteristic of a building which met and continues to meet the requirements of Part M of the Building Regulations in force at the time of building (DD(E) Regs 1996, reg 8, and see p 246 below).

If an employer is required by a legally binding obligation not contained in a lease to obtain the consent of any person to any alteration of any premises occupied by him, it is deemed always to be reasonable for an employer to take steps (other than an application to a court or tribunal) to obtain that consent and never to be reasonable for the employer to make the alteration before consent is obtained (DD(E) Regs 1996, reg 10(1), and see p 234 below).

It is deemed never to be reasonable for an employer to make any alteration to any premises occupied by him under a lease which is contrary to the terms of that lease if he has applied for and has been refused consent to make the alteration and has informed the disabled person of the refusal of his application (DD(E) regs 1996, reg 15, and see p 244 below).

Other matters to be taken into account in deciding reasonableness

As noted above, other factors not expressly referred to in the DDA may be relevant. The Employment Code refers to some other factors which may be relevant (para 4.32). In particular, it suggests that the extent to which the disabled employee is willing to co-operate with the adjustment should be taken into account. If an employee refused to move to a more easily accessible office on the ground floor, it would not be reasonable for the employer to have to relocate that employee to that office. It also notes that whilst the effect on other employees may be relevant, their adverse reaction to an adjustment being made because they too would like the benefit of, say, a special working arrangement is unlikely to be significant. It also states that whilst adjustments made for other disabled employees may be relevant, an employer will not be obliged to make an adjustment which goes beyond the duty of reasonable adjustment for a particular employee simply because he has chosen to make that adjustment for other disabled employees.

One matter which may be of particular importance is the advice sought and obtained by an employer. Although there is no general duty on employers to seek advice, they would be best advised to do so. Otherwise, they may decide that an adjustment is too expensive when funds are available from an outside agency so that the step could be taken at little or no cost to the employer (but see justification below at p 59). Alternatively, it could assist in identifying steps that could be taken in order to overcome any practical difficulties. Irrespective of any potential liability for discrimination under the DDA, this will often allow an employer to employ the best person for the job:

> If employers make a decision about reasonable adjustment off the top of their head, for want of a better phrase, tribunals will be able to take that into account. We do not propose to make the taking of advice a prerequisite—but not doing so could be taken into account by the tribunal in considering whether the employer had acted reasonably in all the circumstances.
> (*Hansard*, Report SC E, 14 Feb 1995, col 222, Paice).

Other statutory obligations upon employers may be relevant. If an employer is required to take a particular step by other legislation or by a different part of the DDA, it is more likely to be reasonable for the purposes of the DDA. For example, there may be an obligation upon an employer under the Chronically Sick and Disabled Persons Act 1970 to make provision for sanitary conveniences, parking, and means of access for people with disabilities. Alternatively, once the provisions of s 21(2) of the DDA come into force, there may be an obligation upon an employer who is also a service provider to make alterations to premises to make them more accessible for disabled persons. See also art 20 of the Workplace Directive (89/654/EEC), which provides that:

> [W]orkplaces must be organised to take account of handicapped workers, if necessary. This provision applies in particular to the doors, passageways, staircases, showers, washbasins, lavatories and workstations used or occupied directly by handicapped persons.

Although no specific mention is made of 'handicapped workers' in the Workplace (Health, Safety and Welfare) Regulations 1992, (SI No 3004) which implemented the Workplace Directive, the regulations should be interpreted so as to accord with the Directive (see *Litster v Forth Dry Dock and Engineering Co Ltd* [1989] ICR 341 and *Webb v Emo Air Cargo (UK) Ltd* [1993] ICR 175). In any event, the Directive will be directly enforceable against an employer that is an emanation of the State (see *Marshall v Southampton and South West Hampshire Area Health Authority* [1986] ICR 335).

Equally, other legislation may prevent it being reasonable for an employer to have to make an adjustment. An adjustment 'would not be reasonable if it is impossible because the employer would be in breach of the Health and Safety or fire laws were it to be made' (*Hansard*, HL, 18 July 1995, Vol 566, col 185, Henley).

And the employer 'cannot show that his failure to comply with the section is justified'

Even if it is established that the employer failed to comply with a duty, discrimination under s 5(2) is only made out if the employer cannot show that the failure was 'justified' under s 5(2)(*b*). Section 5(4) provides that treatment can only be justified 'if the reason for it is both material to the circumstances of the particular case and substantial'. This provision is very similar to the justification provisions under s 5(1) and 'material' and 'substantial' will have the same meaning in both (see p 15 above). The duty to adjust only arises if it is reasonable for the employer to make the adjustment. If it is not reasonable for an adjustment to be made, it will not be necessary to justify the failure to adjust. An employer will only need to show that the failure was justified if it was otherwise reasonable for him to take that step. The Employment Code, at para 4.34, suggests that an employer may be justified in failing to adjust where:

1   he was unaware of the appropriate adjustment or of the availability of financial or other assistance to make the adjustment, provided he had made a reasonable effort to obtain proper information;

2   the disabled person refuses to co-operate with a reasonable adjustment proposed by the employer, even if other steps could be taken; and

3   the need for the adjustment resulted from the disabled person's refusal to follow specific advice offered by the employer in the past.

However, in each case it could be argued that it was not reasonable for the employer to have to make the adjustment in the circumstances. In practice, there will often be a large overlap between matters that make it unreasonable for an employer to adjust and matters which justify a failure to take a step.

Deemed justification

Regulations may prescribe circumstances in which a failure to adjust is and is not justified (s 5(6)(*b*) and (*d*)). No regulations have been made deeming any such failure to be unjustified. Regulation 6(*b*) of the DD(E) Regs 1996 deems a failure to adjust to be justified in circumstances covered by a permit under s 5 of the Agricultural Wages Act 1948 (or s 5 of the Agricultural Wages (Scotland) Act 1949) (see p 80 below).

Checklist on the duty to adjust

Was there a relevant disadvantage?

—Was the disabled person caused a disadvantage in comparison with persons who were not disabled?

—Was the disadvantage substantial?

—Was any disadvantage deemed not to be a substantial disadvantage because it resulted from performance related pay?

—Was the substantial disadvantage caused by:

- any arrangements made by or on behalf of an employer for determining to whom employment should be offered?
- any term condition or arrangements on which employment, promotion, a transfer, training or any other benefit is offered or afforded?
- any physical feature of premises occupied by the employer?

—In a case involving an applicant, did the employer know that the disabled person may be an applicant for employment?

—If not, should the employer have known that the disabled person may be an applicant for employment? If so, why and how?

—In any case, did the employer know that the disabled person was placed at a substantial disadvantage by the arrangement or feature?

—If not, should the employer have known that the disabled person was placed at a disadvantage by the arrangement or feature? If so, why and how?

Could the employer have taken a step to remove or reduce that disadvantage?

—Could the employer have taken a step to remedy the substantial disadvantage, by:

- Making adjustments to premises?
- allocating some of the disabled person's duties to another person?
- transferring them to fill an existing vacancy?
- altering their working hours?
- assigning them to a different place of work?
- allowing them to be absent during working hours for rehabilitation, assessment or treatment?
- giving them, or arranging for them to be given, training?
- acquiring or modifying equipment?
- modifying instruction or reference manuals?
- modifying procedures for testing or assessment?
- providing a reader or interpreter?
- providing supervision?
- taking some other step, and if so what?

Was it reasonable for the employer to take that step?

—Is the step deemed not to be reasonable on the ground that the step was altering premises and:
  • the premises complied with the Building Regulations?
  • the employer had sought and been refused consent to make the alteration by its landlord and the employer had told the disabled person concerned of the landlord's refusal?
  • the employer had sought and been refused consent of a person required under a legally binding obligation?
—Unless the step is deemed not to be reasonable, consider the following:
  • to what extent would taking the step have prevented the disadvantage?
  • to what extent was it practicable for the employer to take that step?
  • would taking the step have had financial costs? If so, what? If there would have been savings—such as the cost of training a replacement—or tax benefits, what would the net cost have been?
  • would taking the step have had other costs If so, what?
  • would taking the step have caused disruption to the employer? If so, what disruption and to what extent?
  • what financial and other resources did the employer have?
  • was financial and other assistance available to the employer? If so, what?
  • are any other circumstances relevant: such as the service record of the disabled person, the attitude of the disabled person, the advice sought and received by the employer, the impact of other legislation etc?

Discrimination by failing to comply with the duty to adjust

—Was there a duty to take a step?
—Did the employer take that step?
—If not, was the failure to adjust deemed to be justified because of a permit under the Agricultural Wages Act 1948?
—If not, what was the reason for the failure to take that step?
—Was the reason substantial?
—Was the reason material to the particular circumstances?
—Was the failure justified?

Chapter 6

The Unlawful Acts

Section 4 of the DDA 1995 provides that it is unlawful for an employer to discriminate against employees and applicants for employment in various respects. The discrimination can be by way of unjustified less favourable treatment, an unjustified failure to adjust or victimisation (see p 251 below).

Employees and applicants

A disabled person can only bring a claim for discrimination under Pt II of the DDA if he is an employee, an applicant or prospective applicant for employment or a contract worker at an establishment in Great Britain. There are special rules relating to small employers, some 'employment' by or for the Crown or various other parts of the government and charities. The law relating to contract workers is dealt with at p 66 below.

Employment

'Employment' means 'employment under a contract of service or of apprenticeship or a contract personally to do any work' (s 68). There is no material difference between this definition and its equivalents in ss 82 of the SDA 1975 and s 78 of the RRA 1976 (both of which refer to 'a contract personally to do any work *or labour* (emphasis added) (although nothing seems to turn upon the omission of those words in this section).

The definition thereby includes many people who would generally be regarded as self employed, but only if they are under an obligation to carry out the work themselves (*Tanna* v *Post Office* [1981] ICR 374). However, whilst a 'contract personally to do any work' is a wide and flexible concept (see *Quinnen* v *Hovells* [1984] IRLR 227), the obligation to carry out the work personally must be the dominant purpose of the contract (see *MGN* v *Gunninig* [1986] IRLR 27).

Employment will probably not include working pursuant to arrangements made by a statutory scheme conferring rights and obligations, such as the relationship between a doctor and a Medical Practices Committee (*Wadi* v *Cornwall & Isles of Scilly Family Practitioner Committee* [1985] ICR 492 and *Ealing, Hammersmith & Hounslow Family Health Services Authority* v

Shukla [1993] ICR 710). If the primary purpose of a training agreement (not an apprenticeship) is to allow a trainee to obtain skills and experience rather than to create the relationship of employee and employer, it will probably not comprise employment within the meaning of the Act (*Daley* v *Allied Suppliers Ltd* [1983] ICR 90).

Illegality

An industrial tribunal has jurisdiction to hear a complaint of discrimination even if the contract of employment is tainted with illegality, such as a fraud on the Inland Revenue by non-payment of tax and national insurance (*Leighton* v *Michael* [1996] IRLR 67, EAT).

Applicants

Section 4(1) of the DDA 1995 applies to people who apply for employment and to prospective applicants who did not make a formal application because of discrimination, for example if they were wrongly told the vacancy had been filled (*Johnson* v *Timber Tailors (Midlands) Ltd* [1978] IRLR 146).

Ex-employees

Section 4(2) of the DDA 1995 applies to someone who is employed at the time of the act complained of. It does not apply to someone who is no longer employed by the employer. In particular, discrimination in the course of an appeal against dismissal after the worker has been dismissed does not fall within the DDA (see *Post Office* v *Adekeye (No.2)* [1995] ICR 540). However, if the dismissal is 'suspended' and the contract of employment continues pending the appeal, the DDA will apply.

Partnerships

Subject to what is said below, the DDA does not prohibit discrimination against partners or persons seeking to become partners. It does prohibit discrimination in relation to people described as partners who are nevertheless employees (eg some salaried partners) and to employees of, or applicants for employment with, partnerships. It will also cover those cases where existing employees are offered partnership as a form of promotion and that promotion is denied to a disabled person for a discriminatory reason (*Hansard*, Report, SC E, col 456, Paice).

At an establishment in Great Britain

The employment or prospective employment must be at an establishment in Great Britain (s 4(6)) (or Northern Ireland, Sched 8 and see p 65 below). 'Employment at an establishment in Great Britain' is to be construed in accordance with s 68(2)–(5). An employee who works wholly or mainly outside Great Britain is deemed not to be employed at an establishment in Great Britain even if he does some of his work at an establishment in Great Britain (s 68(4)).

Establishment
Establishment is not defined in the DDA. In *Secretary of State for Employment and Productivity* v *Vic Hallam Ltd* (1969) 5 ITR 108, QBD Lord Parker CJ said, at p 110:

> I find it quite impossible to give any exclusive definition or test as to what constitutes an establishment. The Tribunal said that they approached the matter as one of broad commonsense. For my part I think that is the correct approach in deciding whether as a matter of fact and degree any particular premises do constitute an establishment. But as it seems to me there are certain indications which help in the matter. The first is one to which I have already referred, exclusive occupation of premises; secondly some degree of permanence ... and thirdly, as it seems to me, some organisation on the premises, an organisation of the men who are working there. Finally, the question of whether a particular premises is an establishment is bound up with the question of where the men who are working there are being employed in or from.

See also *Lord Advocate* v *Babcock & Wilcox (Operations) Ltd* [1972] 1 WLR 488 (HL) and *Haughton* v *Olau Lines (UK)* [1986] 1 WLR 504.

If work is not done at an establishment it is treated as done at the establishment from which it is done; if it is not done from any establishment it is treated as done at the establishment with which it has the closest connection (s 68(5)). For example, employment as a salesperson may involve spending all or most working hours calling on customers. If the salesperson goes into the employer's premises each morning in order to make appointments and pick up samples before going out to make calls, the employment is done 'from' those premises and is treated as being done 'at' those premises. If the salesperson never or rarely goes to the employer's premises, the employment will be treated as being done at the establishment with which it has the closest connection, such as the local administrative centre that he or she deals with.

In Great Britain
Great Britain means England, Scotland and Wales (Union with Scotland Act 1706, art 1).

Northern Ireland

The DDA also applies to employment at an establishment in Northern Ireland. Schedule 8 modifies the DDA in its application to Northern Ireland by substituting or amending provisions as necessary.

Applicants
Applicants for employment that is intended to be wholly or mainly outside Great Britain at the time of the alleged discrimination will not be able to bring a claim under Pt II of the DDA. This is still the case even if the job applied for subsequently changes into one within Great Britain through circumstances

unforeseen at that time (see *Deria* v *General Council of British Shipping* [1986] ICR 172, CA).

Inclusions and exclusions
Regulations may prescribe that certain forms of employment or employment in certain circumstances are to be regarded as not being at an establishment in Great Britain, although no such regulations have been made as yet.

Ships, aircraft and hovercraft
Except in prescribed cases, employment on board a ship, aircraft or hovercraft is to be regarded as not being employment at an establishment in Great Britain (s 68(3)). No regulations have been made prescribing any such employment to constitute employment at an establishment in Great Britain.

Qualifying period and minimum hours

There is no qualifying period of continuous employment or requirement as to the minimum weekly hours.

Special cases

There are special rules in the following cases.

Contract workers
Section 12(1) makes it unlawful for a principal to discriminate against a disabled person who is a contract worker
  (a) in the terms on which he allows him to do that contract work;
  (b) by not allowing him to do it, or continue to do it;
  (c) in the way he affords him access to any benefits or by refusing or deliberately omitting to afford him access to them; or
  (d) by subjecting him to any other detriment (see p 85 below).
Where the principal is concerned with the provision of benefits to the public or a section of the public which includes the contract worker, s 12(1) does not apply to the provision of benefits of that description unless the provision of the benefit by the principal to the (section of the) public differs in a material respect from the provision of the benefits to the contract worker (s 12(2)). (Similar provisions relating to benefits provided to the public are discussed in relation to employees at p 77 below) Section 12(4) makes it unlawful for a principal to victimise any person (whether disabled or not) within the meaning of s 55 (s 12(4) and see p 251 above). The employment provisions of Pt II (other than s 4(1) and (3)) apply to a principal as if he were or would be the employer of the contract worker supplied to do work for him (s 12(3)).
    The section applies only in relation to contract work done at an establishment in Great Britain (s 12(5)) as defined by s 68 (see p 65 above). A principal is a person who makes work available for individuals employed by another person who provides the workers under a contract with the principal.

A contract worker is someone who is supplied to the individual under such a contract. Contract work is work made so available (s 12(6)). These provisions are broadly comparable to those of s 9 of the SDA 1975 and s 7 of the RRA 1976. The provision rendering unlawful discrimination by a principal against contract workers will only apply if the employer is contractually obliged to supply the worker to the principal and the work is done for the principal and not for the employer. In *Rice v Fon-a-Car* [1980] ICR 133 a firm operated a number of taxi cabs driven by owner-drivers. The drivers paid a weekly sum to the firm and were provided with a telephone link with the firm's office. Customers contacted the firm who then contacted the driver. One driver (E) was given leave to engage a relief driver and proceeded to engage a woman. When the firm discovered she was a woman they told E to dismiss her. The EAT held that the equivalent provisions of the SDA relating to discrimination against contract workers did not apply because E was under a contractual obligation to supply a worker to the firm.

Regulation 7 of the DD(E) Regs 1996 applies where a contract worker is likely to be placed at a similar substantial disadvantage by premises occupied by or arrangements made by or on behalf of all or most of the principals to whom they are or might be supplied. It provides that in such a case it is reasonable for the sending employer to have to take such steps as are within his power as would be reasonable for him to have to take if the premises were occupied by him, or the arrangements were made by him or on his behalf (Reg 7(1) and (2) and see para 7.6 of the Employment Code at p 311). It is not reasonable for any principal to take any step which it is reasonable for the sending employer to have to take (Reg 7(3)). Nonetheless, subject to the exclusion of small employers (see p 69 below), the principal may be made under a duty to co-operate with the reasonable adjustment made by the sending employer, to make an adjustment that was outside the power of, or not reasonable for, the sending employer to take (see Employment Code, para 7.6).

Supported Placement Schemes

The rules on contract workers will apply to the Employment Service's Supported Placement Schemes, with the contractor being the sending employer and the 'host employer' being the principal. However, note the effect of s 10(3)(*a*) of the DDA on providers of supported employment under s 15 of the Disabled Persons (Employment) Act 1944 (see p 86 below).

The Crown, Parliament and statutory office holders

Part II of the DDA applies to service for the purposes of a Minister of the Crown or Government office, other than service *as* a person holding a statutory office and other specified exceptions (s 64(2)(*a*)). However, service on behalf of the crown *for the purposes of* a person holding a statutory office is covered by the employment provisions, again subject to specified exceptions (s 64(2)(*b*)). 'Service for purposes of a Minister of the Crown or government department' does not include service in any office for the time being mentioned in Sched 2 (Ministerial offices) to the House of Commons Disqualification Act 1975 (s 64(8)). (See para 2.7 of the Employment Code).

However, even where the employment provisions do not apply, a Minister of the Crown or government department must not act in a way that would contravene those provisions in making an appointment or in making arrangements for determining to whom the post should be offered, save in respect of any appointments that may be prescribed (s 66).

Police

Express provision is made excluding service as members of the Ministry of Defence Police, the British Transport Police, the Royal Parks Constabulary or the United Kingdom Atomic Energy Authority Constabulary from Pt II (s 64(5)(a)). They are defined by s 64(8) as follows. 'Ministry of Defence Police' means the force established under s 1 of the Ministry of Defence Police Act 1987. 'British Transport Police' means the constables appointed, or deemed to have been appointed, under s 53 of the British Transport Commission Act 1949. 'Royal Parks Constabulary' means the park constables appointed under the Parks Regulation Act 1872. 'United Kingdom Atomic Energy Authority Constabulary' means the special constables appointed under s 3 of the Special Constables Act 1923 on the nomination of the United Kingdom Atomic Energy Authority.

Other police constables hold a statutory office and are not employees. As a result of this, and the effect of s 64(2)(a), service as a police constable is excluded from Pt II of the DDA 1995. This contrasts with the position under the SDA 1975 and RRA 1976 where police service was expressly brought within the ambit of those Acts (ss 17 and 16 respectively). Civilian employees of the police force work under a contract of employment and are not covered by this exclusion. The DDA 1995 applies to such employment.

Prison Officers

Part II of the Act does not apply to service as a prison officer (s 64(5)(b)). 'Prison officer' means a person who is a prison officer within the meaning of s 127 of the Criminal Justice and Public Order Act 1994 (CJPOA 1994) other than a custody officer within the meaning of Pt I of that Act. Section 127(4) defines 'prison officer' as

any individual who—

(a) holds any post, otherwise than as a chaplain or assistant chaplain or as a medical officer, to which he has been appointed for the purposes of section 7 of the Prison Act 1952 or under section 2(2) of the Prison Act (Northern Ireland) 1953 (appointment of prison staff),

(b) holds any post, otherwise than as a medical officer, to which he has been appointed under section 3(1) of the Prisons (Scotland) Act 1989, or

(c) ... a prisoner custody officer, within the meaning of Part IV of the Criminal Justice Act 1991 or Chapter II or III of this Part.

This provision therefore excludes prisoner custody officers certified as such under s 89 of the Criminal Justice Act 1991 or s 114 or s 122 of the CJPOA 1994 even though they are not members of the prison service but work for contracted out services. However, the DDA 1995 will apply to custody officers within the meaning of s 12(3) of the CJPOA 1994, namely officers at secure training centres who are not members of the prison service.

Firefighters

Service as a member of a fire brigade maintained in pursuance of the Fire Services Act 1947 who is or may be required by his terms of service to engage in fire fighting is excluded from Pt II of the DDA (ss 64(6), (8)). Similarly, service for the purposes of a Minister of the Crown or government department having functions with respect to defence as a person who is or may be required by his terms of service to engage in fire fighting is excluded (s 64(5)(c)).

Armed forces

Service in any of the naval, military or air forces of the Crown is excluded from Pt II of the DDA.

Small employers

One of the most hotly debated issues during the passage of the Bill concerned the exclusion of small employers from Pt II of the DDA. (For the debate on this clause see *Hansard*, HL, 15 June 1995, Vol 564, col 1903 to 1929 and *Hansard*, HL, 18 July 1995, Vol 566, col 126 to 140.) The employment provisions do not apply to an employer who has fewer than 20 employees (s 7). There is no further definition of employees, so that everyone employed by the employer (as defined in s 68) will count. Moreover there is no requirement in s 7 that the other employees are employed at an establishment in the UK. Thus representatives of an overseas company in the UK may have the employment of those employed in other countries taken into account in calculating the total, provided they are employees within the meaning of s 68. In contrast to the old provisions of s 6(3)(b) of the SDA 1975 and s 56A of the Employment Protection (Consolidation) Act 1978 (both provisions now repealed), there is no provision to allow account to be taken of the employees of associated employers.

It is the number of employees at the date of the act complained of that is relevant (Employment Code, para 2.6). Discrimination may be a continuing act (see *Barclays Bank* v *Kapur* [1991] IRLR 136, HL and *Sougrin* v *Haringey Health Authority* [1992] IRLR 416, CA, and *Littlewoods Organisation* v *Traynor* [1993] IRLR 154). In such a case, where there is a fluctuating workforce, the employer will be acting unlawfully under the DDA during those periods for which he has 20 or more employees.

In the case of contract workers, the DDA will not apply to a principal if the principal has less than 20 employees, including contract workers, although it will apply to the employer unless the employer has less than 20 employees, including contract workers supplied to others (Employment Code, para 7.7 and see *Hansard* HL Debs, Vol 566, col 222 and p 66 above). The Secretary of State is under an obligation to review this section before 2 December 2000 and may by Order reduce (but not increase) the figure of 20 (s 7(2)–(9)).

Unlawful acts against applicants

Section 4 of the DDA makes it unlawful for employers to discriminate against applicants and employees in various respects. These provisions are similar to those found in s 6 of the SDA 1975 and s 4 of the RRA 1976 and the authorities under those Acts will often be applicable here.

Discrimination against applicants ...

(1) It is unlawful for an employer to discriminate against a disabled person
   (a) in the arrangements which he makes for the purpose of determining to whom he should offer employment;
   (b) in the terms on which he offers that person employment;
   (c) by refusing to offer or deliberately not offering him employment.

Arrangements made to determine to whom employment should be offered

The term 'arrangements' is to be read broadly and will cover all stages of the recruitment process from inception until the applicant is rejected or an offer is made (see p 50 above). It covers the use of standards, criteria and administrative methods. It will include operating non-discriminatory arrangements in a discriminatory way, (*Brennan* v *J H Dewhurst Ltd* [1984] ICR 52).

Job specifications
The inclusion of unnecessary, marginal or blanket requirements in job and person specifications can result in unlawful discrimination (Employment Code, para 5.3/4). The employer should seek to produce a clear job description and person specification identifying the core elements of the job to be advertised. The employer should also consider whether the core elements of the job could be performed in different ways.

Advertisements
In contrast with the SDA 1975 and RRA 1976, the DDA 1995 does not make discriminatory advertisements unlawful in themselves. Section 11 of the DDA provides that a tribunal shall assume (unless the contrary is shown) that the reason that an employer did not offer a disabled applicant employment was a reason which related to his disability in certain circumstances. Those circumstances are that the employer had advertised the job in an advertisement which 'indicated, or might reasonably be understood to have indicated, that the success of any application would or might be determined to any extent by

reference to one of the matters specified in s 11(1)(e)'. Those matters are:

(1) the applicant not having any disability;
(2) the applicant not having a category of disability which includes the disabled person's disability; and
(3) the employer's reluctance to make any reasonable adjustment.

The subjective intention of the person who compiled the advertisement is not relevant to determining whether the advertisement indicated one of those matters. The question is: 'what would an ordinary reasonable person understand by the words?' (*Race Relations Board* v *Associated Newspapers Group Ltd* [1978] 3 All ER 419). However, that intention will often be relevant to decide whether the reason for the decision not to offer employment was in fact related to the disability. The advertisement relied on may be dated either before or after the disabled person applied for the job (s 11(1)(d)). Any advertisement or notice suffices, whether it was made to the public or not (s 11(3)), so that internal vacancy lists comprise an advertisement for the purposes of this provision (Employment Code, para 5.8). This provision simply reverses the burden of proof in relation to the reason for the failure to appoint. An employer will still avoid a finding of discrimination if he can prove, on the evidence, that the reason for refusing to offer the person the job did not relate to the disability or that the refusal was justified within the meaning of s 5(1)(b).

However, advertisements may have an independent importance in a claim for discrimination. Although an advert which discloses an intention to discriminate against people with disabilities is unlikely in itself to amount to less favourable treatment (see *Cardiff Women's Aid* v *Hartup* [1994] IRLR 390), the form of an advert may place a disabled person at a substantial disadvantage in comparison to others. For example a list of vacancies posted on a notice board will probably not come to the attention of a blind employee. In such a case, the employer is likely to be under a duty to adjust by ensuring that the blind employee is given notice of the vacancies by other means and an unjustified failure to do so will amount to discrimination under s 5(2).

Recruitment agencies

An employer should ensure that any recruitment or employment agency does not discriminate against disabled persons during the selection process, as the employer may be held liable for any unlawful discrimination by its agents (see p 249 below).

Information and application forms

A failure to provide information about a vacancy in alternative formats for applicants unable to read because of a disability may amount to discrimination. Likewise, requiring application forms to be handwritten may discriminate (Employment Code, paras 5.9, 5.13). Some applicants may have difficulty in reading and comprehending written applications, especially those that are heavily loaded with complicated English unfamiliar terms.

Thus, a reasonable adjustment may involve allowing the person to take an application and obtain assistance in filling it out, allowing more time for completion, or providing a sign language interpreter. A person with a vision impairment will be discouraged from applying for a job which does not require much sight if he or she cannot read the application form. An employer should be prepared to make available to the person a large print form which can be read by persons or allow oral applications to be made to a personnel officer or other employee who can then reduce the application to writing.

Interviews
Interviews form part of the arrangements. If an employer is aware that an applicant or potential applicant has a disability and will be placed at a substantial disadvantage by existing interview practices and procedures, there may be a duty to adjust, to remove or reduce that disadvantage (Employment Code, para 5.15–5.18). The Employment Code states that employers should think ahead for interviews. They should give applicants the opportunity to indicate any relevant effects of a disability and to suggest adjustments to help overcome any disadvantages the disability may cause. This may assist the interviewer avoid discriminating in interview, and may assist to clarify whether any adjustments may be required (Employment Code, para 5.16). This approach to interviews will require the interviewer to be clear on the purpose of the questions he is asking. He or she should guard against making assumptions about the person's disability. The time of an interview may have to be altered in the case of a disabled person if, because of a reason related to his disability, the candidate cannot make the time fixed for the interview (para 5.17). An employer may have to pay for special requirements of a disabled candidate, including payment (if necessary) for a support worker or taxi/travel.

Asking questions about the disability at an interview
It will not usually be unlawful in itself to ask a disabled applicant about his disability or general health, although it may evidence discrimination (*Saunders* v *Richmond-upon-Thames London Borough Council* [1978] ICR 75). Unlike race and sex discrimination, questions about the effects of a disability will often be relevant rather than discriminatory, as they may identify steps that need to be taken in accordance with the duty to adjust (Employment Code, para 5.20). Questions should only be raised about a disability if it may be relevant to the person's ability to do the job once a reasonable adjustment has been carried out. Although it may be relevant to ask a person suffering from a progressive illness about any potential need for time off for treatment or recuperation, an employer should not automatically ask any disabled applicant about their absence record. Furthermore, it may amount to discrimination if the interview is conducted so as to discourage the applicant for a reason related to his disability (*Simon* v *Brimham Associates* [1987] IRLR 307).

Interviews with people with hearing impairment
Interviews should be conducted in a quiet, well-lit environment that minimizes visual distractions. The interviewer should avoid sitting in front of bright lights or windows which make it difficult to lip read. The interviewer should be willing to utilise the interviewee's hearing aid, if one is used. The interviewer should talk at a normal pace and at a normal volume, but be prepared to repeat questions, converse at a different pace or volume, or try other strategies like note writing if asked. Professional sign language interpreters could be used if a presentation is made to a group of candidates including a person who is hard of hearing or deaf. In group interviews, the interviewer should speak with one person at a time and ensure that any deaf or hard-of-hearing applicant knows that the interviewer is speaking before the interviewer or other persons in the room speak (see also the Employment Code, para 5.17). It will normally be reasonable to allow a longer time for an interview with someone with a hearing impairment, using a sign language interpreter to communicate (Employment Code, para 5.18).

Interviews with people with vision impairment
If a person with vision impairment is to be interviewed, an employer should consider asking the applicant if they need directions to the site of the interview. If the candidate is travelling by public transport, indicate which bus stop or station is closest and give directions from there to the interview. Once the applicant is in the interview room, the interviewer should place his or her hand onto the back of the chair the applicant is going to sit on.

Interviews with people with mobility impairments
Interviews should be held in an accessible place. Interviewers should ensure that there is an entry which can be used by those with mobility problems. Parking should be made available near the entry. If there is no permanent ramp, a temporary one should be made available. If the interview is to be conducted other than on the ground floor, those conducting it should ensure that there are ramps or lifts available. In any case there should be accessible toilets.

Medical checks
Medical examinations are not automatically unlawful. It is not discriminatory for an employer to require all prospective employees to have an examination. It would probably be discriminatory to require someone with a disability (and no-one else) to have a medical check unless it was justified by the nature of both the disability and the employment (Employment Code, para 5.23). Furthermore, medical evidence about an applicant's disability will not usually justify a decision not to offer her the job unless there is a substantial adverse effect on her ability to do the job which cannot be overcome by a reasonable adjustment (Employment Code, para 5.24). For example, if there is evidence that the condition will only have a substantial effect upon the applicant in the

long term the employer would not be justified in rejecting a candidate for that reason in the absence of exceptional circumstances. However, if the job was for a single project that genuinely required that the candidate be available for two years, but the medical evidence showed that it is unlikely that he will be able to work for more than one year, the employer will be justified in rejecting him. Even when an employer has the advice of an expert that an applicant is unable to perform a particular job, the employer should still consider if the applicant would be able to do the job if a reasonable adjustment was made.

Aptitude and other tests
Where the form or nature of a test would place a disabled applicant at a disadvantage, the employer may need to revise the way in which it is conducted or assessed. For example, an applicant who cannot write easily may be tested orally or allowed longer to finish. A candidate with a stammer may be given longer to complete the test or given a written test. Alternatively, a lower 'pass' rate could be accepted, provided the applicant is otherwise suited to the job. The Employment Code points out that routine testing of all candidates may discriminate against particular individuals or substantially disadvantage them (Employment Code, para 5.21).

Test results should accurately reflect the applicants' ability, skills and aptitude for the job rather than simply reflecting the effect of any impairment upon the ability to complete the test. Employers should consider the following questions. Firstly, what is the purpose of the test? Secondly, does the test relate to the ability of the candidates to do the core functions/main purpose of the job? Thirdly, does the test relate to an ability of the candidates which is relevant to the job? Finally, is there an adjustment which it would be reasonable to carry out in relation to the particular candidate with the particular disability in the circumstances? If the form of the test is directly relevant to the job in question, such as a typing test for a job as a typist, it will not be reasonable to require an oral test to be offered as an alternative, although there may still be a need to provide adapted equipment, such as an adapted keyboard.

Qualifications
It may be discriminatory to refuse to employ someone who does not have a particular qualification because of their disability if they can show their competence by other means. However, where a qualification is essential to the job irrespective of any reasonable adjustment, it will not be unlawful to reject an applicant without that qualification (Employment Code, para 5.22). If the qualification is sought simply as evidence of competence (for example a GCSE in mathematics as evidence of numeracy) alternative evidence of competence should be accepted. In cases where the possession of a particular qualification is essential to the performance of certain parts of the job, the duty to adjust may require an employer to reallocate those functions to other employees.

The terms on which he offers that person employment

It is unlawful for an employer to discriminate against an applicant by offering employment on less favourable terms without justification, such as lower pay, longer hours or less favourable benefits than others (Employment Code, para 5.27, 5.28, and see Chap 4 above). In addition, it may be unlawful discrimination to offer terms which place the disabled person at a substantial disadvantage where there is a duty to adjust, for example by offering an employee a job with standard hours or at a place of work which places him at a substantial disadvantage when a reasonable adjustment could be made. This provision covers the offer of employment, and will apply even if the offer is rejected. If the offer is accepted on the discriminatory terms and conditions, the disabled person should claim under s 4(2). There must be an offer of employment for s 4(1)(*b*) to apply (*Ogilvie* v *Harehills Conservative Club Ltd & Parry* EAT 449/92). There are special rules relating to pensions, insurance and performance related pay (see p 77 below).

Refusing or deliberately not offering employment

An employer can discriminate by refusing or deliberately not offering employment. There is no need for an express refusal to employ. There is no need to show that the post was filled (*Roadburg* v *Lothian Regional Council* [1976] IRLR 283).

Unlawful acts and employees

Once a disabled person has become employed he is entitled to rely on section 4(2) if he experiences discrimination whether by failure to make adjustments or less favourable treatment.

Discrimination against ... employees

4(2)   It is unlawful for an employer to discriminate against a disabled person whom he employes—
  (a)   in the terms of employment which he affords him;
  (b)   in the opportunities which he affords him for promotion, a transfer, training or receiving any other benefit;
  (c)   by refusing to afford him, deliberately or not affording him, any such opportunity; or
  (d)   by dismissing him, or subjecting him to any other detriment.

Terms of employment
This applies to all contractual terms and conditions of employment including pay, hours and a wide range of fringe benefits. (See p 50 above). The special rules relating to occupational pension schemes and insurance services are discussed below at p 77. Performance related pay is considered at p 79 below.

Opportunities for promotion, a transfer, training or receiving any other benefit
This is a wide provision which will cover discrimination in relation to matters that are not based on contractual rights, including opportunities for promotion, training, working overtime etc. It does not require an applicant to prove that they would have obtained the benefit provided they can show that they have lost or been denied an opportunity for promotion.

Promotion and transfer
'Employers must not discriminate in assessing a disabled person's suitability for promotion or transfer, in the practical arrangements necessary to allow the promotion to take place, in the operation of the appraisal, selection and promotion or transfer process or in the new job itself' (Employment Code, para 6.4). Opportunities may be denied to a disabled person by omissions occurring as a result of an employer having stereotypical views about disability. Discrimination may also occur where an employer fails to make an adjustment to internal procedures which would give the disabled person the opportunity to seek a transfer. To take an extreme example, if the vacancy is advertised only on a notice board which is in part of the building to which there is no wheel chair access, the employee using a wheel chair is placed at a substantial disadvantage. Similar issues arise when considering applicants for employment (see p 71) and Employment Code, para 6.5). It may be that an employer will be required to transfer an employee to a more suitable position by the duty to adjust (see p 53).

Training
Employers must not discriminate in selection for training. They must make any alterations to the training provided that are required by the duty to adjust. An employer may be required to provide a disabled employee with special training as part of the duty to adjust (Employment Code, para 6.6).

Any other benefit
Benefits include facilities or services (s 4(4)). It is to be construed widely and will include anything that could fairly be described as an 'advantage' (*Peake* v *Automotive Products Ltd* [1977] ICR 480, EAT). It will include (but is not limited to) a very wide range of fringe benefits, such as a staff canteen and workplace nurseries (Employment Code, para 6.7). It would include the provision of laundry facilities, free or subsidised work clothing, membership of a social club, subsidised travel or loans. A refusal to investigate a complaint of unfair treatment may itself amount to a refusal of access to 'any other benefits, facilities or services' (*Eke* v *Commissioners of Customs and Excise* [1981] IRLR 334, EAT). Occupational pension schemes and insurance services are dealt with below at p 77. Performance related pay is considered at p 79 below.

Benefits provided to the public

Where a benefit is provided to members of the public, or, to a section of the public which includes the employee, s 4(3) excludes that benefit from the operation of s 4(2) unless one of three conditions is satisfied. Firstly, s 4(2) will still apply if the provision of the benefit to the public differs in a material respect from the provision of the benefits by the employer to his employees (s 4(3)(a)). A difference is material if it is signifcant and relevant (*Rainey v Greater Glasgow Health Board* [1987] ICR 129) such as where a benefit is made available to employees on significantly more favourable terms than are available to the public. Secondly, s 4(2) will apply if the provision of the benefits services and facilities to the employee is regulated by the relevant employee's contract of employment (s 4(3)(b)). Finally, s 4(2) will apply to a benefit which relates to training (s 4(3)(c)).

Occupational pensions

Occupational pension schemes (OPS) are deemed to include a non-discrimination rule which relates to the terms on which persons become members of the scheme and are treated as members of the scheme (s 17(1)(a)). That rule requires the trustees or managers of the scheme to refrain from any act or omission which, if done in relation to a person by an employer, would amount to unlawful discrimination against that person for the purposes of Pt II of the DDA (s 17(1)(b)). The other provisions of the scheme take effect subject to the non-discrimination rule (s 17(2)). By s 68(1), 'occupational pension scheme' has the same meaning as in s 1 of the Pension Schemes Act 1993, namely:

> ... any scheme or arrangement which is comprised in one or more instruments or agreements and which has, or is capable of having, effect in relation to one or more descriptions or categories of employment so as to provide benefits, in the form of pensions or otherwise, payable on termination of service, or on death or retirement, to or in respect of earners with qualifying service in an employment of any such description or category.

This allows a disabled person who is a member of the scheme to seek redress for discrimination by the managers or trustees or by the rules of the scheme through the existing dispute resolution mechanisms for pension schemes or the Pensions Ombudsman. Such dispute resolution schemes will be made compulsory from April 1997 by s 50 of the Pensions Act 1995. If the complaint is that an employer is discriminating against a disabled person by refusing or restricting his access to a scheme, the disabled person will be able to bring a discrimination claim before a tribunal under the ordinary rules. Paragraphs 6.9 to 6.16 of the Employment Code concern Occupational Pension Schemes.

Less favourable treatment

The DDA does not prevent an employer or the operators or rules of a scheme treating a disabled person less favourably provided the treatment can be shown to be justified under s 5(1)(*b*). For example, account could be taken of a pre-existing medical condition which is likely to increase the risk of ill-health retirement or death whilst in employment, provided any decisions are based upon sound actuarial and medical evidence or advice. Regulation 4 of the DD(E) Regs 1996 applies benefits provided under an occupational pension scheme in respect of termination of service; retirement, old age or death; or accident, injury, sickness or invalidity (reg 4(3)). It provides that less favourable treatment resulting from the application of eligibility conditions for, or from determining the amount of, benefit is taken to be justified in certain circumstances (reg 4(2)). Those circumstances are that by reason of the disabled person's disability (including any clinical prognosis flowing from that disability) the cost of providing any such benefit is likely to be substantially greater than it would be for a comparable person without that disability (reg 4(2)). The burden of proof is on the employer or operator of the scheme to show that a case falls within the circumstances set out in reg 4(2).

Uniform rates of contribution
For the purposes of s 5(1) an employer is deemed to be justified in requiring a disabled person to make contributions to an occupational pension scheme at the same rate as other employees (or class of employees including the disabled person that is not defined by reference to any disability) even though the disabled person is not eligible to receive a benefit or benefits at the same rate as others for a reason relating to his disability (DD(E) Regs 1996, reg 5). Unlike the deeming provision under reg 4 above, this regulation expressly refers to employers. Nonetheless, it would appear to apply indirectly to the operators and rules of an OPS on the grounds that such treatment, if done in relation to a person by an employer, would not amount to unlawful discrimination, but see s 17(3)(*a*).

The duty to adjust
There is no duty to adjust in relation to any benefit under an occupational pension scheme in respect of termination of service; retirement, old age or death; or accident, injury, sickness or invalidity and any matters that may be prescribed in the future (s 6(11)).

Insurance Services
Section 18 of the DDA 1995 applies where a provider of insurance services ('the insurer') enters into an arrangement with an employer under which the employer's employees (or a class of those employees) receives insurance services from the insurer or are given an opportunity to receive such services (s 18(1)). 'Insurance services' means benefits in respect of termination of service; retirement, old age or death; or accident, injury, sickness or invalidity and any matters that may be prescribed in the future (s 18(3)). In such a case, an insurer discriminates against a relevant employee if the insurer treats him in such a way as would be unlawful discrimination for the purposes of Pt III

(provisions of goods, facilities and service) if the insurer were providing the service to members of the public and the employee was provided with or trying to obtain that benefit as a member of the public (s 18(2)). Such treatment is deemed to be discrimination for the purposes of Pt II so that any complaint is to be made to a tribunal rather than a county court under Pt III. A 'relevant employee' is an employee who is in the class of employees who are covered by the arrangement concerned (s 18(3)), or someone who has applied for or is contemplating applying for such employment (s 18(4)). If all employees are covered by the arrangement concerned, all employees (or actual or potential applicants for employment) are 'relevant employees' (s 18(3)(a)). Where the disabled person is not a relevant employee, he may still have a right of action under Pt III.

The duty to adjust

There is no duty to adjust in relation to any benefit payable in money or money's worth under a scheme or arrangement for the benefit of employees in respect of termination of service; retirement, old age or death; or accident, injury, sickness or invalidity and any matters that may be prescribed in the future (s 6(11)).

Performance related pay

Regulation 3 of the DD(E) Regs 1996 provides that less favourable treatment is justified if it results from the application of 'a term or practice (a) under which the amount of a person's pay is wholly or partly dependent on that person's performance and (b) which is applied to all of the employer's employees or to all of a class of his employees which includes the disabled person, but which is not defined by reference to any disability'. 'Pay' means remuneration of any kind including any benefit (DD(E) Regs 1996, reg 2). Furthermore, any such term or practice is not to be taken to place a disabled person at a substantial disadvantage (DD(E) Regs 1996, reg 3(2)) so that a duty to adjust will not arise in relation to the term or practice itself. However, this does not prevent a duty to adjust from arising where any arrangements or physical features place the disabled person at a disadvantage by causing a reduced performance (DD(E) Regs 1996, reg 3(3)).

'Performance'

' ''Performance'' includes performance as assessed by reference to any measure, whether relative or absolute, of output, efficiency or effectiveness in an employment' (DD(E) Regs 1996, reg 2). Unlike the other matters defined in the interpretation regulation, the definition of 'performance' is inclusive. It would apply to piece rate and performance related pay which can be measured by objective means (eg number of items produced, income generated, targets met etc).

It is not clear whether it would apply to performance bonuses that are not paid by reference to any (objective) measure of output, efficiency or effectiveness but which simply depends upon a manager's subjective view as to effort or ability. That subjective view may be shaped, consciously or unconsciously, by the fact of the employee's disability. For example a manager may be prejudiced against people who are HIV positive and deliberately or otherwise underestimate their effort or ability so that they receive less performance-related pay. Such behaviour would clearly contravene the purpose of the DDA 1995. As such, it may be that wholly subjective performance related pay is not within the provision. Alternatively, the disabled person could argue that his complaint was not about the application of the practice to all persons but about the particular decision made in his case.

Agricultural wages and conditions

Section 5 of the Agricultural Wages Act 1948 (or s 5 of the Agricultural Wages (Scotland) Act 1949) concerns an agricultural worker who is 'so affected by any physical injury or mental deficiency, or any infirmity due to age or to any other cause' that:

(1) he cannot earn the minimum rate fixed under that Act (s 5(1)); or
(2) it is inappropriate for any of the terms and conditions (other than those regarding pay or holidays) fixed by an order under the Act to apply to him (s 5(2A)).

Such a worker can obtain a permit from an agricultural wages board which allows his employer to pay him less than the minimum rate or dispenses with the inappropriate term or condition over such periods and on such conditions as are specified in the permit.

Regulation 6(a) of the DD(E) Regs 1996 provides that less favourable treatment is taken to be justified to the extent that it relates to a matter within the terms and conditions of such a permit and accords with those terms and conditions. Failure to take a step in relation to a matter within the terms or conditions of such a permit is deemed to be justified if the steps would exceed the requirements of the terms and conditions specified in the permit (DDE Regs 1996, reg 6(b)).

Refusing to afford, or deliberately not affording him, any such opportunity

An important difference between the DDA 1995 and the race and sex discrimination legislation is that the duty to adjust under the DDA may require an employer to alter existing duties or working hours for an applicant or employee. An employer may discriminate by failing to make a reasonable adjustment to allow a disabled person to work a different shift pattern or by failing to provide training that had not previously been available (*Clymo* v *Wandsworth LBC* [1989] IRLR 241 and *Mecca Leisure Group plc* v *Chatprachong* [1993] IRLR 531).

Dismissal

Dismissal for a reason relating to the employee's disability will amount to unlawful discrimination unless it is justified and could not be avoided by a reasonable adjustment (Employment Code, para 6.19/21).

Unfair dismissal and disability discrimination

Many claims for discriminatory dismissals will be made in conjunction with a claim for unfair dismissal under Pt X of the Employment Rights Act 1996 (ERA 1996) and there will be substantial interplay between the two statutory codes. In an unfair dismissal claim, it is for the employer to show the reason or principal reason for the dismissal and that that reason is a potentially fair reason for dismissal (ERA 1996, s 98(1)). One potentially fair reason is a reason that 'relates to the capability or qualifications of the employee for performing work of the kind which he was employed by the employer to do' (ERA 1996, s 98(2)). 'Capability' means the employee's capability 'assessed by reference to skill, aptitude health or any other physical or mental quality' (ERA 1996, s 98(3)(a)). If the employer establishes a potentially fair reason for dismissal, the tribunal must decide if the dismissal was 'fair or unfair (having regard to the reason shown by the employer)' (ERA 1996 s 98(4)). That decision will depend upon whether '(a) ... in the circumstances (including the size and administrative resources of the employer's undertaking) the employer acted reasonably or unreasonably in treating it as a sufficient reason for dismissing the employee, and (b) shall be determined in accordance with equity and the substantial merits of the case' (ERA 1996, s 98(4)). Although a dismissal in breach of the DDA 1995 is not automatically unfair for the purposes of s 98(4) of the ERA 1996, in practice it will be held to be unfair. However, an unfair dismissal will not necessarily be discriminatory. Capability dismissals can be divided into three broad categories: dismissals for incompetence; dismissals for long term absence; and dismissals for persistent intermittent absence.

Incompetence

In unfair dismissal cases, 'it is sufficient that the employer honestly believes on reasonable grounds that the man is incapable and incompetent. It is not necessary for the employer to prove that he is in fact incapable or incompetent' *Taylor* v *Alidair Ltd* [1978] ICR 445, CA. In addition, the degree of incompetence must be such as to make it reasonable for the employer to treat it as a sufficient reason for dismissing the employee (ERA 1996, s 98(4)(a)). Even prior to the DDA 1995, an employer was required to take account of a disabled person's personal circumstances, including the disability itself, and the basis on which they had been employed before deciding to dismiss (*Seymour* v *British Airways Board* [1983] 1RLR 55 and *Post Office* v *Husbands*, EAT 432/80).

There must be some evidence of incompetence to establish reasonable grounds for the belief. Although a genuine conclusion held by managers over a period of time may itself amount to evidence of incapacity, tribunals should consider if there is any objective material to support that belief (*Cook* v *Thomas Linnell & Sons Ltd* [1977] ICR 770, EAT). The evidence available will depend upon the nature of the employment, as many jobs are incapable of precise assessment. It may include a reduction in sales or trade (*Cooke* v *Thomas Linnel & Sons Ltd* [1977 ICR 770 EAT), complaints by customers (*Dunning* v *Jacomb* [1973] IRLR 206 or other employees (*Hooper* v *Feedex Ltd* [1974] IRLR 99).

A dismissal will usually be unfair in the absence of a reasonable procedure. In incompetence cases, this will generally involve making a reasonable appraisal of the employee's work and discussing it with him or her, giving the employee a reasonable opportunity to improve and warning the employee of the consequences of failing to improve (*James* v *Waltham Holy Cross UDC* [1973] ICR 398, NIRC). Although formal warnings will not be necessary in every case, the complaint should be brought to the employee's attention to give him or her an opportunity to improve (*Cook* v *Thomas Linnell*). However, a warning and opportunity to improve may not be necessary in exceptional circumstances, such as where the inadequacy of performance is so extreme that there must be an irredeemable incapability (*James* v *Waltham Holy Cross UDC*); where the consequences of incompetence have been or could be very serious (*Taylor* v *Alidair* and *Turner* v *Pleasurama Casinos Ltd* [1976] IRLR 151, but see *Inner London Education Authority* v *Lloyd* [1981] IRLR 394); where it is clear that the employee is unable to change (*A J Dunning & Sons* v *Jacomb*) or unwilling to change (*Retarded Children's Aid Society Ltd* v *Day* [1978] IRLR 128); or where a senior employee is aware of the consequences of poor performance without the need for a warning (*James* v *Waltham Holy Cross UDC*).

Whether an employee has been given a reasonable opportunity to improve is a question of fact and degree. What is reasonable will depend upon matters such as the employee's length of service, past work record, status and the like (see for example *Evans* v *George Galloway & Co* [1974] IRLR 167). Although an employer should offer guidance by advice or a warning before dismissing for incompetence, there is no general contractual duty upon an employer to 'support, assist, offer guidance and training' and an absence of such assistance will not render every such dismissal unfair (*White* v *London Transport Executive* [1981] IRLR 261) although it may be required in particular cases. However, failing to give adequate training may render a dismissal unfair in particular circumstances (for example where an employee is given insufficient training after promotion *Burrows* v *Ace Caravan Co (Hull) Ltd* [1972] IRLR 4). In some cases, an employer may need to discover if there is suitable alternative employment, particularly where the employee has been promoted into the job that he or she is not competent to perform (*Draper* v *Kraft Foods Ltd* [1973] IRLR 328 and *Kendrick* v *Concrete Pumping Ltd* [1975] IRLR 83).

The impact of the DDA 1995 upon dismissals for incompetence
Where a disabled employee is dismissed for incompetence and the alleged incompetence is unrelated to the disability, the DDA 1995 will have no effect upon the case. In a case where the poor performance is caused by the disability, for example where an employee with a learning difficulty works less quickly than other workers or loses concentration and makes mistakes, the dismissal is for a reason which relates to the disability. As such, it will be discriminatory unless it can be justified under s 5(3) of the DDA 1995. This will require the employer to show that the dismissal was for a substantial and material reason (see p 42 above). On the face of it, this will add little to the test of fairness under s 98(4) of the ERA 1996, as an employer is unlikely to be found to be acting reasonably in treating incompetence as a sufficient reason for dismissal if the incompetence involved was neither more than minor nor material to the circumstances of the particular case. However, if the objective test of justification is adopted (see p 42 above) an employer will have to prove that the person was in fact incompetent in order to avoid a finding of discrimination and, very probably, a consequential finding of unfair dismissal. It will not be enough for the employer to show that he reasonably believed that the employee was incompetent. This would be a significant departure from the current position under the ERA 1996 as set out in *Taylor* v *Alidair Ltd.*

The duty to adjust will also have a substantial impact upon the fairness or otherwise of incompetence dismissals. The onus upon employers to take active steps to remedy poor performance will be far greater in cases involving the DDA 1995 than would otherwise be the case. Where the incompetence is caused by a disability, an employer will not be able to justify the dismissal if he had failed without justification to comply with the duty to adjust or if the dismissal would still have been justified had the duty been complied with (DDA 1995 s 5(5), above at p 59). Where the performance could have been improved by steps such as providing training, support, supervision, modified equipment or other assistance *and* it was reasonable for the employer to take those steps, the dismissal will be discriminatory and therefore unfair *unless* the improved performance would still have been sufficiently poor to justify dismissal. The same will apply if the employer could reasonably have reallocated the duties that were being poorly performed or transferred the employee into an alternative position. The DDA 1995 will therefore increase the onus upon employers to take active steps to help a disabled employee remedy poor performance or to identify and provide alternative employment if a dismissal for incompetence related to a disability is to be fair under the ERA 1996.

Dismissals for long term absence caused by ill health
The leading case in relation to dismissal for long term absence is *Spencer v Paragon Wallpapers Ltd* [1977] ICR 301, in which Phillips J said 'Every case depends upon its own circumstances. The basic question is whether, in all the circumstances, the employer can be expected to wait any longer and, if so,

how much longer?' Phillips J went on to say that 'the nature of the illness, the likely length of the continuing absence, the need of the employers to have done the work which the employee was engaged to do' should be considered in answering that basic question. In addition, and in the absence of exceptional circumstances, an employer should ensure that he is properly informed before deciding to dismiss. The employer should consult with the employee and take steps to ascertain the true medical position (*East Lindsey District Council* v *Daubney* [1977] ICR 566). Often, the medical position will be established by consulting with the employee. Nonetheless, in some cases it will also be necessary to seek medical advice in order to establish the true position (*Patterson* v *Messrs Bracketts* [1977] IRLR 137). A dismissal may be fair in the absence of consultation where the employer has a particular need for a fit and healthy employee (*Taylorplan Catering (Scotland) Ltd* v *McInally* [1980] IRLR 53), particularly if this requirement is part of the contract of employment (*Leonard* v *Fergus and Haynes Civil Engineering Ltd* [1979] IRLR 235).

The impact of the DDA upon dismissals for long term absence

The DDA will not affect the fairness of most dismissals for long term ill-health absence even if the ill-health comprises or is caused by a disability. If the employer cannot reasonably be expected to wait any longer for an employee to return to work under the test set out in *Spencer* v *Paragon Wallpaper*, an employer is very likely to be able to justify dismissing the employee for the purposes of the DDA 1995. The DDA 1995 may have an impact in a case where the employee is unable to attend his or her previous place of work but could work at premises closer to his or her home or even at home. If it was reasonable for the employer to adjust to allow the employee to work at those other premises or at home as an alternative to dismissal, the dismissal will be discriminatory and unfair. Similarly, if the employee would have been able to return to work fewer hours, to perform modified duties or to do a different job *and* it was reasonable for the employer to alter the working hours or duties or transfer the employee to that different job, a dismissal will be discriminatory and unfair.

Dismissals for persistent intermittent absence

The approach taken in cases involving persistent intermittent absences *which do not have a single underlying cause* is set out in *International Sports Co Ltd* v *Thomson* [1980] IRLR 340, EAT. In that case Waterhouse J said

> In such a case, it would be placing too heavy a burden on an employer to require him to carry out a formal medical investigation and, even if he did, such an investigation would rarely be fruitful because of the transient nature of the employee's symptoms and complaints. What is required, in our judgment, is, firstly, that there should be a fair review by the employer of the attendance record and the reasons for it; and, secondly, appropriate warnings after the employee has been given an opportunity to make representations. If then there is no adequate

improvement in the attendance record, it is likely that in most cases the employer will be justified in treating the persistent absences as a sufficient reason for dismissing the employee.

A similar approach was adopted in *Rolls Royce Ltd* v *Walpole* [1980] IRLR 343, EAT and *Lynock* v *Cereal Packaging Ltd* [1988] ICR 670, EAT. Where the bulk of the absences have the same underlying cause, the proper approach will be more akin to that with long term absences, and the employer will be under an obligation to consult and ascertain the true medical position so that the likely future attendance rate can be assessed and taken into consideration before any decision is made to dismiss.

The impact of the DDA upon dismissals for persistent intermittent absence
Where a disabled employee is dismissed for persistent intermittent absence and those absences are unrelated to the disability, the DDA 1995 will have no effect upon the case. If the absences are related to the disability, either directly or as a result of secondary infections, the employer should seek to identify the true medical position so that any decision is properly informed. The duty to adjust may require the employer to allow a disabled employee to take more time off than other employees (see p 53 above). This is really a difference of emphasis, as matters such as the need of the employer for the work done by the employee and the effect of absences on other employees is to be taken into account in deciding the reasonableness of a dismissal under the ERA 1996 (*Lynock* v *Cereal Packaging Ltd*) and the reasonableness of a proposed adjustment under s 6 of the DDA 1995 (see p 49 above). However, the objective approach of the DDA 1995 (see p 49 above) will place a higher burden on the employer.

Any other detriment

The 'detriment' referred to in s 4(2)(*c*) does not require anything more than 'putting under a disadvantage', provided a reasonable person would or might feel disadvantaged (*Jeremiah* v *Ministry of Defence* [1980] ICR 13). In *Barclays Bank plc* v *Kapur* [1989] ICR 753, CA, Bingham LJ commented that, since 'subjecting to any detriment' was to be given its broad, ordinary meaning, almost any discriminatory conduct by employer against employee in relation to the latter's employment will be rendered unlawful. However, an unjustified sense of grievance does not amount to a detriment (*Barclays Bank* v *Kapur (No 2)* [1995] IRLR 87, CA).

Unjustified warnings given to a disabled worker in order to appease workforce feelings could constitute a detriment under the DDA 1995 (see RRA 1976 claim of *Ramsey* v *John James Hawley (Speciality Works) Ltd* COIT 804/139, IT). A failure to deal with complaints by a disabled worker that he was being subjected to harassment by his fellow workers could constitute a detriment (*Sandhu & Minhas* v *Leicester Foundry Co Ltd* 1563/161, IT).

Harassment

Although not expressly mentioned in the DDA, harassment for a reason relating to an employee's disability is an example of 'any other detriment' in s 4(2)(*d*) (*Strathclyde Regional Council* v *Porcelli* [1986] IRLR 134, CS and *Wileman* v *Minilec Engineering Ltd* [1988] IRLR 144). A single incident of serious harassment may constitute a detriment within the meaning of s 4(2)(*d*) (*Bracebridge Engineering Ltd* v *Darby*) [1990] IRLR 3 and *Insitu Cleaning Co Ltd* v *Head* [1995] IRLR 4, EAT). The Employment Code deals with harassment at para 6.22.

Special cases

Charities

Although the DDA 1995 does not prohibit discrimination against those who are not disabled persons for the purposes of the Act, it can prohibit discrimination against people with one sort of impairment in favour of those with another sort of impairment. In the absence of further provision, it would be unlawful to employ a candidate who was blind in favour of one who was deaf for a reason which related to the deafness of the unsuccessful candidate. Section 10 of the DDA provides that the employment provisions do not:

(1) affect any charitable instrument which provides for conferring benefits on one or more categories of person determined by reference to any physical or mental capacity (s 10(1)(*a*));

(2) make unlawful any act done by a charity or recognised body (for the purposes of Pt I of the Law Reform (Miscellaneous Provisions) (Scotland) Act 1990) in pursuance of its charitable purposes in so far as those purposes are connected with persons determined by reference to any physical or mental capacity (s 10(1)(*b*);

(3) prevent a person who provides supported employment from treating members of a particular group of disabled persons more favourably than other persons in providing such employment (s 10(2)(*a*)). Supported employment means facilities provided or funded under s 15 of the Disabled Persons (Employment) Act 1944 (s 10(3)); and

(4) prevent the Secretary of State from agreeing to arrangements for the provision of supported employment which will or may result in members of a particular group of disabled persons being treated more favourably than other persons in providing such employment (s 10(2)(*b*)).

By s 10(3), 'Charity' is given the same meaning as in the Charities Act 1993. Section 96(1) of the Charities Act 1993 provides that a charity is a body with charitable purposes. In England and Wales 'charitable purposes' means purposes which are exclusively charitable according to the law of England and Wales in both s 10(4) and s 97(1) of the Charities Act 1993. 'Charitable instrument' means an enactment or other instrument (whenever taking effect) so far as it relates to charitable purposes' (DDA 1995, s 10(3)). In Scotland, 'charitable purposes' has the same meaning as in the Income Tax Acts (s 10(5)).

Crown and specified employments: The Crown, Parliament and others
Part II of the DDA 1995 applies to acts done by or for the purposes of a Minister of the Crown or government department (s 64(1)(*a*)) or on behalf of the Crown by a statutory body or a person holding a statutory office (s 64(1)(*b*)) or by or for the purposes of the House of Lords or the House of Commons (s 65).

Local government employment
The Local Government and Housing Act 1989 (LGHA 1989) provides that all staff engaged by a local authority, parish, or community council must be appointed on merit (LGHA 1989, s 7). Before the DDA 1995 this was subject to the quota system for registered disabled persons (see Introduction above) and permitted merit to be ignored in relation to registered disabled persons, if the local authority was below the three per cent quota. However, s 70(4) and Sched 6, para 5 of the DDA 1995 amend s 7 of the LGHA 1989 so that merit is the only criteria that can be taken into account in local government appointments, subject to the duty on the local authority to remove substantial disadvantage to the disabled person in accordance with its duty to make reasonable adjustments. The net effect of these amendments is that a local authority can no longer give disabled persons 'priority interviews' whereby the disabled candidate is considered before any other applicant. However the amendments do not preclude special recruitment drives to encourage applications from disabled persons, preferential training, and guaranteed interviews for all suitable disabled applicants (*Hansard*, HC Debs Vol 265, col 120–121).

Statutory authority or national security
The DDA 1995 excludes discriminatory acts done pursuant to or to comply with statutory enactment or instrument or for the purposes of safeguarding national security (s 59) (see p 250 below).

Victimisation
For the purposes of s 4, it is unlawful to discriminate against a person, whether disabled or not, by way of victimisation as defined in s 55. (See the Employment Code, para 4.53 and p 251 below.)

Checklist on unlawful acts

Employees and applicants

Does the person have a right to make a claim under the DDA?

—Does the claim relate to employment under:
  • a contract of service or of apprenticeship?
  • a contract personally to do any work?
—Was the employment at an establishment in Great Britain or Northern Ireland?
—Is the person entitled to claim under the DDA 1995 as:
  • an applicant, or prospective applicant?
  • an employee?
  • a contract worker?

Excluded employments

—Was the employment excluded from the DDA 1995 as employment:
  • on a ship, aircraft or hovercraft?
  • as a person holding a statutory office?
  • service as a police officer?
  • as a prison officer?
  • as a firefighter?
  • in the armed forces?
  • for a small employer

Was the person discriminated against?

—Was the disabled person unjustifiably treated less favourably for a reason related to his or her disability? (See the checklist on less favourable treatment?)
—Did the employer fail to comply with the duty to adjust justification? (See the checklist on the duty to adjust?)
—Was the person, whether disabled or not, victimised?

Was the discrimination against an applicant unlawful?

—Did the discrimination involve:
  • the arrangements made for the purpose of determining to whom employment should be offered?
  • terms on which employment was offered?
  • refusing to offer or deliberately not offering the person employment?

Was the discrimination against an employee unlawful?

—Did the discrimination involve:
- the terms of employment afforded to the employee?
- in the opportunities for promotion, a transfer, training or receiving any other benefit afforded to the employee?
- refusing to afford or deliberately not affording the employee any such opportunity?
- dismissing the employee?
- subjecting the employee to any other detriment?

—Does the case involve the special rules relating to:
- Benefits provided to the public
- Occupational pensions
- Insurance services
- Performance related pay
- Agricultural wages and terms
- Charities
- Crown and unspecified employments
- Local government employment
- Statutory authority or national security

Chapter 7

Trade Organisations

Sections 13 to 15 of the DDA 1995 prohibit discrimination by trade organisations against disabled members and applicants for membership. These provisions made it unlawful to discriminate against a person who has a disability as defined in s1 (see Chap 1, p3 above) or someone who had a disability (s2, and see p22). The provisions also render it unlawful to discriminate against any person by way of victimisation whether that person is disabled or not (see p251 below). Many of these provisions parallel those made in relation to discrimination by employers which are discussed in detail above. The provisions of the DDA may be supplemented by regulations. Some specific practical guidance is given by para7 of the Employment Code. Furthermore, given the similarity between many of the provisions, the remainder of that code will also be of some assistance here. Subject to the different definitions of discrimination, these provisions are broadly similar to those in s12 of the SDA 1975 and s11 of the RRA 1976. It must be remembered that a trade organisation's relations with applicants for employment and with its employees will be governed by the same provisions as apply to other employers.

The meaning of trade organisation

'Trade organisation' is defined as meaning 'an organisation of workers, an organisation of employers, or any other organisation whose members carry on a particular profession or trade for the purposes of which the organisation exists' (s13(4)). 'Profession' includes any vocation or occupation and 'trade' includes any business (s 68(1)). This would include a trade union, an employer's association or a professional body such as the Institute of Personnel and Development or the Law Society.

Definition of discrimination

The meaning of discrimination in relation to trade organisations is defined by s14. It mirrors the definition of discrimination by employers found in s5. Discrimination may comprise of unjustified less favourable treatment or of a failure to comply with the duty to adjust.

Discrimination by way of less favourable treatment

The provisions relating to discrimination by way of less favourable treatment follow closely those in s 5(1) and (3).

Meaning of discrimination in relation to trade organisations

14(1) For the purposes of this Part, a trade organisation discriminates against a disabled person if—

(a) for a reason which relates to the disabled person's disability, it treats him less favourably than it treats or would treat others to whom that reason does not or would not apply; and

(b) it cannot show that the treatment in question was justified.

Discriminates against a disabled person

See Chap 1 for the definition of disabled person. A person who had, but no longer has, a disability is deemed to be a disabled person for the purposes of these provisions (s 2(1)). Where the discrimination is by way of victimisation, the discrimination is unlawful whether or not the person victimised is a disabled person (s 13(3) and see p 251 below).

For a reason which relates to the disabled person's disability
This is identical to the equivalent provision in s 5(1)(*a*) (see p 36 above).

It treats him less favourably than it treats or would treat others to whom that reason does not or would not apply
This is also identical to the equivalent provision in s 5(1)(*a*) (see p 36 above).

It cannot show that the treatment in question was justified
As with the provisions of s 5, discrimination is only established if the trade organisation cannot show that the less favourable treatment was justified. Sub-section 14(3) provides that treatment is justified 'if, but only if, the reason for it is both material to the circumstances of the particular case and substantial'. This is identical to the equivalent provision in s 5(3) (see p 42 above). For example, the Employment Code suggests that a trade organisation may well be justified in excluding a member who uses a wheelchair from a trip to some workplaces where too many of the sites are inaccessible to that person (para 7.11).

Relationship with the duty to adjust
As under s 5(5), less favourable treatment cannot be justified where the trade organisation is under a duty to make a reasonable adjustment but fails (without justification) to make it *unless* the less favourable treatment would have been

justified even after that adjustment (s 14(5)) (see p 42 above). However, this sub-section will not come into force until the provisions imposing a duty to adjust on trade organisations is brought into effect.

Discrimination by way of a failure to adjust

These provisions are in the same terms as those in ss 5(2) and 5(4) (see p 48 above). At the time of writing they have not been brought into force. Once brought into force, they will place an obligation upon trade organisations to take reasonable steps to adapt their arrangements and premises where they place a disabled person at a substantial disadvantage.

Meaning of discrimination in relation to trade organisations

14(2)   For the purposes of this Part, a trade organisation also discriminates against a disabled person if—
   (a)   it fails to comply with a section 15 duty imposed on it in relation to the disabled person; and
   (b)   it cannot show that its failure to comply with that duty is justified.

Discriminates against a disabled person
See p 36 above.

Fails to comply with a section 15 duty imposed on it in relation to the disabled person
This is identical to the equivalent provision in s 5(2)(*a*) (see p 49 above). The nature and extent of the duty to adjust under s 15 is dealt with below.

It cannot show that its failure to comply with that duty is justified
Discrimination by a failure to adjust will be established unless the trade organisation can show that the failure was justified. Sub-section 14(4) provides that treatment is justified 'if, but only if, the reason for it is both material to the circumstances of the particular case and substantial'. This is identical to the equivalent provision in s 5(4) (see p 42 above).

The duty to adjust

The DDA 1995 makes provisions to place trade organisations under a duty to take reasonable steps to remove or reduce disadvantages to a disabled person that result from the arrangements made or premises occupied by the trade organisation. These provisions have not been brought into force at the time of writing and no commencement date has been set for doing so. Once in force, the nature and extent of the duty to adjust will be substantially similar to that imposed on employers by s 6. As such, they will not require a trade organisation to treat a disabled person more favourably than it treats or would treat others (s 15(6)), although they will not make it unlawful to treat disabled applicants and members more favourably.

The duty

The duty of trade organisations to adjust is set out in s 15 of the DDA.

Duty of trade organisations to make adjustments

15(1) Where
  (a) any arrangements made by or on behalf of a trade organisation, or
  (b) any physical feature of premises occupied by the trade organisation,

place the disabled person concerned at a substantial disadvantage in comparison with persons who are not disabled, it is the duty of the employer to take such steps as it is reasonable, in all the circumstances of the case, for him to have to take in order to prevent the arrangements or feature having that effect.

Any arrangements made by or on behalf of a trade organisation
The duty to adjust in s 15(1)(*a*) only applies to arrangements for determining who should become or remain a member of the organisation (s 15(2)(*a*)) or any term, condition or arrangements upon which membership or any benefit is offered or afforded (s 15(2)(*b*)). The word 'arrrangements' is to be broadly construed (see p 49 above). It will apply to arrangements made by the trade organisation itself and those made on behalf of the organisation by its agents.

Arrangements for determining who should become or remain a member of the organisation (s 15(2)(a))
This provision is self explanatory. It will apply to the practices, procedures and criteria used for processing and determining applications for membership. It will include the organisation's disciplinary procedures in so far as they may result in the expulsion of a member.

Any term, condition or arrangements on which membership or any benefit is offered or afforded (s 15(2)(b))
This provision is somewhat similar to that in s 6(2)(*b*) (see p 49 above). It would include arrangements made for providing members with training facilities, welfare and insurance schemes, invitations to attend events, processing of grievances, assistance provided to members in disciplinary or grievance procedures with their employer or employees (Employment Code, para 7.10).

Any physical feature of premises occupied by the employer
'Premises' includes land of any description (s 68) and will be given the same meaning under ss 6 and 15. The DD(E) Regs 1996 define 'physical features' only in relation to s 6(1) (see p 49 above). However, that phrase is likely to be

similarly defined by regulations when the duty of trade organisations to adjust is brought into force. The duty to adjust in relation to premises held under a lease is discussed in detail at p 233 below.

'The disabled person concerned' and the question of knowledge

The duty under s 15 will be a specific and individualised duty. Adaptations will be required only in relation 'to the disabled person concerned' and a trade organisation is not required to make general adaptations to its premises and practices accessible to disabled people in general. The duty to adjust will arise only relation to the 'disabled person concerned'. In cases involving arrangements for determining to whom membership should be offered, 'the disabled person concerned' is any person who is or who has notified the organisation that he is or may be, an applicant for that employment (s 15(4)(*a*)). In any other case, this means either an applicant for membership or a member of the organisation concerned (s 15(4)(*b*)). Furthermore, the duty will not arise if the organisation does not know and could not reasonably be expected to know that the disabled person concered:

    (a) is or may be an applicant for membership; or

    (b) has a disability and is likely to be placed at a substantial disadvantage (s 15(5)).

At a substantial disadvantage in comparison with persons who are not disabled

A disadvantage is substantial if it is more than minor or trivial. Regulations may be made to prescribe circumstances in which arrangements or features are or are not to be taken to place a disabled person at a substantial disadvantage (ss 15(7) and 6(8)) but no regulations have been made to date.

It is the duty of the organisation to take such steps as it is reasonable, in all the circumstances of the case, for him to have to take in order to prevent the arrangements or feature having that effect

There is no list setting out examples of the steps that s 15 may require an organisation to take. However, the steps that will be required in practice are likely to include some of the examples given under s 6(3) (see p 52 above). In particular, there may be a need to make adjustments to premises occupied by a trade organisation to allow a disabled member to gain access to them (see p 49 above and p 233 below). An organisation may be required to provide modified instructions or reference manuals, a reader or interpreter to allow a disabled person to make use of services (see p 54 above). For example, a trade union may be required 'to ensure that, where it is reasonable, visually impaired members could get union literature in braille and members with hearing impairments could have signers at meetings' (*Hansard*, HL, 18 July 1995, Vol 566, col 225, Henley). Similarly, it may be necessary for an organisation to provide special equipment to allow a disabled person to utilise the organisation's services (see p 53 above), such as providing a minicom for use by deaf members.

The extent of the duty

The organisation is only under a duty to make the adjustment if it is reasonable for it to have to do so. A list of some of the matters to be taken into account is provided in s 15(3) of the DDA 1995. This provision, and the list of matters to be taken into account, is identical to that in s 6(4). The matters are:

(1) the extent to which taking the step would prevent the effect in question (s 15(3)(a)) (see p 55);

(2) the extent to which it is practicable for the organisation to take that step (s 15(3)(b)) (see p 55);

(3) the financial and other costs which would be incurred by the organisation in taking the step and the extent to which taking it would disrupt any of his activities (s 15(3)(c)) (see p 56);

(4) the extent of the organisation's financial and other resources (s 15(3)(d)) (see p 56); and

(5) the availability of financial and other assistance to the organisation with respect to taking that step (s 15(3)(e)) (see p 57).

Regulations may make provisions as to circumstances in which it is or is not reasonable for organisations to have to take steps of a prescribed description (ss 15(7) and 6(8)(c) and (e)) and as to steps which it is always or never reasonable for an employer to have to take (s 6(8)(d) and (f)). No regulations have been made yet (although see the regulations made in relation to alterations to premises occupied by employers at p 233 as equivalent provisions are likely to be made in relation to trade organisations once the duty to adjust premises is brought into force). Again, other matters may be taken into account even if they are not listed in para 15(3) provided they are relevant to the question of reasonableness (see p 52 above).

And the organisation 'cannot show that his failure to comply with the section is justified'

Even if it is established that the organisation failed to comply with a duty, discrimination under s 14(2) will not be established if the organisation can show that the failure was 'justified' under s 14(2)(b)). Section 14(4) provides that treatment can only be justified 'if the reason for it is both material to the circumstances of the particular case and substantial'. This provision is identifical to the justification provisions under ss 5 and 14(1)(b) above (see p 59). Regulations may prescribe circumstances in which a failure to adjust is and is not justified (ss 15(7) and 6(8)) but none have been made to date.

Consequences of a failure to adjust

A failure to make a reasonable adjustment only allows a disabled person to bring a discrimination claim against the trade organisation. It does not give rise to an independent right of action for breach of statutory duty (s 15(10)).

Unlawful discrimination by trade organisations

Section 13 of the DDA 1995 provides that it is unlawful for a trade organisation to discriminate against members and applicants for membership in various respects. There is no geographical limitation upon this provision. There is no need for a disabled person to establish that their trade or profession is carried out at an establishment in Great Britain or Northern Ireland in order to obtain the protection of the DDA (compare the provisions in relation to employees at p 64 above). Therefore, a worker whose employment is excluded from the DDA because, for example, it is on a hovercraft (see p 66 above) is still entitled to the protection of s 13.

Unlawful acts against applicants

Section 13(1) makes it unlawful for a trade organisation to discriminate against an applicant or potential applicant for membership.

Discrimination by trade organisations

13(1)   it is unlawful for a trade organisation to discriminate agaisnt a disabled person—
   (a)   in the terms on which it is prepared to admit him to membership of the organisation; or
   (b)   by refusing to accept, or deliberately not accepting, his application for membership.

In the terms on which it is prepared to admit him to membership of the organisation
It is unlawful for a trade organisation to discriminate against a disabled applicant by offering membership on less favourable terms, such as requiring higher membership fees, offering membership subject to more stringent or onerous conditions, or by offering only restricted or associate membership. Similarly, it would be unlawful to require a disabled person (but no-one else) to pass a medical test prior to admission unless the organisation could prove that such treatment was justified. This provision covers the offer of membership, and will apply even if the offer is rejected. If the offer is accepted on the discriminatory terms and conditions, the disabled person will also be able to claim under s 13(2), in so far as those discriminatory terms are applied after membership commences. There is some similarity with s 4(1)(*b*) of the DDA 1995 which is discussed at p 70 above. Once the duty to adjust is

brought into force, a trade organisation may be under a duty to make reasonable alterations to any terms which place a disabled person at a substantial disadvantage.

By refusing to accept, or deliberately not accepting, his application for membership
It is unlawful for a trade organisation to discriminate by refusing to accept or deliberately not accepting the disabled person as a member. There is no need for an express refusal of membership provided the failure to accept the application was deliberate. It would be unlawful for a professional organisation to refuse to accept a person with mental health problems as a member because of those problems unless it could show that the decision was justified. There is some similarity with s 4(1)(c) of the DDA 1995 which is discussed at p 75 above.

One difference between this section and that of s 4 is that there is no express provision in s 13 making it unlawful to discriminate in the arrangements made for determining who should be accepted as a member. However, where those arrangements consist of criteria or conditions which result in the rejection of the application, the disabled person will have a cause of action under s 13(1)(b). For example, a trade organisation may have a rule that it will only consider written applications for membership and therefore refuse to accept an oral application from a disabled person. If the disabled person was unable to complete a written application because of his disability, the refusal would amount to less favourable treatment for a reason related to that disability. Therefore, if the insistence on a written application cannot be justified, it would amount to discrimination under s 14(1) and would be made unlawful by s 13(1)(b).

In addition, s 15(2) makes express reference to the arrangements made for determining who should become or remain a member. Once in force, trade organisations will be under a duty to take reasonable steps to alter those arrangements where they place the disabled person concerned at a substantial disadvantage. To some extent, this would overlap with the less favourable treatment provisions. It would require the modification of criteria and conditions which result in less favourable treatment of a disabled person for a reason related to his disability, when the application of such criteria and conditions is already unlawful under s 14(1). In the example given above, the duty to adjust would very probably oblige the organisation to modify the insistence upon written applications or to provide assistance to allow a written application to be completed by a member of staff on behalf of a disabled applicant, even though the enforcement of that rule is already made unlawful by s 14(1). However, the duty to adjust will also require adjustments to matters which do not in themselves result in or amount to unlawful less favourable treatment, such as providing recruitment literature in accessible formats upon request.

Unlawful acts against members

Section 13(2) makes it unlawful for a trade organisation to discriminate against an applicant or potential applicant for membership.

Discrimination by trade organisations

13(2)   It is unlawful for a trade organisation, in the case of a disabled person who is a member of the organisation, to discriminate against him—

(a)   in the way it affords him access to any benefits or by refusing or deliberately omitting to afford him access to them;

(b)   by depriving him of membership, or varying the terms on which he is a member; or

(c)   by subjecting him to any other detriment.

In the way it affords him access to any benefits or by refusing or deliberately omitting to afford him access to them

This is a wide provision which will cover discrimination in relation to the benefits available to members of trade organisations. 'Benefits' is to be construed widely and will include anything that could fairly be described as an 'advantage' (*Peake v Automotive Products Ltd* [1977] ICR 480, EAT). It includes arrangements made for providing members with training facilities, welfare and insurance schemes, invitations to attend events, processing of grievances, and assistance provided to members in disciplinary or grievance procedures with their employer or employees (Employment Code, para 7.10). It does not require an applicant to prove that they would have obtained the benefit provided they can show that they have lost or been denied an opportunity to take advantage of that benefit.

Once the duty to adjust provisions come into force, a trade organisation may be required to make adjustments to the way in which benefits are provided and to those benefits themselves. For example, it may be required to alter means by which training courses are advertised to members and by which members are selected to attend such courses. Therefore, a practice under which training courses are advertised on a notice board at the organisation's premises and places distributed to those who attend the training department on a 'first come first served' basis may place a member with mobility difficulties at a substantial disadvantage and require modificiation. In addition, it may be necessary to alter the format of the training itself so that it is accessible to the disabled person concerned, eg by providing training materials in an appropriate format.

Occupational pension schemes

Where an occupational pension scheme is available to members of a trade organisation, it will be subject to the non-discrimination rule implied by s 17 (see p 77 above). In contrast to s 6(11), the duty on trade organisations to adjust does not expressly exclude occupational pension schemes, although such provision may be made by way of regulations before the duty to adjust is brought into force (s 157)).

Insurance services
There are no special rules relating to insurance services provided to members of a trade organisation. Section 17 applies only to arrangements made between insurers and employers.

By depriving him of membership
This will include both a discriminatory expulsion and a discriminatory refusal to renew membership.

Varying the terms on which he is a member
This provision will encompass any discriminatory changes to the terms of membership adverse to the disabled person. As with the other provisions of the DDA, there is nothing to prevent the organisation giving better treatment to a disabled person.

By subjecting him to any other detriment
This provision will be widely construed to encompass anything that puts the member under a disadvantage (see p 85 above). It would include disciplinary action short of expulsion. It could also include harassment of a member by, for example, officials of an organisation.

Ex members
Presumably s 13(2) will not apply to someone who has been expelled from the organisation and complains of discrimination in the course of an appeal against that expulsion (see *Post Office v Adekeye (No 2)* [1995] ICR 540), although it would apply where the expulsion is 'suspended' pending the appeal.

Statutory authority or national security

The DDA excludes discriminatory acts done pursuant to or to comply with statutory enactment or instrument (s 59) (see pp 250–251 below).

Victimisation

For the purposes of s 14, it is unlawful for a trade organisation to discriminate against a person, whether disabled or not, by way of victimisation as defined in s 55 (see pp 251–252 below).

Checklist on Trade Organisations

—Was the organisation a trade organisation?
—Was the complainant an applicant or prospective applicant for membership or member of the trade organisation?
—Was there discrimination against a disabled person by way of:
  • unjustified less favourable treatment?
  • an unjustified failure to comply with the duty to adjust?
—Was there discrimination against any person by way of victimisation?
—Did the discrimination against an applicant involve:
  • the terms on which the organisation was prepared to admit the applicant to membership?
  • refusing or deliberately not accepting the application for membership?
—Did the discrimination aainst a member involve:
  • the way the organisation affords the member access to any benefits or by refusing or deliberately omitting to afford him access to them?
  • depriving the member of membership?
  • varying the terms of membership?
  • by subjecting the member to any other detriment?

The checklists given at the end of Chaps 4 and 5 can be modified and used in assessing if there has been unjustified less favourable treatment and, once the provisions are in force, an unjustified failure to comply with the duty to adjust.

Chapter 8

Enforcement and Remedies

Introduction

The employment provisions can be enforced only by individual claims. There is no equivalent of the Commission for Racial Equality (CRE) or the Equal Opportunities Commission (EOC) with responsibility for enforcing Pt II of the DDA. The status and role of the National Disability Council (NDC) is discussed in the Introduction. Section 8 of the DDA deals with claims, enforcement, remedies and procedure in relation to Pt II, covering employment, contract work and discrimination by trade organisations. The procedure to be followed in the tribunal itself is largely determined by the Industrial Tribunal (Constitution and Rules of Procedure) Regulations 1993 (IT Regs 1993), which apply to all tribunal claims. Save where the contrary appears from the context, references to the rules in the remainder of this chapter are references to the provisions of those regulations.

The appropriate forum

Proceedings for breach of Pt II of the DDA must be brought by way of a complaint to an Industrial Tribunal, to be renamed Employment Tribunals, (Employment Rights (Dispute Resolution) Bill 1996, cl 1) under s 8 of the DDA. No other civil, or criminal, proceedings may be brought against any person in respect of an act merely because the act is unlawful under the employment provisions of the DDA (Sched 3, para 2(1)). This does not prevent an application for judicial review in appropriate circumstances (para 2(2)). Judicial review will not be appropriate where there is an alternative remedy available, such as a right of application to an industrial tribunal, or other private law remedy (see e.g. *R v East Berkshire Health Authority, ex p Walsh* [1984] IRLR 278, and *MacLaren v Home Office* [1990] ICR 824). In *R v Hammersmith & Fulham London Borough, ex p NALGO* [1991] IRLR 249 at para 35, Nolan LJ was prepared to assume 'that if a public authority proposes to embark upon an employment or redeployment policy which is in breach of the SDA or the RRA, or is otherwise unlawful, the public law remedies should be available to the unions and employees affected'. Judicial review may be available where there is no or no adequate alternative means of challenge through the Industrial Tribunal. For example, although many government appointments are not subject to Pt II of the DDA, the relevant Minister or department is under a duty not to act in a way that would contravene Pt II in making appointments or selection arrangements to those posts (s 66, and see p 67 above). In such a case, there would be no right to make an application to a tribunal under s 8 and an unlawful decision or policy could be challenged by way of judicial review.

Questionnaire

The questionnaire procedure has been developed to assist those who believe they have been discriminated against to decide whether or not to institute proceedings and, if proceedings are commenced, to formulate and present a case in an effective manner. The purpose of a questionnaire is to elicit evidence from the respondent to enable the aggrieved person to decide whether or not to bring the claim, and also to gather information which will assist in the effective presentation of the case if a claim is made. The respondent's replies are admissible in proceedings (s 56(3)(*a*)). Questionnaires procedures have been included in both the sex and race discrimination legislation (see SDA 1975, s 74 and the Sex Discrimination (Questions and Replies) Order 1975 (SI No 2048); RRA 1976, s 65 and the Race Relations (Questions and Replies) Order 1977 (SI No 842)). Section 56 of the DDA allows the Secretary of State to make similar regulations for a questionnaire procedure under the DDA.

Under these provisions, a person who considers that he may have been discriminated against may use a prescribed form to question the respondent on his reasons for doing any relevant act or on any other matter which may be relevant (s 56(2)). The forms are available from Jobcentres. The questionnaire can be served on a potential respondent before proceedings are commenced or an actual respondent after the commencement of proceedings. Questionnaires served before issue must be served within three months of the date of the discriminatory act alleged (Disability Discrimination (Questions and Replies) Order 1996, r 3(*a*)). A questionnaire presented after a complaint is presented to a tribunal must be presented within 21 days of the complaint unless the tribunal give leave for service outside of that period (r 3(*b*)). The granting of leave to serve a questionnaire late is a matter for the tribunal's discretion, and it may properly be refused where there is no satisfactory explanation for the delay (*Williams* v *Greater London Citizens Advice Bureaux Service* [1989] ICR 545) although a tribunal would err if it failed to recognise that it has a discretionary power to extend the time limit (*Simpkin* v *JET Ltd* unreported, EAT 606/84). The EAT has warned against using or allowing questionnaires that are oppressive or prolix, but noted that in an appropriate case more than one questionnaire may be used, with leave being sought on notice to serve additional questionnaires after the complaint has been presented, particularly after discovery (*Carrington* v *Helix Lighting Ltd* [1990] ICR 125).

If it appears to the tribunal that there has been a deliberate failure to reply without reasonable excuse, or that any reply is evasive or equivocal, then it may draw such inference as it considers just and equitable, including an inference that the respondent has commited an unlawful act under the employment provisions of the DDA (s 56(3)). Care should be taken both over the drafting of the questionnaire and the response. A carelessly drafted questionnaire will allow a respondent the opportunity give unhelpful replies to an ill-chosen question. Similarly, a vague reply to a well drafted questionnaire will permit the tribunal to draw inferences against the employer.

In *Carrington v Helix Lighting Ltd* [1990] ICR 125, the EAT said that 'it is true that any unsatisfactory answering of questionnaires does not lay the party open to being struck out, as it would be in the case of a failure to answer interrogatories, but by section 65(2) of the Race Relations Act 1976 a tribunal is encouraged to take a serious view of the conduct of a respondent in this respect.' In *King v Great Britain–China Centre* [1992] ICR 516 the Court of Appeal emphasised it is unusual to find direct evidence of discrimination as few employers will be prepared to admit such discrimination even to themselves. In some cases the discrimination will not be ill-intentioned but merely based on an assumption 'he or she would not have fitted in'. The outcome of the case will therefore usually depend on what inferences it is proper to draw from the primary facts found by the tribunal. These inferences can include, in appropriate cases, any inferences that it is just and equitable to draw from an evasive or equivocal reply to a questionnaire.

It is not necessary to serve a questionnaire before commencing proceedings. However the procedure may be particularly useful in disability discrimination cases. A recalcitrant employer who is not prepared to make reasonable adjustments may be encouraged to do so when asked to explain his failure in a questionnaire. Suggestions as to the kinds of information that could be sought in the questionnaire are contained in Appendix 5.

Presentation of a complaint to the tribunal

Section 8(1) provides that a complaint by any person that another has discriminated against him (or is to be treated as having discriminated against him) in a way which is unlawful under Pt II of the DDA, may be presented to an Industrial Tribunal. The complaint should be sent to the Regional Office of the Tribunal.

Time Limits

As a general rule, an Industrial Tribunal must not consider a complaint under s 8 unless it is presented before the end of the three-month period beginning when the act complained of was done (Sched 3, para 3). It only has jurisdiction to consider a complaint which is out of time if, in all the circumstances of the case, it considers that it is just and equitable to do so (para 3(2)).

The date of presentation

Presentation is complete when an application is received or communicated through what is indicated as an acceptable channel of communication, such as a post box (*Hetton Victory Club* v *Swainston* [1983] ICR 341). A claim is presented when it is received by the tribunal, whether or not it is dealt with immediately upon receipt. A claim delivered to the tribunal office by post on a Saturday is presented on that day, even if it is not registered until the following Monday. A claim is not presented by the act of posting it addressed to the tribunal (*Hammond* v *Haigh Castle & Co Ltd* [1973] IRLR 91 at 92).

The date of the discriminatory act

In many cases it will be clear when the act complained of took place. If the discrimination consists of dismissing the disabled person, the act took place on the date of the dismissal and the time limit runs from that date. If the employee was dismissed with notice, the time limit still runs from the date on which the notice expires and the dismissal takes effect (*Lupetti* v *Wrens Old House Ltd* 1984 [ICR] 348). There are statutory rules for the following situations (Sched 3, para 3(3).

Contractual terms

If the unlawful act of discrimination is attributable to a term in a contract, that act is to be treated as extending throughout the duration of the contract (para 3(3)(*a*)). Therefore, a complaint concerning the application of a less favourable contractual term to a disabled employee, such as a lower rate of pay, contractual bonus or contractual overtime, may be made at any time up to the end of three months from the termination of that contract.

Continuing acts

Any act extending over a period shall be treated as done at the end of that period (para 3(3)(*b*)). In *Barclays Bank plc* v *Kapur* [1991] ICR 208 the House of Lords held that maintaining a discriminatory regime, rule, or practice can be an 'act extending over a period' within the equivalent provision in s 68(7)(*b*) of the RRA 1976. The three-month time limit runs from the end of the period during which the regime, rule or practice is operated. This must be distinguished from a single act which simply has consequences over a period of time. In such a case, the time limit runs from the date of the act. Where the rules of a mortgage subsidy scheme were discriminatory, the denial of access to the scheme was held to be a continuing act extending over the period of employment in *Calder* v *James Finlay Corporation* (Note) [1989] ICR 157. However, the appointment of a male rather than a female teacher (*Amies* v *Inner London Education Authority* [1977] ICR 308) or a decision not to regrade a nurse (*Sougrin* v *Haringey Health Authority* [1992] IRLR 416) were single acts, even though the consequences of those acts were continuous.

In *Littlewoods Organisation plc* v *Traynor* [1993] IRLR 154 the EAT upheld an Industrial Tribunal's decision that a failure by employers to implement fully remedial measures they had promised in response to the complainant's complaint of racial abuse against a colleague consitituted a continuing act of discrimination rather than a single act having consequences extending over a period of time.

Deliberate omissions
A deliberate omission shall be treated as done when the person in question decided upon it (para 3(3)(*c*)). In the absence of evidence establishing the contrary, a person shall be taken to decide upon an omission:
  (a) when he does an act inconsistent with doing the omitted act; or
  (b) if he has done no such inconsistent act, when the period expires within which he might reasonably have been expected to do the omitted act if it was to be done (para 3(4)).
In *Barclays Bank plc* v *Kapur* [1991] ICR 208 Lord Griffiths said at 213f:

> It would probably be unwise to attempt to define a 'deliberate omission' but I get the distinct impression that it was included by the draftsman as a sweeping-up provision intended for the protection of employees and addressed to activities peripheral to the employment rather than to the terms of the employment itself and intended to cover a one-off rather than a continuing situation: for example, a deliberate failure to notify a coloured employee of a vacancy for a better job in the company when all his white comparators were invited to apply for the job ...

The provisions relating to deliberate ommissions create particular difficulties in relation to a decision not to offer an applicant employment. In such a case, the decision may be made long before it is communicated to the employee. *Swithland Motors plc* v *Clarke* EAT 329/92 concerned the equivalent provision in s 76(6)(*c*) of the SDA 1975. Swithland Motors was purchasing the assets of an insolvent company. The applicants sought employment prior to the completion of the transfer of assets. The decision not to offer them employment was made prior to the transfer although they were not informed that they had been unsuccessful until afterwards. The EAT held time started to run only after the transfer rather than upon the decision being made, as decides means 'decides at a time and in circumstances when he is in a position to implement that decision'. In most cases, the employer will be in a position to implement a decision immediately, whether or not it is communicated to the complainant at that time. Where a applicant was unaware that an adverse decision had been made, an Industrial Tribunal may extend the time limit on the grounds that it is just and equitable to do so (see p 106 below). Nevertheless, in the absence of any suggestions to the contrary (such as an interview or date for the close of applications) it may be reasonable to assume that a decision not to offer employment is made soon after the date of the application. In those circumstances, complainants should try to present their claims within three months of that date.

Time limits and Internal Appeals

In *The Post Office* v *Adekeye (No 2)* [1995] ICR 540, the EAT held that a discrimination claim could not be brought in relation to a post dismissal appeal as the complainant was not an employee at the date of the appeal. Therefore, the claim must be made in relation to the dismissal and time starts to run from the date of the dismissal. However, if a disabled person remained an employee at the date of the appeal, for example if he was reinstated but demoted or if the dismissal would only take effect after the appeal if it were unsuccessful, a claim could be made in relation to the appeal itself. In such cases, time starts to run from the date of the appeal (*Adekeye* v *The Post Office* [1993] IRLR 324).

Extending the time for making an application

The tribunal may extend time for presenting a claim where it considers that it is just and equitable in all the circumstances of the case to do so (Sched 3, para 3(2)). The same form of words is used in the other discrimination legislation (see s 76(5) of the SDA 1975 and s 68(6) of the RRA 1976). In *Hutchinson* v *Westward Television Ltd* [1977] ICR 279 the EAT upheld a refusal to extend time where the complainant knew of the SDA and consciously decided not to pursue a claim. The EAT held that the tribunal had a wide discretion to do what is fair in all the circumstances, that will rarely be challengeable on appeal. The words 'in all the circumstances of the case' refer however only to circumstances relating to the late presentation of the claim and do not require the tribunal to consider the merits of the case as a whole. However, this does not preclude a tribunal from considering the merits, though they should invite the parties to make submissions before doing so (*Lupetti* v *Wrens Old House Ltd* [1984] ICR 348, EAT). In *Callahan* v *East Sussex County Council* EAT 587/76 the EAT held that a tribunal's refusal to extend time where the lateness of the claim resulted from the applicant's failure to check her information, either by using the questionnaire procedure or by other easily accessible means, could not be challenged. By contrast, an extension was granted where a complainant did not present a claim because of a request by the respondent to wait until a committee had met to reconsider the matter (*Farrar* v *GLC* COIT 785/193).

The tribunal should consider all of the reasons for the delay. In particular, the fact that an applicant has been sick may be relevant, especially if he acts promptly once he has recovered, as in *Butler* v *J & Y Plastics Ltd* COIT 1095/240. Although there is no rule of law which prevents time running under Sched 3, para 3 during periods of incapacity, mental illness or disability has often been held sufficient to establish that it was not practicable for a complaint of unfair dismissal to be presented in time and to justify an extension of time (see *Newell* v *Snow & Partners* COIT 982/229; *Theobald* v *Trustees of the Borough Market* COIT 1531/113 and *Martin* v *Broxtowe BC* COIT 1507/40).

The originating application

Complaints to an Industrial Tribunal are usually made on a form known as an IT1, available from Department for Education and Employment Offices and offices of the Industrial Tribunals and many advice agencies. However, a letter will be accepted provided it contains the information required by r 1(1) below (*Smith* v *Automobile Proprietary Ltd* [1973] ICR 306). In either case, the document on which the complaint is made is called an originating application. The originating application must be in writing and contain:

(a) the name and address of the applicant and, if different, his address for service of documents;

(b) the name(s) and address(es) of the person(s) against whom relief is sought; and

(c) the grounds, with particulars, on which relief is sought (r 1(1) of the Industrial Tribunals (Constitution and Rules of Procedure) Regulations 1993 (SI No 2687)).

A failure to provide grounds of complaint in the appropriate place was held not to render an originating application a nullity in *Dodd* v *British Telecommunications plc* [1988] ICR 116, EAT as the nature of the complaint in that case was made clear elsewhere on the form. Where the Secretary to the tribunal is of the opinion that the application does not raise an issue on which the tribunal has jurisdiction, he may notify the applicant accordingly with reasons, and decline to register the claim unless the applicant insists (r 1(2)). If no reply is received the claim is not registered and proceeds no further, but if the applicant so requires it must be registered (r 1(3)).

Very often the grounds of an application concerning unfair dismissal are set out briefly. However, in discrimination cases it will often be advisable to present a reasonably detailed account of the matters on which the complainant is going to rely at the hearing. This does not require the complainant to present all his evidence on the grounds, but enough information should be presented so that the respondent to the case cannot complain of being taken by surprise or have to seek further particulars of the complaint. Time spent on the grounds at the start of a case may save interlocutory stages in a case which otherwise lengthen proceedings. Furthermore, applicants should remember that their credibility may suffer if the case presented at the tribunal differs significantly from the account given in the originating application.

In a case under the DDA, it will be necessary to consider including the following details in an IT1 in addition to the mandatory requirements set out above. Firstly, a statement of facts showing that the complainant is a disabled person for the purposes of s 1 or 2 of the DDA 1995, including a reference to the nature of the complainant's condition or impairment and the normal day-to-day activities affected. If a case relates to less favourable treatment, the originating application should identify the less favourable treatment, state that (and if possible how) the reason for the treatment related to the disability, and say how others were or would have been treated more favourably. Where a case relates to a failure to adjust, the IT1 should identify the nature of the

substantial disadvantage and the arrangement or physical feature that gave rise
to it. In addition, it should identify any measures which were reasonable for
the employer to take to remove that disadvantage. Any measures taken that
were ineffective should be explained. The consequences of the less favourable
treatment or the failure to adjust should be set out. Finally, the application
should state the remedy sought, although this will not present the complainant
from seeking a different remedy thereafter (see below).

The notice of appearance

A respondent to proceedings under the DDA 1995 will reply to the complaint
in a notice of appearance or IT3. Upon receipt of an originating application,
the Secretary of the Tribunals enters the application in the Register (which is
public) and sends a copy to the respondent(s), together with information as to
the time limit for entering an appearance (IT Regs 1993, r 2(1) and (2)). Notice
of the application is sent on standard form IT2. The respondent is sent the IT3
with this. The notice of appearance must be returned within 21 days and must:

  (a) set out the respondent's full name and address (and address for ser-
       vice, if different);
  (b) state whether or not he intends to resist the application; and
  (c) if he does intend to resist, state the grounds of resistance with suffi-
       cient particulars (IT Regs, r 3(1)).

The notice of appearance should attempt to deal with the defences to be
raised by the respondent to the claim. If the respondent leaves out a ground and
wishes to raise it at any subsequent tribunal hearing, the applicant may
successfully resist an application to amend the notice of appearance or obtain
an adjournment so that he can deal with the new allegation (*Hotson* v *Wisbech
Conservative Club* [1984] ICR 859) possibly with costs. The notice of
appearance should try to deal with some or all of the following issues in
sufficient detail to avoid unnecessary interlocutory steps. Sufficient particulars
should be given to allow the complainant and the tribunal to understand the
nature of the defence. Firstly, issues going to the jurisdiction of the tribunal
should be raised. For example:

  (1) the person complaining is not a disabled person within the meaning
       of the Act;
  (2) the complaint is time barred;
  (3) the complainant was not applying for employment;
  (4) the complainant was not an employee; or
  (5) the complainant's employment was not at an establishment in the
       UK.

In cases relating to less favourable tratment the IT3 should attempt to deal
with the issues raised in the IT1. For example, it might state that there was no
less favourable treatment, that any such treatment was not for a reason relating
to the disabled person's disability or that the treatment was justified. In a
failure to adjust case, it may be useful to concede or dispute that the complaint
relates to an arrangement or physical features within the meaning of s 6 or that

the complainant was at a substantial disadvantage in comparison to non-disabled persons. Finally, consider if the steps which it is alleged the employer should have taken were reasonable. For example, it may be useful to raise the effectiveness, practicability and cost of the step or the availability of resources to take the step. In either case it may be relevant to state that the employer did not know (or could not reasonably have known) that the complainant was a disabled person or that he was disadvantaged by a feature or arrangement (see p 51).

Time limit for the notice of appearance

The notice of appearance must be presented within 21 days of receipt of the originating application (r 3(1)). A chairman has a power for extending the time for doing any act appointed under the rules and may do so either before or after the time limit has expired (r 15(1)). This power was regularly used to allow 'late' notices of appearance before the time limit was extended to 21 days from 14 by the Industrial Tribunal (Constitution and Rules of Procedure) (Amendment) Regulations 1996 (SI No 1757). It may be that it will no longer be exercised so readily. If a notice of appearance is sent to the tribunal after expiry of the 21 days it is treated under the rules as containing an implicit application for an extension of the time limit if it sets out the reasons why the notice has been presented late (r 3(3)). Even if the chairman grants an extension of time, he is to consider whether it would have been reasonably practicable for the notice to have been presented in time. If he determines that timely presentation was reasonably practicable, the respondent is deemed to have acted unreasonably for the purposes of r 12(1) and the chairman must make an order for costs under r 12(1) if he considers it appropriate (r 3(4)). The respondent must be given the opportunity to show cause why he should be granted the extension before an application for an extension is refused (rr 3(5) and 15(1)). In the event of an appeal to the EAT against a refusal to extend time to lodge a notice of appeal, an affidavit should be provided dealing with the reasons for failure to enter the appearance in time, and exhibiting draft grounds of resistance that show at least an arguable case on the substantive claim (*Charlton v Charlton Thermosystems (Romsey) Ltd* [1995] IRLR 79).

If the respondent does not enter a notice of appearance he is not entitled to take further part in the proceedings except to:
(a) make application for an extension of time for entering a notice of appearance;
(b) apply for futher particulars of the originating application;
(c) apply for a review on the grounds that he did not receive notice of the proceedings;
(d) be called as a witness by another person; and
(e) receive a copy of the decision (r 3(2), and see *Comber v Harmony Inns* [1993] ICR 15).

Pre-hearing review

A Pre-Hearing Review (PHR) may be held where a complaint to a tribunal is unlikely to succeed, or where any contention made by a party has no reasonable prospect of success. A PHR may be held upon the application of a party or by the tribunal of its own motion (r 7(1)). The PHR may be heard either by a full tribunal or (more usually) by a Chairman sitting alone (r 13(8)). The tribunal will consider the contents of the originating application and the notice of appearance, written submissions from the parties and oral argument from any party that chooses to appear (r 7(1)). No oral evidence is taken, although the written submissions may include documents related to the case. If the tribunal determines that the claim or contention has no reasonable prospect of success it can order the contending party to make a deposit (not exceeding £150) as a condition of being permitted to take part in the proceedings (r 7(4)). The tribunal must have regard to the party's means in fixing the sum, so far as they are reasonably ascertainable (r 7(5)).

The tribunal must record the order for a deposit. It must also record its reasons in summary form in a document signed by the Chairman. Copies of the document must be sent to all parties, along with a note, which states that, if the party against whom the order is made persists in participating in proceedings, or (as the case may be) making the contention which has no reasonable prospect of success, an award of costs may be made against him should he lose the full hearing (r 7(6)). The document also points out that the party could lose the deposit (r 7(6)). The decision from the PHR becomes available to the tribunal which hears the substantive case after it has reached its decision on liability. If a deposit is ordered it must be paid within 21 days (extendable by up to another 14 days upon representations made within the initial period of 21 days); if it is not so paid the application or notice of appearance is struck out (r 7(7)). The deposit paid by a party is refundable unless at the main hearing an order for costs is made against that party (rr 7(8) and 12(8)). A tribunal member who hears a PHR is not permitted to hear the full hearing, regardless of whether a deposit was ordered (r 7(9)).

Amendments

The originating application or the notice of appearance can only be amended by consent or with leave of the tribunal. While leave is generally given, the later the request for leave to amend is made, the less likely leave is to be granted. In some cases, if the amendment is made at the hearing, the complainant may have to pay the respondent's costs if an adjournment is caused by the respondent needing an adjournment to deal with the matters raised in the amendment (see below). There is a wide power to allow such amendments as are required by the justice of the case, and a complainant may be allowed to amend to substitute a different respondent if he had wrongly identified the employer in the originating application (*Cocking* v *Sandhurst (Stationers) Ltd* [1974] ICR 650, and see *Linbourne* v *Constable* [1993] ICR 698).

Joinder of parties

A tribunal has the power of its own motion, or upon the application of any person at any time, to direct that any person against whom any relief is sought be joined as a party to the proceedings (r 17(1)). The tribunal may also dismiss a respondent from the proceedings who appears to the tribunal not to be, or to have ceased to be, directly interested in the proceedings (*Reddington* v *Straker & Sons* [1994] ICR 172).

Premises occupied under a lease

Joinder will be particularly important in cases involving the duty to adjust physical features in premises occupied under a lease. If the adjustment was not made because a lessor unreasonably refused to consent to the occupier making the alteration, the lessor may be liable instead of the occupier (see generally pp 126 below). Where a disabled person brings a complaint against the occupier under s 8, either the occupier or the complainant can ask the tribunal to join the lessor (including the superior lessor) to the proceedings (Sched 4, para 2(1)). Such a request must be granted if made before the hearing of the complaint begins (Sched 4, para 2(2)); may be granted if made after the hearing begins (para 2(3)); but must not be granted if made after the tribunal has determined the complaint (para 2(4)). However, where an application is made so late as to necessitate an adjournment, for example on the morning of the hearing itself, it may be that there will be a penalty in costs under r 12(4) (see p 126 below). Where the lessor has been joined to the proceedings, the tribunal may determine whether or not the lessor unreasonably refused consent or consented subject to unreasonable conditions (para 2(5)). See p 126 below as to the consequences of such a determination.

Further interlocutory matters

The tribunal has various interlocutory powers which are exercisable by the tribunal either of its own motion or on the application of a party. Such applications may, and usually are, made in writing, although they are sometimes made orally at a directions or other hearing. These powers play a particularly important role in discrimination cases, because of the lack, in most cases, of significant direct evidence. From the respondent's point of view the powers are useful to ensure that there are no surprises in the complainant's case. The tribunal has a general power to give directions (r 16(1)). Otherwise the powers are as follows.

Further particulars

The tribunal has the power to require a party to give further particulars of the grounds on which he relies and on any facts and contentions relevant thereto (r 4(1)(*a*)). Further particulars of the notice of appearance or the originating application will be ordered where:

(a) a party would otherwise be taken by surprise at the last minute;
(b) they are necessary to do justice in the case;
(c) the order would prevent an adjournment; or
(d) they would identify the issues in the case.
Further particulars can be required where:
(a) insufficient detail has been given in the document to enable another party to know the case to be met by him;
(b) clarification is needed of the facts alleged or legal basis of the case; or
(c) an allegation of bad faith has been made which is not detailed.
Further particulars will not be ordered where
(a) the order would be oppressive;
(b) the particulars sought seek evidence;
(c) the order would result in protracted and complicated pleadings battles (see *Byrne* v *Financial Times Ltd* [1991] IRLR 417).

Particulars may be ordered by the tribunal of its own motion, and will be where the application is very vague. Otherwise the request should be made in the first instance by letter to the other party containing a list of the required particulars. The letter should also contain a time limit after which an application will be made to the tribunal for an order that the particulars be supplied. Once that time limit has passed without (sufficient) particulars being supplied, an application should be made to the tribunal in writing for the particulars requested in the letter to be ordered (r 4). The application should set out the justification for the request. If a party fails to comply with an order requiring him to serve particulars, the tribunal may strike out the whole or part of his originating application or the notice of appearance and, if appropriate, debar a party from defending altogether (r 4(7)). Such an order can only be made if the tribunal has first sent the party a written notice giving him the opportunity to show cause why the pleading should not be struck out (r 4(7)). This requirement is mandatory, and if the tribunal fails to send the notice after the date for compliance, the defaulting party is entitled to have the pleading reinstated. If the tribunal sends out the notice before the date of compliance, it does not conform to the requirements of r 4(7) and the order is invalid (*Bearcard Property Managment and Construction Ltd* v *Day* [1984] ICR 837). The power should not be used to punish the party in default, except where the defaulting party has deliberately not complied with the order. The power to strike out may be exercised in particular where the failure to comply will prevent proper and fair disposal of the proceedings (*National Grid Co plc* v *Virdee* [1992] IRLR 555).

Discovery and inspection of documents

The tribunal has the power to require a party to give discovery and inspection of documents (r 4(1)(*b*)). Discovery of documents will assume as great an importance under the DDA as it has in other discrimination cases and will often be the most important phase of proceedings prior to the hearing.

Tribunals faced with a conflict between oral testimony and documentary evidence will often prefer the documentary evidence. There is no provision for the automatic discovery of documents. Where disclosure is made voluntarily there is a duty not to give a misleading impression by selective disclosure. If non-disclosure of a particular document would render a disclosed document misleading, it should be disclosed (*Birds Eye Walls Ltd* v *Harrison* [1985] ICR 278). In the absence of automatic discovery, specific or generic requests for documents should be made. Initially voluntary discovery should be requested by letter to the opposing party. Where that request is not fully complied with, a written appliation should be made to the tribunal for an order. That application should explain why the documents are sought and how they are relevant to the issues before the tribunal. The tribunal's power to order discovery upon such an application is the same as that of the county court. Normally, copies of all the documents concerned should be provided to the other party (see CCR Ord 14, r 5A). Again, this power is enforceable by an order striking out all or part of an originating application or notice of appearance once the party has been given an opportunity to show cause why such an order should not be made (r 4(7), and see p 112 above). In addition, failure to comply with such an order without reasonable excuse renders a person liable on summary conviction to a fine.

To be discoverable, a document (or category of documents) must be:

(a) relevant;

(b) not excessive, and

(c) necessary for the fair disposal of the case (see CCR Ord 14, r 8.

These factors must be weighed against one another. Relevance in this context signifies that a document either helps the complainant's or respondent's case or hinders it, or would lead to a chain of enquiry having one of those two effects. Where the documents are relevant only to a subsidiary issue in the case, but discovery would require disclosure of a very large amount of documentation, discovery is unlikely to be ordered. It has been the practice of the tribunals to allow a broad application for discovery in discrimination cases due to the need for inferences to be drawn from peripheral evidence (*West Midlands Passenger Transport Executive* v *Singh* [1988] ICR 614). Discovery can only be ordered of existing documents. It cannot be used to require the creation of a document (e.g. by compiling statistics; *Carrington* v *Helix Lighting Ltd* [1990] ICR 125). However a party may require such information under the questionnaire procedure in discrimination cases or by use of the written questions procedure (see interrogatories at p 114 below).

Discovery may be resisted on the basis that a document is privileged, or is subject to public interest immunity. Legal professional privilege applies only to communications with and from professional legal advisers, not, for instance, a lay adviser including a professional consultant or trade union adviser who is not legally qualified (*New Victoria Hospital* v *Ryan* [1993] ICR 201). The ambit of public interest immunity is discussed in *R* v *Chief Constable of West Midlands, ex p Wiley* [1994] 3 WLR 433).

Confidentiality

The fact that a document is confidential does not render it immune from disclosure. Various methods are available to respect confidentiality, and documents may be altered (by agreement or with leave of the tribunal) so that identifying material can be removed if it is not also necessary to the case. Alternatively, the tribunal may inspect the documents and decide whether their relevance to the fair disposal of the case overcomes the need to respect confidentiality (*Science Research Council* v *Nassé; Leyland Cars Ltd* v *Vyas* [1979] ICR 921).

Medical records

Medical records may be required in order to establish whether or not an applicant is a disabled person or in relation to other issues. Obtaining medical records is discussed in more detail at p 27 above.

Witness orders

The tribunal has the power to make an order requiring any person within Great Britain to attend as a witness, and if the order so requires, to produce documents (r 4(2)). Most applications for a witness order are made because a witness is unwilling or unable to attend for work-related reasons, such as where an employer would not otherwise permit his attendance. For example, orders are always needed to secure the attendance of a police officer. It will often be counterproductive to use a witness order to require the attendance of a witness who is simply unwilling to give evidence for a party. An order can be obtained on the grounds that:

(a) the witness is believed to have relevant knowledge or information to give; and

(b) the party seeking his attendance believes he may not attend voluntarily.

The party who obtains the order must serve it. Before the hearing at which he is to attend to give evidence, the witness may apply to have the order set aside (r 7(5)(*b*)). Failure to comply with such a witness order without reasonable excuse renders that person liable on summary conviction to a fine.

Interrogatories

The tribunal has the power to require a party to furnish it with answers in writing to questions (r 4(3)). This power is separate to the questionnaire procedure considered at p 102 above. If a tribunal is asked to make such an order, it must first consider:

(a) whether the answer to that question may help to clarify any issue likely to arise for determination in the procedings; and

(b) whether it is likely to assist the progress of the proceedings for the answer to be available to the tribunal before the hearing.

The tribunal may specify a time within which the written answer is to be furnished. The tribunal copies the order and the written answers to all the parties. By r 4(4) the tribunal must take account of a written answer in the same way as it takes account of representations in writing presented by a party. Thus the tribunal considers the written answer as evidence and may consider it where a party does not attend a hearing. This power is also enforceable by a striking out order (r 4(7), and see p 112 above).

Orders made in the absence of a party

Where an order for particulars, discovery or inspection or interrogatories is made in the absence of a party (for example, by post) that party may, before the time for compliance specified in the order, make an application to the tribunal to vary or set aside the requirements of the order (r 4(5)). Notice of such an application will be given to each other party.

Expert medical evidence

In certain cases it may be necessary to obtain expert evidence to establish whether or not a person is or was a disabled person within the meaning of ss 1 and 2. Obtaining such evidence is discussed in detail at p 25 above.

The hearing

A hearing in an industrial tribunal will normally be before a panel of three persons, a legally qualified chairman and two industrial members selected from either side of industry for their experience in industrial relations. Proceedings before them are supposed to be informal (r 9(1)). In practice, the parties make submissions and give evidence sitting down, and the tribunal may be more inquisitorial than a criminal or civil court would be. Members of the tribunal should be addressed as 'Sir' or 'Madam' as appropriate. Advisers should note that the inquisitorial nature of the tribunals means that the tribunal may intervene with questions at any point. Representatives, and witnesses, should be made aware of this before the hearing.

Public or private hearings

Hearings are usually held in public. The tribunal may sit in private for reasons of national security (r 8(3)(a)) and may be ordered to do so by a Minister of the Crown (EP(C)A 1978, Sched 9, para 1(4A)). A private hearing may also be ordered where the evidence to be given would in the opinion of the tribunal be likely to consist of information which could not be disclosed without causing:
  (a) a breach of a statutory prohibition; or
  (b) breach of confidence; or
  (c) substantial damage to the witness's undertaking for commercial reasons (r 8(3)(b)).

Conduct of the hearing

The tribunal is free to regulate its own procedure within the framework of the Rules of Procedure (r 13(1)). Tribunals are enjoined by the rules to 'make such inquiries of persons appearing before it and witnesses as it considers appropriate' and to conduct the hearing in such manner as it considers most appropriate for the clarification of the issues before it and generally to the handling of the proceedings (r 9(1)). A party is entitled to give evidence, call witnesses, question witnesses and address the tribunal (r 9(2)).

Nonetheless, too much informality can be counter-productive and tribunals should normally adhere to the generally recognised rules of procedure (*Aberdeen Steak Houses Group plc* v *Ibrahim* [1988] ICR 550). The tribunal is bound by natural justice and should, for example, alert the parties before deciding a point which has not been raised or addressed by the parties (*Laurie* v *Holloway* [1994] ICR 32).

Normal procedure

Generally the party on whom the overall burden of proof lies will commence proceedings. In DDA cases, the complainant will usually start. An opening statement will often be advisable whilst claims under the DDA are novel or if the claim raises a complicated issue of law or fact. Once tribunals have become comfortable with DDA cases a formal opening statement may not be necessary and should be avoided in a simple case with little documentation. The opening statement should make clear what the issues are between the parties and how the party opening seeks to establish his case. The documents to which (most) reference will be made should be identified if the tribunal has not had the opportunity of familiarising itself with the papers. The opening statement should be kept as short as possible.

Evidence

The parties present their evidence in turn. Evidence is taken orally, although increasingly evidence in chief is given by witnesses reading out prepared witness statements (copies of which are supplied to the members of the tribunal and the other party) and are then cross examined on the contents of that statement and any other relevant matters. This will often save substantial time. In addition, written representations may be submitted if served on the tribunal and other parties not less than seven days before the hearing (r 8(5)).

Tribunals will have to adapt their procedures where the complainant's disability makes it impossible for him to attend the hearing physically, or where he requires a reader etc. This may be of particular significance in cases involving progressive illnesses. Arrangements may have to be made where there is a need to take the evidence of such a person away from the tribunal.

In the industrial tribunals the formal rules of evidence are relaxed. If a piece of evidence is not relevant it will not be admitted. Ideally evidence should be given from a first hand source because the tribunal can then determine its weight properly. Nonetheless, hearsay evidence including multiple hearsay, is generally admissible if relevant. Although the weight to be attached to such evidence is a matter for the tribunal, a failure to admit such evidence may amount to an error of law (*Coral Squash Clubs Ltd* v *Matthews* [1979] ICR 607).

Certificates

A certificate of registration issued to a disabled person on the register of disabled persons maintained under s 6 of the Disabled Persons (Employment) Act 1944 will be conclusive evidence of the matters certified (DDA 1995, Sched 1, para 7(3)). A document purporting to be a certificate of registration shall be taken to be a certificate validly issued unless the contrary is shown (Sched 1, para 7(4)).

A certificate signed by or on behalf of a Minister of the Crown certifies that:
(a) any arrangements or condition specified in the certificate were made, approved or imposed by a Minister of the Crown and were in operation at a time or throughout a time so specified; or
(b) that an act specified in the certificate was done for the purpose of safeguarding national security (para 4(1)) of Sched 3 and see p 87 above).

A document purporting to be a certificate must be received in evidence and, unless the contrary is proved, be deemed to be such a certificate (Sched 3, para 4(2)).

Restricted reporting orders

Rule 14(1A) of the rules (inserted by para 15 of the Industrial Tribunal (Constitution and Rules of Procedure) (Amendment) Regulations 1996 (SI No 1757) made under s 62 of the DDA, now replaced by s 12 of the Industrial Tribunals Act 1996 (ITA 1996)) allows a tribunal to make a restricted reporting order in relation to claims made under the DDA. Such an order can be made at any time before the promulgation of a decision in a case where 'evidence of a personal nature' is likely to be heard (r 14(1A)). ' "Evidence of a personal nature" means evidence of a medical, or other, intimate nature which might reasonably be assumed to be likely to cause significant embarrassment to the complainant if reported' (ITA 1996, s 12(7)). Where such a claim under the DDA is made in conjunction with any other claim or claims, the order will apply to all or part of the other claims if the tribunal so directs (r 14(1B)). The restricted reporting order prohibits the identification of the person specified in the order, or the publication of any identifying matter, in any written publication or broadcast programme in Great Britain prior to the promulgation of the tribunal's decision (ITA 1996, s 12(7)). It is a criminal offence to publish such matter in contravention of a restricted reporting order, punishable on summary conviction by up to a level 5 fine (ITA 1996, s 12(3)), although it is a defence for the alleged publisher that he was not aware, and neither suspected nor had reason to suspect that the publication was of restricted matter (ITA 1996, s 12(4)).

Similar provisions will be made in relation to proceedings before the EAT under s 32 of the ITA 1996.

Conciliation

Where a complaint has been presented to an industrial tribunal under s 8 a copy of it is sent to a conciliation officer. The conciliation officer shall try to promote a settlement of the complaint without its being determined by an industrial tribunal provided he is requested to do so by one of the parties or if he considers that he has a reasonable prospect of success (ITA 1996, s 18(2)). The Secretary to the tribunal will notify the parties of the availability of the Conciliation Officer's services (r 2(3)). Where someone is contemplating presenting a complaint, a conciliation officer may try to promote a settlement if asked to do so by a prospective complainant or respondent (ITA 1996, s 18(3)). Conciliation officers are members of the ACAS staff. They are impartial and independent. They promote settlements of employment disputes by means of informal discussions with the parties. Generally, they do not (or should not) give a view on the merits of either party's case or state how the dispute should be settled although they may provide other relevant information. In *Duport Furniture Products* v *Moore* [1982] IRLR 31 the House of Lords held that the statutory duty of a conciliation officer to 'endeavour to promote' settlement covers whatever action is thought applicable to the case. He is under no duty to ensure that a settlement is fair to both sides.

If the parties reach an agreement via the Conciliation Officer the agreement is recorded on a form known as a COT3 and will be binding upon the parties (see p 119 below). However, the ACAS officer must facilitate the agreement in some way. ACAS will not become involved in settlements if the conciliation officer is merely asked to rubber stamp an agreement already reached between the parties. The COT3 may be signed by any authorised representative (*Freeman* v *Sovereign Chicken Ltd* [1991] ICR 853). The agreement will be binding once the parties endorse the COT3 (*Duport Furniture Products Ltd* v *Moore* [1982] ICR 84) and is generally taken to be binding from the time oral agreement is reached via the ACAS officer (*Gilbert* v *Kembridge Fibres Ltd* [1984] IRLR 52). However, in *Slack* v *Greenham (Plant Hire) Ltd* [1983] IRLR 271 the EAT held that only if the Conciliation Officer acted in bad faith or adopted unfair methods could the agreement be set aside once he had taken action. In *Hennessy* v *Craigmyle & Co Ltd and ACAS* [1986] ICR 461 the Court of Appeal recognised that economic duress can in theory provide a basis for avoiding an agreement. However the party alleging it must have had no real alternative to signing the agreement. In *Trafford Carpets Ltd* v *Baker* EAT 206/90 the EAT held that it is no part of the statutory machinery for protecting conciliated settlements to lend validity to sham and misleading agreements, so that an agreement which was designed to mislead the Department for Education and Employment would not be binding. A COT3 agreement will be taken to include only matters within the presumed contemplation of the parties at the time of signature. Thus a claim under another Act may not be compromised even if the settlement uses the phrase 'all claims that the complainant may have against the respondent' (*Livingstone* v *Hepworth Refractories plc* [1992] ICR 287).

Anything communicated to a conciliation officer endeavouring to promote a settlement is not admissible in evidence in any proceedings before a tribunal without the consent of the person who communicated it to the officer (ITA 1996, s 18(6)). Documents that are not otherwise privileged in themselves do not become privileged simply because they are sent to the ACAS officer. (*M & W Grazebrook Ltd* v *Wallens* [1973] ICR 256).

Appeals

An appeal lies to the Employment Appeal Tribunal, but only on a question of law (ITA 1996, s 21)).

Validity of certain agreements

As a general rule, any term in a contract of employment or other agreement is void so far as it purports to exclude or limit the operation of any provision of Pt II of the DDA or prevent any person from presenting a complaint to an employment tribunal (s 9(1)(*b*),(*c*)). Subject to the following paragraph, this allows a party to pursue a claim under the DDA despite agreeing not to make or continue such a claim if already made (*Naqvi* v *Stephens Jewellers Ltd* [1978] ICR 631), even if there is a clear agreement to give up the right to claim disability discrimination in return for a sum of money (*Council of Engineering Institutions* v *Maddison* [1976] IRLR 389). This remains the case even if the sum of money specified under the agreement is offered and accepted.

However, such agreements are valid if either a conciliation officer has acted under para 1 of Sched 3 in relation to the matter (see p 118 above), or if the three conditions set out hereafter are satisfied. The first condition is that the complainant has received independent legal advice from a qualified lawyer as to the terms and effect of the proposed agreement (and in particular its effect on his ability to pursue his complaint before an industrial tribunal). Secondly, at the time the advice was given, the qualified lawyer must have been covered by a policy of insurance covering the risk of a claim by the complainant in respect of loss arising in consequence of the advice. Thirdly, the agreement must be made in writing, related to the particular complaint, identify the lawyer and state that the conditions were satisfied (s 9(3)).

In England and Wales a 'qualified lawyer' is either a barrister in private practice or employed to give legal advice, or a solicitor of the Supreme Court who holds a practising certificate. In Scotland, a 'qualified lawyer' is an advocate in private practice or employed to give legal advice or a solicitor who holds a practising certificate. To be 'independent', the lawyer advising the complainant must not be acting for the other party or for a person who is connected with that other party (s 9(4)). Two persons are connected if:

(a) one is a company of which the other (directly or indirectly) has control; or

(b) both are companies of which a third person (directly or indirectly) has control (s 9(5)).

Remedies

Under s 8(2) of the DDA 1995, where an industrial tribunal finds that a complaint presented to it is well-founded, it must take such of the following steps as it considers just and equitable:

(a) make a declaration as to the rights of the complainant and the respondent in relation to the matters to which the complaint relates;

(b) order the respondent to pay compensation to the complainant; or

(c) recommend that the respondent take, within a specified period, action appearing to the tribunal to be reasonable, in all the circumstances of the case, for the purpose of obviating or reducing the adverse effect on the complainant of any matter to which the complaint relates.

Declaration

A declaration is a statement that, and if necessary how, the respondent violated the complainant's rights.

Recommendations

The tribunal may make a recommendation that the respondent take action to remove or reduce the effect of discrimination on the applicant. This power will be particularly useful in relation to the duty to adjust, as a tribunal can recommend that a particular step be taken as a reasonable adjustment. If a recommendation is made, there should be a time limit within which the recommended action is to be taken (*Irvine* v *Prestcold Ltd* [1981] IRLR 281, CA). A recommendation can only be made in relation to the complainant. A tribunal cannot make a general recommendation that the respondent alter practices which do not affect the complainant (*Ministry of Defence* v *Jerimiah* [1978] IRLR 402, EAT). It seems that a tribunal should not make a recommendation that the complainant's pay should be increased as the remedy for future loss of wages is an award of compensation, and if the wages remain discriminatory beyond the period for which compensation was awarded, the complainant could make a further complaint to the tribunal (*Irvine v Prestcold Ltd* [1981] IRLR 281, CA, and in the EAT at [1980] IRLR 267). See p 124 for the consequences of an unjustified failure to comply with a recommendation.

Compensation

The amount of compensation is to be determined by applying the principles used to calculate damages in claims in tort or (in Scotland) in reparation for breach of statutory duty (s 8(3)). This will include a sum in respect of any loss of earnings or loss of an opportunity (such as an opportunity to obtain employment, promotion, a bonus or other benefit) in an attempt to place the complainant in the position he would have been in had he not been subject to unlawful discrimination. The award can include a sum for injury to feelings (s 8(4)). A general assessment on a commonsense basis is required. There is no upper limit on the sum that can be awarded.

Financial loss
This will include compensation for any actual or possible loss flowing directly from the unlawful discrimination. If someone was dismissed unlawfully, they will be entitled to their lost earnings. If someone was unlawfully denied an opportunity to obtain work or a promotion, they will be entitled to recompense for the loss of that opportunity. For example, if the tribunal decides they had a 50 per cent chance of being appointed in the absence of discrimination, they will be awarded 50 per cent of the sums they would have earned. If the tribunal concludes that someone who was unlawfully discriminated against would not have been appointed even in the absence of discrimination, the only award will be for injury to feelings. This may be the case where, for example, a person in a wheelchair is wrongly told that a job had been filled because the employer does not want any disabled employees, although that person would not have been appointed even had his application been considered because he lacked essential qualifications that did not relate to his disability.

In *Stone* v *Hills of London Ltd* EAT 12/83 the EAT, under Balcombe J, held that damages for someone refused employment on racial grounds should be assessed as in personal injury claims on the basis that the complainant would have continued working and should be compensated for lost wages. A tribunal would err in law if they acted on an assumption that the complainant would not have remained in employment when he had a good employment history and there was no reason to suppose he would have left in the short term. When assessing the applicant's loss of future earnings, a tribunal may have to consider hypothetical questions such as (in cases where the disabled person has needed time off) whether the applicant would have returned to work following a bout of sickness had he been allowed to do so, how long he would have remained in work, and whether or to what extent he would have achieved promotion.

The principle that damages should place the complainant in the position he would have been in but for the respondent's unlawful act applies to compensation for a breach of the duty to make reasonable adjustments. The tribunal must consider what the loss to the complainant is in such cases. The DDA contemplates that reasonable adjustment may consist of additional training. Should the complainant be provided with compensation to enable him to take the additional training, or merely for the effects of failing to have that training in terms of additional promotional opportunities? The principle that the employee should be placed so far as possible in the position he would have been but for the unlawful act requires no more than that the benefits of the training that would have accrued to him should be quantified. In some cases compensation may include an element representing the cost of training. For example, if the only benefit from training would have been to allow the complainant to obtain or keep a particular job, the only loss is the loss of wages and other benefits and there is no need for additional compensation in respect of the failure to provide training in itself. However, where the training would have provided the disabled person with transferable skills that could have been used elsewhere in the labour market, it may be argued that compensation should include a sum in respect of the failure to provide the training itself (see also p 53 above).

The DDA envisages damages being awarded where there is discrimination consisting of both less favourable treatment and a failure to adjust. The tribunal will have to consider what the effect of the adjustments would have been as well as considering the effects of the less favourable treatment, and award compensation based on the income the disabled person would have received had the adjustments been carried out. For an example (in the context of unfair dismissal) of a decision based on what would have happened had a person obtained a different job as a result of consultation in a redundancy situation, see *Red Bank Manufacturing Co Ltd* v *Meadows* [1992] IRLR 209. There the EAT held that in a redundancy situation which is unfair for lack of consultation, the tribunal is required to ask:

(1) if the proper procedure had been followed would it have resulted in an offer of employment? and

(2) if it would, what would the employment have been, and what wage would have been paid in respect of it?

Compensation is then awarded on the basis of the wage that would have been attracted by the new job. The process of awarding compensation on the basis of a job which would probably have been obtained had reasonable adjustments been carried out should take a similar form.

Injury to feelings
Compensation for injury to feelings may be awarded even if no other compensation is awarded (s 8(4)). Such a claim is fundamental to discrimination cases and will almost inevitably arise (*Murray* v *Powertech (Scotland) Ltd* [1992] IRLR 257). Although injury to feelings may be intangible, they are real and substantial elements and should be reflected as such in the assessment of damages (*Sharifi* v *Strathclyde Regional Council* [1992] IRLR 259). In *Alexander* v *Home Office* [1988] ICR 685, May LJ said, at 692:

> As with any other awards of damages, the objective of an award for unlawful racial discrimination is restitution. Where the discrimination has caused actual

pecuniary loss, such as the refusal of a job, then the damages referable to this can be readily calculated. For the injury to feelings, however, for the humiliation, for the insult, it is impossible to say what is restitution and the answer must depend on the experience and good sense of the judge and his assessors. Awards should not be minimal, because this would tend to trivialise or diminish respect for the public policy to which the Act gives effect. On the other hand, just because it is impossible to assess the monetary value of injured feelings, awards should be restrained. To award sums which are generally felt to be excessive does almost as much harm to the policy and the results which it seeks to achieve as do nominal awards. Further, injury to feelings, which is likely to be of a relatively short duration, is less serious than physical injury to the body or the mind which may persist for months, in many cases for life.

The factors to be considered in making an award under this head were discussed in *MOD* v *Cannock* [1994] ICR 918, *North West Thames Regional Health Authority* v *Noone* [1988] ICR 813, *Alexander* v *the Home Office* (above) and *Duffy* v *Eastern Health & Social Services Board* [1992] IRLR 251). They include the following:

(1) shock at the treatment, unlawful behaviour and frustration, anger and bitterness at having legitimate aspirations thwarted;

(2) loss of congenial employment or more senior position; and

(3) the degree to which the complainant has been held up to 'hatred, ridicule or contempt' by the discriminator.

The level of the award is to be determined by the subjective effect of the discrimination upon the complainant (see *Wileman* v *Minilec Engineering Ltd* [1988] ICR 318) and no award can be made if the complainant was not aware that the respondent's conduct was discriminatory (*Skyrail Oceanic Ltd* v *Coleman* [1981] ICR 864).

Aggravated damages
An award of aggravated damages may be made where the respondent has acted in a high-handed, malicious, insulting or oppressive manner (*Alexander* v *the Home Office* (above)).

Exemplary damages
An award of exemplary damages almost certainly cannot be made under the DDA. This is because disability discrimination was not unlawful when the House of Lords decided *Rookes* v *Barnard* [1964] AC 1129 (see *AB* v *South West Water Services Ltd* [1993] 1 All ER 609, followed in *Deane* v *Ealing London Borough Council* [1993] ICR 329 and *Ministry of Defence* v *Meredith* [1995] IRLR 539). Earlier suggestions in *City of Bradford Metropolitan Council* v *Arora* [1991] IRLR 164 and *Alexander* v *Home Office* (above) that such an award could be made are unlikely now to be followed.

Mitigation
The complainant is under a duty to mitigate his loss. The complainant must act as a reasonable person would act if he had no hope of seeking compensation from the respondent. He must take all reasonable measures to mitigate the loss

to him consequent upon the respondent's wrong. He cannot recover damages for any loss which he failed through unreasonable action or inaction. The duty is only to act reasonably, and the standard of reasonableness is not high in view of the fact that the respondent is a wrongdoer (*Banco de Portugal* v *Waterlow & Sons Ltd* [1932] AC 452). Where a complainant fails to take reasonable steps to find other work, the tribunal should decide when he would have found work had he taken reasonable steps and calculate loss to that date, rather than reducing the award by a percentage (*Peara* v *Enderlin Limited* [1979] ICR 804, and see also *Gardiner-Hill* v *Roland Berger Technics Limited* [1982] IRLR 498). Loss which is caused by the failure of the complainant to take a reasonable offer of employment from the respondent may be seen either as flowing from the complainant's own act, and not the act of discrimination, or from a failure to mitigate his loss (*Sweetlove* v *Redbridge & Waltham Forest Area Health Authority* [1979] IRLR 195). The complainant is under no duty to take the first job that comes along irrespective of pay and prospects (*A G Bracey* v *Iles* [1973] IRLR 210). Setting up in self-employment may be a reasonable act of mitigation in the circumstances of the given case (*Gardiner Hill* v *Roland Berger Technics* (above)). Questions of mitigation of loss are questions of fact to be decided by reference to what the complainant did or did not do following the unlawful act (*Ministry of Defence* v *Cannock* [1994] ICR 918). The complainant will not fail to mitigate loss by declining to follow internal appeals procedures before making a complaint to the Industrial Tribunal (*William Muir (Bond 9) Ltd* v *Lamb* [1985] IRLR 95 and *Seligman and Latz* v *McHugh* [1979] IRLR 130).

A difficult question will be whether a disabled person who does not continue to work as a result of his employer's refusal to make an adjustment has mitigated his loss or not. The question may arise where certain steps have been taken, but have (rightly) not been regarded as sufficient to comply with the s 6 duty by the disabled person. Should the disabled person have continued working at the substantial disadvantage if that was possible? It is unlikely that a tribunal would listen sympathetically to that argument as the employer would in essence be relying on his own wrong doing to argue that the disabled person has failed to mitigate his loss (see *Banco de Portugal* (above)).

Benefits

The Recoupment Regulations 1977 do not apply to compensation under the discrimination legislation. However, all benefits received during the material period should be taken into account in assessing the level of the complainant's loss so that the complainant is not put in a better position than he or she would have been in had he or she not been discriminated against.

Compensation for failure to carry out recommendations

If the respondent to a complaint fails, without reasonable justification, to comply with a recommendation made by an Industrial Tribunal the tribunal may, if it thinks it just and equitable to do so:

(a) increase the amount of compensation required to be paid to the complainant; or

(b) make an order for compensation if it had not already done so (s 8(5)).

Where the tribunal recommended, for example, that particular adjustments be made to working practices but the employer fails to make those adjustments, it would normally be just and equitable to make an order for, or increase, compensation payable to the complainant to take account of any continuing loss or disadvantage of the complainant. In an appropriate case that compensation could reflect the cost of the employee having to take steps to overcome any disadvantage himself. For example, if the recommendation was that the employer provide training which is only available from a source outside the employing organisation, the tribunal could award such compensation as would give the employee the money to attend the course.

In *Nelson* v *Tyne & Wear Passenger Transport Executive* [1978] ICR 1183 the EAT held that the tribunal may take account of practical, industrial realities when considering whether there was a 'reasonable justification' for not implementing a recommendation.

> Tribunals ought to be careful, having found discrimination established, not, by too mild orders, to allow it to continue unchecked for too long in the future. On the other hand it would be most unreasonable not to take into account practical realities and not to allow a period of time to sort out the difficulties consequent upon the finding, and would not be in the interests of the cause of eliminating . . . discrimination.

Interest

Interest on sums may form part of the award of compensation itself. Interest will also be payable on tribunal awards. Both of these powers are subject to regulations being made. Section 8(6) provides for regulations to be made to make provision:

(a) for enabling a tribunal, where compensation is awarded, to include in the award interest on that amount; and

(b) specifying, for cases where a tribunal decides that an award is to include an amount in respect of interest, the manner in which and the periods and rate by reference to which the interest is to be determined:

Section 8(7) provides for regulations to be made to modify the operation of Orders made under para 6A of Sched 9 to the Employment Protection (Consolidation) Act 1978, giving the Secretary of State power to make provision as to interest on sums payable in pursuance of Industrial Tribunal decisions.

Costs

Cost are not usually awarded in proceedings before a tribunal. They can only be awarded against a party if that party has acted frivolously, vexatiously, abusively, disruptively or otherwise unreasonably in bringing or conducting proceedings (r 12(1)), or if the tribunal has postponed or adjourned a hearing at the application of that party (r 12(4)). In addition, a tribunal must consider making a costs order where it finds against a party in relation to a matter (which may not be the entire claim or defence) and that party had been ordered to pay a deposit at a PHR in relation to that matter (r 12(7)). Such an order will only be made where the tribunal considers that the party acted unreasonably in persisting with that matter after the PHR and is of the opinion that the reasons which caused it to find against the party were substantially the same as those recorded in the document recording the order for a deposit at the PHR (r 12(7), and see p 110 above). Finally costs may be awarded where the IT3 was returned late (see above).

Remedies and premises occupied under a lease

In a case where a lessor has been joined as a respondent, and the tribunal decides that the lessor had unreasonably failed to give consent to an alteration required under the duty to adjust or imposed unreasonable conditions (Sched 4, para 2(6), and see pp 243) the tribunal may:

(1) make such declaration as it considers appropriate (para 2(6)(*a*); and/ or
(2) make an order authorising the occupier to make the alteration specified in the order (para 2(6)(*b*); and/or
(3) order the lessor to pay compensation to the complainant (para 2(6)(*c*)).

An order authorising an alteration under para 2(6)(*b*) may require the occupier to comply with conditions specified in the order (para 2(7)). This appears to refer to conditions to be complied with if the occupier chooses to make the authorised alteration rather than requiring the occupier to make such an alteration. However, the tribunal could still recommend that such an alteration was made (see p 120 above). Any such orders may be made in substitution for or in addition to an order under s 8(2), save that if the lessor is ordered to pay compensation the tribunal cannot also order the occupier to pay compensation to the complainant (para 2(8)(9) of Sched 4).

Part 3

Goods, Services and Premises

Chapter 9

Overview

Introduction

Part III of the DDA 1995 deals with discrimination in the provisions of goods and services and in relation to premises. Similar provisions exist in the Sex Discrimination Act 1975 (ss 29–36) and the Race Relations Act 1976 (ss 20–27). Goods and services are dealt with in ss 19 to 21. Section 19 makes specified discriminatory acts by service providers unlawful. Discrimination is defined in s 20. The definitions of discrimination are modelled on those used in the employment provisions, except that the concept of justification is very different, and depends upon the service provider (or owner or manager of premises) reasonably holding a particular opinion. Section 21 provides for service providers to make reasonable adjustments to prevent disadvantage to people with disabilities. Sections 22 to 24 concern discrimination against disabled persons in connection with the disposal and management of premises. Section 22 makes unlawful specified acts of discrimination by those who have the power to dispose of premises, those who manage premises and those whose licence or consent is required for the assignment of premises held under a lease. Discrimination is defined in s 24. Small premises are defined and exempted from these provisions by s 23. Section 26 provides that agreements are made void in so far as they purport to require a person to contravene the DDA or limit or exclude its application or the right of any person to make a claim under the DDA. The enforcement provisions relating to goods, services and premises are found in ss 25 to 28.

Further provisions are found in the Disability Discrimination (Services & Premises) Regulations 1996 (SI No 1836) (DD(SP) Regs 1996). In addition, practical assistance is found in the *Code of Practice on Rights of Access: Goods, Facilities, Services and Premises* ('the Services and Premises Code') (July 1996, London, HMSO) prepared by the NCS and issued by the Secretary of State for Social Security pursuant to s 51(2) of the DDA. It is similar in status and effect to the Codes issued by the Equal Opportunities Commission and Commission for Racial Equality under the sex and race discrimination legislation. It gives practical guidance to service providers and those concerned with the disposal and management of premises in eliminating discrimination. The Services and Premises Code is admissible in evidence in any proceedings under the Act before a county court or sheriff court (s 51(4)), who must take into account such parts of the Code as they consider relevant to any question arising in proceedings under the DDA (s 51(5)). Although a failure to observe the provisions of the Code is not automatically unlawful (s 51(3)), such a failure may assist a court to conclude that there has been a breach of the DDA, particularly where liability depends upon determining what is reasonable, practicable or justified. The Code is set out in full in Appendix 3, at p 315.

Commencement

These provisions came into force on 2 December 1996 (DDA(C No 3) Order 1996), with the exception of the duty upon service providers to adjust which is not in force. The duty to adjust will be brought in in stages. In the timetable proposals issued by the NDC (contained in the Consultation Pack DL140 (HMSO)), it was suggested that the duty to adjust practices, policies and procedures may be brought into force in 1998, the provision of auxiliary aids and services would be required from 2000, and the removal of physical barriers would be required from 2005.

Chapter 10

Unlawful Acts Relating to Goods and Services

Section 19 provides that it is unlawful for a provider of services to discriminate against a disabled person in a number of specified ways. It also renders it unlawful for a provider of services to discriminate against a person, whether disabled or not, by victimising him (s 19(4) and see p 25). It provides a definition (s 19(2)(*a*)) and a non-exhaustive list of the services which are encompassed by provisions (s 19(3)). Certain services are excluded from these provisions of ss 19–22 (s 19(5)).

Goods, Facilities and Services

For the purposes of ss 19–22, the provision of services includes the provision of any goods or facilities (s 19(2)(*a*)). It is irrelevant whether a service is provided on payment or without payment (s 19(2)(*c*)). It expressly encompasses services provided by public authorities (s 19(3)(*h*)). This is a very broad provision. It was intended to provide 'a universal, all-embracing right of non-discrimination against disabled people ... applicable to all providers of goods, facilities and services to the general public, with the specific exclusions of transport and education' (*Hansard*, Report SC E, 16 February 1995, col 290, Hague). The provisions only apply to services provided to the public or a part of the public within the UK (see p 135 below).

Goods

There is no definition of goods in the DDA, but the term is intended to be used widely. The OED defines 'goods' as 'saleable commodities, merchandise, wares (now chiefly applied to manufactured articles)'. Note that it is the provision of goods that is subject to the DDA and not the design of the goods involved. 'It is one thing to give an individual a legal right of access to goods and services as the [Act] does; but it is quite another to give him a right to products of a certain type or design' (*Hansard*, HL, 18 July 1995, Vol 566 col 241, Mackay). For example, it would be unlawful to refuse to deliver a newspaper to a disabled person. However, there is no requirement to produce the newspaper in a form that is accessible to the disabled person, for example on tape or in large print (see *Hansard*, HL, 18 July 1995, Vol 566, col 251, Mackay).

Services and facilities

Numerous examples of services covered by the provisions were given during passage of the Bill through Parliament. They included all medical and health care service (*Hansard*, HL, 15 June 1995, Vol 564, col 1952, Mackay). Also included were the services provided to the public by courts, tribunals, the Legal Aid Board and the agencies of the criminal justice system (*Hansard*, HL, 18 July 1995, Vol 566, col 260, Mackay). However, jurors, and probably witnesses, would not be covered as they are performing a duty rather than receiving a service within the meaning of the DDA (*Hansard*, HL, 18 July 1995, Vol 566, col 261–2, Mackay).

' "Facility" is a slippery word' (*R* v *DSS, ex p Overdrive Credit Card Ltd* [1991] 1 WLR 635). The OED defines facilities as 'opportunities, favourable conditions for the easier performance of any action *spec* (Orig U.S.) the physical means for doing something; *freq* with qualifying word: eg educational, postal, retail facilities. *Also in sing* of a specified amenity service etc'. This definition was relied upon in *Ex p Overdrive Credit Card Ltd* and in *Midland Greyhound Racing Co Ltd* v *Foley* [1973] 1 WLR 324. The provision of physical aids and services comes within the ordinary meaning of the word 'facilities' (*Midland Greyhound Racing Co Ltd* v *Foley*). A charge card is something which renders easier the performance of an obligation to pay for items, and therefore falls within the OED definition of 'facility' (*Ex p Overdrive Credit Card Ltd*). A club does not provide facilities to become a member when it permits members of the public to apply for membership (*Race Relations Board* v *Charter* [1972] 2 WLR 190). The distinction between facilities and services was considered, albeit in a different context, in *Westminster City Council* v *Ray Alan Ltd* [1982] 1 WLR 383:

> Perhaps one can illustrate the difference in this way. Hotels or businesses of all kinds provide services, meaning that they do something for the customer. Others provide facilities in the sense that various things are made available to customers to use if they are so minded in a more passive sense than the activities implied in the word 'services'.

However, as both facilities and services are covered by the DDA, the dividing line is not of practical importance.

The statutory examples

Section 19(3) provides a non-exhaustive list of facilities or services to which the section applies. Many of the examples are identical to those provided in the equivalent provisions of the SDA 1975 (s 29(2)) and RRA 1976 (s 20(2)) and authorities under those statutes are of assistance here. The only differences between the DDA and the provisions of the SDA and RRA are that the DDA includes means of communication (s 19(3)(*b*), and information services (s 19(3)(*c*)), and excludes education and transport (s 19(5) and see p 134 below). The statutory examples given in the DDA are set out below. Some further examples are set out in the Services and Premises Code at para 2.4.

(a) *access to and use of any place which members of the public are permitted to enter*

This would include access to a public park, church, theatre or cinema.

(b) *access to and use of means of communication*

This would include access to telephone, postal and similar services.

(c) *access to and use of information services*

This would include formal advice agencies and information services such as advice lines.

(d) *acommodation in a hotel, boarding house or other similar establishment*

This is self explanatory. There may be some overlap with the provisions relating to premises (see p 161 below), for example in relation to long stay 'residential' hotels.

(e) *facilities by way of banking or insurance or for grants, loans, credit or finance.*

This would encompass a wide range of financial services, including hire purchase facilities offered by retailers (*Quinn* v *Williams Furniture Ltd* [1981] ICR 328, CA). Where the right to participate in the government of a friendly society providing mutual insurance comprises an integral part of what is offered to the public, the opportunity to participate in meetings is part of the 'facilities' provided (*Jones* v *Royal Liver Friendly Society* (1982) *The Times*, 2 December, CA).

(f) *facilities for entertainment, recreation, or refreshment*

This would include things like theatres, cinemas, football stadia, swimming pools and sports facilities, restaurants and pubs.

(g) *facilities provided by employment agencies, or under section 2 of the Employment and Training Act 1973*

This would apply to both public funded employment agencies, such as Job Centres and to private recruitment agencies. Employment agency is not defined under the DDA. It was defined in both the SDA (s 82(1)) and RRA (s 78(1)) as meaning 'a person who, for profit or not, provides services for the purposes of finding employment for workers or supplying employers with workers'.

(h) *the services of any profession or trade, or any local or other public authority*

This would include the services offered by members of the medical, legal and other professions. It would include the services of any trade, such as plumbers, electricians, caterers, hairdressers and the like. This includes services provided by local and other public authorities such as the provision of foster care to children (*Applin* v *Race Relations Board* [1974] 2 WLR 541, HL); the providing of advice about and granting of tax relief by the Inland Revenue (*Savjani* v *Inland Revenue Commissioners* [1981] 2 WLR 636, CA); the functions performed for members of the public by the registrar of births, deaths and marriages (*Tejani* v *Superintendent Registrar for the District of Peterborough* [1986] IRLR 502, CA); and access to a public swimming pool (*James* v *Eastleigh Borough Council* [1990] ICR 554). Work provided to prisoners was conceded to fall within the equivalent provisions of the RRA in *Alexander* v *Home Office* [1988] All ER 118. Those parts of a police officer's duties involving assistance to or protection from members of the public will be covered (*Farah* v *Commissioner of Police of the Metropolis* (1996) *The Times*, 10 October. However, activities carried out by public bodies that are not akin to the provision of goods or services will not be covered (*R* v *Immigration Appeal Tribunal, ex p Kassam* [1980] 1 WLR 1037, CA and *Amin* v *Entry Clearance Officer, Bombay* [1983] 2 All ER 864, HL). Therefore, the grant of leave to enter or remain in the UK under the Immigration Act 1971 or Immigration Rules is not a service for these purposes (*ex p Kassam*) and nor is the grant of a work permit (*R* v *Immigration Appeal Tribunal and Department of Employment, ex p Bernstein* [1987] Imm AR 182). Similarly, other acts of a governmental nature, such as making regulations, fall outside of the DDA (see *R* v *Secretary of State for Social Security, ex p Nessa* (1994) *The Times*, 15 November).

Exclusions

The provisions of Pt III do not apply to most forms of education or to such other services as may be prescribed (s 19(5)). The only matters to have been prescribed under s 19(5)(*c*) at the date of writing are certain services ancillary to education. In addition, acts done pursuant to statutory authority or for the purposes of national security are excluded from the DDA.

Education
Most educational and ancillary services are excluded from Pt III by s 19(5)(*a*). In addition, some express provision is made in relation to education in Pt VI of the DDA. These matters are considered in detail in Chap 14 below.

Transport
Section 19(5)(*b*) excludes 'any service so far as it consists of the use of any means of transport' from Pt III of the DDA. This will include, for example, the use of trains, buses, taxis, private hire vehicles, aircraft, ships and hovercraft. However, the exclusion relates only to the means of transport, ie the vehicle itself. The provisions of ss 19 to 22 do apply to the infrastructure of the transport system, such as stations and ticket offices. In Parliament, William Hague said

> The new right of access will apply to stations. The duties in [s 21] must be complied with and policies that make it impossible or unreasonably difficult for disabled people to use stations must be changed' (*Hansard*, Report SC E, 21 February 1995, col 337, Hague).

Part V of the DDA allows regulations to be made affecting certain forms of public transport, namely public service vehicles (buses and coaches), taxis, some private hire vehicles, trains and trams. These provisions are dealt with in Chap 15 below.

Statutory Authority and national security.
See p 250 below.

Service Providers

'A person is "a provider of services" if he is concerned with the provision, in the United Kingdom, of services to the public or to a section of the public' (s 19(2)(*b*)). The United Kindom means England, Wales, Scotland, and Northern Ireland.

'Concerned with the provision'

Section 19(2) is intended to deal with a person who holds him or herself out as engaged regularly, or at least recurrently, in the activity of providing a particular service (*Hector* v *Smethwick Labour Club and Institute* (1988) unreported, Court of Appeal Civil Division, Association Transcript, 28 November 1988 and Lexis). It is not intended to cover a person who provides, or is minded to provide, a particular service upon one isolated occasion. A person is 'concerned with the provision' of services only if he or she is already providing those services at the time of the incident complained of or is holding him or herself out as willing to provide such services (see *Hector* v *Smethwick*). A person is not concerned with the provision of particular services if he or she is neither providing those services to others nor holding him or herself out as willing to provide those services to others at the material time.

For example, a restaurant may run a party catering service. If it is already providing that service to the public, it is concerned with the provision of party catering for the purposes of s 19(2)(*b*). If the service is a new venture and has not yet had any bookings, the restaurant is still concerned with the provision of party catering if it is holding itself out as providing that service, for example by advertising the service. In either case, discrimination provisions will apply to the party catering service offered by the restaurant. However, if the restaurant does not provide or hold itself out as providing a party catering service, it is not concerned with the provision of such a service for the purposes of s 19(2)(*b*). This will be so even if it had provided such a service on isolated previous occasions. In these circumstances, a restaurant will not act unlawfully in refusing to provide such a service to a disabled person.

To the public or to a section of the public

The provisions of Pt III only apply where the goods and services concerned are provided to the public or a section of the public. Similar restrictions apply to s 29 of the SDA and s 20 of the RRA. Foster children were found to be sections of the public for the purposes of the RRA in *Applin* v *RRB* [1975] AC 259. It was conceded that prisoners were a section of the public in *Alexander* v *Home Office* [1988] All ER 118, another case under the RRA. The provisions do not apply to relationships of a purely private character (see *Dockers' Labour Club and Institute Ltd* v *RRB* [1976] AC 285, HL, *per* Lord Diplock at 297E). The limitation will affect the application of the DDA to clubs and manufacturers.

Clubs

Much of the caselaw under the SDA 1975 and RRA 1976 concerned whether and when members of a club constituted a section of the public. In summary, if entry into the club is a mere formality, the members of the club are a section of the public. If the rules provide for a true selection of the members and they are not in practice disregarded, the members are not a section of the public (*Charter* v *RRB* [1973] AC 868). Associate members of a club belonging to a union of working men's clubs, whose associate membership of one gave access to all, were held not to be a section of the public (*Dockers' Labour Club and Institute Ltd* v *RRB*). However, the provisions will apply if a private club also provides services to the public, for example a private golf club hiring out its facilities for a wedding reception (Services and Premises Code, para 2.6) or allows non-members to use its course on payment of a fee (see Lord Reid in *Dockers' Labour Club and Institute Ltd* v *RRB* at p 292).

Manufacturers

The provisions will not apply to manufacturers who provide goods to retailers or other intermediaries and not direct to the public. However, they will apply to a mail order service provided by a manufacturer directly to the public (Services and Premises Code, para 2.6) or a factory shop that is open to the public.

Small businesses

Small businesses are not excluded from ss 19 to 21 of the DDA. Even if a service provider is exempt from the employment provisions on the grounds that it has fewer than 20 employees (see s 7 and p 69 above), it will still be covered by the goods and services provisions.

The Prohibited Acts

Section 19 of the DDA provides that it is unlawful for a provider of services to discriminate against a disabled person in a number of specified ways.

Discrimination in relation to goods, facilities and services

> 19(1) It is unlawful for a provider of services to discriminate against a disabled person—

(a) in refusing to provide, or deliberately not providing, to the disabled person any service which he provides, or is prepared to provide to members of the public;

(b) in failing to comply with any duty imposed on him by section 21 in circumstances in which the effect of that failure is to make it impossible or unreasonably difficult for the disabled person to make use of any such service;

(c) in the standard of service which he provides to the disabled person or the manner in which he provides it to him;

(d) in the terms on which he provides a service to the disabled person.

Provider of services

See p 135 above.

Disabled person
See Chap 1 above.

In refusing to provide, or deliberately not providing a service to the disabled person (s 19(1)(*a*))

This will cover express refusals, such as refusing a person access to a cinema or restaurant. It will also apply where there has been a deliberate failure to provide a service without an express refusal. For example, it would make it unlawful for a publican to discriminate against a disabled person by refusing to serve him at the bar, even if the person was not refused entry or asked to leave. See *Gill* v *El Vino Co* [1983] QB 425. This provision only applies if the service provider already provides, or is prepared to provide, the relevant service to others (see p 135 above).

In failing to comply with any duty imposed on him by section 21 in circumstances in which the effect of that failure is to make it impossible or unreasonably difficult for the disabled person to make use of any such service (s 19(1)(*b*))

A failure to comply with a s 21 duty to adjust only renders a service provider liable to proceedings if, as a consequence of that failure, it is impossible or unreasonably difficult for a particular disabled person to make use of the relevant service. There is some overlap with s 19(1)(*c*) and (*d*), in that the test is whether it is impossible or unreasonably difficult for the disabled person to make use of a comparable service. Therefore, it will be necessary to consider the standard, manner and terms of a service made available to a person in considering whether there has been a breach of the duty to adjust actionable under this provision. Lord Mackay said, on behalf of the government,

> Service providers will not be able to get away with treating disabled people without the same dignity and respect as any other customer ... in this context, the term 'service' includes the concept of service as far as possible to the same standard as that received by other people. There is no question of service providers

being able to get away with providing access to a lower standard than normal unless there are inescapable reasons (*Hansard*, HL, 18 July 1995, Vol 566, col 266).

Discrimination by a failure to make adjustments is considered in Chap 11 below. This provision is not in force at the time of writing (see p 130 above).

In the standard of service which he provides to the disabled person or the manner in which he provides it to him (19(1)(*c*))

This makes it unlawful to discriminate against a disabled person by offering that person only a lower or less favourable standard of service. In addition, offering only a higher, and more costly, standard of service could be unlawful, in that it denies a disabled person the option of taking advantage of the cheaper standard of service. The manner of service could include such things as allowing a person with a severe disfigurement into a restaurant to eat the same meal as others and at the same price, but requiring him to sit in a remote seat or separate room away from most other customers. In addition, it would render unlawful the adoption of a deliberate policy of discouraging disabled customers by surly, slow or poor quality service.

In the terms on which he provides a service to the disabled person (19(1)(*d*))

This makes it unlawful to discriminate against a disabled person by providing the service only on less favourable or more onerous terms, such as requiring a disabled person to pay a higher price, provide a larger deposit or enter into a longer or more expensive maintenance contract in relation to hired goods.

Discriminatory terms and agreements

Any term in an agreement is void in so far as it purports to:
  (a) require a person to do anything which would contravene any of the provisions of Pt III;
  (b) exclude or limit the operation of Pt III; or
  (c) prevent any person from making a claim under Pt III (s 26(1)).
For example, a term in an agreement between a theatre and a ticket agency prohibiting the ticket agency from selling any tickets to people with learning difficulties is void and of no effect. Similarly, a provision in a hire agreement under which a hirer purported to agree to waive any rights under the DDA would be void. A county court may make such order as it thinks just for modifying an agreement which contains such a term upon the application of any person interested in the agreement (s 26(3)). Such a modification may involve striking out a discriminatory term or modifying the term so as to prevent it from having a discriminatory effect (see p 197 below).

Checklist of unlawful acts relating to goods, facilities and services

—Does the claim involve the provision of goods, facilities or services consisting of:
- access to and use of any place which members of the public are permitted to enter?
- access to and use of means of communication?
- access to and use of information services?
- accommodation in a hotel, boarding house or other similar establishment?
- facilities by way of banking or insurance or for grants, loans, credit or finance?
- facilities for entertainment, recreation or refreshment?
- facilities provided by employment agencies, or under s 2 of the Employment and Training Act 1973?
- the services of any profession or trade, or any local or other public authority?
- any other form of goods, facilities or services, and if so what?

—Are the services excluded from Pt III of the DDA because they involve:
- educational or ancillary services?
- the use of any means of transport?
- Statutory Authority and national security?

—Is the service provider concerned with the provision of those services to the public or to a section of the public?

—Does the service provider provide (or is it prepared to provide) those services to the public or to a section of the public?

The prohibited acts

—Does the discrimination involve:
- refusing to provide or deliberately not providing any service to the disabled person or persons victimised?
- failing to comply with any duty to adjust imposed by s 21 in circumstances in which the effect of that failure is to make it impossible or unreasonably difficult for the disabled person to make use of any such service?
- the standard or manner of service provided to the person or persons victimised?
- the terms on which he provides a service to the disabled person or persons victimised?

See the checklist at the end of Chap 11 to establish if there has been discrimination.

Chapter 11

The Meaning of Discrimination in Relation to Goods and Services

As with the employment provisions, there are three forms of discrimination under the goods and services provisions of Pt III. Firstly, discrimination may be by way of unjustified less favourable treatment for a reason relating to the disabled person's disability (s 20(1)). Secondly, once the relevant provisions are brought into force, a provider of services will also discriminate against a disabled person if he or she fails to comply with the duty to adjust and the failure was not justified (s 20(2)). Thirdly, it is unlawful for a provider of services to discriminate against any person (whether disabled or not) by victimising him (s 19(4) and s 55; see p 251 below). The provisions regarding vicarious liability and the liability of those (such as agents) who aid unlawful acts are dealt with from p 248.

Discrimination by less favourable treatment

Discrimination by unjustified less favourable treatment is defined by s 20(1). The same approach is to be taken in establishing if there is less favourable treatment for a reason which relates to the disabled person's disability as is taken in employment cases under s 5(1) (see p 36 above). However, the approach to be taken in deciding if the service provider was justified in treating the disabled person less favourably is markedly different to that set out by s 5(3).

Meaning of 'discrimination'

20(1) A provider of services discriminates against a disabled person if—
  (a) for a reason which relates to the disabled person's disability, he treats him less favourably than he treats or would treat others to whom that reason does not or would not apply; and
  (b) he cannot show that the treatment in question is justified.

A provider of services

See p 135 above.

Against a disabled person

These provisions make it unlawful to discriminate against a person who has a disability as defined in s 1 (see Chap 1, p 3 above) or someone who had a disability (s 2 and p 22). The provisions also render it unlawful to discriminate against any person by way of victimisation whether that person is disabled or not (s 19(4) and s 55; see p 251 below). As with the other provisions of the DDA, they do not prevent discrimination against organisations seeking, for example, to obtain finance to be used for the benefit of people with disabilities (see p 23 above).

Less favourable treatment for a reason which relates to the disabled person's disability

This is identical to the equivalent provision in s 5(1)(a) and 24(1)(a) (see p 36 above and p 162 below). It will include less favourable treatment based on the fact of someone's disability, such as refusing to serve someone with a learning difficulty in a pub. It will also apply where the reason relates to the disability. For example, it would be unlawful to refuse to allow a group of deaf people into a nightclub because the doorman thinks sign language might be seen as threatening (Services and Premises Code, para 3.3) even if other deaf people who lip read are allowed in. Similarly, it would be unlawful to refuse to allow a blind person with a guide dog into a restaurant even though a blind person who used a white stick would be allowed in.

He cannot show that the treatment in question is justified

As with the provisions relating to employment and premises, less favourable treatment for a reason relating to the disabled person's disability does not amount to discrimination if the service provider can prove that it was justified. The burden of proving that the treatment was justified is upon the service provider. Treatment is only justified if:
  (1) in the opinion of the service provider, one of the conditions specified in s 20(4) is satisfied *and* it is reasonable in all of the circumstances of the case for him to hold that opinion (s 20(3)); or
  (2) if the case falls within circumstances prescribed by regulations (see p 148 below).
The conditions set out in s 20(4) concern:
  (a) health and safety;
  (b) capacity to contract or consent;
  (c) treatment necessary in order for the provider to be able to provide the service to members of the public;
  (d) treatment necessary in order for the provider to be able to provide the service to the disabled person concerned or to other members of the public; and
  (e) the greater cost of providing the service to the disabled person.

They are set out in full below. Similar provisions are found in relation to premises in s 24(2) and (3) (see p 163 below). Less favourable treatment can only be justified if the service provider reasonably holds the opinion that one of those conditions is satisfied or the treatment is deemed to be justified. Less favourable treatment cannot be justified on the grounds that anyone who behaved in a like manner would be treated in the same way. For example, a restaurant that refused to serve a person who has difficulty eating because of a disability could not justify that behaviour on the grounds that it would have refused to serve anyone who was eating messily (Services and Premises Code, para 2.15). It is not possible to justify discrimination in the provision of goods and services by reference to the service provider's good intentions (Services and Premises Code, para 3.4). Thus, it is not permissible for a shop owner to refuse to serve a deaf customer because another nearby shop owner can use British Sign Language and is therefore better able to serve the customer.

In the opinion of the service provider

The provision is in the present tense and refers to matters as at the time of the less favourable treatment. For this reason, the opinion must be held at the time of that treatment. Matters which did not affect the defendant's mind at that time will not justify that treatment. Nonetheless, in such a case damages may be reduced or limited to those for injury to feelings on the grounds that no other loss flowed from the treatment. For example, a bank may refuse to lend money to a person with learning difficulties because of simple prejudice, without considering the person's capacity to contract. On the analysis above, the less favourable treatment would not be justified even if the person did not have capacity to enter into an enforceable agreement. However, although discrimination will be proven, it can be argued that the only loss that flowed from the refusal was injury to feelings as the loan could lawfully have been refused had the bank considered the matter properly (see also p 163 below).

Reasonable for him to hold that opinion

The opinion must be reasonably held. Of course, more than one opinion may be reasonable and an opinion may be reasonably held even if it is incorrect. It may be that a genuinely held opinion will be reasonably held unless no reasonable person would have held that belief (see, for example, *Associated Provincial Picture Houses Ltd* v *Wednesbury Corporation* [1948] 1 KB 223 and *British Leyland (UK)* v *Swift* [1981] IRLR 91). In addition, the opinion should not be based on general assumptions and prejudice, although it may be argued in appropriate circumstances that it was reasonable for a particular person to hold a generally held assumption, even if it is incorrect. It may be that an opinion is not reasonably held if it is formed and acted upon hastily without making reasonable inquiries (see *W Weddell & Co Ltd* v *Tepper* [1980] ICR 286 at 297). The Services and Premises Code gives the following example in relation to the health and safety condition (see the paragraph below). 'Although there are adequate means of escape, a cinema manager turns away a wheelchair user because he assumes, *without checking*, that she could be in danger in the event of a fire. This is against the law' (Services and Premises Code, para 5.6, emphasis added). The nature of the inquiries, if any, required for an opinion to be reasonable will depend upon all of the circumstances. Furthermore, even though an erroneous opinion was reasonable at the time it was formed, it will not continue to be reasonably held if maintained after evidence is presented which makes it unsustainable. In those circumstances, the service provider will not be able to justify any less favourable treatment after it became unreasonable to hold the relevant opinion. Regulations may prescribe circumstances in which it is or is not reasonable for a person to hold such an opinion (s 20(6)) although no such regulations have been made to date. A similar provision appears in relation to premises (s 24(3)(*a*).

The conditions

The conditions (or relevant opinions) specified in s 20(4) are as follows:

That the treatment is necessary in order not to endanger the health or safety of any person (s 20(4)(a))
This condition applies to any act of discrimination made unlawful under s 19, including a failure to comply with the duty to adjust. 'Any person' expressly includes the disabled person concerned (s 20(3)(*a*)). The Services and Premises Code gives the example of a driving instructor refusing to give lessons to a person with such severely impaired eyesight that he fails the eyesight test even with glasses (para 5.5). As the opinion must be reasonably held, spurious reasons will not provide a defence (see para 5.6 of the Services and Premises Code). A service provider who acts upon assumptions and stereotypes is unlikely to prove that less favourable treatment was justified. Thus, simply assuming that a wheelchair user would be a 'fire risk' will not justify less favourable treatment (Services and Premises Code, para 5.6). The Services and Premises Code states that every opportunity should be taken as far as practicable, to enable disabled people to use cinemas, theatres, leisure centres and other entertainment venues (para 5.7). The less favourable treatment need not be 'necessary' provided it was reasonable to believe it to have been so. Nonetheless, the inclusion of the word 'necessary' was intended to establish a relatively onerous test for justification to be made out (see p 146 below). Arguably, the subsection would not be satisfied unless the service provider reasonably believed that no other less discriminatory treatment would avoid the danger to health or safety. On this basis, if a reasonable adjustment or other modification could have been made to avoid the health and safety risk, the less favourable treatment in question would not be necessary (see below). However, the nature and extent of possible alternatives will depend upon the particular circumstances. Where the less favourable treatment is a continuing act (see p 104 above), it will presumably cease to

be justified and become unlawful once it ceases to be reasonable to believe that the treatment is necessary, either because of a change in circumstances or because further information has been obtained by the person holding the belief. It is to be hoped that an irrational (although common) fear about the risk of violence from people with mental health problems or infection by people with communicable illnesses would be found not to be reasonably held.

That the disabled person concerned is incapable of entering into an enforceable agreement, or of giving an informed consent, and for that reason the treatment is reasonable in that case (s 20(4)(b))
This condition can apply to any act of discrimination made unlawful under s 19, including a failure to comply with the duty to adjust. It can arise in two ways; firstly, where the service provider reasonably believes that the person is incapable of entering an enforceable contract, and secondly, where the service provider reasonably believes that the person is incapable of giving an informed consent.

Capacity to enter an enforceable contract
A person is incapable of entering into an enforceable agreement if his mental state is such that he lacks an understanding of the general nature of what he is doing at the time of the contract. In fact, the contract would bind both parties unless the person incapable of understanding the contract could also prove that other party 'knew him to be so insane as not to be capable of understanding what he was about' (*Imperial Loan Co* v *Stone* [1892] 1 QB 599 at 601). The fact that a person is suffering from delusions is not conclusive evidence that he did not sufficiently understand the contract, even if the delusion is connected with the subject-matter of the contract (*Jenkins* v *Morris* (1880) 14 ChD 674). A person is also incapable of entering into an enforceable agreement for the purposes of this sub-section if he has been found to be incapable of managing his affairs by reason of a mental disorder and/or a receiver has been appointed under Pt VII of the MHA 1983. Although the point has yet to be finally decided, it is likely that this incapacity will continue during lucid intervals if the receiver is still in post, (see *The Law of Contracts*, Chitty, Sweet & Maxwell, 27th edn, para 8–072 and *Re Walker* [1905] 1 Ch 160). Subject to that qualification, a person is capable of entering an enforceable contract during a lucid interval (*Creagh* v *Blood* (1845) 3 Jo & Lat 509).

It is not necessary for the defendant to prove that the disabled person did in fact lack capacity to contract so long as he reasonably believed that there was a lack of capacity. There will need to be some evidence of incapacity before that belief can be reasonably held. A service provider should assume that a disabled person is able to enter into any contract unless there is evidence to the contrary (Services and Premises Code, para 5.9). In addition a person may be able to understand less complicated transactions but have difficulty with more complex ones (Services and Premises Code, para 5.9). The defendant must also be of the opinion that the less favourable treatment is justified because of the absence of capacity and that opinion must be reasonable. In those circumstances, the service provider will be able to justify the less favourable treatment (Services and Premises Code, para 5.8) providing it is reasonable to do so. For example, it may well be reasonable to refuse to enter into a complicated hire purchase or loan agreement with a person reasonably believed to lack the capacity to contract, as the agreement could not subsequently be enforced. However, it would not be reasonable for a shopkeeper to refuse to sell a £1 sandwich to a person with a profound learning difficulty who was offering a £1 coin. Even if that person had no understanding of money and did lack capacity to contract, it would not be reasonable to refuse to serve that person. Once the coin is handed over and the sandwich eaten, no question of further enforcement arises. The government made clear that this form of justification was intended to apply only in limited circumstances. Mr Hague said:

> It will not be reasonable for service providers to cite this justification when the purchase of a product or service would not normally be the subject of a written agreement. For example, it cannot be used in relation to buying groceries in a supermarket. The subsection will apply only to major purchases—a motor car perhaps—or credit agreements, and it is meant to apply only in a few cases (*Hansard*, Report SC E, 21 Feb 1995, col 350).

Even in those few cases where s 20(4)(*b*) would otherwise apply, reg 8 of the DD(SP) Regs 1996 provides that it shall not apply where the disabled person is acting through another person where that other person is:

(1) acting by virtue of a power of attorney;
(2) exercising functions conferred by or under Pt VII of the MHA 1983; or
(3) in Scotland, exercising powers in consequence of the appointment of a *curator bonis*, tutor or judicial factor.

The Services and Premises Code gives the example of a salesman refusing to rent a television to a person simply because he is legally acting on behalf of someone with a mental illness and notes that this is unlawful (para 5.10).

Capacity to give informed consent

The doctrine of informed consent is usually used in the context of consent to medical treatment, although it is not recognised as such in English law (see *Sidaway v Board of Governors of the Bethlem Royal Hospital and Maudsley Hospital* [1985] AC 871). In order to give informed consent, a patient must be given sufficient information to allow him or her, albeit in broad terms, to understand what material risks the treatment will involve. This may be relevant to the provision of medical services. For example, it may allow a doctor to refuse to carry out a termination, sterilisation or elective surgery on a person reasonably believed not to understand the material risks involved in the procedure. As the concept of informed consent has developed in relation to medical treatment, it would not seem inappropriate to apply it outside the field of medical or similar services. The expression 'informed consent' is also found in the provisions relating to premises (see s 24(3)(*b*) and p 164 below). This suggests that the application of this concept will not be limited to justifying acts that would otherwise be unlawful in relation to medical services although it is not clear when else it may be invoked.

That the treatment is necessary because the provider of services would otherwise be unable to provide the services to members of the public (s 20(4)(c))
This condition applies only in relation to a refusal to provide or deliberate failure to provide services to a disabled person under s 19(1)(*a*). As with the other conditions, there is no need to prove that the treatment was in fact necessary provided the service provider reasonably believed that it was necessary. Nonetheless, the inclusion of the word 'necessary' was intended to limit the availability of this condition of justification. The Minister for Social Security and Disabled People said that it provided 'the strictest test of all. It applies only in circumstances in which, if a service provider were to serve a particular disabled person, he would not be able to continue to provide his service at all. ... the use of the word necessary would be a tough test, with a meaning akin to essential. That is intended to be its legal meaning' (*Hansard* Report SC E, 21 February 1995, col 354, Hague). Paragraph 5.11 of the Services and Premises Code gives the following example. A tour guide would be entitled to refuse to allow an unaccompanied wheelchair user on a tour where he has well-founded reasons to believe that the extra help he would have to give him would prevent the party completing the tour. However, the condition would seem not to be satisfied if the guide believed only that other members of the party would merely be inconvenienced or delayed were the wheelchair user to join the tour. 'The distinction is between people who had paid for a service and cannot receive it at all and those who are merely being delayed ... [For example], a clerk in a post office refuses to serve a deaf person because the extra time taken means that other customers have to queue for longer. This is against the law' (Services and Premises Code, para 5.13). Again, the word necessary suggests that the subsection would not be satisfied unless the service provider reasonably believed that no other less discriminatory treatment would allow the service to be provided to others. In particular, if a reasonable adjustment or other modification could have been made at the relevant time to allow the service to be provided to the disabled person and preserved for others, less favourable treatment comprising of a refusal to serve the disabled person would not be necessary (see below).

That the treatment is necessary because the provider of services would otherwise be unable to provide the services to the disabled person or to members of the public (s 20(4)(d))
This condition applies to the provision of services to a different standard, in a different manner or on different terms under s 19(1)(*c*),(*d*). The service provider may be able to justify the provision of a different standard of service

or service on less favourable terms if that is necessary in order to serve the disabled person or another customer (s 20(4)(*d*)). For example, an hotel would be entitled to offer only ground floor rooms for use by wheelchair users because the other floors are not accessible (Services and Premises Code, para 5.12). Again, although the condition will be satisfied if the service provider reasonably believed the treatment was essential even if it was not, the use of the word 'necessary' establishes a strict test (see p 146 above). As with the condition in s 20(4)(*c*) it will be necessary to consider if other, less discriminatory measures, could be taken to allow the service to be provided to the disabled person and others. If it could, the less favourable treatment comprising of a refusal to serve the disabled person would not be necessary).

The difference in the terms on which the service is provided to the disabled person and those on which it is provided to other members of the public reflects the greater cost to the provider of services in providing the service to the disabled person (s 20(4)(e))

Where this condition is made out, the service provider will be able to justify charging a disabled person more than others for a particular service. The additional charge must be reasonably believed to reflect the additional cost of providing the service to the disabled person. Furthermore, it must be due to the individual tailoring of the service in order to meet the needs of the customer and the disabled person's particular requirements increase costs as a result of greater materials of work being needed (Goods and Services Code, para 5.14). Thus, a furniture shop may charge more for an orthopaedic bed made to the disabled person's specification, but may not charge the disabled person more than is charged to non-disabled persons for a standard bed.

This provision will not allow a service provider to pass on the cost of complying with the duty to adjust to the disabled person once that duty comes into force. Any additional cost which results from the service provider's compliance with the duty to adjust is to be disregarded for the purposes of s 20(4)(*e*) (s 20(5)). The government stated that it did not intend to

> allow service providers to charge more to a disabled person where they have to make their services more accessible to suit his or her disability ... It is certainly not our intention that, for example, a large organisation which had to produce information in an alternative format for some of its disabled customers should be able to charge them for it (*Hansard*, HL, Vol 564, col 2009, Mackay).

As a working rule, it will generally be acceptable to pass on the additional costs of providing different goods or services to the disabled person but not the costs of providing the same goods or services in a different, or more accessible, way. However, it will not always be easy to differentiate between the allowable extra costs of providing the service to the disabled person and the disregarded extra costs of complying with the duty to adjust.

Justification and the duty to adjust

There is no express provision limiting the circumstances in which a service provider who has failed to comply with the duty to adjust can justify less favourable treatment. A service provider who fails without justification to comply with the duty to adjust will not have to show that the less favourable treatment would have been justified even if the duty had been complied with. This contrasts with the employment provisions (s 5(5), and see p 44 above). Nonetheless, the availability of alternative measures to avoid a danger to health or to allow the service to be provided to the disabled person or others may prevent a service provider from reasonably holding the opinion that the less favourable treatment in question was necessary in cases under s 20(4)(*a*), (*c*) and (*d*). This will be a question of fact in the circumstances of each case as they existed at the time of the less favourable treatment in question. For example, refusing to allow a wheelchair user into a restaurant in order to avoid a risk to health and safety will not be necessary (and could not reasonably be believed to be necessary) if the risk could easily be avoided by rearranging the furniture. This will be the case even before the duty to adjust is brought into force. However, if the risk could only be avoided by installing ramps or a lift, for example, so that the disabled person did not have to be carried up several flights of stairs, no alternative measures would be available at the time of the less favourable treatment. In such a case it would appear that the service provider would be able to defeat a claim under s 19(1)(*a*) (refusing to provide a service) by establishing that the refusal was justified notwithstanding any existing failure to comply with the duty to adjust (once in force) by providing ramps or a lift. However, this will not be of practical importance because the disabled person would also have a cause of action under s 19(1)(*b*) (failing to comply with a duty to adjust). If the reasonable adjustment would have allowed the disabled person to make use of the service, the service provider will be found to have discriminated against the disabled person unless it establishes that the failure to comply was itself justified (see p 152 below).

Deemed justification

The DD(SP) Regs 1996 make provision deeming some less favourable treatment relating to insurance, guarantees and warranties and deposits to be justified.

Insurance

The DD(SP) Regs 1996 makes provisions in connection with insurance business carried out by the service provider.

Definitions

Regulation 1(2) provides that insurer has the same meaning as 'insurance company' as defined in s 96 of the Insurance Companies Act 1982. Section 96 of that Act defines 'insurance company' to mean a person or body of persons (whether incorporated or not) carrying on insurance business. Regulation 1(2) provides that 'insurance business' has the same meaning as in the Insurance Companies Act 1982, namely:

(a) the effecting and carrying out, by a person not carrying on a banking business, of contracts for fidelity bonds, performance bonds, administration bonds, bail bonds or customs bonds or similar contracts of guarantee, being contracts effected by way of business (and not merely incidentally to some other business carried on by the person effecting them) in return for the payment of one or more premiums;

(b) the effecting and carrying out of tontines;

(c) the effecting and carrying out, by a body (not being a body carrying on a banking business) that carries on business which is insurance business apart from this paragraph, of—
  (i) capital redemption contracts;
  (ii) contracts to manage the investments of pension funds (other than funds solely for the benefit of its own officers or employees and their dependants or, in the case of a company, partly for the benefit of officers or employees and their dependants of its subsidiary or holding company or a subsidiary of its holding company);

(d) the effecting and carrying out of contracts to pay annuities on human life.

Less favourable treatment deemed to be justified
Regulation 2 of the DD(SP) Regs 1996 deems less favourable treatment in connection with insurance business carried out by the service provider to be justified if:

(1) it is based on information which is relevant to the assessment of the risk to be insured (such as actuarial or statistical data or a medical report) and is from a source on which it is reasonable to rely (reg 2(2)(*b*)); and

(2) the less favourable treatment is reasonable having regard to the information relied upon and any other relevant factors (reg 2(2)(*c*)).

The Services and Premises Code states that these regulations recognise the need for insurers to be able to distinguish between individuals on the basis of the risks against which they seek to insure (para 5.19). The Code emphasises that if a disabled person establishes that less favourable treatment has occurred, it will be for the insurer to prove that there is an additional risk associated with the disabled person which arises from his or her disability. The Code gives the example of an insurance company that charges a higher premium to a deaf person for car insurance although it has no evidence of an increased risk, and notes that this was unlawful. An insurer can only refuse to insure or to continue to insure, limit the amount, extent, or kind of coverage available to an individual, or charge a different rate for the same coverage for a reason relating to a disability if that treatment is based on sound actuarial principles or is related to actual or reasonably anticipated experience. Only legitimate actuarial considerations or similar objective good reasons will justify less favourable treatment of individuals with disabilities in insurance.

Transitional provisions for existing policies
There are transitional provisions for policies of insurance which came into effect before 2 December 1996. Less favourable treatment in connection with insurance business carried on by the service provider is deemed to be justified if it relates to an 'existing policy' (DD(SP) Regs 1996, reg 3(1)). 'An existing policy' means a policy of insurance where the liability to risk of an insurer under a policy of insurance commenced before 2 December 1996 (regs 1(2) and 3(4)). However where an existing policy is due to be renewed or the terms of such a policy are to be reviewed on or after 2 December 1996, any less favourable treatment which occurs on or after the date on which the review or renewal is due is not deemed to be justified by reg 3(1) (reg 3(2)). A review of an existing policy as part of or incidental to a general reassessment of the pricing structure of a group of policies is deemed not to be a review for the purposes of reg 3(2) (reg 3(3)).

Transitional provisions for cover documents and master policies
Regulation 4 of the DD(SP) Regs 1996 makes transitional provisions relating to cover documents and master policies. Master policy means a contract issued between an insurer and another person under which the other person is entitled to issue certificates or policies to individuals and which details the terms upon which those certificates or policies may be issued (reg 4(4)). A cover document is a certificate or policy issued under a master policy (reg 4(4)). Less favourable treatment in connection with insurance business carried on by the service provider is deemed to be justified if:
(1) it results in a refusal to issue a cover document to or in respect of the disabled person and the refusal occurs before 2 December 1997 (reg 4(1)(*b*)); or
(2) it relates to a master policy where the liability to risk of the insurer commenced before 2 December 1997 (reg 4(1)(*b*)).
However, where the master policy under which the cover document was (or would have been) issued was entered into or renewed on or after 2 December 1996, or the terms of that master policy were reviewed on or after 2 December 1996, the transitional provisions will not apply and the less favourable treatment will not be deemed to be justified under regulation 4(1) (reg 4(2)). Where a cover document is due to be renewed or its terms reviewed on or after 2 December 1997, less favourable treatment on or after the date of review or renewal will not be deemed to be justified under reg 4(1) (reg 4(3)).

Guarantees and warranties

Regulation 5 of the DD(SP) Regs 1996 deems less favourable treatment in relation to a guarantee to be reasonable in specified circumstances. The circumstances are that:
(1) the service provider provides a guarantee (whether legally enforceable or not) that he or she will either refund the purchase price if the services, goods or facilities are not of satisfactory quality or replace,

or repair goods if they are not of satisfactory quality (reg 5(2)(*a*)). Guarantee is defined to include any document that has such an effect, whether or not it is described as a guarantee by the provider (reg 5(3)); and

(2) the service provider refuses to provide a replacement, repair, or refund under the guarantee, because damage has occurred (reg 5(2)(*b*)); and

(3) the damage occurred for a reason which relates to the disabled person's disability (reg 5(2)(*b*)); and

(4) the damage is above the level at which the provider would normally provide a replacement, repair, or refund under the guarantee (reg 5(2)(*b*)); and

(5) it must be reasonable in all the circumstances of the case for the provider to refuse to provide a replacement, repair, or refund under the guarantee (reg 5(2)(*c*)).

The Services and Premises Code gives the example of a person who buys a pair of shoes but wears out the left one after a few months because his left foot has to bear most of his weight. The retailer may lawfully refuse to provide a new pair because the old pair has undergone abnormal wear and tear (para 5.20).

This deeming provision will not affect a disabled person's rights under s 14(2) of the Sale of Goods Act 1979 and s 4 of the Sale of Goods and Services Act 1982, which require goods sold or transferred in the course of a business to be of merchantable quality and fit for any purpose made known to the seller or transferor. A disabled person who has drawn to the attention of the supplier of goods the purpose to which he intends to put the goods may be able to rely on these implied terms in circumstances in which he could not rely on his rights under the DDA. The details of the law on sale of goods are outside the scope of this book, and reference should be made to *Benjamin's Sale of Goods*, 4th edn, Sweet & Maxwell.

Deposits in respect of goods and facilities

Regulation 6 of the DD(SP) Regulations 1996 deems less favourable treatment in relation to a deposit given in respect of goods or services to be justified in the following specified circumstances. A similar provision is made in relation to deposits given in respect of premises (DD(SP) Regs 1996, reg 7 and p 166 below). The specified circumstances are that:

(1) the disabled person is required to provide a deposit when goods or facilities are provided (reg 6(2)(*a*)); and

(2) the deposit is refundable if the goods or facilities are undamaged (reg 6(2)(*a*)); and

(3) the provider refuses to refund some or all of the deposit because the goods or facilities are damaged (reg 6(2)(*b*)); and

(4) the damage occurred for a reason which relates to the disabled person's disability (reg 6(2)(*b*)); and

(5) the damage is above the level at which the provider would normally refund the deposit in full (reg 6(2)(*b*)); and

(6) the refusal to refund the deposit in full is reasonable in all of the circumstances of the case (reg 6(2)(*c*)).

The deeming provision only applies in relation to a refusal to refund some or all of the deposit and only if the specified circumstances exist. It will not justify requiring a disabled person to provide a deposit when others are not required to provide a deposit. Nor will it justify requiring a disabled person to provide a larger deposit.

Discrimination and the duty to adjust

The introduction of the duty to adjust is intended to require 'positive action which is reasonable and readily achievable to overcome the physical and communication barriers that impede disabled people's access' (*Ending Discrimination against Disabled People*, Cmnd 2729, 1995, HMSO, White Paper). The positive action to be required involves taking reasonable steps to alter exclusionary practices, policies and procedures, to provide auxiliary aids and services and to remove physical barriers. None of the provisions are in force at the date of writing. It is proposed to introduce the duty to take these steps by service providers so as to adjust gradually over the next nine years (see p 130 above).

Discrimination by failing to comply with the duty to adjust

The definition of discrimination in cases involving the duty to adjust is set out in s 20(2).

> 20(2)   For the purposes of s 19, a provider of services also discriminates against a disabled person if—
>> (a)   he fails to comply with a section 21 duty imposed on him in relation to the disabled person; and
>> (b)   he cannot show that his failure to comply with that duty is justified.

In order to establish discrimination by a failure to comply with the s 6 duty to make a reasonable adjustment, a disabled person has to show that:

(1) the service provider was under a duty to adjust; and

(2) the service provider failed to comply with that duty.

If the disabled person can prove those two things, discrimination will be established unless the service provider can show that the failure to comply was justified. The duty is imposed only for the purposes of determining if a service provider has discriminated against a disabled person within the meaning of s 20(2) so that a breach of the duty does not give rise to an independent right of action (s 20(10)). A breach of a duty will only give rise to a cause of action where it results in an act made unlawful by s 19(1)(*b*) (see p 136 above).

The duty

The duty to adjust is set out in s 21. It makes specific provision about practices, policies and procedures (s 21(1)); physical features (s 21(2)); and auxiliary aids and services (s 21(4)). Nothing in s 21 requires service providers to take any steps which would fundamentally alter the nature of the service provided or the nature of the trade, profession or business (s 21(6)).

Fundamental alterations

This is a question of fact and degree. For example, a nightclub which created a special atmosphere by using low level lighting would not have to increase the level of lighting, even if this meant that some people with impaired sight could not use the club, as this would fundamentally change the nature of the nightclub. However, the practice of self service in a restaurant is unlikely to be considered to be fundamental to the nature of the business as an employee could serve someone who had difficulty serving themselves without affecting the nature of the business (Timetable proposals, DL 140, para 2.3, WDC 1996).

Practices, policies and procedures

Section 21(1) provides as follows:

> (1) Where a provider of services has a practice, policy or procedure which makes it impossible or unreasonably difficult for disabled persons to make use of a service which he provides, or is prepared to provide, to other members of the public, it is his duty to take such steps as it is reasonable, in all the circumstances of the case, for him to have to take in order to change that practice, policy or procedure so that it no longer has that effect.

Practice, policy or procedure

These words are not defined in the DDA although regulations doing so may be made (s 21(5)(c), (d)). Examples have been given by the NDC during the consultation process:

> A restaurant may operate a policy of allowing no dogs onto the premises; its procedure would be to prevent anyone with a dog from entering the restaurant while the practice would be to carry out the procedure ...
> A train station has a policy to inform customers of train departures, arrivals and cancellations. The procedure for informing customers is either to put details of departing trains or cancellations on a notice board. This, therefore, is the practice (Para 2.3, DL 140, NDC 1996).

Which makes it impossible or unreasonably difficult for disabled persons to make use of a service

This provision refers to 'disabled persons' in general rather than to a specific 'disabled person concerned' (compare s 6(1) in relation to employment). Therefore, the duty may arise where the practice, policy or procedure has an adverse effect upon disabled persons, or a particular group of disabled persons, even though the service provider is not aware of any specific disabled person who has been so affected. However, a service provider will only be liable for failing to amend the policy, practice or procedure if a particular disabled person has been adversely affected as a result (s 19(1)(b)). In addition, it will often not be reasonable to expect a service provider to make an adjustment if he or she is not aware that the policy has made it impossible or unreasonably difficult for any disabled person to make use of the service, unless the service provider should have known that it had that effect.

The clearest case will be one in which the practice, policy or procedure renders it impossible for disabled persons with a particular disability to use the services in question. For example, an information service provided at a station which adopts the practice of informing customers of details of arrivals, departing trains and cancellations on a notice board makes it impossible for the service to be used by blind people. The words 'unreasonably difficult' raise a question of fact and degree in all of the circumstances. The mere fact that a policy renders use of the service difficult will not render the policy liable to adjustment unless the nature or extent of the difficult is unreasonable.

Note that 'the service' means a comparable service to that used by other people. It is not enough that some services can be used by disabled persons if others enjoy a wider range, or different quality, services. Lord Mackay, on behalf of the government, gave the following example:

> The dining area of a particular cafe may occupy two rooms. In one, where 80 per cent of the tables are accommodated, the management are happy to admit guide gods, but in the other room, where diners are entertained by a pianist, a ban on dogs is applied. In this circumstance, it will not be good enough for the proprietor to suggest that, because a blind person is able to use 80 per cent of the cafe, the service is reasonably accessible. He must consider a reasonable adjustment so that the disabled person can use the service to the full (*Hansard*, HL, 18 July 1995, Vol 566, col 267, Mackay).

It is his duty to take such steps as it is reasonable, in all the circumstances of the case, for him to have to take in order to change that practice, policy or procedure so that it no longer has that effect

The test of whether a measure was a reasonable one for the service provider to take will be an issue of fact for the court. Regulations will make provision for circumstances in which it is reasonable or not reasonable for a service provider to take particular types of steps (s 21(5)). There is no list of matters to be taken into account on the question of reasonableness as there is in relation to the employment provisions (s 6(4) and see p 52 above). Nonetheless, it will often be useful to consider the matters referred to in s 6(4). For example, the efficacy and practicability of a particular step, the cost and disruption of a particular step, size and resources of the service provider and the availability of financial or other assistance should be considered, together with any other factors that may be relevant. In due course a code of practice on the duty to make adjustments in respect of goods, services and facilities is likely to be issued, which will give more detailed practical advice on this area. In addition, there is an express provision relating to the fundamental nature of the service (s 21(6)) above at p 153, and regulations may be made to prescribe circumstances in which it is or is not reasonable for a service provider to have to take steps of a particular description (s 21(5)(a),(b)). Finally, there is likely to be a financial limit upon the expenditure to be required under the duty (s 21(7)). The mechanism by which that limit is to be calculated and applied to particular cases is to be provided by regulations, although no such regulations are available at the date of writing.

Physical features

Section 21(2) provides that:

(2)   Where a physical feature (for example, one arising from the design or construction of a building or the approach or access to premises) makes it impossible or unreasonably difficult for disabled persons to make use of such a service, it is the duty of the provider of that service to take such steps as it is reasonable, in all the circumstances of the case, for him to have to take in order to—
(a)   remove the feature;
(b)   alter it so that it no longer has that effect;
(c)   provide a reasonable means of avoiding the feature; or
(d)   provide a reasonable alternative method of making the service in question available to disabled persons.

Physical feature
'Physical feature' has not been defined for the purposes of s 21(2), although the examples of features arising from the design or construction of a building or the approach or access to premises are given. Regulations may be made defining physical feature (s 21(5)(e),(f)) and they are likely to follow the pattern of those used in relation to employment (see DD(E) Regs 1996, reg 9 at p 50 above).

Makes it impossible or unreasonably difficult for disabled persons to make use of such a service
The duty to adjust arises where the physical feature makes it impossible or unreasonably difficult for disabled persons to use the service in question. For example a building may simply be inaccessible to someone who uses a wheelchair or dangerous and unnavigable by someone with impaired sight. See above at p 153.

It is the duty of the provider of the service to take such steps as it is reasonable in all the circumstances of the case for him to have to take in order to do one of the things specified at s 21(2)(a)–(d)
The things specified are:
(a)   the removal of the feature;

(b) alter the feature so that it no longer has the effect of making it impossible or unreasonably difficult to make use of a service;
(c) provide a reasonable means of avoiding the feature; or
(d) provide a reasonable alternative method of making the service in question available to disabled persons.

Reasonableness is considered above at p 154, although the NDC has suggested that reasonableness in this context will 'primarily be a question of affordability', suggesting a role for the financial limit upon adjustments under s 21(7). Again, the adjustment should allow disabled persons access to services comparable to those enjoyed by others in so far as that is reasonably possible. The following examples were given on behalf of the government:

> ... there will be occasions when physical alterations will be the only reasonable solution because physical access to premises is a fundamental attribute of the service. I am thinking, for example, of restaurants, theatres, art galleries and so on. It would not be reasonable for the proprietor of a café to suggest that a take-away meal was a suitable alternative to making an adjustment to the lay-out or construction of his premises which would allow disabled people to enter (*Hansard*, 15 June 1995, Vol 564, vol 2022, Lord Inglewood).

> ... a cinema will have to make reasonable provision to allow wheelchair users a degree of choice as to where they sit. But all the seats in a cinema would not have to be moveable to leave space for a wheelchair. Of course, this means that a wheelchair user would have less choice than other customers and thus would receive a lower standard of service. The requirement, however, is to provide access to a service as close as it is reasonably possible to get to the standard normally offered. (*Hansard*, 18 July 1995, Vol 566, col 266–7, Lord Mackay)

Alterations to premises are considered in detail in Chap 16 below.

Regulations

Regulations may also be made to prescribe matters to be taken into account in deciding whether the provision of means of avoiding a feature or of an alternative method of making the service available to disabled persons is reasonable (s 21(3)(*a*)). Regulations may also be made to exempt categories of service providers specified in the regulations from the duty to adjust physical features (s 21(3)(*b*)).

Auxiliary aids or services

Section 21(4) provides:

(4) Where an auxiliary aid or service (for example, the provision of information on audio tape or of a sign language interpreter) would—
　　(a) enable disabled persons to make use of a service which a provider of services provides, or is prepared to provide, to members of the public, or
　　(b) facilitate the use by disabled persons of such a service,

it is the duty of the provider of that service to take such steps as it is reasonable, in all the circumstances of the case, for him to have to take in order to provide that auxiliary aid or service.

Auxiliary aids or services
The Act does not define 'auxiliary aid or service' although it gives examples of information on audio tape and a sign language interpreter. These words may be defined by regulations (s 21(5)(g),(h)). They are likely to include things such as:

(1)   qualified interpreters, notetakers, computer-aided transcription services, written materials, telephone handset amplifiers, assistive listening devices, assistive listening systems, telephones compatible with hearing aids, closed caption decoders, open and closed captioning, telecommunications devices for deaf persons (TTDs), videotext displays, or other effective methods of making aurally delivered materials available to individuals with hearing impairments;

(2)   qualified readers, taped texts, audio recorders, brailled materials, large print materials, or other effective methods of making visually delivered materials available to individuals with visual impairments (examples taken from the Technical Assistance Manual for Title III of the Americans with Disabilities Act 1990)

Enable disabled persons to make use of a service which a provider of services provides ... to members of the public or facilitate their use of such a service
The duty to provide auxiliary aids or services will therefore arise where those aids or services will enable disabled persons to use a service they were otherwise unable to use, or where it would make it easier for them to do so. However, a failure to provide such aids will only be unlawful under s 19(1)(b) where it results in it being impossible or unreasonably difficult for the disabled person to make use of the relevant service.

It is the duty of the provider of that service to take such steps as it is reasonable, in all the circumstances of the case, for him to have to take in order to provide that auxiliary aid or service
The auxiliary aid requirement is a flexible one. The duty on the service provider is to take such steps as are reasonable in all the circumstances of the case for him to have to take in order to provide that auxiliary aid or service (see p 154 above for reasonableness). As with the other provisions of s 21, there will be a financial limit on the duty (s 21(7) and p 155 above). As the duty is to take reasonable steps, a service provider could choose among various alternative devices or services as long as the result is to enable or facilitate disabled persons' use of the goods, facilities or services. This means that it is unlikely that a restaurant would be required to provide menus in braille for patrons who are blind, if the waiters in the restaurant are made available to read the menu. Similarly, a clothing boutique would not be required to have brailled price tags if sales personnel provide price information orally upon request, and a book shop would not be required to make available a sign

language interpreter, because the shop's services can be accessed by using a notepad. These examples are adapted from the Technical Assistance Manual for Title III (see above). Auxiliary aids and services include the acquisition or modification of equipment or devices. For example, tape players used for an audio-guided tour of a museum exhibit may require the addition of brailled adhesive labels to the buttons on a reasonable number of the tape players to facilitate their use by individuals who are blind. Similarly, a hotel conference centre may need to provide permanent or portable assistive listening systems for persons with hearing impairments.

Justifying a failure to adjust

If a service provider fails to make an adjustment that it was under a duty to make, the service provider will be found to have discriminated unless it can prove that the failure to make the adjustment was justified (s 20(2)). The test of justification set out in s 20(2),(3) applies equally to discrimination by way of a failure to adjust (s 20(9)). Therefore, other than in relation to failures that are deemed to be justified, the service provider will need to show that it reasonably believed that the failure to adjust was necessary in order not to endanger the health or safety of any person or that it was reasonable because the disabled person lacked the capacity to contract or give informed consent. These are discussed at p 143 above. The forms of justification based on preserving the service (under s 20(4)(c) and (d)) are not available in a claim alleging a breach of the duty to adjust under s 19(1)(b), as they are expressly limited to cases falling within s 19(1)(a),(c) and (d). However, if the failure to take a particular step was necessary in order to preserve the service, a service provider is unlikely to be required to take that step by s 21, either because it was not reasonable or because it would involve fundamentally altering the nature of the service (s 20(6), and see p 153 above). Justification under s 20(4)(e) based on the additional cost of providing the service is not available, as the cost of making reasonable adjustments required by s 21 must not be passed on to the disabled person (s 20(5)). Express provision will be made limiting the expenditure that must be made by the service provider (see p 155 above).

Checklist on the meaning of discrimination in relation to goods and services

Discrimination by less favourable treatment

—What is the less favourable treatment alleged?
—Did the service provider treat someone else more favourably:
- someone without a disability?
- someone with a different disability?
- someone with the same disability to whom the reason for the treatment did not apply?

—If not, would the service have treated others more favourably in the same circumstances?
—Was the reason for the less favourable treatment:
- the fact of the disability?
- related to the disability?

—Did the service provider know of the disability?
—Did the service provider know the reason for the treatment related to the disability?

Was the less favourable treatment justified?

—Was the less favourable treatment deemed to be justified by the rules relating to:
- insurance?
- guarantees?
- deposits?

—Did the service provider believe that:
- the treatment was necessary in order not to endanger the health or safety of any person?
- the disabled person concerned was incapable of entering into an enforceable agreement, or of giving an informed consent, and for that reason the treatment was reasonable?
- (in a case under s 19(1)(a)) the treatment was necessary because the provider of services would otherwise have been unable to provide the services to members of the public?
- (in a case under s 19(1)(c) or (d)) the treatment was necessary because the provider of services would otherwise have been unable to provide the services to the disabled person or to members of the public?
- (in a case under s 19(1)(d)) the difference in the terms on which the service is provided to the disabled person and those on which it is provided to other members of the public reflects the greater cost (other than any cost incurred in complying with the duty to adjust) to the provider of services in providing the service to the disabled person?

—If so, was the belief reasonable?

—If the belief related to the disabled person's capacity to contract or give an informed consent, is the defence of justification unavailable because someone was:

- acting by virtue of a power of attorney?
- exercising functions conferred by or under Pt VII of the MHA 1983?
- (in Scotland) exercising powers in consequence of the appointment of a *curator bonis*, tutor or judicial factor?

A checklist has not been provided in relation to the duty to adjust as the provisions are not yet in force and the regulations and code of practice that will flesh out the duty to adjust in relation to goods and services are not yet available.

Chapter 12

Discrimination in the Disposal and Management of Premises

Sections 22 to 24 of the DDA make discrimination against disabled persons in connection with the disposal or management of premises unlawful. The provisions are based on the corresponding provisions of the SDA 1975 and the RRA 1976 (*Hansard*, Report SC E, 28 Feb 1995, col 453, Hague). Section 22 renders unlawful specified acts of discrimination by those who have the power to dispose of premises, those who manage premises and those whose licence or consent is required for the assignment of premises held under a lease. Discrimination is defined in s 24. Small premises are exempted from these provisions by s 23. Any term in a lease which would require a person to contravene these provisions is made void by s 26. The enforcement provisions are the same as for discrimination relating to goods, facilities and services and are considered at pp 181. Further provisions relating to premises are found in reg 7 of the DD(SP) Regs 1996. In addition, practical assistance is found in the *Code of Practice on Rights of Access: Goods, Facilities, Services and Premises* ('the Services and Premises Code') (HMSO, July 1996, London) issued by the Secretary of State for Social Security pursuant to s 51(2) of the DDA. The origins and status of the Code are discussed in more detail at p 129 above and it is set out in full in Appendix 3 at p 315 below.

In addition to these specific provisions, the duty to adjust imposed on employers (p 52) and to be imposed upon service providers (p 155) will have a substantial impact upon the liabilities of landlords (p 234).

The meaning of discrimination

The meaning of discrimination in relation to the disposal and management of premises follows that of the unjustified less favourable treatment provisions of ss 5(1) and 20(1), although there is a different test for establishing if such less favourable treatment is justified. There is no duty to adjust in relation to the management or disposal of premises. It is unlawful for a person disposing or managing premises to discriminate against any person (whether disabled or not) by victimising him (s 22(7) and s 55, see also p 251 below). The provisions regarding vicarious liability and the liability of those (such as agents) who aid unlawful acts are dealt with at p 248.

Meaning of 'discrimination'

24(1)   For the purposes of section 22, a person ('A') discriminates against a disabled person if—

(a)   foi a reason which relates to the disabled person's disability, he treats him less favourably than he treats or would treat others to whom that reason does not apply; and

(b)   he cannot show that the treatment in question is justified.

Against a disabled person

Sections 22 and 24 make it unlawful to discriminate against a person who has a disability as defined in s 1 (see Chap 1, p 3 above) or someone who had a disability (s 2, and see p 22). The provisions also render it unlawful to discriminate against any person by way of victimisation whether that person is disabled or not (s 22(7) and s 55, and see p 251 below). They do not prevent discrimination against organisations seeking, for example, to acquire premises for use as residential accommodation by people with disabilities (see p 23 above).

Less favourable treatment for a reason relating to the disabled person's disability

There is no material difference between this part of the definition and that found in ss 5(1)(a) and 20(1)(a). See generally pp 36 and 140 above. It will include less favourable treatment based on the fact of someone's disability, such as refusing to let premises to a person because he has a learning difficulty or mental health problems. It will also apply where the reason relates to the disability, for example refusing to let premises to a person who has a guide dog.

The absence of a duty to adjust and the limited circumstances in which less favourable treatment can be justified (see below) make it particularly important to establish how closely connected the reason must be to the disability in order to come within s 24(1)(a). For example, if a peson has been excluded from employment because of his disability, the fact that he has little or no money and is unable to pay a deposit and a month's rent in advance is, to an extent, related to his disability. As the comparison is to be made with someone 'to whom that reason does not apply' rather than someone without that (or any) disability, it is to be made with someone who is able to pay a deposit and a month's rent. Presumably the DDA does not require landlords to let premises to those unable to pay sums that would be required of any tenant. The less favourable treatment will not be justified as the circumstances do not match those set out in s 24(3) (see below). In such a case the link between the disability and the reason for the treatment is likely to be too remote to satisfy the first part of the definition. Other cases may be less straightforward. For example, someone who lost his job and now receives incapacity benefit as a direct result of a disability will be excluded by a landlord or letting agency with a 'No DSS' rule. Alternatively, a requirement that prospective tenants provide a reference from their last landlord may exclude someone who has just left a long stay institution. Finally, less favourable treatment of a tenant with mental health problems because of behaviour caused by or related to those mental health problems should fall within this provision (see p 176 below).

He cannot show that the treatment in question is justified

As with the employment and goods and services provisions, less favourable treatment for a reason relating to the disability constitutes unlawful discrimination unless the defendant can show that the treatment was justified (see p 141 above). The burden of proving that the treatment was justified is upon the defendant. Treatment is only justified if, in the opinion of the person disposing of, managing, or required to consent to the disposal of the premises, one of four conditions specified in s 24(3) is satisfied *and* it is reasonable in all of the circumstances of the case for him to hold that opinion (s 24(2)) or the case falls within circumstances prescribed by regulations. The four conditions set out in s 24(3) bear some similarity to the goods and services provisions (s 20(4)) (see p 143 above).

In the opinion
The provision is in the present tense and refers to matters as at the time of the less favourable treatment. Matters which did not affect the service provider's mind at the material time will not justify less favourable treatment although they may have an impact upon damages awarded (see p 142 above). For example, a landlord may refuse to accept a person with mental health problems as a tenant because of simple prejudice, without addressing his mind to whether the person was able to enter an enforceable agreement. Even if the person did not have capacity to enter into a lease the less favourable treatment would not be justified as the landlord did not hold an opinion at the material time. However, although discrimination will be proven, it can be argued that the only loss that flowed from the refusal to grant a lease (that could not validly be granted) was injury to feelings.

Reasonable for him to hold that opinion
The opinion must be reasonably held (see p 142 above). Provided the opinion is reasonably held, it does not matter if it is, in fact, incorrect. It should not be based on general assumptions and prejudice.

The specified conditions
The conditions specified in s 24(3) are as follows.

That the treatment is necessary in order not to endanger the health or safety of any person (s 24(3)(a))

This condition applies to any act of discrimination made unlawful under s 22. 'Any person' expressly includes the disabled person concerned (s 24(3)(a)). It is in the same terms as s 20(4)(a) of the goods and services provisions (see p 143 above). This would include refusing to let premises to a person who could not safely use the fire escape or negotiate the stairs. It would not include refusing to let a flat to a person because they have AIDS, despite knowing that there is no risk (Services and Premises Code, para 5.6). 'Disabled people should not be prevented from living where they choose through unfounded concerns for safety (Services and Premises Code, para 5.7). Although there is no duty to adjust, if the danger could be readily avoided by other less discriminatory measures it could be argued that the treatment was not 'necessary'. The treatment need not be 'necessary' provided it was reasonable to believe it to have been so. Where the less favourable treatment is a continuing act (see p 104 above), it will presumably cease to be justified and become unlawful once it ceases to be reasonable to believe that the treatment is necessary, either because of a change in circumstances or because further information has been obtained by the person holding the belief. Given the purpose of the DDA, it may be that irrational (although common) fears about the risk of violence from people with mental health problems or infection by people with communicable illnesses would be found not to be reasonably held even in the absence of such specific advice. Regulations may prescribe circumstances in which it is or is not reasonable for a person to hold such an opinion (s 24(4)). No such regulations have been made to date.

That the disabled person concerned is incapable of entering into an enforceable agreement, or of giving an informed consent, and for that reason the treatment is reasonable in that case (s 24(3)(b))

This condition applies to any act of discrimination made unlawful under s 22. This is in the same terms as s 20(4)(b) in the goods and services provisions and is discussed in detail at p 144 above. It is particularly difficult to envisage what role informed consent will play in this context. As under s 20(4)(b), it is not necessary for the defendant to prove that the disabled person did in fact lack capacity to contract so long as he reasonably believed that there was a lack of capacity. The landlord must also be of the opinion that the less favourable treatment is justified because of the absence of capacity and that opinion must be reasonable. This will be important where the person is acting through someone holding a power of attorney, performing functions conferred by or under Pt VII of the Mental Health Act 1983 or using powers exercisable in Scotland in consequence of the appointment of a *curator bonis*, tutor or judicial factor. In such a case, that person would be able to make a binding agreement on behalf of the disabled person. Regulation 8 of the DD(SP) Regs 1996 (which provides that incapability cannot justify discrimination in relation to goods and services where the disabled person is acting through another person in this way—see p 145) does not apply to s 24(3)(b). It will be a question of fact whether, in those circumstances, it was reasonable for the defendant to believe that the less favourable treatment was reasonable because of the disabled person's incapacity when a binding contract could have been made.

That the treatment is necessary in order for the disabled person or the occupiers of other premises forming part of the building to make use of the benefit or facility (s 24(3)(c)

This condition applies only in relation to less favourable treatment by a manager of premises who treats a disabled person less favourably in the way he permits that person to make use of any benefits or facilities under s 22(3)(*a*). As with the other conditions, there is no need to prove necessity provided the belief was reasonably held. Again, the absence of a duty to adjust may be tempered by the argument that the treatment could not reasonably have been thought necessary if alternatives were readily available. See p 164 above in relation to continuing acts.

Part of a building

There is no statutory definition of the term 'part of a building'. It is a question of fact whether something comprises a single building (see *Bardrick* v *Haycock* (1976) 2 HLR 118, CA). Extensions have generally been considered to form part of the building to which they are added, even in the absence of internal connections with the main property (*Bardrick* v *Haycock* above, *Griffiths* v *English* (1981) 2 HLR 126 and *Lewis-Graham* v *Conacher* (1991) 24 HLR 132). A pair of semi-detached houses has been held to comprise two separate buildings (*Humphrey* v *Young* [1903] 1 KB 4 and to comprise a single building (*Cook* v *Minion* (1978) 37 P&CR 58). In *Guppy* v *O'Donnell* (1979) 129 New LJ 930 formerly adjoining buildings which had been connected by the demolition of walls were held to comprise a single building.

That the treatment is necessary in order for the occupiers of other premises forming part of the building to make use of the benefit or facility (s 24(3)(d))

This condition applies only in relation to a manager of premises who treats a disabled person less favourably by refusing or not permitting that person to make use of any benefits or facilities under s 22(3)(*b*). For example, it may be necessary to prevent a person with mental health problems from using laundry facilities if he repeatedly damages them, putting them out of action and thereby preventing other occupiers from using them (Services and Premises Code, para 5.15). The condition only applies where not treating the disabled person less favourably would prevent the use of benefit or facility. It will not apply to justify treatment imposed simply to reduce inconvenience or delay to others. For example, it would be unlawful for a landlord to refuse 'to allow a mentally ill tenant to use a shared kitchen because he sometimes takes a little longer and so delays other tenants' (Services and Premises Code, para 5.17).

Regulations

Regulations may make provision as to other circumstances in which treatment is to be taken to be justified (s 24(5)). Regulation 7 of the DD(SP) Regs 1996 provides that less favourable treatment consisting of a refusal to return all or part of a deposit paid by a disabled person is justified in specified circumstances. Those circumstances are that:

(a) the person with power to dispose of the premises ('the provider') has granted the disabled person a right to occupy the premises (whether by means of a formal tenancy agreement or otherwise);

(b) the disabled person has paid a deposit that was refundable at the end of the occupation provided there was no damage to the premises or their contents;

(c) the premises were damaged for a reason which relates to the disabled person's disability and the damage was above the level at which the provider would normally refund the deposit in full; and

(d) it is reasonable in all of the circumstances for the provider to refuse to refund the deposit in full.

For example, if a tenant with epilepsy falls during a seizure, dropping and smashing a cup, it will not be deemed to be reasonable to deduct the cost of the cup from the deposit if the landlord would not usually deduct the cost of such minor breakages. Alternatively, if the person fell and broke the bannisters, it probably would be reasonable to deduct the cost of replacing the bannisters unless it was unreasonable in all of the circumstances. It may be unreasonable to deduct the cost of more serious damage if, for example, the landlord was going to demolish the premises anyway once the tenant gave up possession. A similar provision is made in relation to deposits for goods and services (DD(SP) Regs 1996, reg 6, and see p 151 above).

Unlawful acts

Section 22 makes it unlawful for a person to discriminate against a disabled person (or to victimise any person) in specified ways in disposing of premises, managing premises or by withholding a licence or consent for the disposal of any premises to that person. Equivalent provisions are found in ss 30 and 31 of the SDA and ss 21 and 24 of the RRA 1976.

Premises

'Premises' includes land of any description (s 68(1)). It includes both residential and commercial premises and even, it seems, a prison (see *Alexander* v *Home Office* [1988] 2 All ER 118). The Services and Premises Code states, at para 4.7, that the hire of premises or rooms booked in hotels and guest houses falls outside these provisions and is to be dealt with under the goods and services provisions (p 133 above). However, there may be some cross-over here, particularly with long stay or residential hotels. This may be of importance, as there is no duty to adjust under ss 22 and 24. Once s 21 is brought into force, hoteliers will be under such a duty under the goods and services provisions (see p 133 above). The section applies only to premises in the UK (s 22(8)).

Small dwellings
Small dwellings are exempted from s 22, provided:
  (a) the relevant occupier resides, and intends to continue to reside, on the premises;
  (b) the relevant occupier shares accommodation on the premises with persons who reside on the premises and are not members of his household;
  (c) the shared accommodation is not storage accommodation or a means of access; and
  (d) the premises are small premises (s 23(2), and see the Services and Premises Code, para 2.10).

There are equivalent exemptions for small dwellings under s 32 of the SDA 1975 and s 22 of the RRA 1976, although this has generated no useful authorities. There is some broad similarity between the purpose and nature of this exemption and those under the Rent Acts and Housing Acts, particularly as regards resident landlords (see s 21 of the Rent Act 1977 prior to its repeal by the Housing Act 1988). The authorities under those Acts may be of some assistance here.

The relevant occupier
In a case involving someone with power to dispose of any premises under s 22(1), 'the relevant occupier' is the person with that power or a near relative of that person (s 23(6)(*a*). In a case involving someone whose licence or consent is required for the disposal of premises let on or subject to a tenancy under s 22(4), 'the relevant occupier' is the person whose licence or consent is required or a near relative of that person (s 23(6)(*b*)). In a case involving the manager of premises, there is no definition of 'the relevant occupier'. This appears to have been an oversight. The legislative intention appears to have been to encompass such cases in the small premises exception, as s 23(1) expressly refers to cases involving the manager of premises. Furthermore, the person with power to dispose of premises may become the manager of premises once the right to occupy them has been granted. If this is correct, the courts may fill the legislative lacunae by defining the relevant occupier as the manager or a near relative in order to mirror the provisions relating to cases under s 22(1) and (4).

A near relative
Section 23(7) defines 'near relative' to mean 'a person's spouse, partner, parent, child, grandparent, grandchild, or brother or sister (whether of full or half blood or by affinity)'. 'Partner' means the other member of a couple consisting of a man and a woman who are not married to each other but are living together as husband and wife' (s 23(7)). A shared household is

necessary but not sufficient of itself to establish this (*City of Westminster* v *Peart* (1992) 24 HLR 389). All of the circumstances must be considered and no one factor will be decisive in every case. However, the consideration of the following 'signposts' may assist in analysing the nature of the relationship: the stability of the relationship; the financial arrangements; the existence of a sexual relationship; children; public acknowledgment (see *Crake* v *Supplementary Benefits Commission* [1982] 1 All ER 498). The express reference to 'a man and a woman' excludes the 'other' member of a same sex couple from the meaning of 'partner' and thereby 'near relative'. However, this will only be material if the couple live together somewhere other than at the premises in question but the person who does not have the power of disposal or management also resides on the relevant premises. 'Child' probably includes a foster child treated in all respects as the natural child of the foster parents (*Reading BC* v *Ilsley* [1981] CLY 1323). An adopted child is to be treated as a natural child of the adoptive parent or parents (Adoption Act 1976, s 39(1)).

The relevant occupier resides, and intends to continue to reside, on the premises (s 23(2)(a))
A person resides at premises if they occupy those premises as a home (*Hampstead Way Investments Ltd* v *Lewis-Weare* [1985] 1 All ER 564 at 568A). This is a question of fact and degree for the trial judge, to be determined applying ordinary common-sense (*Palmer* v *McNamara* (1990) 23 HLR 168). There is no requirement for the relevant occupier to reside in the premises as his only or principal home (see *Wolff* v *Waddington* [1989] 47 EG 148). The relevant occupier may reside in two places, provided it can properly be said that each was a home (*Hampstead Way Investments Ltd* v *Lewis-Wear* above, *Blanway Investments* v *Lynch* (1993) 25 HLR 378). Use for occasional visits or holidays will not be sufficient (*Spraggs* v *Prentice* [1950] EGD 313; *Walker* v *Ogilvy* (1974) 28 P&CR 288). If there is more than one landlord or manager, it probably only requires one of them (or a near relative of one of them) to reside on the premises, *Cooper* v *Tait* (1984) 15 HLR 98.

A person does not cease to reside on premises because of a temporary absence. In cases of extended absence, the proper approach is as follows:
(1) it is a question of fact and degree as to whether the absence is sufficiently prolonged as to infer cesser of occupation, with the burden of proof lying on the person alleging cesser;
(2) if it is, the burden of proof is on the person claiming residence to prove that residence has not ceased by establishing both an intention to return to the premises *and* some outward sign of that intention, such as the presence of furniture or a 'caretaker' on the premises;
(3) residence continues so long as both that intention and the manifestation of that intention are present (see *Brown* v *Brash* [1948] 2 KB 247).

If the conditions are satisfied, residence may continue during protracted absences. See for example *Gofor Investments* v *Roberts* (1975) 29 P&CR 366,

CA where residence continued despite the tenant leaving for France with an intention to return permanently in eight to ten years after the completion of his children's education. See also *Notting Hill Housing Trust* v *Etoria* [1989] CLY 1912, where the tenant continued to occupy premises as his only or principal home whilst serving a life sentence for murder with a prospect of release on licence after nine years, when his brother was living at the flat to look after the premises and furniture until his return.

On the premises
There is no statutory guidance as to when the premises on which the relevant occupier resides are the same premises as those being disposed of or managed. If the relevant occupier lives with his household on the ground floor of a house and lets out rooms on the upper floors, with all occupants using a single set of facilities, there is no doubt that only the lower and upper floors comprise one set of premises. However, the position is less clear in relation to a house that has been converted or purpose built to include one or more flats or interconnecting two semi-detached houses. It may be that this will not create practical difficulties, as the greater the separation between the premises the less likely there is to be shared accommodation (but see p 170 below). In any event, this is likely to be a question of fact and degree. The greater the degree of separation between the different parts, the less likely they are to form part of the same premises. This would be consistent with the mischief aimed at by the provision (see *Bardrick* v *Young* (1976) 2 HLR 168), namely avoiding the social embarrassment of requiring a householder to share premises with someone he or she does not wish to share with.

The relevant occupier must share accommodation on the premises with persons who reside on the premises and are not members of his household (s 23(2)(b))
There must be some sharing of accommodation. However, minimal common use, such as a right to make an occasional cup of tea or obtain water from a tap is unlikely to be sufficient (see *Marsh* v *Cooper* [1969] 1 WLR 803, CA). It will be a question of fact and degree whether the joint user is sufficient to amount to sharing. Under the old resident landlord provisions of the Rent Acts, a tenancy was only excluded from protection if there was sharing by concurrent use of the accommodation, as only then would there be the invasion of privacy that the provisions were aimed at (*Goodrich* v *Paisner* [1957] AC 65, HL). Therefore, if accommodation was such that it was only used consecutively, such as a bathroom or spare bedroom, that sharing would not take the tenancy outside of the Rent Acts. However, if, as argued below, 'accommodation' includes a bathroom and lavatory, sharing by consecutive use of that accommodation will suffice. It is not clear if an unexercised right to share the accommodation will suffice, although this was enough to satisfy the resident landlord provisions of the Rent Acts (see *Stanley* v *Comptom* [1951] 1 All ER 859 and *Mortgage Corporation Ltd* v *Ubah* (1996) *The Times*, March 21).

Note that the relevant occupier need not share the accommodation with the disabled person for the premises to be exempted under this rule, provided he shares with someone who resides on the premises and who is not a member of his household. Therefore, it would seem that the letting of a self-contained flat is exempted from the DDA if the relevant occupier shares some of his accommodation with other residents, provided the flat is part of the same premises (see p 169 above). Household is not defined by the DDA. The word is used in legislation relating to houses in multiple occupation (see Housing Act 1985, s 345). The *Houses in Multiple Occupation: Guidance to Local Housing Authorities on Managing the Stock in their Area* (DoE Circ 12/93) suggests, at para 2.2.2, that the following matters are relevant: shared cooking facilities; shared washing facilities; whether the occupants eat together; whether cleaning is carried out individually or shared; whether occupants have separate contracts; whether the vacancies are filled by a landlord or by the occupants; and whether occupants come and go frequently. However, both 'the expression 'household' and membership of it is a question of fact and degree, there being no certain indicia the presence or absence of which is by itself conclusive ... '; *Simmons* v *Pizzey* [1979] AC 37 HL. (See also *Silbers* v *Southwark London Borough* (1977) 76 LGR 421 CA; *London Borough of Hackney* v *Ezedinma* [1981] 3 All ER 438, DC; and *Heglibiston Establishments* v *Heyman* (1977) 36 P&CR 351).

The shared accommodation is not storage accommodation or a means of access (s 23(2)(c))
The shared accommodation must be other than storage space (such as a garage, storage cupboard, coal-house, cellar or loft used only for storage) or a means of access (such as a front or rear entrance door, passageway or staircase). Shared accommodation, such as a kitchen, living room or sitting room will clearly suffice. Under the old resident landlord provisions of the Rent Acts, tenancies were excluded from protection only where there was sharing of living accommodation (see *Cole* v *Harris* [1945] KB 474, CA), although the word 'living' does not appear in the legislation. However, the express exclusion of storage accommodation and means of access will probably prevent this additional requirement being read into the DDA, so that sharing of a bathroom or lavatory or shared use of a spare bedroom will be enough to exclude premises.

The premises are small premises (s 23(2)(d)
'Small premises' can mean one of two things (s 23(3)). They are defined by reference to either a households test or a persons test. The definitions are alternatives. The premises will be small premises if they satisfy the households test even if they do not satisfy the persons test and vice versa.

The households test
Premises are 'small premises' if:

(a) only the relevant occupier and members of his household live in the premises occupied by him;

(b) the premises comprise, in addition to the accommodation occupied by the relevant occupier, residential accommodation for at least one other household;

(c) the residential accommodation for each other household, is let or available on a separate tenancy or similar agreement; and

(d) there are not normally more than two other such households (s 23(4).

Therefore, a house converted into two or three flats will be excluded from the DDA if the relevant occupier lives in one of them with his household and lets out the other flat (or each of the other flats) on a separate tenancy agreement, provided there is sufficient sharing of accommodation.

The persons limit

Premises are also 'small premises' if there is not normally residential accommodation on the premises for more than six persons in addition to the relevant occupier and his household (s 23(5)). If members of the relevant occupier's family live in the premises but are not part of his household, for example if they live separately in a different room or rooms, they are to be counted towards the six. Therefore, premises will satisfy this test if they comprise of six or fewer single rooms let out by the relevant occupier in addition to the relevant occupier and his household.

Disposal of premises:

Section 22(1) of the DDA makes it 'unlawful for a person with power to dispose of any premises to discriminate against a disabled person—

(a) in the terms on which he offers to dispose of those premises in relation to the disabled person;

(b) by refusing to dispose of those premises to the disabled person;

(c) in his treatment of the disabled person in relation to any list of persons in need of premises of that description.'

To dispose

'Dispose' is defined to include granting a right to occupy the premises (s 22(6)). This inclusive definition appears to include granting a licence to occupy the premises in addition to granting a tenancy of the premises. Where the premises are comprised in, or (in Scotland) are the subject of a tenancy, 'dispose' includes (a) assigning, and (b) sub-letting or parting with possession of the premises or any part of the premises (s 22(6)). See the Services and Premises Code, para 4.7.

'Tenancy' means a tenancy created:

(a) by a lease or sub-lease;

(b) by an agreement for a lease or sub-lease;

(c) by a tenancy agreement; or

(d) in pursuance of any enactment (22(6)).

The terms lease and tenancy are interchangeable, although lease is more frequently used where the term has been created by deed under seal or to refer to the deed itself. An agreement for a lease is an instrument which binds one party to create and the other to accept a lease in the future (see *Halsbury's Laws*. 4th Edn Reissue, Butterworths, 1994, para 50). A tenancy agreement may be oral where the term is for three years or less (Law of Property Act 1925, s 54(2)). Periodic tenancies (ie yearly, monthly or weekly tenancies) can be created by oral agreement even though they may last for more than three years (*Hammond v Farrow* [1904] 2 KB 332, DC). A statutory tenancy created by s 2 of the Rent Act 1977, a periodic assured tenancy created by s 5 of the Housing Act 1988 and a secure periodic tenancy created under s 86 of the Housing Act 1985 fall within the meaning of tenancy as being created by statutory enactment.

A person with power to dispose of any premises
There is no need for the person to have any interest in the premises, and it will cover managing agents and others with power to dispose of premises on behalf of others. In any event, both the owner and the managing agent may be liable under the secondary liability provisions of ss 57 and 58 discussed at p 248 below.

The terms on which he offers to dispose of those premises (s 22(1)(a))
This would include all of the terms on which premises are offered to the disabled person; see the Services and Premises Code, para 4.10. For example, it would be unlawful to discriminate against a disabled person in the following ways: by setting a higher rent or sale price than would be required from others; requiring a larger deposit than would be sought from others; requiring a guarantor only from a disabled tenant; offering the premises only for a shorter (or longer) term or making the agreement subject to a break clause; offering to grant a different form of tenancy than would be granted to others, such as an assured shorthold under s 20 of the Housing Act 1988 rather than an ordinary assured tenancy. It would also apply to terms restricting the use of the premises or associated facilities, such as those limiting or preventing the disabled person's use of communal facilities in a block of flats.

Refusing to dispose of those premises to the disabled person (s 22(1)(b))
This would include refusing to grant a right to occupy the premises or otherwise dispose of them to the disabled person (see the Services and Premises Code, para 4.11). In contrast to s 4(1)(c) of the employment provisions (see p 70 above) and s 22(3)(b) below, there is no reference to 'deliberately not offering' to dispose of the premises. However, as an 'act' includes a deliberate omission (s 68(1)) it is unlikely to require an express refusal. It may be that this sub-section would apply to a refusal to let premises unless a third party becomes a joint tenant with the disabled tenant. Alternatively, such treatment could also be unlawful under s 22(1)(a) above. It would include refusing to grant an interest to the disabled person even if the

disposer was willing to grant such an interest to a third party on behalf of the disabled person, unless that third party was acting on behalf of the disabled person under, for example, Pt VII of the MHA 1983 (see also p 164 above as to when incapacity will justify less favourable treatment).

Treatment in relation to any list of persons in need of premises of that description (s 22(1)(c))
In particular, this applies to housing lists kept by local authorities or housing associations. It is unlawful to discriminate against disabled persons by refusing to register them on housing lists or treating them less favourably, for example by keeping them at the bottom of the list, once they were registered (Services and Premises Code, para 4.12). It would only apply to housing lists kept by agents if they had power to dispose of the premises themselves or were keeping the list for a person with power to dispose of the premises, in which case the secondary liability provisions of ss 57 and 58 of the DDA would apply (see p 248). If the list was kept for the benefit of the agent itself, rather than the property owners, it would probably be outside of s 22(1)(c). However, such discrimination by property agents would probably be rendered unlawful by the goods and services provisions of ss 19 to 21. A person who does not have the mental capacity to make an application for housing as a homeless person under Pt III of the Housing Act 1985 or to authorise an agent to do so is not entitled to make such an application (*R v London Borough of Tower Hamlets, ex p Begum* (1993) 25 HLR 319). A local authority declining to accept an application from or on behalf of such a person would have a defence under s 59 (see p 250) on the grounds that the refusal was in pursuance of a statutory enactment (as construed in *ex p Begum*) in addition to showing that the refusal was justified under s 24(3)(*b*).

Exception for private disposals
Section 22(1) does not apply to a person who owns an estate or interest in the premises and wholly occupies them unless he uses the services of an estate agent or publishes (or causes to be published) an advertisement for the purposes of disposing of the premises (s 22(2)). ' "Estate agent" means a person who, by way of profession or trade, provides services for the purpose of finding premises for persons seeking to acquire them or assisting in the disposal of premises' (s 22(6)). ' "Advertisement" includes every form of advertisement or notice, *whether to the public or not*' (s 22(6)). For this reason, the suggestion in the Services and Premises Code at para 2.11 that the exemption applies if the disposer does not 'advertise *publicly*' is contrary to the statute and is wrong. A notice circulated to all the occupiers of a block of flats would probably comprise an advertisement for the purposes of this provision, even though it was not directed to the public. A 'For Sale' notice outside the premises or a card in a newsagent's window would certainly comprise an advertisement.

Managers

It is unlawful for a person managing any premises to discriminate against any disabled person occupying those premises—
  (a) in the way he permits the disabled person to make use of any benefits or facilities;
  (b) by refusing or deliberately omitting to permit the disabled person to make use of those facilities; or
  (c) by evicting the disabled person, or subjecting him to any other detriment (s 22(3)).

Manager
There is no definition of 'a person managing any premises'. The Services and Premises Code suggests that it could 'include actions by accommodation agencies, housekeepers and estate agents who, for example, may collect the rent or provide access to particular benefits or facilities' (para 4.8). There is little doubt that commercial managing agents would be within these provisions. However, it is submitted that the expression 'person managing any premises' is to be construed widely. It should not be limited to those who manage premises as the agent of the owner. Instead, it should include any person who makes or implements decisions and arrangements in relation to the premises, including the owner if the owner is the person who makes and implements those decisions and arrangements. Subject to the exemption for small premises, this would include all landlords who 'manage' premises themselves, from a private landlord letting out a single flat to large commercial and local authority landlords who 'manage' their housing stock directly through their own employees. The reason for this wide construction is as follows. Any narrow construction would exclude all property owners who manage property themselves without the benefit of an agent. If this were the case, it would be unlawful for an 'owner-manager' to discriminate against a disabled person by refusing to let him premises, but not unlawful for him to discriminate against a disabled person by evicting him after he has let the premises to him. This would be absurd. As against this, a property owner who sets and collects rent and service charges, arranges repairs, implements rules, maintains facilities and decides when and if to evict manages his own property. The Services and Premises Code assumes that a landlord will fall within the 'managing' provisions (see paras 4.13 and 4.14).

In the way he permits the disabled person to make use of any benefits or facilities (s 22(3)(a))
Although benefits and facilities are not defined in the DDA, the Services and Premises Code gives the examples of laundry facilities, access to a garden and parking facilities (para 4.9), or shared recreational facilities (para 4.13). In common with the employment provisions, the word 'benefit' is likely to be interpreted widely to include anything that could fairly be regarded as an advantage or of value by the disabled person (see p 76 above). It is unlawful to

discriminate against a disabled person by permitting them to use any such benefits or facilities on less favourable terms than others. For example, it would be unlawful to limit the hours or circumstances in which a disabled person could use cooking or laundry facilities when those restrictions are not applied to others, or to require an additional payment from the disabled person for using those facilities (Services and Premises Code, para 4.13). Note that in common with the rest of the DDA, there is nothing to prevent a disabled person being given access on more favourable terms than others (Services and Premises Code, para 4.15). It was conceded that allowing a prisoner to do, or be placed on a waiting list to do, a specific job in prison fell within the equivalent provision of the RRA in *Alexander* v *Home Office* [1988] 2 All ER 118.

By refusing or deliberately omitting to permit the disabled person to make use of those facilities (s 22(3)(b))
This provision will cover any refusal to permit a disabled person from using any such benefits or facilities, such as where a person with a severe disfigurement is prevented from using the swimming pool in a block of flats (Services and Premises Code, para 4.13). If such a person was told that he could use the pool, but only early in the morning, there would be a breach of s 23(3)(*a*) above. There need not be an express refusal. The deliberate omission to permit will include circumstances in which all other occupiers are told that a facility is available but the disabled person is deliberately not told (see *Barclays Bank* v *Kapur* [1991] ICR 208, HL at 213).

By evicting the disabled person, s 22(3)(c)
It will be unlawful to evict a disabled person by evicting him, unless that treatment is justified. Although this provision is relatively straightforward, it could be of substantial practical importance. It will apply to all evictions, whether effected by proceedings in court or not. In fact, most evictions have to be effected by proceedings in court (see Pt I of the Protection from Eviction Act 1977) if they are to be lawful. However, a discriminatory eviction will not be rendered lawful for the purposes of the DDA simply because it was carried out under a court order, even if the order was granted following proof of one of the statutory grounds for possession under the Rent Act 1977, or the Housing Act 1985 or the Housing Act 1988. The statutory authority defence in s 59 will not apply because even if the eviction was allowed under an enactment, it was not required (see p 250 below). To put it another way, the court order (and/or any statutory ground for possession) constitute the means by which the eviction is carried out. It is not, or is not necessarily, the reason the eviction is carried out. It is the discriminatory reason for an eviction that makes the eviction unlawful under the DDA.

This is best illustrated by the following example. Where the necessary formalities have been complied with under ss 20 and 21 of the Housing Act 1988, a landlord is entitled to a possession order against an assured shorthold tenant as a matter of right once the fixed term has expired. However, a landlord is not required to recover possession at the expiry of the fixed term and may, for example, offer to renew the fixed term or allow a periodic tenancy to arise under s 5(2) of the Housing Act 1995. If the tenant can prove that the reason the landlord sought to recover proceedings was that the landlord had discovered that he (the tenant) was suffering from AIDS, the reason for the eviction would be a reason relating to the disabled person's disability. As such it would be unlawful under s 22(3)(c) of the DDA even though it would be lawful under the law of landlord and tenant. The position is similar to the employment provisions, in which a dismissal may be contractually 'lawful' in that proper notice was given to terminate the contract but still be unlawful discrimination under the RRA or SDA.

This may have far reaching consequences for landlords or managers seeking to evict occupiers with mental health problems by reason of their behaviour, such as repeatedly shouting or screaming through the night. If that behaviour is caused by or is a manifestation of the person's illness, it is 'a reason which relates to the person's disability'. Therefore, an eviction for that reason would be unlawful under the DDA unless the landlord or manager could show that the treatment was justified under s 24(2). This would be so even where the landlord was entitled to recover possession under the law of landlord and tenant because the behaviour gave rise to grounds for possession under ground 2 of Sched 2 to the Housing Act 1985 (or ground 14 of Sched 2 to the Housing Act 1988 or case 2 of Sched 15 to the Rent Act 1977) because that behaviour was causing 'nuisance or annoyance' to the disabled person's neighbours. Furthermore, the fact that the behaviour was causing nuisance or annoyance to neighbours would not, of itself, justify the eviction for the purposes of s 24(2) of the DDA. In such a case, the eviction would only be justified where the behaviour was such that the landlord or manager reasonably believed that the eviction was necessary in order not to endanger the health or safety of one of the neighbours under s 24(3)(a). Whilst this may be possible in extreme cases, it will not always be so.

It remains to be seen whether and to what extent the DDA will provide a defence to a claim for possession when eviction is made unlawful by s 22(3)(c). In cases where the court must be satisfied that it is reasonable to make an order for possession before doing so (as with many claims under the Rent Act 1977 and the Housing Acts 1985 and 1988) it could be argued that it is not reasonable to make an order where the eviction would be unlawful under the DDA. However, in 'nuisance and annoyance' claims, the court must take into account the effect of the behaviour upon neighbours (see *Woking Borough Council* v *Bistram* (1995) 27 HLR 1, CA and *Kensington & Chelsea Royal London Borough Council* v *Simmonds* (1996) *The Times*, July 15) so the effect of the DDA may not be decisive. The position is equally unclear where, as a matter of landlord and tenant law, the landlord has a right to possession and need not establish reasonableness. This is the position in relation to the mandatory grounds for possession and also where the occupier has no statutory security of tenure. Whilst the fact that an eviction would be unlawful under the DDA will not provide a defence as such, it may be possible to strike out the claim under CCR Ord 13, r 5(1)(*d*) as an abuse of the process of the court and/or seek an injunction restraining the landlord from evicting the tenant. Alternatively, it may be that the landlord would be granted possession of the premises and the occupier left to his remedy in damages. In *Ivory* v *Palmer* [1975] ICR 340 a landlord/employer was held to be entitled to an order for possession of premises when he had brought the occupier's contractual licence to an end by unlawfully terminating the occupier's contract of employment. However, as the decision in that case rested upon the special nature of an employment contract, it may not be of assistance in other cases. These issues await authoritative determination by the courts.

Or subjecting him to any other detriment (s 22(3)(c)
Presumably this provision will be interpreted widely and will include disadvantaging the disabled person in any way in relation to the premises (see Services and Premises Code, para 4.14 and p 85 above). It will include such things as charging higher rent or service charges for a reason related to the disabled person's disability. It would include harassment by the manager's employees and agents. However, it would not include harassment by other tenants save where those other tenants were acting as agents for the manager. Only in rare circumstances will a landlord be liable to a disabled person in nuisance for the acts of other tenants (see *Smith* v *Scott* [1973] Ch 314; *Page Motors Ltd* v *Epsom and Ewell BC* (1981) 80 LGR 337; and *O'Leary* v *London Borough of Islington* (1983) 9 HLR 81).

Licence or consent to assign

It is unlawful for any person whose licence or consent is required for the disposal of any premises comprised in a tenancy to discriminate against a disabled person by withholding his licence or consent for the disposal of the premises to the disabled person (s 22(4)). In this context disposal means assigning the tenancy, or subletting, or parting with possession of all or some of the premises to the disabled person (s 22(6)). This provision applies to tenancies created before and after the DDA (s 22(5)). It will not apply to tenancies which contain an absolute prohibition against assignment, subletting or parting with possession. Consent can only be withheld if it has been asked for (*Bilson* v *Residential Apartments Ltd* [1991] 3 WLR 264 CA, reversed on other grounds by the House of Lords). A refusal to consent except on unreasonable terms is probably a withholding of consent (*F W Woolworth & Co* v *Lambert* [1936] 2 All ER 1523), although this would only be made unlawful by the DDA if the requirement for terms or the terms themselves were discriminatory. Other statutes also affect the circumstances in which a landlord can withhold his licence or consent to a tenant assigning, underletting or parting with possession of the premises. Where a tenancy agreement contains a provision prohibiting such a disposal without the landlord's licence or consent, that licence or consent must in any event not be unreasonably refused (Landlord and Tenant Act 1927, s 19(1)(*a*)). The Landlord and Tenant

Act 1988 (LTA 1988) has placed express statutory duties upon landlords in relation to covenants against without the consent of the landlord, such consent not to be unreasonably refused. Those duties include the duty to reply within a reasonable period and, if consent is withheld, to state the reason for that refusal (LTA 1988, s 1). See also SDA 1975, s 33 and RRA 1976, s 24. There is no provision in the DDA allowing a court to consent to the disposal in place of the party unlawfully withholding consent (compare the provisions in relation to altering premises occupied under a lease at p 197 below). However, it is probable that a withholding of consent made unlawful by s 22(4) frees the tenant from the burden of the covenant and puts him at liberty to dispose of the premises to the disabled person without consent. Such a withholding would almost certainly be unreasonable for the purposes of s 19(1) of the LTA 1927 (and see *Treloar* v *Bigge* (1874) LR 9 Exch 151 and *Lewis* v *Allenby (1909) Ltd* v *Pegge* [1914] 1 Ch 782 CA for the effect of an unreasonable withholding of consent). In any event, the tenant could seek a declaration in the county court or, if appropriate, the High Court as to his right to assign without consent (*Young* v *Ashley Gardens Properties* [1903] 2 Ch 112 and *Evans* v *Levy* [1910] 1 Ch 452). Note that those proceedings would have to be brought by the tenant under the law of landlord and tenant (albeit in the light of s 22(4)) rather than directly under the DDA by the disabled person.

Discriminatory terms in leases and other agreements

Any term in a lease or other agreement is void in so far as it purports:
  (a) to require a person to do anything which would contravene any of the provisions of Pt III;
  (b) to exclude or limit the operation of Pt III; or
  (c) prevent any person from making a claim under Pt III (s 26(1)(a)).

Therefore, any provision in a tenancy agreement prohibiting a person from disposing of premises to a disabled person for a reason which related to his disability would be void. For example, a term in a lease forbidding the tenant from subletting to people with learning disabilities would not be legally binding (Services and Premises Code, para 6.6). Similarly, a provision in a tenancy agreement under which the tenant purported to agree not to bring a claim or to waive any rights under the DDA would be void. A county court may make such order as it thinks just for modifying an agreement which contains such a term upon the application of any person interested in the agreement (s 26(3)). Such a modification may involve striking out a discriminatory term or modifying the term so as to prevent it from having a discriminatory effect (see p 138 below).

Checklist on discrimination in the disposal and management of premises

The defendant and the premises

—Was the defendant:
- a person with the power to dispose of premises?
- the manager of premises?
- a person whose licence or consent was required for the disposal of any premises comprised in a tenancy?

—Were the premises:
- in the UK?
- exempted from s 22 by the rules on small dwellings?
- exempted from the provisions relating to the disposal of premises by the rules on private sales?

Was there discrimination?

Was there victimisation?
Was there less favourable treatment for a reason related to the disability?
- —What is the less favourable treatment alleged?
- —Did the defendant treat someone else more favourably:
  - someone without a disability?
  - someone with a different disability?
  - someone with the same disability to whom the reason for the treatment did not apply?
- —If not, would the defendant have treated others more favourably in the same circumstances?
- —What was the reason for the less favourable treatment?
- —Was the reason for the less favourable treatment:
  - the fact of the disability?
  - related to the disability?
- —Did the defendant know of the disability?
- —Did the defendant know that the reason related to the disability?

Was the treatment justified?
- —Was the less favourable treatment deemed to be justified by the rules relating to deposits?
- —Did the defendant believe that:
  - the treatment was necessary in order not to endanger the health or safety of any person?
  - the disabled person concerned was incapable of entering into an enforceable agreement, or of giving an informed consent, and for that reason the treatment was reasonable?

- (in cases under s 23(3)(*a*)) the treatment was necessary in order for the disabled person or the occupiers of other premises forming part of the building to make use of the benefit or facility?
- (in cases under s 23(3)(*b*)) the treatment was necessary in order for the occupiers of other premises forming part of the building to make use of the benefit or facility?

—If so, was the belief reasonable?

Was the discrimination unlawful?

—In a case involving the disposal of premises, was the disposal exempted from s 22(1) by the rules on private sales?

—In a case where the defendant has power to dispose of premises, did the discrimination involve:

- the terms on which the defendant offered to dispose of the premises in relation to the disabled person or the person victimised?
- the defendant refusing to dispose of those premises to the disabled person or the person victimised?
- the defendant's treatment of the disabled person or the person victimised in relation to any list of persons in need of premises of that description?

—In a case where the defendant is the manager of premises, did the discrimination involve:

- the way the defendant permitted the disabled person or person victimised to make use of any benefits or facilities?
- the defendant refusing or deliberately omitting to permit the disabled person or person victimised to make use of those facilities?
- the evicting of the disabled person or person victimised?
- subjecting the disabled person or person victimised to any other detriment

—In a case involving a person whose licence or consent is required for the disposal of any premises comprised in a tenancy, did the defendant discriminate by withholding his licence or consent for the disposal of the premises to the person discriminated against?

Chapter 13

Enforcement and Remedies

Introduction

Although the NDC has a monitoring role in relation to goods and services that it does not presently have in relation to employment provisions, it still does not have any powers to bring proceedings under or otherwise enforce Pt III of the DDA. Any claim for unlawful discrimination in relation to goods, services or premises must be brought by the disabled person concerned under s 25 of the DDA (para 5 of Sched 3) in either the county court or the sheriff court, although there may be a right to make an application for judicial review in limited circumstances. Save where express provision is made by the DDA, the practice and procedure for such claims will follow the usual rules of civil litigation under the County Courts Act 1984 (CCA 1984) and the County Court Rules 1981 (SI No 1687) (CCR) (or their Scottish equivalents). It is beyond the scope of this book to discuss those rules in any depth (for a detailed analysis see *Civil Litigation*, O'Hare and Hill, 7th edn, 1996, FT Law and Tax). This chapter will provide only a broad overview of practice and procedure in civil litigation save in respect of those aspects which have particular significance for claims under the DDA. In addition to court proceedings, arrangements are to be made to promote the settlement of disputes arising under Pt III without recourse to the courts.

Advice, assistance, assistance and settlement without recourse to the courts

The Secretary of State may make arrangements for the provision of advice and assistance to persons with a view to promoting the settlement of disputes arising under Pt III without recourse to the courts. This advice and assistance will be available to both disabled people who consider they have been discriminated against in contravention of Pt III and to service providers and others who are subject to the provision of Pt III. The government has said that it envisages 'the provision of a second tier advice and assistance service which will be available to disabled people and small businesses ... and in certain circumstances large businesses ...' (*Hansard*, HL Debate, Vol 566, col 988, Lord Mackay). In addition, 'it will seek a resolution which ensured that disabled person's rights were met' (*Hansard*, HL Debate, Vol 566, col 1029, Lord Mackay). As such, its role will be similar to that provided by ACAS in employment cases (see p 118) rather than that of an enforcement agency like the CRE or EOC. No such arrangements have been made at the time of writing. If an approach is made to a person appointed by the Secretary of State in connection with these arrangements in relation to proceedings or prospective proceedings, the time limit for issuing a claim is extended by two months (see p 187 below).

The validity of agreements

Any agreement which seeks to exclude or limit the operation of Pt III or to prevent any person from making a claim under Pt III is void (s 26(1)(*b*)(*c*)). Therefore, a clause in an agreement which states that a disabled person agrees to waive any rights under the DDA or to refrain from issuing proceedings under the DDA will be void and will not prevent such a claim from being made. However, this provision does not prevent any agreement settling a claim made or which could be made under s 25 (s 26(2)). Therefore, it is possible for the parties to reach a binding settlement of any claim which could be or has been made under Pt III without recourse to the courts or, if proceedings have been issued, prior to judgment. The parties do not need to use the arrangements for promoting settlement made under s 28 for any such agreement to be binding.

Questionnaires

There is no questionnaire procedure to assist those who believe they have been discriminated against in contravention of Pt III. The questionnaire procedures applies only to employment claims (see p 102 above).

Forum and venue

Any claim for unlawful discrimination in relation to goods, services or premises must be brought under s 25 of the DDA (para 5 of Sched 3). In England and Wales the cause of action is in tort (s 25(1)). In Scotland, the claim is for reparation for breach of a statutory duty (s 25(1)). A claim under s 25 (including a claim for victimisation) can only be brought in a county court in England and Wales (s 25(3)) or a Sheriff Court in Scotland (s 25(4)). If the only remedy sought in an action under the DDA is compensation, the action will be a default action (CCR Ord 3, r 2(2)) and can be issued in any county court (CCR Ord 4, r 2(1)(*c*)). However, if there is a claim for an injunction or a declaration in addition to or instead of a claim for compensation, it will be a fixed date action (CCR Ord 3, r 2(1)) and must be issued in either the county court where the defendant resides or carries on business, or in the county court for the district in which the cause of action wholly or partly arose (CCR Ord 4, r 3(1)(*a*),(*b*)). Either party may apply for transfer to a more convenient court after issue (CCR Ord 16, r 1). An application for the modification of an agreement made void by s 26 (see p xx) should be commenced by an originating application under Ord 3, r 4 in the court for the district in which the respondent, or any of the respondents, resides or carries on business, or in the court for the district in which the contract was made. All persons who would be affected by any modification should be made respondents to or given notice of the application (s 26(4)). A reference to the court made by a service provider occupying premises under a lease or by a disabled person made under para 6 of Sched 3 in relation to a proposed alteration (see p 245) should also be made by way of an originating application under Ord 3, r 4.

Arbitration

Small claims in the county court are dealt with by references to arbitration under CCR Ord 19. This provides a procedure to deal with claims with less formality and is often known as the 'small claims court'. Many claims under Pt III of the DDA are likely to be referred to arbitration on the grounds that they involve less than £3,000. In fact, one purpose of the power (as yet unexercised) to limit compensation for injury to feelings was 'to help ensure that the vast majority of cases can be dealt with under the small claims procedure' (*Hansard*, HL, Vol 566, col 1065).

The reference to arbitration

Where the claim does not exceed £3,000 (see p 189 below in relation to the statement of the value of the action), the district judge will refer the claim to arbitration upon the receipt of a defence (Ord 19, r 3(1)). The procedure is not restricted to monetary claims and an injunction may be granted in an action that has been referred to arbitration (*Joyce* v *Liverpool* [1995] 3 All ER 110). Presumably a declaration may also be made. Therefore, the inclusion of claims for those remedies will not prevent a reference to arbitration. However, the district judge may rescind the reference by ordering a trial of the action in court if he is satisfied:

(a) that the claim involves a difficult question of law or a complex question of fact;
(b) an allegation of fraud;
(c) that the parties agree that the dispute should be tried in court; or
(d) that it would be unreasonable for the claim to proceed to arbitration given the subject matter, the size of any counterclaim, the circumstances of the parties or the interests of any other person likely to be affected by the award (CCR Ord 19, r 3(2)).

'The circumstances of the parties [to be taken into account under Ord 19, r 3(2)(*d*)] may, for example, include physical disability, poor sight, pronounced stammer or inability to read' (*Afzal* v *Ford Motor Co Ltd* [1994] 4 All ER 720, CA). If a plaintiff considers that there are grounds for rescinding a reference to arbitration, they may be set out in the particulars of claim. It is a misuse of the process of the court for a plaintiff to claim more than £3,000 in order to avoid a reference to arbitration when he does not reasonably and genuinely expect to recover more than that sum (*Afzal* v *Ford Motor Co Ltd* above). Where an action is not referred to arbitration because of such an inflated claim, the plaintiff may be penalised in costs (*Barrowclough* v *British Gas Corpn* [1986] CLY 459). Where the defendant alleges that the claim involves less than the £3,000 despite the plaintiff claiming damages in excess thereof, the defendant should plead this in his defence (*Afzal* v *Ford Motor Co Ltd* above), although a failure to apply for a reference to arbitration will not prevent a plaintiff from being penalised in costs (*Motley* v *Courtaulds plc* [1990] 12 LS Gaz R 39, CA).

The procedure
The simplified procedure applicable once proceedings have been referred to arbitration is governed by CCR Ord 19, r 6. The usual rules regarding discovery and inspection, further and better particulars, interrogatories, notices to admit, expert evidence and the exchange of witness statements do not apply (CCR Ord 19, r 9). Fourteen days before the hearing, parties must send every other party copies of all documents that they intend to rely on at the hearing (CCR Ord 19, r 6(3)(*a*)). Seven days before the hearing, parties must send every other party copies of any expert report they intend to rely on and a list of the witnesses they intend to call CCR Ord 19, r 6(3)(*b*)). A district judge may decide to hold a preliminary appointment and/or to give further directions if necessary or desirable, including a direction that a party should clarify his claim or his defence (CCR Ord 19, rr 5, 6).

The hearing
Although hearing will usually be held in chambers at the court house, it may be held at any other place convenient to the parties (CCR Ord 19, r 7(2)). This power will be useful when the disabled person is unable to travel to the court house. The hearing is conducted informally and the strict rules of evidence do not apply (CCR Ord 19, r 7(3)). The hearing will be in private unless the arbitrator (usually a district judge) orders otherwise (CCR Ord 19, r 7(3)). The arbitrator may assist a party by putting questions to witnesses or the other party and should explain any legal terms used (CCR Ord 19, r 7(4)). Where the parties consent, the arbitrator may consult an expert, call for an expert report or invite an expert to attend the hearing as an assessor before giving his decision (CCR Ord 19, r 6). This may be useful where there is a dispute as to whether a plaintiff has or had a disability within the meaning of s 1.

Appeals
A final decision made in proceedings referred to arbitration may only be set aside on appeal on the grounds of an error of law or misconduct by the arbitrator (CCR Ord 19, r 8(1)), although there is a wider power to set aside orders made in the absence of a party (CCR Ord 19, r 8(2) and Ord 37, r 2).

Costs and representation

If the proceedings are referred to arbitration, only limited costs may be awarded or recovered (CCR Ord 19, r 4). As a result, legal aid will not be available for representation at such hearings. Although a party may be legally represented, he or she need not be and may act in person or be represented by a lay representative (such as a friend or lay adviser) at a small claims hearing (Lay Representatives (Rights of Audience) Order 1992 (SI No 1966)). A lay representative only has rights of audience if the person represented attends the hearing (1992 SI No 1966, r 7, para 2(2)). As a corporate body cannot attend, it cannot be represented by a lay representative under that Order and nor can a company represented by a director be regarded as a litigant in person (*Jonathan Alexander Ltd* v *Proctor* (1966) *The Times*, 3 January, CA). However, the arbitrator has a discretion to allow the company to be represented by a person other than a lawyer (Courts and Legal Services Act 1990, s 27(2)(*c*), and *Charles P Kinnell & Co Ltd* v *Harding Wace & Co* [1918] 1 KB 405, CA).

Judicial review

The restriction on civil proceedings in para 5 to Sched 3 does not prevent the making of an application for judicial review. It will not be granted where alternative means of relief are available and will not be granted where the applicant could have issued proceedings in the county court or sheriff court under s 25. Such a claim may be made where, for example, a local authority adopts a policy contrary to the DDA, for example a policy reducing the number of offers made to disabled applicants for housing. An organisation of or for disabled people may be able to bring such a claim where it has sufficient interest for the purposes of RSC Ord 53, r 3 (see *R* v *Inland Revenue Commissioners, ex p National Federation of Self-Employed and Small Businesses* [1982] AC 617 at 659). See p 101 above.

Commencement of proceedings

Proceedings in the county court should be commenced by action and brought by plaint (CCR Ord 3, r 1). The plaintiff should file summons or a request for the issue of a summons together with particulars of claim and copies thereof (ie a copy for each defendant) as required by CCR Ord 6 (CCR Ord 3, r 3(1), (1A)). In addition, any fee payable under s 128 of the CCA 1984 and the County Court Fees Order 1982 (SI No 1706) must be paid at the time of filing the documents or the proceedings will not be instituted (CCR Ord 50, r 7). No fee is payable where the person is on income support at the material time and the fee can be remitted in exceptional circumstances if payment would cause undue financial hardship (CCFO 1982, r 4). These documents and the court fee may be filed in person, by post or document exchange (CCR Ord 2, rr 4, 5).

Time limits

As a general rule, a county court shall not consider a claim under s 25 unless proceedings are instituted before the end of the period of six months beginning when the act complained of was done (para 6(1) of Sched 3). The time limit may be extended in the circumstances set out below.

The date proceedings are instituted

Where the necessary documents and any court fee are filed in person, the proceedings are instituted on the day they are filed. Where documents and fee are sent by post, the claim will be treated as having been instituted on the day that the documents are received in the court office even though there may be a delay in acting upon them (*Aly* v *Aly* (1984) 128 Sol Jo 65, CA). CCR Ord 3, r 5(1) makes clear that documents sent by post will only institute a claim if the documents are actually received. If the time limit expires on a day on which the court office is shut, the proceedings will probably be treated as having been issued in time if they are instituted on the day that the office reopens (*Pritam Kaur* v *S Russell & Sons Ltd* [1973] 1 QB 336, and see *Hodgson* v *Armstrong* [1967] 2 QB 299 in relation to documents not delivered to a court office on a Saturday or Easter Monday because of a direction of the county court to the Post Office).

The date of the discriminatory act

As with employment cases, it will usually be clear when the act complained of took place. If the discrimination consists of refusing to serve someone in a restaurant, the act took place on the date of the refusal. There are statutory rules for the following situations which mirror the employment provisions (para 6(3) of Sched 3).

Contractual terms

If the unlawful act of discrimination is attributable to a term in a contract, that act is to be treated as extending throughout the duration of the contract (para 6(4)(*a*) and see p 104 above).

Continuing acts

Any act extending over a period shall be treated as done at the end of that period (para 6(4)(*b*) and see p 104 above).

Deliberate omissions

A deliberate omission shall be treated as done when the person in question decided upon it (para 6(4)(*c*)). In the absence of evidence establishing the contrary, a person shall be taken to decide upon an omission:
    (a) when he does an act inconsistent with doing the omitted act; or

(b) if he has done no such inconsistent act, when the period expires within which he might reasonably have been expected to do the omitted act if it was to be done (para 6(5) (and see p 105 above).

Extending the time limit

That time limit will be extended by two months where a person appointed in connection with the arrangements made under s 28 for the provision of advice or assistance is approached before the end of the initial six-month period (para 6(2) of Sched 3). Paragraph 6(2) does not expressly refer to an approach by the disabled person and it may be that an approach by either the prospective plaintiff or prospective defendant will be sufficient to extend the time limit under this provision. In addition, a court may consider a claim instituted after the expiry of the time limit if, in all the circumstances of the case, it considers that it is just and equitable to do so (para 6(3) of Sched 3). Tribunals hearing employment cases under Pt II have the same power to hear claims made out of time if it is just and equitable to do so and is discussed in detail at p 106 above.

The particulars of claim

The particulars of claim must specify the cause of action and the relief and set out the material facts relied upon (CCR Ord 6, r 1(1)). Although the facts relied on must be pleaded, the evidence relied on to prove those facts does not. If insufficient particulars are given, further particulars may be ordered on the defendant's application or of the court's own motion (CCR Ord 6, r 7(1)). However, parties must ensure that the case is properly pleaded and should not rely upon further particulars being ordered or requested. A party will often not be allowed to raise matters that should have been but were not pleaded. The rules of pleading are enforced much more strictly in the county court than they are in employment cases before tribunals. In general, the particulars of claim should deal with the following matters, although each case must be considered individually. A precedent is at appendix 8.

The right to bring the claim

The plaintiff will need to establish his or her right to bring a claim under Pt III. Unless the claim is for victimisation, the particulars should state that the plaintiff is or was a disabled person within the meaning of ss 1 or 2 of the DDA (see p 3 above) and should give sufficient particulars to allow the defendant to know how the plaintiff claims to satisfy the definition. Where the claim is for victimisation by reference to s 55 (below at p 251) that should be stated and particulars given of the matters referred to in s 55 (for example stating when and where the plaintiff gave evidence in proceedings under the DDA and identifying those proceedings).

The status of the defendant and the nature of the transaction

It will be necessary to show that the defendant was subject to the relevant provisions of the DDA. For example, it may be necessary to plead that the defendant was a provider of services within the meaning of s 19(2) or a person with power to dispose of premises within the meaning of s 22(1). Again, sufficient particulars should be given of the facts relied on to establish that the defendant was such a person. It will often be useful to refer to the relevant sections of the DDA in the pleading. In addition, the plaintiff will need to set out the nature of the relevant transaction in order to establish that it was covered by Pt III. Where the case concerns the goods and services provisions, the particulars of claim should state that the plaintiff sought to make use of a service provided by the defendant to members of the public and identify the service in question. For example, if the case involves a refusal to serve a disabled person in a restaurant, the particulars of claim should state when and where the disabled person sought to use the restaurant. If the claim concerns the premises provisions, the particulars may need to identify the premises in question and state that the plaintiff sought to obtain a tenancy of them or was in occupation of them as appropriate. In a claim relating to s 22(1)(c), the particulars will set out that the details of any application by the plaintiff to be registered on the defendant's waiting list (eg 'On 30 March 1997 the plaintiff delivered a written application for registration on the defendant's housing waiting list to the defendant's offices at ...').

The facts comprising discrimination

Particular care should be taken to plead the facts alleged to comprise the unlawful acts, to ensure that, as pleaded, they fall within the provisions of Pt III that are relied upon. If the claim is for less favourable treatment, the treatment complained of should be identified.

The duty to adjust

Where the claim is made under s 19(1)(b) and concerns a failure to comply with the duty to adjust, the circumstances giving rise to the duty to adjust, the step that should have been taken and the consequences of failing to take it should be set out. In particular, sufficient particulars should be given of why the failure to take that step made it impossible or unreasonably difficult for the plaintiff to make use of the service.

The loss

Particulars must be given of any loss suffered by the plaintiff. In many cases, the only loss will be injury to feelings but particulars should still be given. If there are any special damages, such as the costs of any alternative arrangements, they must be particularised or they will not be recoverable (*Ilkiw* v *Samuels* [1963] 2 All ER 879). A plaintiff must plead any aggravated damages (Ord 6, r 1B and see p 197 below).

The remedy sought

The remedy sought must be set out in the particulars of claim, and is usually done in the prayer. This will usually be for damages and may also be for a declaration or an injunction. A plaintiff must plead any claim for interest (Ord 6, r 1A).

A statement of the value of the claim

The pleading should contain a statement of the value of the claim. This should either be damages limited to £3,000 (the limit for a reference to arbitration); damages limited to £5,000 (the limit for a hearing before a district judge); or damages in excess of £5,000. If there is no statement of value, it will be treated as limited to £5,000 (CCR Ord 6, r 1(1A) and Ord 21, r 5(1)(*b*)). The consequences of limiting (or not limiting) a claim to £3,000 are dealt with above at p 183.

Defence

The defence should be delivered to the court within 14 days of service of the summons (CCR Ord 9, r 2). Although a defence delivered late will be valid if judgment has not been entered (CCR Ord 9, r 1), a defendant will be at risk of judgment in default (CCR Ord 9, rr 4A and 6) and could be ordered to pay the costs incurred as a consequence of the delay (CCR Ord 9, r 3) including the costs of any application to set aside judgment. A default action will be automatically struck out if no defence has been delivered and no judgment has been entered and 12 months have expired from the date of service of the default summons (CCR Ord 9, r 10). The defence should make clear what factual allegations in the particulars of claim are disputed and what are admitted. It should also set out any positive case. Some examples follow below.

The right to bring the claim

Unless the claim is for victimisation, the defence should state whether it is admitted, not admitted or denied that the plaintiff is or was a disabled person (see p 3 above) and should give sufficient particulars to allow the plaintiff to know why the defendant says the definition is not satisfied. For example, it may be necessary to deny that the plaintiff suffers from the condition stated in the particulars of claim and/or assert that the condition is not a clinically well-recognised mental illness. If the court does not have jurisdiction to hear the claim because it was made outside the time limit in Sched 3 para 6, this should be raised in the defence.

The status of the defendant and the nature of the transaction

Indicate whether it is agreed that the defendant and the transaction is subject to the relevant provisions of the DDA. There will often be no dispute on this point. However, if the service provider denies that it provided or was prepared to provide the relevant service to members of the public or at all for the purposes of s 19, this should be pleaded. Similarly, if the transaction is said to be excluded, for example on the grounds that the service concerned the use of means of transport under s 19(5)(b) or that the premises concerned were small premises under s 23, the facts relied on should be set out.

The facts comprising discrimination

The defence should make clear the extent to which the facts alleged by the plaintiff as comprising discrimination are admitted, not admitted or denied. For example, the defence may admit not providing a service to the plaintiff but deny that this was deliberate. Alternatively, it may deny that the reason for refusing to provide a service or grant a tenancy was related to the disability. If a positive case is to be relied upon, this should be pleaded. For example, if the defendant's case is that the plaintiff was refused entry to a restaurant because he was drunk, this should be stated. In particular, if the defendant's case is that the treatment was justified under s 20(2) or 24(2), the defence should state the opinion that was held and provide sufficient particulars of the grounds for that opinion to establish that it was reasonable.

The duty to adjust

The defence should state whether it is admitted that the defendant was under any duty to adjust or was under a specific duty to take the step referred to in the particulars of claim. If the step relied on by the plaintiff was unreasonable, give particulars of why it was unreasonable. Refer to any alternative step that had been taken. Again, any positive defence, such as justification, the financial limit or an averment that the alteration would have resulted in a fundamental alteration in the nature of the service should be pleaded and particularised.

The loss and value of the claim

As a general rule it is unnecessary to plead in detail to the allegations of loss. In most cases, it will be enough to not admit any loss was suffered and to deny that any loss suffered was caused by any unlawful act by the defendant. However, if the claim is for damages in excess of £3,000, and the defendant considers this figure to be inflated, the defence can deny that there is any reasonable prospect of recovering £3,000 and aver that the matter should be referred to arbitration (see *Afzal* v *Ford Motor Co Ltd* [1994] 4 All ER 720 CA). Even if the matter is not in fact referred to arbitration, this can be of assistance in relation to costs.

Proceedings by persons under a disability

For the purposes of the County Court Rules, a person is a 'person under a disability' if he or she is either:
  (a) under 18 years of age; or
  (b) a person who is incapable of managing his or her property and affairs by reason of mental disorder within the meaning of the MHA 1983 is a 'mental patient' (CCR Ord 1, r 3).

A 'person under a disability' cannot bring or make a claim in the county court except by his next friend (CCR Ord 10, r 1). Where a person is authorised under Pt VII of the MHA 1983 to conduct legal proceedings in the name of a mental patient, that person is entitled to be the next friend unless the court appoints some other person to act (CCR Ord 10, r 1(3)). If the person so authorised wishes to act as next friend, an office copy of the order or other authorisation under Pt VII, sealed by the Court of Protection, should be delivered at the court office prior to the commencement of proceedings (CCR Ord 10, r 2(*a*)). If the person wishing to be appointed as next friend is not so authorised under Pt VII, he or she should deliver to the court office a written undertaking to be responsible for any costs which the person under a disability may be ordered and fail to pay (CCR Ord 10, r 2(*b*)). The undertaking should be attested by a solicitor or officer of the court authorised to take affidavits. If proceedings are issued by a 'person under a disability' without a next friend, the court may either order the proceedings to be struck out or, upon application, appoint as next friend a person authorised under Pt VII or a person giving the application referred to above (CCR Ord 10, r 3). Proceedings that are referred to arbitration are still proceedings for the purpose of this rule. There is nothing in the County Court Rules to require a next friend to act by a solicitor, although such a rule exists under the RSC Ord 80, r 2(3).

'Where in any proceedings money is claimed by or on behalf of a person under a disability, no settlement, compromise or payment and no acceptance of money paid into court ... shall ... be valid without the approval of the court' (CCR Ord 10, r 10(1)). A claim for compensation under the DDA is a claim for money. The settlement may be approved by either a judge or district judge (CCR Ord 10, r 10(3)). Where money is recovered by a 'person under a disability' the money is to be paid into or remain in court and not to be paid to the next friend or person under a disability unless the court so directs (CCR Ord 10, r 11(1)). Where the plaintiff is a mental patient, the proper practice is to pay the money into court or to the Court of Protection (see *Leather* v *Kirby* [1965] 3 All ER 927n and *Practice Note: Mental Health Transfer of Damages* [1991] 1 WLR 2).

Interlocutory steps and directions

County court claims made under the DDA will be subject to the automatic directions under CCR Ord 17, r 11. This makes provision for various matters, such as discovery, the disclosure of expert reports, exchange of witness statements and requesting a date for trial. In particular, they provide that a hearing date should be requested six months after pleadings are deemed to be closed (Ord 17, r 11(3)(d)). If no such request is made 15 months after the pleadings are deemed to be closed, the action is automatically struck out and will not easily be reinstated (*Rastin v British Steel plc* [1994] 2 All ER 641). Pleadings are deemed to be closed 14 days after the delivery of a defence (28 days where there is a counterclaim) (Ord 17, r 11(11)(a)). In addition, the county court has a wide power to give such directions as it thinks proper with regard to any matter arising in the course of proceedings (CCR Ord 13, r 2).

Hopeless claims or defences

A claim or defence may order the whole or part of any pleading to be struck out on the grounds that:

(a) it discloses no reasonable cause of action or defence;
(b) it is scandalous, frivolous or vexatious;
(c) it may prejudice, embarrass or delay the fair trial of the action; or
(d) it is otherwise an abuse of the process of the court.

As a general rule, a claim will only be struck out as disclosing no cause of action where it is plain and obvious that it will not succeed (*Lonrho plc v Fayed (No 2)* [1991] 4 All ER 961). Alternatively, a plaintiff can make an application on affidavit for summary judgment where there is no real defence (CCR Ord 14, r 9). However, an application for summary judgment is unlikely to be appropriate in many claims under the DDA. Summary judgment is not available where the claim has been referred to arbitration (CCR Ord 9, r 14(1)(a)).

Further particulars

The court may order either party to deliver any pleading or give any particulars that it thinks necessary to define the issues in the proceedings (CCR Ord 13, r 2(2)(a)). The principles on which they will be ordered are broadly similar to those in tribunal proceedings (see p 111 above). A party seeking further particulars should initially make a formal request under cover of a letter. If the other party fails to reply adequately or at all, an application should be made on notice for an order (Ord 13, r 1(2)). If there is still no reply, or no adequate reply, an application for an order striking out the claim or debarring the defendant from continuing in default of compliance (an 'unless order' under Ord 13, r 2(2)(b)) should be made, again on notice.

Amendment

Any pleading may be amended with the leave of the court (Ord 15, r 1(*a*)) or with the consent of the other party (CCR Ord 15, r 2(1)(*b*)). Trivial errors, such as misspellings and clerical mistakes may be corrected under CCR Ord 15, r 5, often known as 'the slip rule'. An amendment will generally be granted if it can be allowed without injustice to the other side, although the party amending will usually bear the costs.

Joinder of parties

A court has power to add, strike out or substitute parties (CCR Ord 15, r 1(1)(*b*)). This may be used where the plaintiff has wrongly identified the defendant in the summons.

Premises occupied under a lease

Joinder will be particularly important in cases involving the duty to adjust physical features in premises occupied under a lease, once the relevant provisions come into force. If the adjustment was not made because a lessor unreasonably refused to consent to the occupier making the alteration, the lessor may be liable instead of the occupier (see generally p 245 below). Where a disabled person brings a complaint against a service provider under s 25 either the occupier or the plaintiff (pursuer in Scotland) can ask the court to join the lessor (including the superior lessor) to the proceedings (Sched 4, para 7(1)). Such a request must be granted if made before the hearing of the claim begins (Sched 4, para 7(2)); may be granted if made after the hearing begins (para 7(3)); but must not be granted if made after the tribunal has determined the complaint (para 7(4)). Where an application is made so late as to necessitate an adjournment, for example on or shortly before the date fixed for the hearing of the action, it may be that there will be a penalty in costs. Where the lessor has been joined to the proceedings, the court may determine whether or not the lessor unreasonably refused consent or consented subject to unreasonable conditions (para 7(5)). See p 197 below as to the consequences of such a determination. In addition, the occupier *or* the disabled person will be able to issue proceedings against the lessor directly under Sched 4, para 6 (see p 245).

Discovery and inspection of documents

Unless the action is referred to arbitration, a party will be ordered to provide discovery and inspection of relevant documents (see generally Ord 14, rr 1–9). However, discovery will not be ordered if the court is satisfied that it is not necessary either for disposing fairly of the action or for saving costs (CCR Ord 14, r 8). Where a party fails to comply with an order for discovery, an application may be made for an order striking out the claim or debarring the defendant from continuing in default of compliance (an 'unless order' under

Ord 14, r 10(1)). Again, the application should be made on notice (Ord 13, r 1(2)). As in tribunal proceedings, discovery may be resisted on the grounds that it is unnecessary, or that documents are privileged or protected by public interest immunity (see p 112 above).

Witness orders

A court has the power to make an order requiring any person within Great Britain to attend as a witness, and if the order so requires, to produce documents in his possession (CCR Ord 20, r 12).

Interrogatories

A court has the power to require a party to answer interrogatories served on it by the other party (CCR Ord 14, r 11).

Notices to admit

A party may serve on another party a notice to admit facts or such parts of that party's case as are specified in the notice not less than 14 days before the trial or hearing (CCR Ord 20, r 2(1)). If the party served does not admit in writing the facts specified within seven days of service, and those facts are proven, the party served will bear the costs of proving those facts unless the court otherwise directs, even if successful overall (CRR Ord 20, r 2(2)). For example, where a defendant has denied or not admitted that a plaintiff is a disabled person for the purposes of the DDA, the plaintiff could serve the defendant with a notice to admit that the plaintiff is a disabled person for the purposes of the DDA. If the defendant did not make an admission in writing within seven days and it is established that the plaintiff was a disabled person at trial, the defendant will usually bear the costs of that issue even if he successfully defends the claim (see p 24 above).

Expert evidence

The use of all expert evidence, for example medical evidence, evidence from a surveyor as to the feasibility of altering premises, or from a communications expert as to the use of auxiliary aids, is governed by CCR Ord 20, r 27. In summary, such evidence may only be adduced if:
- (1) the party adducing the evidence has complied with the automatic directions relating to experts reports in CCR Ord 17, r 11; or
- (2) the party adducing the evidence has applied to the court for directions under CCR Ord 20, rr 27 and 28; or
- (3) all parties consent; or
- (4) if the court grants leave.

See p 25 above in relation to expert evidence for the purposes of establishing whether or not a person is a disabled person within the meaning of ss 1 and 2 of the DDA.

Assessors

Although there is no express provision in the DDA relating to assessors (compare SDA 1975, s 66(6) and RRA 1976, s 67(4)) the judge (or district judge) may, upon the application of either party, summon one or more persons of relevant skill and experience to act as assessors under s 63 of the County Courts Act 1984. The assessors will advise the judge, although it is still for the judge to decide upon the law and merits (*The Aid* (1881) 6 PD 84). An application for an assessor must be made not less than 14 days before the hearing in accordance with the procedure set out in CCR Ord 13, r 11.

The hearing

The action may be heard by a judge or district judge (sitting with any assessors that have been appointed) unless the claim is in excess of £5,000 when it can only be heard by a judge. The hearing will be relatively formal. Evidence is given on oath or affirmation. The plaintiff will usually go first, unless the only burden of proof falls upon the defendant. For example, a defendant will go first if he has admitted that the plaintiff is a disabled person and that he treated the plaintiff less favourably for a reason that relates to his disability and defends the claim only on the basis that the less favourable treatment was justified. Hearings are usually held in public unless there are compelling reasons not to (CCR Ord 20, r 4). A person is competent to give evidence notwithstanding any mental disorder unless he cannot understand the oath and the matters in question (*R v Hill* (1851) 20 LJMC 222). There is no power to restrict the reporting of a county court action on that grounds that it involves evidence of a personal nature (see p 117 above for the powers in cases before tribunals).

Certificates

A certificate of registration issued under the Disabled Persons (Employment) Act 1944 is conclusive (see p 117 above). A certificate signed by or on behalf of a Minister of the Crown certifying that matters were imposed by a Minister of the Crown or were done for the purposes of safeguarding national security are conclusive (see p 251 below).

Appeals

An appeal from a final order of a district judge is made to a judge (CCR Ord 39, r 6). Any appeal from a judge is made to the Court of Appeal. Where the value of the claim is less than £5,000, the appeal may be made only with the leave of the judge or the Court of Appeal (RSC Ord 59, r 3A and County Court Appeals Order 1991 SI No 1877).

Remedies

The remedies available to a county court or sheriff court in a claim under s 25 are those exercisable by the High Court or Court of Session (s 25(5)), namely an award of damages, the making of a declaration or the grant of an injunction. There will be special provisions relating to premises occupied under a lease once the duty to adjust by adapting premises comes into effect. Finally, a county court has power to make such order as it thinks just to modify an agreement which contravenes s 26(1).

Declaration

A declaration is a statement of the plaintiff's rights, and, if appropriate, a statement that (and if necessary of how) the defendant violated those plaintiff's rights.

Injunction

The county court may grant an injunction restraining the defendant from infringing the plaintiff's rights in future or requiring him to take any step necessary to prevent such an infringement in the future. It is a discretionary remedy. Although there is no power under the DDA to increase the award of compensation if an injunction is breached, the injunction can be enforced by a fine or committal to prison as contempt of court (CCR Ord 29) and a summary award of damages made where the contempt amounts also to a breach of contract in relation to the other party (*Midland Marts Ltd* v *Hobday* [1989] 3 All ER 246.

Compensation

The amount of compensation is to be determined by applying the ordinary principles used to calculate damages in claims in tort or (in Scotland) in reparation for breach. This can (and usually will) include a sum for injury to feelings (s 25(2)). The principles for assessing damages for injury to feelings is considered in detail at p 122 above. In cases under Pt III, a maximum amount of damages to be awarded for injury to feelings may be prescribed under para 7 of Sched 3. This would include any award of aggravated damages. Although no figure has been prescribed at the time of writing, it is likely that such damages will be limited to £3,000, the maximum figure for references to arbitration (see p 183 above). However, this limit will not apply to damages for financial loss caused by the discrimination. Although financial loss in cases under Pt III is likely to be encountered less frequently or to involve smaller sums than in employment cases, it is recoverable if proven. All losses flowing directly from the unlawful discrimination should be compensated in damages. For example, where a person is refused access to a particular service, there may be additional costs of obtaining alternative services at short notice. However, the plaintiff would be under a duty to mitigate his or her loss.

Aggravated damages and exemplary damages

An award of aggravated damages may be made where the defendant has acted in a high-handed, malicious, insulting or oppressive manner (*Alexander* v *the Home Office* [1988] 2 All ER 118). However, it is almost certain that an award of exemplary damages cannot be made.

Interest

Although interest can be awarded under s 69 of the County Courts Act 1984, it will not generally be awarded in relation to damages for non-economic loss such as injury to feelings (*Holtham* v *Metropolitan Police Comr* (1987) *The Times*, 28 November, CA). Interest, currently at 8 per cent, will accrue on judgment debts of £5,000 or more (County Courts Act 1984, s 74 and the County Courts (Interest on Judgment Debts) Order 1991 SI No 1184).

Remedies and premises occupied under a lease

In a case where a lessor has been joined as a defendant to a claim under s 25, and the court decides that the lessor had unreasonably failed to give consent to an alteration required under the duty to adjust or imposed unreasonable conditions (para 7(5) of Sched 4, and see p 193) the court may

(1) make such declaration as it considers appropriate (para 7(6)(*a*); and/ or
(2) make an order authorising the occupier to make the alteration specified in the order (para 7(6)(*b*)); and/or
(3) order the lessor to pay compensation to the plaintiff (para 7(6)(*c*)). If the court orders the lessor to do so, it may not order the occupier to do so (para 7(8)).

An order authorising an alteration under sub-para 7(6)(*b*) may require the occupier to comply with conditions specified in the order (sub-para 7(7)). This appears to refer to conditions to be complied with if the occupier makes the authorised alteration. It does not allow the court to require the occupier to make the alteration. It is uncertain whether the court's general powers to grant an injunction would allow it to require the occupier to make such an alteration, or on what principles any such powers should be exercised.

Modifying agreements

A county court or sheriff court may make such order as it thinks just for modifying an agreement affected by s 26(1) (see p 138 above). This may involve deleting the offending clause (although this is not strictly necessary as it is made void by s 26(1)), or altering it so that it no longer purports to require any person to do anything in contravention of, limit the operation of or restrict claims under the legislation. Such an order will only be made if all persons who would be affected by the order have been given notice of the application and afforded an opportunity to make representations to the court (s 26(5) subject to the court's powers to dispense with notice (s 26(5)). Such an order may have retrospective effect (s 26(6)).

Costs

Costs usually follow the event, such that a successful party recovers his or her costs from the unsuccessful party.

Part 4

Education and Transport

Chapter 14

Education

Introduction

The DDA makes only limited provision relating to education. In Part IV, it requires schools colleges and universities in England and Wales to inform parents, pupils and students about the facilities available for disabled people. Education is currently excluded from the provisions relating to goods, services and facilities, although the Secretary of State has the power to bring education within those provisions by regulations (s 19(5)). The rationale for the exclusion is that other legislation such as the Further and Higher Education Act 1992 (FHEA 1992), the Education Act 1996 (EA 1996) and the *Code of Practice on the Identification and Assessment of Special Educational Needs* already deals with the needs of disabled people in this area. The provisions of Pt IV are intended to supplement the Education Act 1996 in relation to schools. Children (defined as including those aged 19) with special educational needs must be placed in mainstream schools subject to parental wishes, provided the placement is appropriate to the child's needs, does not conflict with the interests of other children in the school, and is an efficient use of the resources of the Local Education Authority (LEA). The school must publish the Special Educational Needs (SEN) policy. The DDA requires schools to include information concerning the following:

(a) arrangements for admission of disabled pupils;
(b) ways in which they will ensure disabled pupils receive the same treatment as other pupils; and
(c) the facilities provided to enable disabled pupils to access the school's education.

Under the Further and Higher Education Act 1992, further education providers are already required to take account of the needs of students with learning and other disabilities when fulfilling duties to provide education. The DDA requires them further to publish disability statements, and report to the government on their progress, and future plans for providing students with disabilities with education. In Scotland the Secretary of State for Scotland and individual college management boards are responsible for meeting the educational needs of disabled students. In Northern Ireland the Education and Library Boards fund further education institutions, and they have a duty to take the needs of disabled students into account when providing educational facilities.

The DDA also requires Higher Education Funding Councils (England, Wales and Scotland) to take account of the needs of disabled students, and to requires institutions funded by them to provide disability statements. The Teacher Training Agency will also be required to take account of the needs of disabled people when funding teacher training courses.

The core of the education provisions for further education is the disability statement. This must give information about their facilities for disabled people. They may include for example information about access for disabled students, specialist equipment, and available counselling. Regulations are to be made to govern the contents of these statements for England and Wales. In relation to such statements for further education institutions see Education (Disability Statements for Further Education Institutions) Regulations 1996 (SI No 1664).

Relationship with Pt III (Goods and Services)

The goods and services provisions of DDA 1995, ss 19–21 do not apply to education:

(a) which is funded or secured by a relevant body or provided at an establishment which is funded by a relevant body or Minister of the Crown; or

(b) any other establishment which is a school as defined in s 4(1) of the Education Act 1996 or s 135(1) of the Education (Scotland) Act 1980 (DDA 1995, s 19(5)(a)).

Although the Secretary of State may prescribe circumstances in which the provisions of ss 19 to 21 will apply to such education, no such regulations have yet been made. Regulations have provided that certain ancillary services to education are also excluded from the goods and services provisions.

Education

The term 'education' is not defined in the Act. There is no reason why it should include anything which goes beyond teaching itself. This would limit the effect of s 19(5)(a) to courses of instruction. Subject to the regulations relating to ancillary services referred to below (at p 203), the other services provided by the relevant body, establishment or school are covered by the goods and services provisions. Some services provided to students are likely to be services subject to the goods and services provisions. If a school provides catering facilities, it is arguable that these are not education, and therefore are subject to the provisions relating to goods and services.

Relevant body

'Relevant bodies' are listed in s 19(6):

(a) a local education authority in England and Wales;

(b) an education authority in Scotland;

(c) the Funding Agency for Schools;

(d) the Schools Funding Council for Wales;
(e) the Further Education Funding Council for England;
(f) the Further Education Funding Council for Wales;
(g) the Higher Education Funding Council for England;
(h) the Scottish Higher Education Funding Council;
(i) the Higher Education Funding Council for Wales;
(j) the Teacher Training Agency;
(k) a voluntary organisation; or
(l) a body of a prescribed kind.
In addition, the term 'relevant body' includes an Education and Library Board in Northern Ireland (Sched 9, para 9(3)).

School

School is defined in s 4(1) of the Education Act 1996 or s 135(1) of the Education (Scotland) Act 1980 (s 19(5)(*a*)). By s 4(1), for the purposes of the Education Acts 'school' means an educational institution not within the further education sector or the higher education sector, being an institution for providing any one or more of the following:
(a) primary education;
(b) secondary education, which is defined as full-time education suitable to the requirements of pupils of compulsory school age; and
(c) further education, which is defined as full-time education suitable to the requirements of persons over compulsory school age who have not attained the age of 19 years;
whether or not the institution also provides part-time education suitable to the requirements of junior pupils further education or other secondary education.

Other educational services

The DD(SP) Regs 1996 exempts certain other educational services from ss 19 to 21 of the DDA. In summary, those educational services are:
(a) some services provided by an LEA;
(b) the provision of social, cultural and recreational activities and facilities for physical education and training by voluntary organisations;
(c) the provision of facilities for research at relevant establishments; and
(d) some assessments of pupils (reg 9(1)).
Each class of services is discussed in more detail below.

Services provided by an LEA under s 15 of the Education Act 1996
Regulation 9(1)(*a*) of the DD(SP) Regs 1996 exempts services provided by a LEA in carrying out its functions under s 41 or 53 of the Education Act 1944, (now EA 1996, s 15) or by an Education Authority in Scotland carrying out its functions under s 1(3) of the Education (Scotland) Act 1980. Section 15 deals with the functions of LEAs in respect of further education. In this context 'further education' means:

(a) full-time and part-time education suitable to the requirements of persons over compulsory school age (including vocational, social, physical and recreational training); and

(b) organised leisure-time occupation provided in connection with the provision of such education (s 2(3)). 'Organised leisure time' means leisure-time occupation, in such organised cultural training and recreative activities as are suited to their requirements, for any persons over compulsory school age who are able and willing to profit by facilities provided for that purpose (s 2(6)).

'Further education' does not include higher education or secondary education (s 2(3)).

The functions of the LEA are set out in s 15. It is the duty of every LEA to secure the provision for their area of adequate facilities for further education (s 15(1)). This duty does not apply to education to which ss 2(1) or 3(1) of the Further and Higher Education Act 1992 applies (s 15(3)). A LEA may secure the provision of further education for persons from other areas (s 15(4)). The LEA has a duty to publish disability statements at such intervals as may be prescribed by the Secretary of State. A 'disability statement' means a statement containing information of a prescribed description about the provision of facilities for further education made by the local education authority in respect of persons who are disabled persons for the purposes of the DDA 1995 (EA 1996, s 528). In exercising their functions under s 15 a LEA must have regard to any educational facilities provided by institutions within the higher education sector or the further education sector, and other bodies, which are provided for, or available for use by persons in, their area (s 15(5)). Further, in exercising these functions the LEA must have regard to the requirements of persons over compulsory school age who have learning difficulties (s 15(5)). For these purposes a person has a 'learning difficulty' if:

(a) he has a significantly greater difficulty in learning than the majority of persons of his age; or

(b) he has a disability which either prevents or hinders him from making use of facilities of a kind generally provided in pursuance of the duty under s 15(1) (see above) for persons of his age (s 15(6)). However, a person is not to be taken as having a learning difficulty solely because the language (or form of language) in which he is, or will be, taught is different from a language (or form of a language) which has at any time been spoken in his home (s 15(7)).

Finally, the LEA may do anything which appears to them to be necessary or expedient for the purposes of or in connection with the exercise of their functions under s 15 (s 15(8)). Services provided in connection with the exercise of these functions under s 15(8) will be exempted from the goods and services provisions of the DDA.

By s 3(1) of the FHEA 1992 a council must secure the provision, for the population of its area, of adequate facilities for part-time education suitable for persons of any age over compulsory school age, and full-time education suitable for persons of 19 and upwards. In respect of such education a LEA has power to do any of the following:

(1)   secure the provision for their area of such facilities as appear to them to be appropriate for meeting the needs of the population of their area; and

(2)   do anything which appears to them to be necessary or expedient for the purposes of or in connection with such provision.

The duty to secure such provision arises only under s 3(1). Therefore the provisions of the goods and services duties under the DDA applies to services or facilities to secure the provision for the population of a LEA's area adequate facilities for part-time education suitable for persons of any age over compulsory school age, and full-time education suitable for persons of 19 and upwards.

Arguably, where the LEA makes available catering facilities which are provided in connection with educational provision for those under compulsory school age, the goods and services provision do not apply. However where those catering facilities are provided in securing the provision of full time education suitable for those of 19 years and upwards, the goods and services provisions do apply. Section 508 of the Education Act 1996 provides that it is the duty of every local education authority to secure that the facilities for primary, secondary and further education provided for their area include adequate facilities for recreation and social and physical training. A local education authority may establish, maintain and manage, for that purpose (or assist in these activities in relation to) camps, holiday classes, playing fields, play centres, and other places (including playgrounds, gymnasiums, and swimming baths not appropriated to any school or other educational institution), at which facilities for recreation and training are available for persons receiving primary secondary or further education. The LEA may organise games expeditions and other activities for such persons. The LEA may defray or contribute towards the expenses of the activities. These facilities will not be subject to the goods and services provisions of the DDA 1995. However a local education authority, when making arrangements for the provision of facilities or the organisation of such activities must have regard to the expediency of co-operating with any voluntary societies or bodies whose objects incude the provision of facilities or the organisation of activities of a similar character. It is for this reason that the exemption also applies to such voluntary organisations. Dual use of school premises is governed by EA 1996, ss 149–152. Finally, leisure facilities provided in accordance with s 145 of the Local Government Act 1972 or s 19 of the Local Government (Miscellaneous Provisions) Act 1976 are covered by Pt III of the DDA 1995.

Voluntary organisations and recreational activities and facilities
Regulation 9(1)(*a*) of the DD(SP) Regs 1996 exempts the provision by a voluntary organisation of social, cultural and recreational activities and facilities for physical education and training, where such activities are designed to promote the personal or educational development of persons taking part in them.

Research facilities
The provision of facilities for research (including the supervision of or guidance of research) at relevant establishments is exempt from ss 19 to 21 of the DDA (DD(SP) Regs 1996, reg 9(1)(c)). A relevant establishment is an establishment referred to in s 19(5)(a)(ii) or funded by a body mentioned in para 19(6)(a) to (k) of the DDA (see p 202 above) or by a Minister of the Crown (DD(SP) Regs 1996 reg 9(2)).

Assessment
Regulation 9(1)(d) of the DD(SP) Regs 1996 exempts the assessment at a relevant establishment of pupils or students in connection with education provided to them by the establishment or by another relevant establishment, whether or not education has been provided to them by the establishment carrying out the assessment. Relevant establishment has the same meaning as in relation to research (DD(SP) Regs 1996, reg 9(2), see above). Assessment is dealt with below at p 209.

Teacher Training Agency
The DDA amends the Education Act 1994. Section 1 of that Act deals with the Teacher Training Agency. In exercising its functions it must 'have regard to' the requirements of disabled persons (DDA 1995, 29(3)).

The DDA and schools

We first consider the general structure of the process of assessing the needs of children with SEN, and drafting a statement setting out the assessed needs and the provision to be made in order to meet those needs. Clearly not every child with a Statement is disabled within the DDA 1995. The local education authority is obliged to make SEN provision to meet the needs of the child. This does not oblige the local education authority to make available the best possible education (*R* v *Surrey Heath County Council Education Committee, ex p H* (1984) 83 LGR 219). By s 324 of the EA 1996, the local education authority must specify the type of school or institution appropriate to meet the SEN and to specify the name of a particular school. Once a school is named in the statement the LEA is to arrange that the special educational provision specified in the statement is made for the child. It is not obliged to do this if the child's parents have made suitable arrangements. If a maintained sector school is specified, the governing body of that school is obliged to admit the child. The LEA may pay the fees, including board and lodging fees, of a child sent to a non-maintained school if that school is named in a statement, or if the LEA considers it to be in the child's interests for provision to be made for him at a school which is not a maintained school (EA 1996, s 348). A parent is entitled to a choice within maintained education, and effect is to be given to that choice by the school being named in the statement unless it is unsuitable to his age ability or aptitude or special educational needs, or if his attendance there would be incompatible with the provision of efficient education for all the children with whom he would be educated or the efficient use of resources (EA 1996, Sched 27).

Governing bodies of maintained schools should secure that provision is made for any pupil who has special educational needs (see EA 1996, s 317(1)(a)) They should secure that, if the head teacher or the appropriate governor has been informed by the LEA that a pupil has special educational needs, those needs are made known to all who are likely to teach him (see EA 1996, s 317(1)(b)). Governing bodies should secure that teachers in the school are aware of the importance of identifying, and providing for, those pupils who have special educational needs (see EA 1996, s 317(1)(c). If necessary or desirable to coordinate provision for pupils with SEN, the governing bodies should consult the LEA, the Funding Authorities and the governing bodies of other schools (EA 1996, s 317(3)). Governing bodies should ensure that the pupil joins in the activities of the school together with pupils who do not have SENs, so far as that is reasonably practical and compatible with the pupil receiving the necessary special educational provision, the efficient education of other children in the school and the efficient use of resources (see s 317(4)). The Governors should draw up and report annually to parents on their policy for pupils with special educational needs (s 161(5)).

Section 29(1) of the DDA amends s 161 of the Education Act 1993 (but now see EA 1996, s 317) by adding a new subs (6). The new duty on each county, voluntary or grant maintained school is that it should include in the annual report a report containing information as to the arrangements made for the admission of disabled pupils and the steps taken to prevent disabled pupils being treated less favourably than other pupils, together with the facilities provided to assist access to the school by disabled pupils. These are defined as pupils who are disabled persons under the DDA. The governing body's annual report must include information on the success of the SEN policy. If there have been any significant changes in policy it should identify these. It should record any consultation with the LEA, the Funding Authority and other schools and show what resources have been allocated to and amongst children with SEN over the year.

The School's SEN policies should contain:
(a) the objectives of the school's SEN policy;
(b) name of coordinator or teacher responsible;
(c) arrangements for coordination of provision;
(d) admission arrangements;
(e) any specialist provision; and
(f) any special units or special facilities to increase access to the school by pupils with SEN.

The policy should deal with the identification, assessment, provision and allocation of resources to and amongst pupils with SEN. The elements of the policy may result in less favourable treatment to a disabled person with one type of disability for a reason relating to that disability in comparison with how a person with a different treatment would have been treated. All the elements of the policy except education and assessment are amenable to the provisions on goods and services. Thus, if the school allocates resources so as to favour wheelchair users, at the expense of persons with reduced vision the school will discriminate and will have to justify that less favourable treatment.

The policy should also deal with the arrangements and review procedures for access to a balanced and broadly based curriculum including the National Curriculum. It should state how children with SEN are integrated and the criteria for the evaluation of the success of the school's SEN policy. A policy should deal with arrangements for considering complaints about special educational provision within the school.

The policy should state its staffing policies and name partnerships beyond the school, (ie the schools arrangements for in-service training on SEN use of teachers, facilities, support services from outside the school, arrangements for partnership with parents, links with other schools, including arrangements for transfer and transition links with health, social services, educational welfare and voluntary organisations). Such links, and in particular the transition links, are likely to be covered by the provisions relating to goods and services.

The intention behind s 317 of the EA 1996 can be seen from the promoting minister's comments when introducing the provision:

> One of the major themes in the Education Act 1996 was that mainstream schools should play their full part in providing for pupils with special needs at every stage; and that school's duties should be clarified though the code of practice for the identification and assessment of such children. ... Local accountability is ensured through the requirement on schools to formulate and publish information about their policy for children with special needs, keeping parents and prospective parents informed. The publication of SEN policies will help to prevent the possibility that parents could feel inclined to send their child to a special school on the basis that they did not know enough about the SEN provision in local mainstream schools. (*Hansard*, HL, 15 June 1995, Vol 564, col 1993, Mackay)

The aim of the provision relating to the annual report is to ensure that disabled pupils are integrated into mainstream education as far as possible (see *Hansard*, HL, 15 June 1995, Vol 564, col 1994, Mackay). Governing bodies exercising functions under Pt IV of the 1996 Act must have due regard to the provisions of the *Code of Practice for the Identification and Assessment of Special Educational Needs*. In addition, a parent who considers that the policies stated in the annual report are not being complied with in a particular case may appeal to the Special Educational Needs Tribunal (see Pt IV of the EA 1996 and p 214 below). In limited cases judicial review of the policy may be possible or the parent may complain under EA 1996, ss 496 and 497 to the Secretary of State.

The duties towards children with special educational needs in s 161 apply to governing bodies of county, voluntary or grant-maintained schools, together with LEAs. By s 312(1) of the EA 1996 'a child has a special educational need if he has a learning difficulty which calls for special educational provision to be made for him or her'.

A child has a learning difficulty if he:

a) has a significantly greater difficulty in learning than the majority of
    children of the same age;
b) has a disability which either prevents or hinders him from making
    use of educational facilities of a kind provided for children of the
    same age in schools within the area of the LEA;
c) is under five and falls within the definition (a) or (b) above or would
    do if special educational provision was not made for the child
    (s 312(2))

A child must not be regarded as having a learning difficulty solely because
the language of the home is different from the language in which he will be
taught (s 312(3)).

Special educational provision means:
a) for a child over two, educational provision which is additional to, or
    otherwise different from, the educational provision made generally
    for children of the child's age in maintained schools other than spe-
    cial schools, in the area; and
b) for a child under two, educational provision of any kind. (s 312(4)).

A LEA conducts an assessment of the child to ascertain whether he has
special educational needs. Although the wording of reg 9(1)(d) of the DD(SP)
Regs 1996 is sufficiently broad to cover other sorts of assessment, the main
assessments to be affected are the special needs and assessment and
transitional plan assessments. In order to understand the scope of the
exemption it is necessary to examine the process of assessment as set out in
the *Code of Practice on the Identification and Assessment of Special
Educational Needs* (see also EA 1996, Sched 26). There is a five stage
model of assessment and management of SEN pupils:

(1) the class or subject teachers should identify or register a child's SEN and
     consult the school's SEN coordinator to take initial action. The coordinator is
     a designated teacher responsible for the day-to-day operation of the school's
     SEN policy by liaising with and advising fellow teachers. He must also
     coordinate provision for children with SEN; maintain the SEN register and
     oversee records on all pupils with SEN. The coordinator is responsible for
     liaising with parents of children with SEN, and for contributing to the in-
     service training of staff, and liaising with external agencies including
     Educational Psychologists, medical and social services and voluntary
     bodies (Stage 1);
(2) working with the child's teachers, the coordinator takes the principal
     responsibility for obtaining information and for coordinating the child's
     special education provision (Stage 2);
(3) the Teachers and the Co-ordinator should be supported by specialists from
     outside the school (Stage 3);
(4) the LEA should consider the need for a statutory assessment of the child and
     make a multidisciplinary assessment if appropriate (Stage 4); and
(5) The LEA should consider the need for a statement of special educational
     needs and, where appropriate, should make a statement and arrange, monitor
     and review provision of special education (Stage 5).

Such (Stage 4) assessments are exempted by reg 9 of the DD(SP) Regs 1996
(see above). However, note that it is only the assessment which is exempted by

reg 9(1)(*d*). Management of SEN pupils will not be covered by this exemption unless it constitutes education under the DDA. This distinction can be seen clearly in the wording of the EA 1996, s 326(1):

> The parent of a child for whom a local education authority maintains a statement under section 168 of this Act may ... appeal to the Tribunal against the description in the statement of the authority's assessment of the child's special educational needs, the special educational provision specified in the statement or, if no school is named in the statement, that fact.

The *Code of Practice on the Identification and Assessment of Special Educational Needs* identifies a process of assessment (see also EA 1996, Sched 26). It operates by way of three stages. During the first stage information is gathered about the pupil by the teacher, and there is increasing differentiation in the child's classroom work. It is the role of the teacher, form or year tutor to identify the child's special educational needs and consult the child's parents and the child. The teacher consults the coordinator who registers the needs. The teacher will work closely with the child in the normal classroom context and monitor/review the child's progress. At the second stage an individual education plan is produced. The coordinator must coordinate the child's special educational provision. The coordinator should marshal information including, if appropriate, any information from sources outside the school. The coordinator ensures that the individual education plan is drawn up and ensures that the child's parents are informed. He is responsible for monitoring and reviewing the child's progress. He informs the head teacher. At the third and last stage specialists from outside the school are involved. The coordinator takes the leading role, working closely with the child's teachers. He keeps the head teacher informed and draws on the advice tendered by outside specialists, eg Educational Psychologists and Advisory Teachers. At this stage the coordinator ensures that the child and his parents are consulted. Finally the coordinator monitors and reviews the child's progress at this stage, together with the outside specialists.

During the school-based assessment social services departments will need to have arrangements for liaising with schools determining how to register concern about a child's welfare. They are responsible for putting into practice child protection arrangements; for liaising with schools if the child is looked after by a local authority and giving schools information on services provided by the local authority for 'children in need'. These services will be subject to the provisions of the DDA on goods and services.

In conducting an assessment, if it appears to the authority, in consequence of medical advice or otherwise, that the child being assessed is:

   (a) hearing impaired; or

   (b) visually impaired; or

   (c) both hearing impaired and visually impaired,

and any person from whom educational advice is sought is not qualified to teach pupils who are so impaired then the advice sought shall be advice given after consultation with a person who is so qualified. A person is considered to be qualified to teach such pupils if he is qualified to be employed at a school as a teacher of a class for pupils who are so impaired otherwise than to give instruction in a craft, trade, or domestic subject. (Education (Special Educational Needs) Regulations 1994 (SI No 1047), reg 7).

Contents of the statement

The contents of the statement itself show that not all of the matters being assessed could be classified as 'education' within the meaning of the DDA or as the 'assessment' in DD(SP) Regs 1996, reg 9. The statement of a child with SEN gives details of each of the child's special educational needs as identified by the LEA during statutory assessment. Certain requirements of the statement are mandatory and are set out in the Education (Special Educational Needs) Regulations 1994 (SI No 1047) and are mirrored in the *Code of Practice on the Identification and Assessment of Special Educational Needs*. It must contain the advice received and attached as the appendices to the statement. The statement should contain the special educational provision which the LEA considers necessary to meet the child's special educational needs. It should identify the objectives which the special educational provision should aim to meet and the special education provision which the LEA considers appropriate to meet.

In *R v Secretary of State for Education and Science, ex p E* [1992] 1 FLR 377, the Court of Appeal held that the statement must deal, in the 'provision' section, with all matters identified in the 'needs' section of the statement, that is the arrangements to be made for monitoring progress in meeting those objectives, particularly for setting short-term targets for the child's progress and for reviewing his or her progress on a regular basis.

Part 5 of the statement deals with non-educational needs of the child. These may be agreed between the health service or other agencies and the LEA, although the LEA may make its own provision such as that for transport or health. Part 6 of the statement deals with non-educational provision. This part of the statement sets out a specification of relevant non-educational provision required to meet the non-educational needs of the child as agreed between the health services and/or social services and the LEA, including the agreed arrangements for its provision.

The advice attached to the statement must include the advice the LEA is obliged to seek for the purpose of making an assessment under EA 1996 s 323. Under the Education (Special Educational Needs) Regulations 1994 (SI No 1047) an authority must seek:

(a) advice from the child's parent;
(b) the educational advice set out in reg 7;
(c) medical advice from the district health authority as provided for in reg 8;
(d) psychological advice as provided for in reg 9;
(e) advice from the social services authority; and
(f) any other advice which the authority consider appropriate for the purpose of arriving at a satisfactory assessment.

The advice must be written advice relating to the educational, medical, psychological or other features of the case (according to the nature of the advice sought) which appear to be relevant to the child's educational needs (including his likely future needs). The advice should deal with how those features could affect the child's educational needs. Finally, the advice should deal with the provision which is appropriate for the child in the light of those features of the child's case, whether by way of special educational provision or non-educational provision (Education (Special Educational Needs) Regulations 1994, reg 6).

The transition plan

The first annual review meeting after the pupil's fourteenth birthday must include a transition plan. A transition plan must include the child's parents, relevant teacher and others as appropriate. The views of the pupil should be sought where possible, and information should be sought from the Social Services Department as to whether the pupil is a disabled person under the Disabled Persons Act 1986. The careers service must be invited to the meeting. There should be a review report and transition plan after the meeting. The effect of the DDA on such transition plans is unclear, but they probably form part of the assessment for the purposes of reg 9 of the DD(SP) Regs 1996. The careers service is arguably not providing an educational service (or an assessment), but a service facilitating the entry of young persons into the employment market. It may be that discrimination against disabled persons by careers advisers would be unlawful under the provisions of the Act relating to goods and services.

Children under five

Regulation 9 of the DD(SP) Regs 1996 exempts the assessment of pupils who have not been provided with education by the LEA. This would include a child under six who has not yet started education. A child under six years of age who has an impairment which does not have an effect on his ability to carry out normal day-to-day activities, is to be taken to have an impairment which has a substantial and long term adverse effect on his ability to carry out normal day-to-day activities, where it would normally have a substantial and long term adverse effect on the ability of a person aged six years or over to carry out normal day-to-day activities (Disability Discrimination (Meaning of Disability) Regulations 1996, reg 6).

Non-school authorities in SEN provision

There are other authorities involved in the process of provision of SEN services. The LEA policies should state the arrangements for identifying children with SEN, including any staged approach (see above). The policies should deal with the role of schools, LEA central staff, the health services, social services, voluntary organisations, primary, secondary and special schools. A LEA policy should cover the arrangements for placing and monitoring pupils in independent and non-maintained special schools, and the arrangements for coordination and collaboration with neighbouring LEAs, the health services and social services. The LEA should have arrangements for monitoring the performance of schools maintained by them, and of support services provided by them. They should ensure that children with statements receive the provision specified in their statements. The LEA is responsible for ensuring that the child's statement is reviewed annually.

By EA 1996, s 315, a LEA must keep under review the arrangements made by them for special educational provision. To the extent that it appears necessary or desirable for the purpose of coordinating provision for children with SEN, they must consult the funding authority and the governing bodies of county, voluntary, maintained special and grant maintained schools in their area in order to keep such arrangements under review. By EA 1996, s 317, duties are imposed on governing bodies and the LEA to consult one another to the extent that it appears necessary or desirable for the purpose of coordinating provision for children with SEN.

The District Health Authority should consider with the LEA and relevant social services departments how to collaborate in meeting their joint responsibilities under s 27 of the Children Act 1989 and s 322 of the Education Act 1996. Section 27 of the Children Act 1989 provides that if it appears to a local authority that another authority could, by taking any specified action, help in the exercise of any of their functions they may request the help of that other authority specifying the action in question. Another authority, including a Health Authority, Special Health Authority or National Health Service trust must comply with the request if it is compatible with its own statutory or other duties and obligations and does not unduly prejudice the discharge of any of its functions. Section 322 of the Education Act 1996 provides that if it appears to a local education authority that any Health Authority or local authority could, by taking any specified action, help in the exercise of any of their functions under the relevant part of the Education Act 1996 they may request the help of the authority, specifying the action in question. An authority whose help is requested must comply with the request unless they consider that the help requested is not necessary for the purpose of the exercise by the local education authority of those functions. The authority may not refuse to comply where the Health Authority considers that, having regard to the resources available to them for the purpose of the exercise of their functions under the National Health Service Act 1977, it is not reasonable for them to provide the service (see *R* v *Brent Health Authority ex p Harrow LBC* (1996) *The Times*, 15 October). Where a local authority, considers that the request is not compatible with their own statutory or other duties and obligations or unduly prejudices the discharge of any of their functions, it may not refuse to comply or delegate (see *R* v *Harrow LBC*, above). It is clear that these powers to refuse will be subject to the provisions of the DDA as regards goods, services and facilities (see *Hampson* v *DES* [1989] IRLR 69).

The District Health Authority should consult with the LEA and any other relevant bodies to ensure that commissioning arrangements take account of the needs of those with the responsibility for identifying, assessing and making provision for children with SEN. The District Health Authority should appoint a designated medical officer for SEN to coordinate activities across the variety of medical authorities that deal with the child. Those contributing medical evidence should provide information on:

(1) any medical condition likely to affect future learning ability;

(2) any medical treatment likely to affect a child's learning ability; and

(3) any general health or development problems which may be related to family or social circumstances or any mental health problems which may lead to emotional or behavioural difficulties.

For children under five the medical authorities must determine the arrangements to be made by them for the early identification and assessment of children under five who may have special educational needs; the arrangements they will make to provide information to parents and to provide early counselling and support; and the procedures they will implement in order to refer children to the LEA. These services, except the assessment of the child, will be subject to the provisions relating to goods and services under the DDA.

Further information which the medical authorities must determine include the information the Health Service will provide about local and national voluntary organisations who might help and advise parents; the health services that should be provided for children with special needs in nursery schools or classes and how these services should be specific within any service-level agreement. Such services provided in nursery schools will not be education, and therefore will be subject to the provisions of the DDA.

Special Educational Needs Tribunals

The detail of an application to the SEN Tribunal is outside the scope of this work. The relevant statutory framework is contained mainly in Pt IV of the Education Act 1996. Section 312 defines special educational needs and special educational provision. Section 316 imposes on a local education authority a duty to provide for pupils with special needs. Section 323 provides for an assessment of educational needs to be made by the local education authority. Section 324 provides for a statement of special needs to be compiled in an appropriate case. Subsection (3) of that section makes provision for the contents of the statement, and subsection (5) imposes on the local education authority an obligation to make special educational provision in accordance with the statement of special needs. Section 325 provides for an appeal to the Special Educational Needs Tribunal against a decision not to make a statement in accordance with the above sections (s 325(2)). Under s 326 there is an appeal to the SEN Tribunal against the contents of a statement. Section 328 makes provision for reassessment of educational needs in relation to a particular child, and there is a right of appeal to the tribunal against a refusal to review those needs following a reassessment (see also other appeal rights in s 329(2) and in Sched 27, para 8(3) and para 11 of the EA 1996). The tribunal is established under s 333 of the 1996 Act. There is a president of the tribunal, a panel of persons who may serve as chairmen, and a panel of persons who serve as the other two 'lay' members of the tribunal. The president and those who may serve as chairmen are required by s 334 of the Act to have legal qualifications.

By reg 3 of the Special Educational Needs Tribunal Regulations 1995 (SI No 3113), lay members are not appointed unless the Secretary of State for Education is satisfied that the person has knowledge and experience of children with special educational needs, or with local government.

The tribunal has jurisdiction to hear three types of case in relation to statements:

(a) where a LEA makes an assessment of a child's educational needs pursuant to its power under s 323 of the Act of 1996, and finds that it is not necessary to determine special educational provision for that child in a statement made under s 324 of the Act, and notifies a child's parents to that effect, the child's parents may appeal (s 325);

(b) if the LEA determines that special educational provision is required, and makes and maintains a statement of the child's special educational needs under s 324 of the Act, the parent of the child may appeal to the tribunal:
   (i) when the statement is first made;
   (ii) when an amendment is made, and if and when a local education authority determines not to amend a statement (s 326);

(c) against a refusal by a local education authority to make an assessment in respect of a child for whom a statement is maintained, in the circumstances set out in the section; and the parent of a child for whom a local education authority is not maintaining a statement may appeal to the tribunal if a request for an assessment has not been met in the circumstances set out in the section (s 328).

The tribunal's jurisdiction can only be invoked by an appeal brought by a parent. A child for these purposes includes any person who has not attained the age of 19 years and is a registered pupil at a school (s 312(5)). An adult affected by any of the above decisions would only be able to appeal through his parents. By reg 7 of the Special Educational Needs Tribunal Regulations an appeal is constituted by a notice of appeal signed by the parent, identifying the name of the child and the name of the authority which made the disputed decision. Regulation 8 makes provision for a reply by the education authority. In reg 27 provision is made for persons other than the parties to attend, but does not include the child.

The High Court deals with appeals from the tribunal (s 11 of the Tribunals and Inquiries Act 1992). The tribunal is included in the category of tribunals which are to be under the supervision of the Council on Tribunals in para 15 of

Pt I of Sched 1 to the Tribunals and Inquiries Act 1992. RSC Ord 55, r 1(1) deals with the procedure for appeal to the High Court from the tribunal. Section 11 of the Tribunals and Inquiries Act 1992 has the effect that, for the purposes of the 1996 Act, the appeal can be made either by way of case stated, or by appeal. Rules of the Supreme Court determine the procedure to be adopted and are set out in Ord 94, rr 8 and 9. An appeal under Ord 55 may be brought by a parent in relation to a decision of the tribunal. The tribunal may of its own motion or at the request of either party state a case on any question of law arising in the course of the proceedings. One of these two methods will generally be preferable to judicial review (*R* v *The Special Education Needs Tribunal, ex p South Glamorgan County Council*, (1995) *The Times*, 12 December).

A tribunal has no right to appear in an appeal by the parent to the High Court. However the High Court has power to permit the tribunal to appear and be heard in appeals where issues of general principle arise, and will permit the tribunal to put before it any relevant material to show what was or was not taken into account by it (*S* v *Special Educational Needs Tribunal* [1995] 1 WLR 1627).

Further education

The Further and Higher Education Act 1992 is amended by the DDA. Funding councils for further education institutions and colleges are required to place certain conditions on the funding they give to educational establishments under s 5 of the FHEA 1992. Without prejudice to the funding council's other powers to impose conditions on funding, the conditions subject to which a council gives financial support under s 5 to the governing body of a further education institution:

   (a)   shall include a requirement that the governing body publish disability statements at prescribed intervals; and
   (b)   may include conditions relating to the provision made or to be made by the institution in respect of disabled persons.

A disability statement is a statement containing information of a prescribed description concerning the provision of facilities for education made by the institution in respect of disabled persons (FHEA 1992, s 8 as amended by DDA 1995, s 30). The information which is likely to be required under regulations relates to physical access, the provision of specialist equipment, facilities which may help students with particular disabilities, admission policies, counselling and welfare arrangements (see *Hansard*, HL, 15 June 1995, Vol 564, col 1991 Mackay).

Where the information provided in the statement does not match the provision made, it is arguable that the disabled student would have sufficient *locus* to apply for judicial review of the decision to provide funding by the funding council, thus threatening the college with repayment of the grant to the funding council (see *Hansard* above, and see *Covent Garden Community Association* v *GLC* [1981] JPL 183, and *Inland Revenue Commission* v

National Federation of Self-employed and Small Businesses Ltd [1982] AC 617). The funding council may stipulate a condition of a grant that if certain actions are not taken the grant is to be repaid.

The supplementary functions of the funding councils are also enhanced. Section 8(6) of the FHEA 1992 is added. This provides that as soon as is reasonably practicable after the end of its financial year, each council shall make a written report to the Secretary of State concerning the following:

(a) the progress made during the year to which the report relates in the provision of further education for disabled students in their area; and

(b) their plans for the future provision of further education for disabled students in their area.

A necessary precondition of s 8(6)(*b*) is that there should be some future provision. This would suggest that it would be unlawful for the funding council to make no provision for disabled students at all. In the exercise of their functions the funding councils must have regard to the requirements of disabled persons for the purposes of the DDA (s 62(7A) and (7B)).

Section 30(7) of the DDA amends s 41 of the Education Act 1944 (now consolidated in EA 1996, s 15). The LEA comes under a duty to publish a disability statement at intervals to be prescribed. The statement must contain information about the provision of facilities for further education made available by the LEA for disabled persons.

Universities

The Universities Funding Council, was dissolved on 1 April 1993 and by s 63(1) of the Further and Higher Education Act 1992, rights and liabilities were transferred to the Higher Education Funding Council for England and a similarly named council for Wales. Sections 65 and 66 of the Further and Higher Education Act 1992 confer upon the bodies functions broadly similar to those of their predecessor. Section 65 of the FHEA 1992 deals with the administration of funds by councils. It draws the distinction between education and research. However reg 9(1)(*c*) of the DD(SP) Regs 1996 provides that the provision of facilities for research, including the supervision or guidance of research, is to be exempt from the goods and services provisions.

Section 65(2) of the FHEA 1992 provides for the following activities to be eligible for funding:

(a) the provision of education and the undertaking of research by higher education institutions in the council's area;

(b) the provision of any facilities, and the carrying on of any other activities, by higher education institutions in their area which the governing bodies of those institutions consider it necessary or desirable to provide or carry on for the purpose of or in connection with education or research;

(c) the provision:

    (i) by institutions in their area maintained or assisted by local education authorities; or

    (ii) by such institutions in their area as are within the further education sector;

of prescribed courses of higher education, and

    (d) the provision by any person of services for the purposes of, or in connection with, the provision of education or the undertaking of research by institutions within the higher education sector.

A council may:

    (a) make grants, loans or other payments to the governing body of any higher education institution in respect of expenditure incurred or to be incurred by them for the purposes of any activities eligible for funding; and

    (b) make grants, loans or other payments to any persons in respect of expenditure incurred or to be incurred by them for the purposes of certain courses of higher education or the provision of services of education or the undertaking of research by institutions within the higher education sector.

The HEFC has a free hand in devising proper means of arriving at its decisions on the funding of research in higher education (see *R* v *Higher Education Funding Council, ex p Institute of Dental Surgery* [1994] 1 WLR 242). The HEFCs are required, by amendments to the FHEA 1992, s 62, to have regard to the requirements of disabled persons when exercising their statutory functions. The higher education councils may make grants, loans or other payments to the governing body of a university, conditional upon a requirement to publish a disability statement at an interval to be prescribed. The information to be provided in such statements includes information concerning the provision of facilities for education and research made by the university or institution in respect of disabled persons (Further and Higher Education Act 1992, s 65(4A) and (4B)). Unlike in relation to further education, the government made it clear that the intention was that disability statements were to assist disabled students and funding councils generally in understanding the provision available for education and research. The government stressed that the provision of information in this context would not '*ipso facto* require any changes in the nature of the facilities offered by the institution' (*Hansard*, HL, 15 June 1995, Vol 564, col 1993, Mackay).

The exempting provisions do not exempt 'the provisions of any facilities, and the carrying on of any other activities, by higher education institutions in their area which the governing bodies of those institutions consider it necessary or desirable to provide or carry on for the purpose of or in connection with education or research' (FHEA 1992, s 65(2)(*b*)). Arguably activities 'in connection with education' are subject to the provisions relating to goods, facilities and services in the DDA. Such activities and facilities will clearly be ancillary to education or research.

Chapter 15

Transport

Part V of the DDA establishes a framework for making some forms of transport more accessible to people with disabilities. In particular, it allows regulations to be made to ensure that certain vehicles are designed, constructed and equipped in such a fashion as to allow people with disabilities to travel in safety, in reasonable comfort and without unreasonable difficulty. Different regulations will apply to taxis, public service vehicles (buses and coaches) and rail vehicles. In addition, duties are to be placed on taxi drivers to assist some categories of disabled people to use taxis. These provisions are enforced by a combination of licensing or certification schemes and criminal penalties. As any service consisting of the use of means of transport is excluded from the goods and services provisions of Pt III of the DDA (s 19(5)(b), and see p 134 above), a disabled person cannot bring a civil claim because he or she is prevented from using a vehicle which does not comply with the relevant provisions.

Taxis

The DDA will make taxis more accessible to people with disabilities in two ways. Firstly, the Secretary of State has power to make regulations relating to the construction and equipment of taxis to make them safe for and accessible to people with disabilities. In addition, duties are placed upon taxi drivers to assist and carry people with disabilities who use a wheelchair or have a guide or hearing dog. These provisions are to be enforced by a combination of criminal penalties and by requiring compliance with the accessibility standards as a condition of obtaining a licence. There are specific provisions for private hire vehicles operating from designated transport facilities. There is a limited power to extend these provisions to private hire care services used in designated transport facilities.

Definition of taxi and regulated taxi

For the purposes of the DDA, a taxi is a vehicle licensed under s 37 of the Town Police Clauses Act 1847 or s 6 of the Metropolitan Public Carriage Act

1986 unless it is drawn by a horse or other animal (s 32(5)). A regulated taxi is a taxi to which the regulations are expressed to apply (s 32(5)). The provisions will not apply to minicabs or private hire vehicles unless they are used in designated transport facilities (see p 225 below).

The taxi accessibility regulations

The Secretary of State may make regulations (the taxi accessibility regulations) for the purpose of securing that it is possible for disabled persons to get in and out of and to be carried in taxis in safety and to be carried in taxis in safety and reasonable comfort (s 32(1)(a)). In addition, regulations may be made for the purpose of securing that disabled persons in wheelchairs may be conveyed in safety into and out of taxis while remaining in their wheelchairs and can be carried in safety and in reasonable comfort while remaining in their wheelchairs (s 32(1)(b)).

Physical accessibility: regulations affecting the construction of taxis
Regulations may be made to ensure that taxis are accessible to disabled people. The regulations may, in particular, require any regulated taxi to comply with prescribed requirements as to:
  (a) the size of any door opening to be used by passengers;
  (b) the floor area of the passenger compartment;
  (c) the amount of head room in the passenger compartment; and
  (d) the fitting of restraining devices designed to ensure the stability of a
       wheelchair while the taxi is moving (s 32(2)(a)).

Physical accessibility: regulations affecting taxi drivers
Regulations may be made, in particular, to require the driver of any regulated taxi which is plying for hire, or which has been hired, to comply with prescribed requirements as to the carrying of ramps or other devices designed to facilitate the carrying of wheelchairs (s 32(2)(b)). Regulations may also require the driver of a regulated taxi in which a disabled person is being carried while remaining in his wheelchair to comply with the provisions of the regulations as to the position in which the wheelchair is to be secured (s 32(2)(c)).

Exemptions
Existing taxis are very likely to be exempt from these regulations for the foreseeable future. Furthermore, the licences of existing taxis may be renewed notwithstanding that they fail to meet the accessibility regulations.

Enforcement
The taxi accessibility regulations are to be enforced by making the driver of a taxi guilty of a criminal offence where the regulations are breached and by way of the licensing scheme.

Criminal offence

A driver of a regulated taxi which is plying for hire, or has been hired, is guilty of a summary offence if the taxi fails to comply with any requirements imposed upon it by regulations made under s 32 or if he fails to comply with any requirement imposed upon him by regulations made under s 32 (s 32(3)). A person guilty of such an offence is liable to a fine not exceeding level 3 on the standard scale (s 32(3)).

Licensing scheme

Section 34 of the DDA will prevent a licensing authority from granting a taxi a licence to ply for hire unless the vehicle conforms with the taxi accessibility regulations. This section will not apply if a taxi was licensed at any time during the 28 days immediately before the day on which a (renewal) licence is to be granted (s 34(2)). This transitional provision is designed to exempt existing taxis, which may have been built and purchased long before the DDA and any regulations made thereunder, from the new standards set by the regulations. However, an old taxi is only assisted by the transitional provision of s 34(2) if a licence was in force within the 28 days prior to the day on which the new licence would be granted. If the old licence had lapsed before the start of that period, the taxi can only be granted a licence if it complies with the taxi accessibility regulations, irrespective of the age of the taxi. Finally, the Secretary of State may by order provide that the provision of s 34(2) will cease to have effect on a day specified (s 34(3)). After that date all taxis will need to comply with the accessibility regulations if they are to be granted a new or renewal licence, subject to the exemption provisions of s 35 (below). Separate orders may be made under s 34(3) with respect to different areas.

Section 35 enables the Secretary of State to make regulations enabling a licensing authority to apply for an order exempting the authority from s 34. A licensing authority can only apply for an exemption order if it is satisfied that:

(a) having regard to the local circumstances it would be inappropriate for the requirements of s 34 to apply; and

(b) that the application of s 34 would result in an unacceptable reduction in the number of taxis in its area.

The regulations may make provision requiring a licensing authority to carry out prescribed consultations and to publish the proposal in a prescribed manner prior to making any application and to make the application in a prescribed form (s 35(2)).

The Secretary of State is to consult with the Disabled Persons Transport Advisory Committee and such other person as he considers appropriate before deciding to:

(a) make an exemption order in the terms of the application;

(b) make an exemption order in such other terms as he considers appropriate; or

(c) refuse to make an exemption order (s 35(4)).

A licensing authority granted such an exemption order will be entitled to license taxis which do not comply with the accessibility regulations. However, regulations may be made requiring any taxi plying for hire in such an area to conform with provisions relating to the fitting and use of 'swivel seats' (s 35(5)). Regulations may also provide that a licensing authority that holds an exemption order may only grant a licence to a taxi that conforms to swivel seat regulations, again subject to transitional provisions (s 35(6)).

Duties upon taxi drivers in relation to passengers in wheelchairs

Once in force, s 36 will impose duties upon the driver of a regulated taxi which has been hired by or for a disabled person in a wheelchair or by a person who wishes a disabled person in a wheelchair to accompany them in the taxi. For the purposes of s 36, 'carry' means carry in the taxi concerned and 'passenger' means the disabled person concerned (s 36(2)). The duties are:

   (a) to carry the disabled person in the taxi concerned while they remain in their wheelchair (s 36(3)(a));
   (b) not to make any additional charge for doing so (s 36(3)(b));
   (c) if the passenger chooses to sit in the passenger seat, the driver is under a duty to carry the wheelchair in the taxi concerned (s 36(3)(c));
   (d) to take such steps as are necessary to ensure the passenger is carried in safety and reasonable comfort (s 36(3)(d));
   (e) to give such assistance as may be reasonably required:
        (i)   to enable the passenger to get in and out of the taxi;
        (ii) if the passenger wishes to remain in his wheelchair, to enable the passenger to be conveyed in or out of the taxi in the wheelchair;
        (iii) to load the luggage into and out of the taxi;
        (iv) to load the wheelchair into and out of the taxi if the passenger does not wish to remain in the wheelchair (s 36(3)(e)).

These provisions do not currently require a driver of any taxi to carry more than one person in a wheelchair, or more than one wheelchair, in any journey, although regulations may be made to require drivers of taxis of a prescribed description to do so. The section does not require a taxi driver to carry any person in circumstances in which it would otherwise be lawful for him to refuse to carry that person.

Exemptions

A driver can apply to a licensing authority for a certificate exempting him from the duties imposed by s 36. The licensing authority shall grant the applicant a certificate of exemption if it is satisfied that it is appropriate for the driver to be exempt either on medical grounds or because the driver's 'physical condition makes it impossible or unreasonably difficult for him to comply with the duties imposed by the section' (s 37(5)). For example, a certificate shall be granted where the authority is satisfied that the driver has a back condition that makes it impossible or dangerous for him to lift heavy luggage or push a person in a wheelchair into the taxi. The certificate is to be issued for such period as may be specified in the certificate. Section 38 provides a right of appeal against the refusal of a licensing authority to issue an exemption certificate under s 36. The appeal must be made to the appropriate court before the end of the period of 28 days beginning with the date of the refusal (s 38(1)). The appropriate court is the magistrates' court for the petty sessions area in which the licensing authority has its principal office. If the appeal is successful, the magistrates' court will direct the licensing authority to issue the appropriate certificate of exemption to have effect for such period as may be specified in the direction. The driver is only exempt if a certificate of exemption issued to him under s 37(5) is in force *and* the prescribed notice of his exemption is exhibited in the taxi in the prescribed manner. The driver will not be exempt from the duties if the notice is not so exhibited.

Enforcement
A taxi driver who fails to comply with any duty imposed by this section is guilty of a summary offence punishable by a fine not exceeding level 3 of the standard scale. However, a taxi driver is not guilty of any offence if he or she can show that the taxi conformed with the provisions of the taxi accessibility regulations that applied to that taxi at the time of the alleged offence and that it would still not have been possible for the wheelchair in question to be carried safely (s 36(6)). This defence may be available where the taxi is exempt from the accessibility regulations or where the particular model of the wheelchair makes it unsafe for it to be carried despite the fact that the taxi is required to and does comply with those regulations.

Forgery and misuse of exemption certificates and notices
A person is guilty of an 'either way' offence if, with intent to deceive, he forges or alters or uses a relevant document, lends a relevant document to any other person, allows a relevant document to be used by any other person, or makes or has in his possession any document which closely resembles a relevant document (s 49(2)). Section 49(1) defines a certificate of exemption issued under s 36 and the prescribed notices of exemption mentioned in s 36(9)(*b*) as 'relevant documents'. Any person guilty of an offence under s 49(2) is liable to a fine not exceeding the statutory maximum on summary conviction (s 49(3)(*a*)). If convicted on indictment, the person may be sentenced to a term of imprisonment of up to two years, fined or both (s 49(3)(*b*)).

Duties placed upon drivers in relation to disabled people with guide dogs or hearing dogs

Once in force, s 37 will impose duties upon the driver of a taxi (not necessarily a regulated taxi) which has been hired by or for a disabled person with a guide dog or hearing dog or by a person who wishes a disabled person with a guide dog or a hearing dog to accompany him in the taxi. In this section, the disabled person is referred to as 'the passenger' (s 37(2)). 'Guide dog' means a dog that has been trained to guide a blind person (s 37(11)). 'Hearing dog' means a dog which has been trained to assist a deaf person (s 37(11)). The Secretary of State has power to prescribe any other category of dog trained to assist a disabled person with a disability of a prescribed kind (s 37(9)). The section will then apply to any category of dog so prescribed as it applies in relation to guide dogs (s 37(10)). The duties are to carry the passenger's dog and allow it to remain with the person during the journey, and not to make any additional charge for doing so (s 37(3)). In contrast with the provisions relating to passengers in wheelchairs, there is no subsection expressly providing that the section does not require a taxi driver to carry any person in circumstances in which it would otherwise be lawful for him to refuse to carry that person. However, it is submitted that nothing will turn on this omission and the duty is likely to be interpreted to be subject to the taxi driver's right to refuse to carry the passenger (with or without the dog) for other lawful reasons.

Exemption

A driver can apply to a licensing authority for a certificate exempting him from the duties imposed by s 37. The licensing authority shall grant the applicant a certificate of exemption if it is satisfied, on medical grounds, that it is appropriate for the driver to be exempt (s 37(5)). In practice, the only medical grounds likely to make it appropriate for the driver to be exempt are that the driver is allergic to dogs or has a condition, such as asthma, which can be aggravated by dog hair. In deciding whether or not to issue a certificate of exemption, the licensing authority shall have particular regard to the physical characteristics of the taxi which the applicant drives or those of any kind of taxi in relation to which he requires the certificate (s 37(6)). This requires the licensing authority to consider if the characteristics are such that the driver would or would not be in such proximity to any dog as to be affected by it. The certificate is to be issued in respect of a particular taxi or a specified type of taxi and for a period specified in the certificate (s 37(8)). Again, the driver is only exempt if a certificate of exemption issued to him under s 37(5) is in force *and* the prescribed notice of his exemption is exhibited in the taxi in the prescribed manner (s 37(9)). There is a right of appeal under s 38 against a refusal to issue a certificate of exemption under s 37.

Enforcement

A taxi driver who fails to comply with any duty imposed by this section is guilty of a summary offence punishable by a fine not exceeding level 3 of the standard scale.

Forgery and misuse of exemption certificates and notices

It is an either way offence for a person to forge or misuse an exemption certificate issued under s 37(5) or a notice of exemption prescribed by s 37(9)(*b*). The same provision applies in relation to certificates and notices issued under s 36 and is dealt with in more detail above at p 223.

Designated transport facilities

Section 33 allows regulations to be made to require hire cars available at some airports and other transport facilities, sometimes to the exclusion of taxis, to be accessible to disabled people. The Secretary of State may extend any of the above provisions to any vehicle (not being a taxi) or driver of any vehicle which is used to provide a hire car service under a franchise agreement at a designated transport facility (s 33(2)). A 'franchise agreement' means a contract entered into by the operator of a designated transport facility for the provision by the other party to the contract of hire car services for members of the public using any part of the transport facility and which involve vehicles entering any part of the facility (s 33(1)). 'Transport facility' means any premises forming part of a port, airport, railway station or bus station and 'designated transport facility' means any such premises which have been designated by the Secretary of State for the purposes of this section (s 33(4)). 'Operator' means any person who is concerned with the management or operation of the facility (s 33(4)).

Scotland

The provisions referred to above relate only to taxis licensed in England and Wales. However, equivalent provisions can be made in Scotland by regulations to be issued under the Civic Government (Scotland) Act 1982 as amended by s 39 of the DDA.

Northern Ireland

Similar provisions may be made in Northern Ireland, subject to the modifications in Sched 8, paras 16–23. The most significant difference is that s 35 does not apply in Northern Ireland and there is no power for a licensing authority to seek an exemption order (see p 221 above).

Public service vehicles

Public service vehicles, such as coaches and buses, are to be made accessible by regulations making it possible for disabled people (including disabled people remaining in their wheelchairs) to get on and off regulated public service vehicles in safety and without unreasonable difficulty and to be carried in them in safety and in reasonable comfort (s 40(1)). The regulations are to be known as the 'PSV accessibility regulations'.

Public service vehicle

'Public service vehicle' means a vehicle which is adapted to carry more than eight passengers and a public service vehicle for the purposes of the Public Passenger Vehicles Act 1981 (PPVA 1981) (DDA 1995, s 40(5)). In so far as is material, s 1 of the PPVA 1981 defines a public service vehicle as 'a motor vehicle (other than a tramcar) which (a) being a vehicle adapted to carry more than eight passengers, is used for carrying passengers for hire or reward . . .'. A 'regulated public service vehicle' is a public service vehicle to which the PSV accessibility regulations apply (s 40(5)).

Public service vehicle accessibility regulations

The regulations may make provisions as to the construction, use and maintenance of regulated public service vehicles (s 40(1)). These regulations may include provision as to the fitting of equipment to vehicles; the equipment to be carried by vehicles; the design of equipment to be fitted to or carried by vehicles; the fitting and use of restraining devices to ensure stability of wheelchairs while vehicles are moving; and the position in which wheelchairs are to be secured (s 40(2)). Different provision may be made for different classes or descriptions of vehicle or for the same class or description of vehicle in different circumstances (s 40(6)). The Secretary of State is to consult the Disabled Persons Transport Advisory Committee and such other representative organisations as he thinks fit before making any regulations under ss 40, 41 or 42 (s 40(7)).

Enforcement

The PSV accessibility regulations are to be enforced by a combination of a system of certification backed up with criminal penalties.

Certification

A regulated public service vehicle shall not be used on a road unless either a vehicle examiner has issued an approval certificate or an accessibility certificate in respect of that vehicle (s 41(1)) or the Secretary of State has granted special authorisation to use that vehicle, or that class or description of vehicle (see p 228).

Accessibility certificates

An accessibility certificate is a certificate issued by a vehicle examiner certifying that a particular vehicle satisfies such provisions of the PSV accessibility regulations as are prescribed (s 41(1)(a)).

Approval certificates

The Secretary of State may approve a type or design of vehicle where he is satisfied that a particular type of vehicle satisfies the PSV accessibility regulations (s 42(1)). A declaration may then be granted, by a person authorised to do so by the Secretary of State, that a particular vehicle conforms in design, construction and equipment to the type of vehicle approved by the Secretary of State (s 42(3)). A vehicle examiner may then issue an approval certificate in certifying that a particular vehicle conforms to the type of vehicle approved by the Secretary of State (s 42(4)). The Secretary of State may withdraw his approval at any time (s 42(6)). After approval is withdrawn, no further approval certificates may be issued but any certificates already issued remain valid (s 42(7)).

Procedure

Following consultation the Secretary of State will issue regulations relating to applications for his approval under s 42(1), applications for accessibility or approval certificates, for the examination of vehicles in respect of which an application has been made, and for the issuing of replacement certificates (ss 41(2) and 42(5)). Provision will be made for reviews and appeals under s 44 and for fees under s 45.

Criminal penalties

Subject to Secretary of State's powers to grant special authorisation to use a vehicle, or a class or description of vehicle, (see p 228 below) a person is guilty of a summary offence punishable by a fine not exceeding level 4 on the standard scale if he:

   (a) contravenes or fails to comply with any provision of the PSV accessibility regulations;

   (b) uses on a road a regulated public service vehicle which does not conform with any provision of the regulations with which it is required to conform; or

   (c) causes or permits to be used on a road such a regulated public service vehicle (s 40(3)).

Corporate liability

Where an offence under s 40 (or s 46 below) is committed by a body corporate with the consent or connivance of, or is attributable to any neglect on the part of, a director, manager, secretary or similar officer of the body, or a person purporting to act in such a capacity, that person is guilty of the offence as well as the body corporate (s 48(1)). Where a body corporate's affairs are managed by its members, 'director' means a member of the body corporate. In Scotland, a partner in a partnership (or a person concerned in the management or control of an unincorporated association other than a partnership) is guilty of an offence as well as the partnership (or unincorporated association) where the partnership (or unincorporated association) commits an offence under s 40 (or s 46) with the consent or connivance, or attributable to any neglect on the part of, that person (s 48(3)).

Furthermore, where a public service vehicle is used on a road without an accessibility certificate, an approval certificate or special authorisation, the operator of the vehicle is guilty of a summary offence and liable to a fine not exceeding level 4 on the standard scale (s 41(3)). For the purposes of s 41(3), 'operator' has the same meaning as in the Public Passenger Vehicles Act 1981. Section 81(1)(b) of that Act defines operator as '(i) the driver, if he owns the vehicle; and (ii) in any other case, the person for whom the driver works (whether under a contract of employment or any other description of contract personally to do any work').

Forgery and misuse of accessibility or approval certificates
A person is guilty of an 'either way' offence if, with intent to deceive, he forges or alters or uses a relevant document, lends a relevant document to any other person, allows a relevant document to be used by any other person, or makes or has in his possession any document which closely resembles a relevant document (s 49(2)). Section 49(1) defines accessibility or approval certificates as 'relevant documents'. Any person guilty of an offence under s 49(2) is liable to a fine not exceeding the statutory maximum on summary conviction (s 49(3)(a)). If convicted on indictment, the person may be sentenced to a term of imprisonment of up to two years, fined or both (s 49(3)(b)).

Making false statements for the purpose of obtaining a certificate
A person who knowingly makes a false statement for the purpose of obtaining an accessibility certificate or an approval certificate is guilty of a summary offence punishable by a fine not exceeding level 4 on the standard scale (s 49(4)).

Special authorisation

The Secretary of State may, by order, authorise any public service vehicle or class or description of vehicle to be used on the road, subject to such restrictions and conditions as may be specified in the order (s 43(1)(2)). Such an order may provide that nothing in ss 40, 41 or 42 prevent the use of such a vehicle on the roads (s 43(1)) or that the PSV accessibility regulations apply to the vehicle subject to the modifications and exceptions specified in the order (s 43(3)).

Rail vehicles

Regulations are to be made to make new rail vehicles accessible to disabled people (including disabled people remaining in their wheelchairs) by making it possible for them to get on and off new rail vehicles in safety and without unreasonable difficulty and to be carried in rail vehicles in safety and in reasonable comfort (s 46(1)). These regulations will be known as the rail vehicle accessibility regulations.

Rail vehicles and regulated rail vehicles

'Rail vehicle' means a vehicle which is adapted to carry passengers on any railway, tramway or prescribed system of guided transport where that vehicle was first brought into use, or belongs to a class of vehicle first brought into use, after 31 December 1998 (s 46(6)). Regulations may make provision as to when a rail vehicle, or class of rail vehicle, is to be treated as having been first brought into use. Railway and tramway have the same meaning as in the Transport and Works Act 1992 (s 46(7)). Section 67(1) of that Act provides that railway means 'a system of transport employing parallel rails which: (a) provide support and guidance for vehicles carried on flanged wheels; and (b) form a track which is of a gauge of at least 350 millimetres or crosses a carriageway (whether or not on the same level)...'. A tramway is defined, again by s 67(1) as 'a system of transport used wholly or mainly for the carriage of passengers and employing parallel rails which: (a) provide support and guidance for vehicles carried on flanged wheels; and (b) are laid wholly or mainly along a street or in any other place to which the public has access...' 'Guided transport' means transport by vehicles guided by means external to the vehicle (DDA 1995, s 46(7) and TWA 1992, s 67(1)), such as rails or overhead tracks or cables. A 'regulated rail vehicle' is any rail vehicle to which the rail vehicle accessibility regulations apply (s 46(6)).

Rail vehicle accessibility regulations

The regulations may make provisions as to the construction, use and maintenance of regulated rail vehicles (s 46(1)). These regulations may include provision as to the fitting of equipment to vehicles; the equipment to be carried by vehicles; the design of equipment to be fitted to or carried by vehicles; the toilet facilities to be provided in vehicles; the location and floor area of the wheelchair accommodation to be provided in vehicles; and assistance to be given to disabled persons (s 46(2)). Different provision may be made for different classes or descriptions of vehicle, for the same class or description of vehicle in different circumstances or as respects different networks (s 46(5)). 'Network' means any permanent way or other means of guiding or supporting rail vehicles or any section of it (s 46(6)). The Secretary of State is to consult the Disabled Persons Transport Advisory Committee and such other representative organisations as he thinks fit before making any regulations under s 46 (s 46(11)).

Exemptions

Firstly, all vehicles in use before 31 December 1998 will be exempt. In addition, the Secretary of State may authorise the use of any regulated rail vehicle which does not conform with the rail vehicle accessibility regulations by granting it an exemption order. Regulations may be made to establish who can apply for such an order, how they are to apply, the information to be provided upon any application, and the duration and revocation of exemption orders (s 47(2)). The Secretary of State is to consult the Disabled Persons Transport Advisory Committee and such other representative organisations as he thinks fit before making any such regulations (s 46(11)). The Secretary of State must also consult the Disabled Persons Transport Advisory Committee and such other persons as he considers appropriate, before either granting the exemption order on the terms sought or other terms or refusing the exemption order (s 47(3)). An exemption order may be granted subject to such restrictions and conditions as are specified in the order (s 47(4)(5)).

Enforcement

The rail vehicle accessibility regulations are to be enforced by way of criminal penalties. If a regulated rail vehicle does not conform with any provision of the regulations, the operator of the vehicle is guilty of a summary offence and liable to a fine not exceeding level 4 on the standard scale (s 46(3),(4)). The operator of a rail vehicle is the person having the management of that vehicle (s 46(6)). Where such an offence is committed by a body corporate with the consent or connivance of, or is attributable to any neglect on the part of, a director, manager, secretary or similar officer of the body, or a person purporting to act in such a capacity, that person is guilty of the offence as well as the body corporate (s 48(1)). The same provisions as to personal liability for offences by bodies corporate apply in relation to offences under s 46 as apply to offences under s 40 (see p 227 above).

No civil cause of action for breach of Pt V

There is no independent civil cause of action arising from a breach of these provisions. A disabled person will not have a right of action against a taxi driver or the operator of a public service vehicle or rail vehicle simply because they are unable to travel in safety and comfort or at all because of a breach of the provisions of the DDA or regulations made under it. However, a disabled person injured as a result of a breach of the regulations—such as a failure to secure a wheelchair in the position required by regulations—is likely to have a very strong claim in negligence and/or under the Occupiers Liability Act 1957.

Commencement and Consultation

At the time of writing none of the transport provisions have been brought into force and no regulations made under Part V. Informal consultation on the contents of regualtions is expected from late 1996. Section 37 should come into force in Spring 1997, with s 36 following later in the year.

Part 5

Common Provisions

Chapter 16

Common Provisions

Several provisions made in or under the DDA are 'common provisions', in that they apply to or are found in more than one part of the Act. Those common provisions relate to alterations to premises, secondary liability of and for agents and employees, and acts carried our pursuant to a statutory requirement or for national security and victimisation.

Alterations to premises and the duty to adjust

An employer may need to make structural or other alterations to its premises in order to comply with the duty to make reasonable adjustment under s 6. The DDA will place similar obligations upon trade organisations (under s 15) and providers of goods and services (under s 21(2)) when those provisions are brought into force. In any case, there may be a need to obtain consent from a third party under a 'binding obligation'. Where the occupier is a lessee or licensee, the right to make the alteration under the lease or licence agreement also needs to be considered. Finally, it will be necessary to consider whether the duty to adjust a particular physical characteristic is deemed not to arise on the grounds that the premises met and continued to meet the standards required by the Building Regulations in force at the time of construction.

Alterations and binding obligations

The DD(E) Regs 1996 make provision for when an employer needs the consent of a third party under a 'binding obligation' before he can make an alteration to premises. These regulations apply only to the duty of employers to adjust under s 6 of the DDA, but similar regulations are likely in relation to both trade organisations and providers of goods and services once the relevant provisions come into force. 'Binding obligation' means a legally binding obligation (not contained in a lease) in relation to the premises whether arising from an agreement or otherwise (DD(E) Regs 1996, reg 2). This could include such things as a consent required under the planning or listed building legislation, or under mortgage, charge, restrictive covenant, or (in Scotland) a disposition not to consent to a particular alteration without the consent of

233

another party. Such a binding obligation may fall upon someone who occupies premises as an owner occupier, tenant or licensee.

Regulation 10(1) of the DD(E) Regs 1996 provides that where an employer is required by a binding obligation to obtain the consent of any person to an alteration to be made under s 6 of the DDA, it is always reasonable for him to have to take steps to obtain that consent and it is never reasonable for the employer to have to make the alteration before that consent is obtained. The steps that it is deemed reasonable for him to take to obtain that consent do not include an application to a court or tribunal (reg 10(2)). This does not mean that it will never be reasonable for such an application to be made, only that it is not necessarily reasonable for such an application to be made. Whether it is reasonable for the employer to make such an application is a question of fact and will depend upon the particular circumstances (Employment Code, para 4.48). This regulation only comes into play if it would be reasonable for the employer to make a particular alteration under s 6 but for the binding obligation. If it was not otherwise reasonable, for example if it was too expensive or unlikely to be effective or practicable, there will be no need to take such steps. It is unclear how diligent the employer must be in attempting to obtain consent in order to satisfy reg 10(1). This is likely to be a question of fact, and an employer who takes only notional steps to obtain consent without making reasonable efforts to follow them up is likely to fall foul of the provision. Note that the DDA does not prohibit the other person from unreasonably refusing consent to the alteration. Furthermore, even if the terms of the obligation require the other person not to unreasonably refuse consent, that other person could not be joined to proceedings in the tribunal under para 2 of Sched 4 (see p 111).

Altering premises held under a lease

The DDA provides a mechanism to enable some lessees to make alterations in some circumstances when they would not be entitled to make those alterations under the terms of the lease. The provision relevant to employers and trade organisations is s 16, supplemented by Pt I of Sched 4. Further guidance in relation to employers is given in the Employment Code at paras 4.40 to 4.48. For the providers of goods and services, the relevant section is s 27 as supplemented by Pt II of Sched 4 neither of which are yet in force. The substantive provisions are in identical terms although there are differences in the enforcement provisions in the respective parts of the Schedule. The DD(SS) Regs 1996 modify s 16 and Pt I of Sched 4. The DD(E) Regs 1996 make additional provision in relation to employers who occupy premises under leases. Presumably similar regulations will be made in relation to providers of goods and services and trade organisations once the relevant provisions of the DDA have been brought into force.

Alterations and leases without the provisions of the DDA

Subject to obtaining the necessary planning and other consents under any binding obligation, the right of a lessee (or tenant) to make alterations usually depended upon the terms of an express covenant in the lease dealing with alterations. In the absence of such a covenant, it will be restricted by the doctrine of waste and, possibly, by the terms of any repairing covenant in the lease.

Waste

A lessee who makes a lasting alteration to the premises to the prejudice of the person with the reversion of the land is guilty of waste. The duty not to commit waste is owed in tort, independent of the terms of the contract. Alterations which do not reduce (or which increase) the value of the land do not usually amount to waste (*Jones* v *Chappell* (1875) LR 20 Eq 539, *per* Jessel MR at 541/2), unless the alteration is so substantial that it alters the nature of the demised premises (*West Ham Central Charity Board* v *East London Waterworks* [1900] 1Ch 624 at 636). Alterations to make the premises suitable for a permitted user do not constitute waste (*Hyman* v *Rose* [1912] AC 623 at 632, *per* Earl Loreburn LC). Any proper and reasonable use of the premises permitted under the lease will not constitute waste (*Saner* v *Bilton* (1878) 7 Ch D 815 at 821 and *Manchester Bonded Warehouse* v *Carr* (1880) 5 CPD 507 at 512). In practical terms, the doctrine of waste is unlikely to have much impact upon an occupier seeking to make a reasonable adjustment. Many adjustments will not be permanent or will not affect the fabric of premises at all, such as using temporary ramps to make premises wheelchair accessible. Many permanent alterations which make premises accessible to people with a mobility disability are more likely to increase rather than significantly reduce the value of the reversion. Furthermore, many such alterations would not amount to waste as they involve a proper and reasonable use of the premises. Finally, the duty of reasonable adjustment is unlikely to require an occupier to take steps so substantial that they alter the nature of the demised premises.

Breach of repairing convenants

Some relatively minor alterations to premises, such as opening a doorway in a wall, have been held to amount to a breach of a covenant to keep premises in repair (see for example *Gange* v *Lockwood* (1860) 2 F&F 115). However, a right to make such alterations as are required to make premises suitable for a user permitted under the lease may be inferred, which can prevent such an alteration from being a breach of covenant (*Hyman* v *Rose* [1912] AC 623 at 632). However, where there is any doubt as to the right to make a desired alteration, an occupier would be best advised to follow the procedure set out below and seek to take advantage of the provisions of s 16 of the DDA.

Common clauses restricting alterations

Most commercial leases will include a covenant which restricts the right of a lessee to make alternations. In its most usual form, this will provide that the lessee shall not 'make any alterations to the structure of the premises nor cut nor maim the main walls or timbers' of the premises, either without the licence or consent of the landlord or at all. Such clauses are generally interpreted to prohibit only those alterations which would affect the structure, construction or fabric of the building (see *Bickmore* v *Dimmer* [1903] 1 Ch 158) and to exclude *de minimis* works (*Hagee (London) Ltd* v *Cooperative Insurance Society Ltd* (1991) 63 P&CR 362). Many alterations made in order to comply with the duty to make reasonable adjustment will not breach such a clause. However, it is dangerous to rely overmuch upon general rules and the exact wording of the covenant and the particular alteration desired should be considered in each case.

Unreasonable refusal of consent

Many clauses prevent the tenant from making alterations without the licence or consent of the landlord. In such a case, consent to an alteration which is 'an improvement' is not to be unreasonably refused (Landlord and Tenant Act 1927, s 19(2)). Section 19(2) does not apply to a lease which places an absolute bar upon alterations. Whether an alteration is an improvement for the purposes of the LTA 1927 is a question of fact (*Balls Bross Ltd* v *Sinclair* [1931] 2 Ch 325) although the word 'improvement' is to be given a wide construction (see *National Electric Theatres Ltd* v *Hudgell* [1939] Ch 533). It is to be considered from the point of view of the tenant. An alteration which does not increase the value of the premises may be an improvement if it allows the tenant a more beneficial use thereof (*F W Woolworth & Co* v *Lambert* [1936] 2 All ER 1523). An improvement which would require a trespass onto land retained by the landlord is not within the section (*Tideway Investment and Property Holdings Ltd* v *Wellwood* [1952] Ch 791).

It is for the tenant to prove that consent is being withheld unreasonably. However, a court may infer that the withholding was unreasonable where the landlord gives no reason for doing so (*Frederick Berry Ltd* v *Royal Bank of Scotland* [1949] 1 KB 619, *per* Lord Goddard CJ at 662) and may even require the landlord to prove that his action was reasonable (*Lambert* v *Woolworth & Co (No 2)* [1938] Ch 883, *per* Slesser LJ at 906). Reasonableness is to be considered from the point of view of the landlord considering his own best interest as a prudent but reasonable man of business (*Lambert* v *Woolworth & Co (No 2)* above) although it is unreasonable for a landlord not to take into account the fact that refusal would have an extreme effect upon the tenant and be of little benefit to the landlord (see *International Drilling Fluids* v *Louisville Investments (Uxbridge) Ltd* [1986] 1 All ER 321, *per* Balcombe LJ at 326). Subsection 19(2) expressly allows the landlord to make any licence or consent conditional upon:

the payment of a reasonable sum in respect of any damage to or diminution in the value of the premises or any neighbouring premises belonging to the landlord, and of any legal or other expenses properly incurred in connection with such licence or consent, [or, where the improvement does not add to the letting value of the premises] an undertaking by the tenant to reinstate the premises ...

Compensation
In addition to prohibiting a landlord from unreasonably refusing consent to an improvement, the LTA 1927 allows some lessees of premises being used wholly or partly for carrying on any trade or business to seek compensation from the landlord at the end of the tenancy for the costs of making the improvement (LTA 1927, s 1), unless the tenant was under an obligation to make that improvement in pursuance of a contract made for valuable consideration (LTA 1927, s 2(1)(*b*)). The right to compensation does not apply to premises held under a mining lease, agricultural holding or those used for the carrying out of a profession (see LTA 1927, s 17). A tenant will only be entitled to compensation if he has followed the procedure set out in s 3 of the LTA 1927. This provides for a tenant to serve notice of an intention to make the improvement upon the landlord, together with a specification and plan showing the proposed improvement and part of the premises to be affected by the improvement. If the landlord serves an objection upon the tenant within three months of the tenant's notice, the tenant must obtain a certificate from the High Court or county court that the improvement is a proper improvement. The matters to be considered by a court in deciding whether or not to grant such a certificate are set out in detail in s 3. The compensation recoverable will not exceed either the net addition to the value of the premises directly attributable to the improvement, or the cost of making the improvement less any sum needed to put the improvement into a reasonable state of repair if necessary and if the tenant is not liable for the costs of putting the improvement into such reasonable repair under the lease (LTA 1927, s 1(1)). The assessment of compensation will take into consideration any benefits received by the tenant or his predecessor in title from the landlord or his predecessor in title in consideration expressly or impliedly of the improvement (LTA 1927, s 2(3)). The fact that compensation may be available at the end of a tenancy may be relevant to the question of whether it is reasonable for an occupier to make a particular alteration for the purposes of ss 6(1), 15(1) or 21(2).

The provisions of the DDA

Section 16 (and 27 once in force) of the DDA entitles some occupiers to make some alterations to premises occupied under a lease in order to comply with the duty to make reasonable adjustments when they would not otherwise be entitled to do so under the lease. Any term of any lease which purports to exclude the operations of the following provisions is void (9(1)(*b*) and s 26(1)(*b*)). The provisions only apply if the following three conditions specified in s 16(1) (or 27(1)) are met.

Lease
Firstly, the premises must be occupied by the employer (or trade organisation or provider of services) under a lease (ss 16(1)(*a*) or 27(1)(*a*)). Lease is defined so as to include a tenancy, sub lease or sub tenancy (ss 16(3) or 27(3)). Sub-lease or sub-tenancy include original or derivative sub-leases and sub-tenancies (DD(SS) Regs 1996, reg 3). The section does not apply to licensees.

Terms of the lease
Secondly, the section only applies if the occupier would not otherwise be entitled to make the alteration (ss 16(1)(*b*) or 27(1)(*b*)). If the occupier is entitled to make the alteration under the lease, the section is not needed and does not apply. The occupier is treated as not being entitled to make the alteration if the lease either imposes conditions which are to apply if the premises are altered or entitles the immediate lessor to impose such conditions upon consenting to an alteration. This seems to apply even if the conditions were nominal, for example requiring the lessee to give notice to or serve plans for the alterations upon the lessor.

The nature of the alteration
Thirdly, the alteration must be one which the occupier proposes to make in order to comply with a duty under s 6 (or ss 15 or 21(2)) (s 16(1)(*c*) or s 27(1)(*c*)). Presumably a lessor could resist the making of an alteration on the grounds that the occupier is not under a duty to adjust because, for example, the person concerned does not have a disability within the meaning of s 1(1) or is not in fact substantially disadvantaged by the particular physical feature concerned. An occupier who wishes to make alterations which go above and beyond those that could be required under the duty to adjust will not be entitled to rely upon s 16 (or s 27) of the DDA. It is unclear to what extent, if at all, a lessor will be able to resist a proposed alteration by arguing that the duty could be satisfied by other methods which would not involve altering the premises. An alteration which would inevitably require a trespass upon or appropriation of land retained by the lessor is probably not covered by s 16 (see *Tideway Investment and Property Holdings* v *Wellwood* [1952] Ch 791).

It is important to note that the duties imposed by ss 6 and 15 are individualised duties. Those duties, and the right to rely upon s 16, will only arise if there is a particular disabled person to whom it can be owed. If an employer or trade organisation occupier simply wishes to make premises more accessible to anyone with a mobility disability, without having a particular disabled person in mind, it will have to rely upon the terms of the lease and s 19 of the LTA 1927. However, the duty in s 21(2) does not require the occupier to have a particular individual in mind before a duty to make reasonable adjustment arises, provided a 'physical feature makes it impossible or unreasonably difficult for disabled persons to make use of' a service. Where an occupier is both an employer and a service provider, he may be able to rely upon the provisions of ss 21 and 27 of the DDA in order to make premises occupied under a lease generally more accessible once that provision is in force.

Implied covenant in occupier's lease
Where the section applies, the lease is treated as though it contained a covenant under which the occupier is entitled to make the alteration with the written consent of the lessor (ss 16(2)(*a*) or 27(2)(*a*)). Although the consent must not be withheld unreasonably ss 16(2)(*c*) or 27(2)(*c*)), it may be made subject to reasonable conditions (ss 16(2)(*d*) or 27(2)(*d*)). Any occupier wishing to take advantage of the provisions must make a written application for consent (s 16(2)(*b*) or 27(2)(*b*)). For the purposes of s 16(2) lessor means 'immediate landlord' (DD(SS) Regs 1996, reg 4(*a*)).

Implied covenant in superior leases
In the absence of further provision, the terms of any superior lease could prevent the immediate lessor of the occupier from giving consent to an alteration without the consent of the superior lessor or at all. The DD(SS) Regs 1996 introduces s 16(2A) into the DDA in order to make similar modifications, if necessary, to any leases superior to that held by the occupier (ie any lease to the immediate lessor from a superior landlord; any lease to that superior landlord from the freeholder etc). Any superior lease will take effect as between the parties to that lease as if it provided:
(1) for the lessee to have to make a written application to the lessor for consent to the alteration;
(2) for the lessor not to withhold his consent unreasonably if such an application is made; and
(3) for the lessor to be entitled to make his consent subject to reasonable conditions (s 16(2A)).

By reg 4(c) of the DD(SS) Regs 1996, the references to lessor in paras 2 and 3 of Sched 4 are modified to include any superior landlord. As result, where, if a disabled person brings a claim on the basis of a failure to adjust by making an alteration to the premises, the superior lessor may be joined and ordered to compensate the disabled person where the adjustment was not made because the superior lessor withheld his consent (see p 244 below).

A written application for consent

If an occupier is to take advantage of s 16 (or s 27), there must be a written application for consent to the immediate lessor of the person seeking consent (ss 16(2)(*b*) and 27(2)(*b*)). Furthermore, unless the occupier makes such an application, any term of the lease restricting the occupier's right to make the alteration is to be ignored in deciding if the occupier was in breach of the duty to adjust in failing to make the alteration (para 1 of Sched 4) and the employer will not be able to rely upon the provisions of reg 15 of the DD(E) Regs 1996 (see p 244 below). There is no prescribed form for the application for consent.

It should state that the occupier proposes to take the step, subject to the consent sought, in order to comply with a s 6 duty to adjust (DD(E) Regs 1996, reg 15)). The application should contain enough information to allow the lessor to know what is proposed. If the lessor requests further information that is not contained in the notice but is relevant to whether consent should be granted, it will probably not be unreasonable for him to refuse to consent until an answer is obtained (*Sood* v *Barker* [1991] 1 EGLR 87). In the absence of any clear statutory guidance, it would be prudent for a person seeking consent to give the lessor as much detailed information as possible in (or annexed to) the notice. It is to be hoped that regulations will provide a clearer answer, preferably with a prescribed form, in due course. If the lease provides that consent shall or will be given to an alteration of the kind in question if consent is sought in a particular way, consent should also be sought in the manner specified in the lease (in addition to the manner required under the DDA if different) so that any refusal of consent will be deemed to be unreasonable (DD(E) Regs 1996, reg 12(b), and p 243 below). If an occupier is intending to seek compensation for the improvement from the lessor at the end of the tenancy under s 1 of the LTA 1927, he will need to serve specifications and plans with the notice of intention to carry our the improvement in order to comply with s 3 of that Act.

Written consent
Although the DDA requires written consent from the lessor (ss 16(2)(*a*) and 27(2)(*a*)), oral consent which is acted upon will often amount to a waiver of any breach of covenant or estop the lessor from subsequently complaining about the failure to obtain written permission (*Richardson* v *Evans* (1818) 3 Madd 218 and *Millard* v *Humphreys* (1918) 62 Sol Jo 505). However, in order to avoid potential disputes and evidential difficulties, written consent should be sought in every case. Once consent has been given, it will probably not usually be revocable (*Mitten* v *Fagg* (1978) 247 EG 901) especially if it has already been acted upon.

Withholding consent
There may be an actual or deemed withholding of consent. When a lessor (including a superior lessor) has received a written application for consent to an alteration made by or on behalf of an occupier he will be deemed to have withheld consent unless he does one of the following things. Firstly, he may reply consenting to or refusing the application (DD(E) Regs 1996, reg 11(2)(*a*)) in which case the deeming provision will not apply as there has been an express grant or withholding of consent. Alternatively, the lessor may reply consenting to the application subject to obtaining the consent of another person required under a superior lease or pursuant to a binding obligation (see p 233 above) *and* seek that other person's consent (reg 11(2)(*b*)). Again, it is unclear how diligent the lessor must be in seeking that consent in order to comply with the regulation, although the Employment Code suggests that it

may, in appropriate circumstances, include an application to a court or tribunal for consent required under a binding obligation (para 4.48).

The reply must be made (and any consent required under reg 11(2)(*b*) sought) within a period of 21 days beginning with the day on which the lessor received the written application for consent or such longer period as is reasonable (reg 11(2)). If this is done, the lessor will not be treated as having withheld consent. Presumably a bona fide request for relevant additional information from the occupier before an answer is given would provide one justification for extending the 21-day period, (see *Sood* v *Barker* above). If the lessor responds (and seeks any necessary consent from another person) in accordance with the requirements of the reg 11(2) but only after expiry of the 21-day or longer reasonable period, he is deemed to have withheld consent from the expiry of that period until he complied with the requirements of reg 11(2) (reg 11(3)). The lessor is to be treated as not having sought any other person's consent unless he had applied in writing to that other person indicating that his (the lessor's) consent has been sought in order to comply with a s 6 duty and has been given conditionally upon obtaining that other person's consent (reg 11(4)).

Presumably an application by a lessor to his own lessor under a superior lease is intended to be treated as an application 'on behalf of' an occupier for the purposes of reg 11(1) as there is no other express provision which would place a time limit requiring a lessor under a superior lease to respond within a time limit or to seek the consent of another person required pursuant to a binding obligation. If this is wrong, then it would still be a question of fact whether prevarication by a superior lessor amounted to a withholding of consent and whether any withholding of consent was unreasonable given the failure to seek the consent required by the binding obligation.

Withholding consent unreasonably

Whether consent was withheld unreasonably or not is a question of fact other than in circumstances where consent is deemed to be or deemed not to be withheld unreasonably. The Employment Code notes that this will depend upon the circumstances, but that a trivial or arbitrary reason would almost certainly be unreasonable (para 4.43). It goes on to say that where a particular adjustment makes a public building more accessible generally, and it is thereby likely to benefit the lessor, it would very probably be unreasonable for consent to be withheld (para 4.43). As against that, a refusal is likely to be reasonable where a particular adjustment is likely to result in a permanent reduction in the value of the lessor's interest or cause significant disruption or convenience to other lessees (Employment Code, para 4.45).

The authorities on the statutory prohibition upon lessors unreasonably refusing a lessee consent to assign or improve demised premises (s 19(1) and (2) of the LTA 1927 and s 1 of the LTA 1988) are probably of some assistance here. As the DDA is silent as to the burden of proof it is probably for the occupier to show that the withholding was unreasonable (*Lambert* v *F*

Woolworth & Co Ltd [1936] 2 All ER 1523, *Pimms Ltd* v *Tallow Chandlers in the City of London* [1964] 2 QB 547 at 564 and s 19 of the LTA 1927; cf s 1 of the LTA 1988). The landlord does not have to show that the conclusions which caused him to withhold consent were justified, provided a reasonable man could have reached those conclusions in the circumstances (*International Drilling Fluids* v *Louisville Investments (Uxbridge) Ltd* [1986] Ch 513). Offering consent only on unreasonable conditions amounts to a withholding of consent (*Lambert* v *F Woolworth & Co Ltd* [1936] 2 All ER 1523).

Although the lessor is not under a duty to give reasons for the withholding of consent, a failure to give reasons may lead the court to draw an inference of unreasonableness so that the lessor has to prove reasonableness (*Frederick Berry Ltd* v *Royal Bank of Scotland* [1949] 1 KB 619 at 662 and *Lambert* v *Woolworth & Co (No 2)* [1938] Ch 883, *per* Slesser LJ at 906). Where two reasons are advanced, and one cannot be sustained or is unreasonable, the withholding of consent may be justified by the other reasons provided it is sufficient in itself and is not tainted by the other (*British Bakeries (Midlands) Ltd* v *Michael Testler & Co Ltd* [1986] 1 EGLR 64). The lessor may rely upon matters not mentioned in correspondence with the occupier to justify the withholding (*Sonnenthal* v *Newton* (1965) 109 Sol Jo 333) but only if those matters did influence the lessor's decision at the time of refusal (*Bromley Park Garden Estates Ltd* v *Moss* [1982] 2 All ER 890 and *CIN Properties Ltd* v *Gill* [1993] EGCS 129). Events after the consent was withheld are immaterial (*Orlando Investments* v *Grosvenor Estates Belgravia* [1989] 43 EG 175). One difference between the provisions of the LTA 1927 and the DDA may lie in the extent to which the lessor must take account of the effect which refusing consent will have upon others. The authorities on the Landlord and Tenant Acts establish that reasonableness is to be considered from the point of view of the lessor considering his own best interest and not the impact of the decision on the tenant, save where the adverse impact upon the tenant is disproportionate to the benefit to the lessor (see *International Drilling Fluids* v *Louisville Investments (Uxbridge) Ltd* above at 326). A lessor's refusal to consent may have adverse consequences for both the occupier and the disabled person. Admittedly, an occupier will not be in breach of the duty to adjust for not making an alteration where the lessor has withheld consent, subject to certain procedural requirements and a tribunal may require the lessor rather than the occupier to pay compensation to the disabled person where the consent was withheld unreasonably (Sched 4, para 2(6) and (9)). However, it may prevent the occupier from employing or continuing to employ the best person or people for the job. In addition, there will be an obvious adverse impact upon the disabled person who is disadvantaged by the physical feature which the occupier had proposed to alter. As the DDA is intended to allow disabled persons to obtain and retain employment irrespective of any disability and to ameliorate the disadvantages caused by architectural barriers, it is submitted that these matters should be taken into account in considering unreasonableness.

Lessor deemed to be withholding consent unreasonably
A lessor is taken to be withholding consent unreasonably where:
  (a) the lease provides that consent shall or will be given to an alteration of the kind in question; or
  (b) the lease provides that consent shall or will be given to an alteration of the kind in question if consent is sought in a particular way and the consent has been sought in that way; or
  (c) the lessor is deemed to have withheld consent by virtue of reg 11 (DD(E) Regs 1996, reg 12)).

Lessor deemed to be withholding consent reasonably
A lessor is taken to be withholding consent reasonably where:
  (a) the lessor is bound by the terms of a binding obligation requiring the consent of any person to the alteration;
  (b) the lessor has taken steps to obtain that consent; and
  (c) that consent had either been refused or has been given subject to a condition making it reasonable for him to withhold his consent (DD(E) Regs 1996, reg 13(1)).
A lessor is also taken to be withholding consent reasonably where:
  (a) the lessor is bound by an agreement which allows him to consent to the alteration in question subject to a condition that he makes a payment; and
  (b) that condition does not permit the lessor to make his own consent subject to a condition that the occupier reimburse him the payment (DD(E) Regs 1996, reg 13(2)).

Reasonable conditions

Whether a condition is reasonable is a question of fact. It is for the lessor to prove the condition is reasonable. It is probably not reasonable to require reinstatement where the alteration adds to the letting value for the premises *James* v *Hutton and J Cook & Sons Ltd* [1950] 1 KB 9, except in the circumstances prescribed by DD(E) Regs 1996, reg 14(2).

Conditions deemed to be reasonable
The following conditions, or conditions to similar effect, are deemed to be reasonable. Firstly, that the occupier must obtain any necessary planning permission and other consent or permission required by or under any enactment (DD(E) Regs 1996, reg 14(1)(*a*)) such as from the Fire Authority or under the Town and Country Planning Act 1971. Secondly, that the occupier must submit any plans or specifications for the alteration for the approval of the lessor (provided that the condition binds the lessor not to withhold approval unreasonably) and that the work is carried out in accordance with such plans or specifications (DD(E) Regs 1996, reg 14(1)(*b*)). Thirdly, that the lessor must be permitted a reasonable opportunity to inspect the work when completed (DD(E) Regs 1996, reg 14(1)(*c*)).

Fourthly, that the occupier must repay to the lessor any costs reasonably incurred by the lessor in connection with the giving of his consent (DD(E) Regs 1996, reg 14(1)*d*)) such as, perhaps reasonable legal costs or any payment made or to be made by the lessor to another party where such payment was or is necessary to obtain the consent of that other party to the alteration. Finally, in a case where it would be reasonable for the lessor to withhold consent to an alteration, a condition that the occupier or any assignee or successor must reinstate any relevant part of the premises which is to be altered to its state before the alteration was made is to be taken as reasonable (DD(E) Regs 1996, reg 14(2)).

Effect of lessor withholding consent

Regulation 15 of the DD(E) Regs 1996 provide that for the purposes of s 6(1) it is not reasonable for an employer to take a step in relation to premises occupied by him which he would otherwise be required to take in order to comply with the duty to adjust where:

   (a) he has applied to the lessor in writing to take that step;

   (b) he has indicated in writing that he proposes to take the step, subject to that consent, in order to comply with a duty to adjust under s 6;

   (c) the lessor has withheld consent; and

   (d) the occupier has informed the disabled person that he has applied for the consent of the lessor and that the lessor has withheld it.

It is not entirely clear whether the employer must give the written indication that he proposes to take the step in order to comply with the duty to adjust (under reg 15(*b*)) to the lessor or the disabled person, although it probably means the lessor. Nonetheless, it may be prudent to serve such notice upon both the lessor and the disabled person, if only to ensure that the disabled person is informed of the employer's intentions. Although there is no time limit within which the disabled person must be notified, the deeming provision will not come into operation until all of the above conditions have been satisfied. If the lessor consents to the alteration after the occupier has informed the disabled person that the lessor refused consent, the deeming provision will cease to apply and it may be reasonable for the employer to make the alteration at that stage. However, the delay in consent may make it unreasonable for the step to be taken after consent is given. For example, the employer may have employed another applicant after consent was refused or after the expiry of the 21-day or longer reasonable period (see p 244 above). In those circumstances the lessor may be liable to the disabled person as a result of the period of actual or deemed refusal.

    Where a disabled person brings a complaint against the occupier under s 8, either the occupier or the complainant can ask the tribunal to join a lessor (including the superior lessor) to the proceedings (Sched 4, para 2(1)). If the tribunal determines that the lessor refused consent unreasonably or imposed unreasonable conditions, it may make a declaration, make an order authorising the occupier to make the alteration, and order the lessor to pay compensation to the disabled person (para 2 to Sched 4, and see further p 126).

Once the relevant provisions come into force, the county court will have equivalent powers in relation to a claim made against a provider of goods or services under s 25 (para 7 of Sched 4, and see p 197). In addition, where a provider of goods and services has applied for consent which has been refused by the lessor or made subject to unreasonable conditions, either the occupier or the disabled person with an interest in the proposed alteration being made may refer the matter to a county court or sheriff court for a determination as to the reasonableness of the refusal or any conditions (para 6 of Sched 4). If the court determines that the refusal or conditions were unreasonable, it may make such declaration as it considers appropriate or an order authorising the occupier to carry our the order (para 6(4) of Sched 4) and requiring the occupier to comply with any conditions specified in the order (para 6(5) of Sched 4).

Pre-emptive action by occupiers/employers

However, an employer may wish to take action without waiting for a disabled person to bring a discrimination claim under the DDA. Although there is no express statutory provision allowing an employer to seek a declaration as to the reasonableness of any refusal of consent or conditions, the authorities on covenants not to assign or make improvements without consent established that an unreasonable refusal of consent by the lessor releases the lessee from the covenant, so that the lessee can then assign or make the improvement without consent (*Treloar* v *Bigge* (1874) LR 9 Exch 151 and *Lambert* v *F Woolworth & Co Ltd* [1936] 2 All ER 1523, *per* Romer LJ at 1536). This construction should be followed under the DDA. In such circumstances, it is submitted that the occupier can seek a declaration in the county court or, if appropriate, the High Court as to his right to have made or to make the alteration without consent (*Young* v *Ashley Gardens Properties* [1903] 2 Ch 112 and *Evans* v *Levy* [1910] 1 Ch 452). The occupier can recover the costs of the action for a declaration (*West* v *Gwynne* [1911] 2 Ch 1) but is unlikely to recover damages for the unreasonable withholding of consent (see *Rendal* v *Roberts & Stacey Ltd* (1959) 175 EG 265; *Rose* v *Gossman* (1966) 201 EG 767). A court will not grant a declaration that a superior lessor has acted unreasonably if he is not a party to the proceedings *Vienit Ltd* v *W Williams & Son (Bread Street) Ltd* [1958] 3 All ER 621. A disabled person who is an employee or potential employee of the occupier would not have sufficient interest to bring such proceedings for a declaration directly against the Lessor, and would have to join the lessor to Industrial Tribunal proceedings brought under s 8. There is no equivalent to para 6 of Sched 4 (see the previous paragraph).

Licensees

Neither ss 16 nor 27 of the DDA nor the provisions of the LTA 1927 apply to those who occupy premises pursuant to a licence rather than a lease or tenancy. The right of such occupiers to make alterations to premises, if any, will depend upon the terms of the licence agreement.

Alterations and building regulations

As with those that relate to binding obligations, the regulations referred to below apply only in relation to the duty to adjust imposed upon employers under s 6. However, similar regulations are expected in relation to trade organisations and providers of goods and services once the relevant sections are in force. Regulation 8 of the DD(E) Regs 1996 applies to a physical characteristic included within building works which:

   (a) was adopted with a view to meeting the requirements for the time being of:
      (i) (in England and Wales) Part M of the building regulations; and
      (ii) (in Scotland) Part T of the Technical Standards, with regard to access and facilities for disabled people; and
   (b) the physical characteristics met and continues substantially to meet the regulations in force at the date the works were carried out (reg 8(1)).

It is never reasonable for an employer to have to alter such a physical characteristic in order to comply with the duty to adjust (reg 8(2)). However, this does not prevent a duty to adjust in relation to matters that were outside of the Building Regulations. The Employment Code says that if a door was constructed at a particular width to comply with the Building Regulations, an employer would not have to widen the door although he may have to alter other aspects of the door, such as the type of handle, that was not governed by the regulations (para 4.35).

Part M of the building regulations

Part M was introduced by the Building (Disabled People) Regulations 1987 (SI No 1445(BDP 1987)) and replaced what was then Sched 2 to the Building Regulations 1985 from 14 December 1987. It is now contained in the Building Regulations 1991 (SI No 2768) (BR 1991). Care should be taken to ensure that the regulations used are those which were in force at the time of the relevant building works. However, each version of Pt M has dealt with broadly similar issues. Paragraph M2 requires reasonable provision to be made for disabled people to gain access to and use buildings to which the Part applied. Paragraph M3 requires reasonable provision for disabled people if any sanitary conveniences are provided in the building. Paragraph M4 requires the provision of adequate wheelchair spaces in buildings providing audience or spectator seating. 'Disabled people' means people who have an impairment which limits their ability to walk or requires them to use a wheelchair and, since 1 June 1992, also includes people with sight or hearing impairments (BDP Regs 1987, para M1). Originally Pt M applied only to factories, schools and other educational establishments, and any premises to which the public were admitted in so far as they were on the storey of the building containing the principal entrance as well as to shops and offices (BDP Regs 1987, para M1). However, since June 1992 it has applied to non-domestic buildings which are newly built or have been substantially constructed and to extensions to a building which include a ground storey extension. They still do not apply to a material alteration, a dwelling, the common parts of a building which are intended for the exclusive use of two or more dwellings, or any part of a building which is used solely to enable the building or any service or fitting in the building to be inspected or maintained (BR 1991, reg 9). Although a certificate issued under reg 15 of the Building Regulations do not automatically bind a tribunal or court for the purposes of the DDA, they will provide compelling evidence of compliance at the date of construction.

Part M is supplemented by Approved Document M (the current edition was published in 1992 (HMSO)) which gives detailed practical guidance on meeting the requirements of the Building Regulations, although there is no legal obligation to adopt a particular solution suggested in the Approved Document, provided the requirements set out above are met by other means. In addition, guidance may be obtained from the Determinations made by the Secretary of State under s 16(10) of the Building Act 1984 published by the Department of the Environment. For example, in a Determination under M2 dated 18 November 1988, it was considered that it was not reasonable to require a ramp to a balcony where the height of the balcony would require a ramp 12.1m long. A determination dated 7 March 1989 (DoE reference K12) concerned a proposal to construct an office block with an underground car park. Under the proposal, a wheelchair user was to obtain access to the principal entrance from the car park via the street pavement by way of a series of ramps. There was direct access to the entrance for able bodied people by way of a staircase. The Secretary of State considered that 'it was unreasonable to expect wheelchair users to have to leave the curtilage when others do not, in order to gain access to the principal entrance. It is even more unreasonable when they would, as well, have to negotiate a series of ramps and a sloping pavement' and that in the circumstances, the plans did not comply with the requirements of M2. An acceptable solution would have been either a lift or wheelchair stairlift from the car park. In a determination dated 20 February 1989 (DoE reference K7) the Secretary of State determined that 'in principle, it is unreasonable to expect that a person in a wheelchair should be required to travel further than an able-bodied person to get to a WC. In addition, there are reasons why disabled persons may need to be able to get to a WC quickly and easily. However, the making of requirements that are unduly onerous should be avoided'.

Physical characteristic

It is important to note the use of the expression 'physical characteristic' which is not defined in the DDA or regulations. Although it appears to have a wider meaning than the expression 'physical feature' that is used in the DDA and defined in reg 9 of the DD(E) Regs 1996, it is unclear how this will be construed. For example, a building may have been constructed with an accessible lavatory on each floor in order to comply with para M3 of the

Building Regulations at the time of construction. Each such accessible lavatory, together with its design features, fixtures and fittings, would comprise a physical feature. If 'physical characteristic' is interpreted to be synonymous with 'physical feature', an employer would not be required to alter any of those lavatories, features and fittings in so far as they were adopted to accord with the building regulations, even if they were unusable by a particular disabled person. This would produce a relatively narrow exception and would not prevent an obligation arising to provide another lavatory that could be used by the individual. However, 'physical characteristic' may be construed widely, as meaning the overall scheme for the provision of sanitary conveniences. If it is, the exception would be much wider in its effect, and would prevent the employer from being under a duty to make any alterations to the overall scheme, either by altering existing provisions or providing an additional lavatory. In relation to accessibility (under para M2 of the building regulations) the narrow construction of 'physical characteristic' would prevent a duty to alter particular features (such as existing doors and ramps) but allow a duty to provide additional means of access to arise. The wider construction would prevent any duty to alter premises to make them more accessible from arising, in so far as they complied with the relevant building regulations at the time of construction. The exact width of this exemption will have to be established by case law.

Certificates

Although a completion certificate issued by a local authority under the Building Regulations or a final certificate issued by an Approved Inspector under Pt II of the Building Act 1984 is not conclusive, it will provide compelling evidence of compliance.

Secondary liability

The DDA sets out the circumstances in which a person is and is not liable for the acts of his employees and agents. In addition, it provides that those who assist another to do an act made unlawful by the DDA are treated as having done the unlawful act, even though they are not directly subject to the substantive provisions of the Act (ie if they are not an employer, provider of goods and services, person with the power to dispose of the premises etc). Although these provisions are similar to the ordinary principles of vicarious liability, a claim under the DDA can only be based on vicarious liability to the extent permitted by s 58 (*Farah* v *Commissioner of Police of the Metropolis* (1996) *The Times*, 10 October).

Vicarious liability for employees

For the purposes of the DDA, an act done by a person in the course of his/her employment is treated as having also been done by the employer, whether or not the act was done with the employer's knowledge or approval (s 58(1)). The provisions of this section are directly comparable to those of s 41 of the SDA 1975 and s 32 of the RRA 1976. This provision is subject to the same principles as apply to the doctrine of vicarious liability at common law for the torts of an employee or agent. As such, an employer is liable both for the authorised acts of his employees and for the way in which those acts are carried out (even if they are unauthorised or improper ways of performing his authorised duties) but not for independent acts of the employee which were outside the sphere of his employment (*Irving* v *Post Office* [1987] IRLR 289). In particular this can restrict an employer's liability for harassment of a disabled person by other employees (see *Tower Boot Co Ltd* v *Jones* [1995] IRLR 529 EAT) unless, for example, the harassers can be said to be carrying out supervisory functions in an improper way (*Bracebridge Engineering Ltd* v *Darby* [1990] IRLR 3).

An employer will have a defence to any proceedings brought under the DDA in respect of an act done by an employee where the employer can prove that s/he took such steps as were reasonably practicable to prevent the employee from doing the act or doing acts of that description in the course of his employment (s 58(5)). In a case where the discriminatory acts were not known to the employer, the defence of having taken such steps as were reasonably practicable to prevent the act or acts of that description can be made out by establishing proper and adequate staff supervision, making an equal opportunities policy known to employees and making staff aware that harassment is a disciplinary matter that will be taken seriously (Employment Code, paras 4.56 and 6.22, and see *Balgobin and Francis* v *London Borough of Tower Hamlets* [1987] IRLR 401).

Vicarious liability for agents

Anything done by a person as agent for another ('the principal') with the express or implied authority of the principal shall be treated for the purposes of the DDA as having also been done by the principal, whether the authority was given before or after the act was done (s 58(2), 3)). There is no statutory defence if a principal can show that he took all practicable steps to prevent the agent from discriminating. Nonetheless, a principal who takes such steps (see Employment Code, para 4.56) and gives an agent clear instructions not to discriminate is likely to avoid being held liable for the agent's discrimination on the grounds that he did not authorise the discriminatory act.

Assisting unlawful acts

Section 57(1) of the DDA provides that 'a person who knowingly aids another person to do an act made unlawful by [the DDA] is to be treated for the purposes of the [DDA] as himself doing the same kind of unlawful act'. Where an employee or agent does an act for which their employer or principal is liable under s 58 (see above), the employee or agent shall be taken to have aided the employer or principal to do the act (s 57(2)). In such cases, the person who knowingly aids the commission of the unlawful act will be personally liable for the discrimination in addition to their employer or principal and both can be ordered to pay compensation (see *Read* v *Tiverton District Council and Bull* [1977] IRLR 202). For example, a recruitment consultant engaged by an employer may be told that the employer does not want to employ anyone with mental health problems. If the consultant then refuses to consider an application by a person with mental health problems, the consultant would be liable for having aided the employer to do something made unlawful by s 4 of the DDA (see the Employment Code, para 4.11). In addition, the employer would also be vicariously liable for the unlawful act carried out by the agent under s 58 (above).

However, a person does not knowingly aid another to do an unlawful act if he acts in reliance on a statement made by the other person that the act would not be unlawful because of any provision of the DDA, provided it is reasonable for him to rely upon that statement (s 57(3)). For example, a receptionist in a hairdresser's may refuse to book an appointment for someone with a disability in accordance with the owner's instructions. If the owner had told the receptionist that the hairdresser's was exempt from the DDA because it had less than 20 employees, provided it was reasonable for the receptionist to rely upon that statement the receptionist would not be liable under s 57, even though the 20 employee limit applies only to Pt II of the DDA and not to the provision of goods and services. The owner would still be vicariously liable for the refusal to book an appointment under s 58 (above).

It is an offence (punishable on summary conviction by a fine not exceeding level 5 on the standard scale) for a person to knowingly or recklessly make a statement that an act would not be unlawful because of any provision of the DDA which is false or misleading in a material respect. The vicarious liability provisions under s 58 (above) do not apply in relation to this offence, so that an employer or principal will not automatically be guilty of an offence because of the statements of an employee or agent (s 58(4)). Therefore, if the owner of the hairdresser's in the above example knew that the 20 employee limit didn't apply to the provision of goods and services, or didn't care if it applied or not, when she told the receptionist that it did, she would be committing an offence (see the Services and Premises Code at para 6.3). However, the DDA does not give anybody responsibility for bringing prosecutions under this section so it is questionable whether it will be enforced in practice.

Statutory authority or national security

The DDA does not make unlawful discriminatory acts done:
   (1) pursuant to any enactment, including those passed or made after the DDA, (s 59(1)(*a*) and (2));
   (2) pursuant to any instrument made under any enactment, including those passed after the DDA (s 59(1)(b) and (2));

(3) to comply with any condition or requirement imposed by virtue of any enactment (s 59(1)(*c*)) or

(4) for the purpose of safeguarding national security (s 59(3)).

Enactment includes subordinate legislation and any Order in Council (s 68(1)). Similar provisions in ss 51, 52 of the SDA 1975 and ss 41, 42 and 69(2)(*b*) of the RRA 1976 have been very narrowly construed. It is not enough to show that the discriminatory act was allowed or permitted by an enactment or that it involved the exercise of a statutory power given under an enactment. An act is only done pursuant to an instrument or enactment if it is done in the necessary performance of an express obligation in the instrument or enactment (*Hampson v Department of Education and Science* [1990] IRLR 302). A certificate signed by or on behalf of a Minister of the Crown certifying that a condition or requirement was imposed by a Minister and was in force at a specified time or that an act was done for the purpose of safeguarding national security is conclusive evidence of the matter so certified (Sched 3, para 4). A document purporting to be such a certificate shall be received in evidence and deemed to be such a certificate unless the contrary is proved (Sched 3, para 4(2)).

Victimisation

In common with the other discrimination legislation, the DDA gives those who make or assist claims of discrimination some protection from reprisals. Section 55(1) of the DDA provides that an employer discriminates against a person if it treats them less favourably than it treats or would treat other persons whose circumstances are the same as theirs because she has done one of the following protected acts:

(1) brought proceedings against [the employer] or any other person under this Act; or

(2) given evidence or information in connection with such proceedings brought by any person; or

(3) otherwise done anything under this Act in relation to [the employer] or any other person; or

(4) alleged that [the employer] or any other person has (whether or not the allegation so states) contravened the Act (DDA, s 55(2)(*a*)).

An employer also discriminates against a person if the employer treats her less favourably because the employer believes or suspects that she has done or intends to do one of the protected acts (s 55(2)(*b*)). It is not discrimination to treat someone less favourably for making an allegation that was false and not made in good faith (s 55(4)). Section 4(5) of the DDA makes clear that the anti-victimisation provisions apply to both non-disabled and disabled persons (see the Employment Code, para 4.53).

This anti-victimisation provision is broadly similar to those in s 4 of the SDA 1975 and s 2 of the RRA 1976. However, the equivalent provisions to s 55(2)(*a*)(iii) under the sex and race legislation read 'otherwise done anything under *or by reference to this Act* ... '. The absence of those words in the DDA may therefore cause the provisions to have a much narrower application. In *Aziz* v *Trinity Street Taxis Ltd* [1988] ICR 534, the Court of Appeal held that

> The phrase 'by reference to' is, in our judgment, a much wider one than 'under' and should be read accordingly. An act can, in our judgment, properly be said to be done 'by reference to the Act' if it is done by reference to the race relations legislation in the broad sense, even though the doer does not focus his mind specifically on any provision of the Act. (at 542c)

Furthermore, in *Kirby* v *Manpower Services Commission* [1980] IRLR 229 the EAT held that there must be 'a reference to a specific statutory provision' for something to be done 'under' the RRA.

Treats less favourably than he treats or would treat other persons whose circumstances are the same

The comparison is made with someone who had not done the protected act. It may be made either with someone who was treated more favourably or with a hypothetical comparator who would have been treated more favourably. If the person victimised is a disabled person, the disability is to be disregarded in comparing his circumstances with those of any other person (s 55(3)).

Causation

It is not enough to prove that the employer would have treated someone more favourably if they had not done the protected act. There must be a causal link between the fact that the act done was a protected act and the less favourable treatment (*Aziz* v *Trinity Street Taxis Ltd* [1988] ICR 534). In that case the employee was dismissed for making secret tape recordings for possible use in a race discrimination claim. However, the court held that as he would have been dismissed for making secret tape recordings for purposes wholly unconnected to the RRA 1976 there was no sufficient conscious link with the race relations legislation in the employer's motive and there was no victimisation. Presumably it is not necessary to show that the conscious link was the sole cause for the less favourable treatment (see p 36 above). The DDA does not prevent an employer from treating someone less favourably because of the manner in which she carried out the protected act (*Re York Truck Equipment Ltd* (1990) unreported, IRLIB 20/2/90, EAT 109/88).

Guidance on Matters to be Taken into Account in Determining Questions Relating to the Definition of Disability

Part I Introduction

Using the guidance

1 Although this guidance is primarily designed for courts and tribunals, it is likely to be of value to a range of people and organisations. **In the vast majority of cases there is unlikely to be any doubt whether or not a person has or has had a disability, but this guidance should prove helpful in cases where it is not clear.**

2 The definition of disability has a number of elements. The guidance covers each of these elements in turn. Each section contains an explanation of the relevant provisions of the Act which supplement the basic definition; guidance and examples are provided where relevant. Those using this guidance for the first time may wish to read it all, as each part of the guidance builds upon the part(s) preceding it.

3 Part II of this guidance relates to matters to be taken into account when considering whether an effect is substantial and/or long term. Most of the examples are to be found here, and particularly in **Section C**. Because the purpose of this guidance is to help in the cases where there is doubt, examples of cases where there will not be any doubt are not included.

4 Throughout the guidance descriptions of the provisions in the legislation are immediately preceded by bold italic text. They are immediately followed by a reference to the relevant provision of the Act or Regulations. References to sections of the Act are marked '*S*'; references to schedules are marked '*Sch*'; and references to paragraphs in schedules are marked '*Para*'. References in footnotes to 'Definition Regulations' mean The Disability Discrimination (Meaning of Disability) Regulations 1996.

Main elements of the definition of disability

5 ***The Act defines*** 'disabled person' as a person with '**a physical or mental impairment which has a substantial and long-term adverse effect on his ability to carry out normal day-to-day activities**' *(S1)*.

6   This means that:
- the person must have an *impairment*, that is either physical or mental (see paragraphs 10–15 below);
- the impairment must have adverse effects which are *substantial* (see **Section A**);
- the substantial effects must be *long-term* (see **Section B**); and
- the long-term substantial effects must be *adverse* effects on *normal day-to-day activities* (see **Section C**).

This definition is subject to the provisions in Schedule 1 *(Sch1)*.

Inclusion of people who have had a disability in the past

7   *The Act says* that Part I of the Act (definition), Part II (employment) and Part III (goods, facilities, services and premises) also apply in relation to a person who has had a disability as defined in paragraphs 5 and 6 above. For this purpose, those Parts of the Act are subject to the provisions in Schedule 2 to the Act *(S2, Sch2)*.

Exclusions from the definition

8   Certain conditions are not to be regarded as impairments for the purposes of the Act. These are:
- addiction to or dependency on alcohol, nicotine, or any other substance (other than in consequence of the substance being medically prescribed);
- the condition known as seasonal allergic rhinitis (eg hayfever), except where it aggravates the effect of another condition;
- tendency to set fires;
- tendency to steal;
- tendency to physical or sexual abuse of other persons;
- exhibitionism;
- voyeurism.

Also, disfigurements which consist of a tattoo (which has not been removed), non-medical body piercing, or something attached th[r]ough such piercing, are to be treated as not having a substantial adverse effect on the person's ability to carry out normal day-to-day activities.[1]

Registered disabled people

9   The introduction of the employment provisions in the Act coincides with the abolition of the Quota scheme which operated under the Disabled Persons (Employment) Act 1944. *The Disability Discrimination Act says* that anyone who was registered as a disabled person under the Disabled Persons (Employment) Act 1944 and whose name appeared on the register both on 12 January 1995 and on 2 December 1996 (the date the employment provisions come into force) is to be treated as having a disability for the purposes of the Disability Discrimination Act during the period of three years starting on 2 December 1996. This applies regardless of whether the person otherwise meets the definition of 'disabled person' during that period. Those who are treated by this provision as being disabled for the three-year period are also to be treated after this period has ended as having had a disability in the past *(Sch1, Para 7)*.

---

[1] Definition Regulations.

Impairment

10   The definition requires that the effects which a person may experience arise from a physical or mental impairment. In many cases there will be no dispute whether a person has an impairment. Any disagreement is more likely to be about whether the effects of the impairment are sufficient to fall within the definition. Even so, it may sometimes be necessary to decide whether a person has an impairment so as to be able to deal with the issues about its effects.

11   It is not necessary to consider how an impairment was caused, even if the cause is a consequence of a condition which is excluded. For example, liver disease as a result of alcohol dependency would count as an impairment.

12   *Physical or mental impairment* includes sensory impairments, such as those affecting sight or hearing.

13   *Mental impairment* includes a wide range of impairments relating to mental functioning, including what are often known as learning disabilities (formerly known as 'mental handicap'). However, *the Act states* that it does not include any impairment resulting from or consisting of a mental illness unless that illness is a clinically well-recognised illness *(Sch1, Para 1)*.

14   *A clinically well-recognised illness* is a mental illness which is recognised by a respected body of medical opinion. It is very likely that this would include those specifically mentioned in publications such as the World Health Organisation's International Classification of Diseases.

15   *The Act states* that mental impairment does not have the special meaning used in the Mental Health Act 1983 or the Mental Health (Scotland) Act 1984, although this does not preclude a mental impairment within the meaning of that legislation from coming within the definition in the Disability Discrimination Act *(S68)*.

Part II   Guidance on matters to be taken into account in determining questions relating to the definition of disability

A   Substantial

Meaning of 'substantial' adverse effect

A1   The requirement that an adverse effect be substantial reflects the general understanding of 'disability' as a limitation going beyond the normal differences in ability which may exist among people. A 'substantial' effect is more than would be produced by the sort of physical or mental conditions experienced by many people which have only minor effects. A 'substantial' effect is one which is more than 'minor' or 'trivial'.

The time taken to carry out an activity
A2   The time taken by a person with an impairment to carry out a normal day-to-day activity should be considered when assessing whether the effect of that impairment is

substantial. It should be compared with the time that might be expected if the person did not have the impairment.

The way in which an activity is carried out
A3   Another factor to be considered when assessing whether the effect of an impairment is substantial is the way in which a person with that impairment carries out a normal day-to-day activity. The comparison should be with the way the person might be expected to carry out the activity if he or she did not have the impairment.

Cumulative effects of an impairment
A4   *The Act provides* that an impairment is to be taken to affect the ability of a person to carry out normal day-to-day activities only if it affects that person in one (or more) of the respects listed in paragraph C4 *(Sch1, Para 4)*. An impairment might not have a substantial adverse effect on a person in any one of these respects, but its effects in more than one of these respects taken together could result in a substantial adverse effect on the person's ability to carry out normal day-to-day activities.

A5   For example, although the great majority of people with cerebral palsy will experience a number of substantial effects, someone with mild cerebral palsy may experience minor effects in a number of the respects listed in paragraph C4 which together could create substantial adverse effects on a range of normal day-to-day activities: fatigue may hinder walking, visual perception may be poor, co-ordination and balance may cause some difficulties. Similarly, a person whose impairment causes breathing difficulties may experience minor effects in a number of respects but which overall have a substantial adverse effect on their ability to carry out normal day-to-day activities. For some people, mental illness may have a clear effect in one of the respects in C4. However, for others, depending on the extent of the condition, there may be effects in a number of different respects which, taken together, substantially adversely affect their ability to carry out normal day-to-day activities.

A6   A person may have more than one impairment, any one of which alone would not have a substantial effect. In such a case, account should be taken of whether the impairments together have a substantial effect overall on the person's ability to carry out normal day-to-day activities. For example a minor impairment which affects physical co-ordination and an irreversible but minor injury to a leg which affects mobility, taken together, might have a substantial effect on the person's ability to carry out certain normal day-to-day activities.

Effects of behaviour
A7   Account should be taken of how far a person can reasonably be expected to modify behaviour to prevent or reduce the effects of an impairment on normal day-to-day activities. If a person can behave in such a way that the impairment ceases to have a substantial adverse effect on his or her ability to carry out normal day-to-day activities the person would no longer meet the definition of disability.

A8   In some cases people have such 'coping' strategies which cease to work in certain circumstances (for example, where someone who stutters or has dyslexia is placed under stress). If it is possible that a person's ability to manage the effects of an impairment will break down so that effects will sometimes still occur, this possibility must be taken into account when assessing the effects of the impairment.

A9   If a disabled person is advised by a medical practitioner to behave in a certain way in order to reduce the impact of the disability, that might count as treatment to be disregarded (see paragraph A11 below).

Effects of environment

A10   Whether adverse effects are substantial may depend on environmental conditions which may vary; for example, the temperature, humidity, the time of day or night, how tired the person is or how much stress he or she is under may have an impact on the effects. When assessing whether adverse effects are substantial, the extent to which such environmental factors are likely to have an impact should also therefore be considered.

Effect of treatment

A11   *The Act provides* that where an impairment is being *treated or corrected* the impairment is to be treated as having the effect it would have without the measures in question *(Sch1, Para 6(1))*. *The Act states* that the treatment or correction measures to be disregarded for these purposes include medical treatment and the use of a prosthesis or other aid *(Sch1, Para 6(2))*.

A12   This applies even if the measures result in the effects being completely under control or not at all apparent.

A13   For example, if a person with a hearing impairment wears a hearing aid the question whether his or her impairment has a substantial adverse effect is to be decided by reference to what the hearing level would be without the hearing aid. And in the case of someone with diabetes, whether or not the effect is substantial should be decided by reference to what the condition would be if he or she was not taking medication.

A14   However, *the Act states* that this provision does not apply to sight impairments to the extent that they are capable of correction by spectacles or contact lenses. In other words the only effects on ability to carry out normal day-to-day activities to be considered are those which remain when spectacles or contact lenses are used (or would remain if they were used). This does not include the use of devices to correct sight which are not spectacles or contact lenses *(Sch1, Para 6(3))*.

Progressive conditions

A15   A progressive condition is one which is likely to change and develop over time. *The Act gives* the following examples of progressive conditions: cancer, multiple sclerosis, muscular dystrophy, HIV infection. *The Act provides* for a person with such a condition to be regarded as having an impairment which has a substantial adverse effect on his or her ability to carry out normal day-to-day activities before it actually does so. Where a person has a progressive condition, he or she will be treated as having an impairment which has a *substantial* adverse effect from the moment any impairment resulting from that condition first has *some* effect on ability to carry out normal day-to-day activities. The effect need not be continuous and need not be substantial. For this rule to operate medical diagnosis of the condition is not by itself enough *(Sch1, Para 8)*.

Severe disfigurements

A16 *The Act provides* that where an impairment consists of a severe disfigurement, it is to be treated as having a substantial adverse effect on the person's ability to carry out normal day-to-day activities. There is no need to demonstrate such an effect *(Sch1, Para 3)*. *Regulations provide* that a disfigurement which consists of a tattoo (which has not been removed) is not to be considered as a severe disfigurement. Also excluded is a piercing of the body for decorative purposes including anything attached through the piercing.[2]

A17 Examples of disfigurements include scars, birthmarks, limb or postural deformation or diseases of the skin. Assessing severity will be mainly a matter of the degree of the disfigurement. However, it may be necessary to take account of where the feature in question is (eg on the back as opposed to the face).

B Long term

Meaning of long-term effects

B1 *The Act states* that, for the purpose of deciding whether a person is disabled, a long-term effect of an impairment is one:
- which has lasted at least twelve months; or
- where the total period for which it lasts, from the time of the first onset, is likely to be at least twelve months; or
- which is likely to last for the rest of the life of the person affected *(Sch1, Para 2)*.

For the purpose of deciding whether a person has had a disability in the past, a long-term effect of an impairment is one which lasted at least 12 months *(Sch2, Para 5)*.

B2 It is not necessary for the effect to be the same throughout the relevant period. It may change, as where activities which are initially very difficult become possible to a much greater extent. The main adverse effect might even disappear—or it might disappear temporarily—while one or other effects on ability to carry out normal day-to-day activities continue or develop. Provided the impairment continues to have, or is likely to have, such an effect throughout the period, there is a long-term effect.

Recurring effects

B3 *The Act states* that if an impairment has had a substantial adverse effect on a person's ability to carry out normal day-to-day activities but that effect ceases, the substantial effect is treated as continuing if it is likely to recur; that is, it is more likely than not that the effect will recur. (In deciding whether a person has had a disability in the past, the question is whether a substantial adverse effect has in fact recurred.) Conditions which recur only sporadically or for short periods (eg epilepsy) can still qualify. *(Sch1, Para 2(2), Sch2, Para 5)*. *Regulations specifically exclude* seasonal allergic rhinitis (eg hayfever) from this category, except where it aggravates the effects of an existing condition.[3]

---

[2] Definition Regulations.
[3] Definition Regulations.

B4   For example, a person with rheumatoid arthritis may experience effects from the first occurrence for a few weeks and then have a period of remission. But, if the effects are likely to recur, they are to be treated as if they were continuing. If the effects are likely to recur beyond twelve months after the first occurrence, they are to be treated as long-term.

B5   Likelihood of recurrence should be considered taking all the circumstances of the case into account. This should include what the person could reasonably be expected to do to prevent the recurrence; for example, the person might reasonably be expected to take action which prevents the impairment from having such effects (eg avoiding substances to which he or she is allergic). This may be unreasonably difficult with some substances. In addition, it is possible that the way in which a person can control or cope with the effects of a condition may not always be successful because, for example, a routine is not followed or the person is in an unfamiliar environment. If there is an increased likelihood that the control will break down, it will be more likely that there will be a recurrence. That possibility should be taken into account when assessing the likelihood of a recurrence.

Effects of treatment

B6   If medical or other treatment is likely to cure an impairment, so that recurrence of its effects would then be unlikely even if there were no further treatment, this should be taken into consideration when looking at the likelihood of recurrence of those effects. However, as **Section A** describes, if the treatment simply delays or prevents a recurrence, and a recurrence would be likely if the treatment stopped, then the treatment is to be ignored and the effect is to be regarded as likely to recur.

Meaning of 'likely'

B7   It is *likely* that an event will happen if it is more probable than not that it will happen.

B8   In assessing the likelihood of an effect lasting for any period, account should be taken of the total period for which the effect exists. This includes any time before the point when the discriminatory behaviour occurred as well as time afterwards. Account should also be taken of both the typical length of such an effect on an individual, and any relevant factors specific to this individual (for example, general state of health, age).

Assessing whether a past disability was long-term

B9   *The Act provides that* a person who has had a disability within the definition is protected from discrimination even if he or she has since recovered or the effects have become less than substantial. In deciding whether a past condition was a disability, its effects count as long-term if they lasted twelve months or more after the first occurrence, or if a recurrence happened or continued until more than twelve months after the first occurrence *(S2, Sch2, Para 5)*.

C   Normal day-to-day activities

Meaning of 'normal day-to-day activities'

C1   *The Act states* that an impairment must have a long-term substantial adverse effect on normal day-to-day activities *(S1)*.

C2   The term 'normal day-to-day activities' is not intended to include activities which are normal only for a particular person or group of people. Therefore in deciding whether an activity is a 'normal day-to-day activity' account should be taken of how far it is normal for most people and carried out by most people on a daily or frequent and fairly regular basis.

C3   The term 'normal day-to-day activities' does not, for example, include work of any particular form, because no particular form of work is 'normal' for most people. In any individual case, the activities carried out might be highly specialised. The same is true of playing a particular game, taking part in a particular hobby, playing a musical instrument, playing sport, or performing a highly skilled task. Impairments which affect only such an activity and have no effect on 'normal day-to-day activities' are not covered. The examples included in this section give an indication of what are to be taken as normal day-to-day activities.

C4   *The Act states* that an impairment is only to be treated as affecting the person's ability to carry out *normal day-to-day activities* if it affects one of the following:
- mobility;
- manual dexterity;
- physical co-ordination;
- continence;
- ability to lift, carry or otherwise move everyday objects;
- speech, hearing or eyesight;
- memory or ability to concentrate, learn or understand; or
- perception of the risk of physical danger *(Sch1, Para 4)*.

C5   In many cases an impairment will adversely affect the person's ability to carry out a range of normal day-to-day activities and it will be obvious that the overall adverse effect is substantial or the effect on at least one normal day-to-day activity is substantial. In such a case it is unnecessary to consider precisely how the person is affected in each of the respects listed in paragraph C4. For example, a person with a clinically well-recognised mental illness may experience an adverse effect on concentration which prevents the person from remembering why he or she is going somewhere; the person would not also have to demonstrate that there was an effect on, say, speech. A person with an impairment which has an adverse effect on sight might be unable to go shopping unassisted; he or she would not also have to demonstrate that there was an effect on, say, mobility.

C6   Many impairments will, by their nature, adversely affect a person directly in one of the respects listed in C4. An impairment may also indirectly affect a person in one or more of these respects, and this should be taken into account when assessing whether the impairment falls within the definition. For example:
- medical advice: where a person has been professionally advised to change,

limit or refrain from a normal day-to-day activity on account of an impairment or only do it in a certain way or under certain conditions;

• pain or fatigue: where an impairment causes pain or fatigue in performing normal day-to-day activities, so the person may have the capacity to do something but suffer pain in doing so; or the impairment might make the activity more than usually fatiguing so that the person might not be able to repeat the task over a sustained period of time.

C7 Where a person has a mental illness such as depression account should be taken of whether, although that person has the physical ability to perform a task, he or she is, in practice, unable to sustain an activity over a reasonable period.

C8 Effects of impairments may not be apparent in babies and young children because they are too young to have developed the ability to act in the respects listed in C4. *Regulations provide* that where an impairment to a child under six years old does not have an effect in any of the respects in C4, it is to be treated as having a substantial and long-term adverse effect on the ability of that child to carry out normal day-to-day activities where it would normally have a substantial and long-term adverse effect on the ability of a person aged six years or over to carry out normal day-to-day activities.[4]

C9 In deciding whether an effect on the ability to carry out a normal day-to-day activity is a substantial adverse effect, account should be taken of factors such as those mentioned under each heading below. The headings are exhaustive—the person must be affected in one of these respects. The lists of examples are not exhaustive; they are only meant to be illustrative. The assumption is made in each example that there is an adverse effect on the person's ability to carry out normal day-to-day activities. A person only counts as disabled if the substantial effect is adverse.

C10 The examples below of what it would, and what it would not, be reasonable to regard as substantial adverse effects are indicators and not tests. They do not mean that if a person can do an activity listed then he or she does not experience any substantial adverse effects; the person may be inhibited in other activities, and this instead may indicate a substantial effect.

C11 In reading examples of effects which it would not be reasonable to regard as substantial, the effect described should be thought of as if it were the only effect of the impairment. That is, if the effect listed in the example were the only effect it would not be reasonable to regard it as substantial in itself.

C12 Examples of effects which are obviously within the definition are not included below. So for example, inability to dress oneself, inability to stand up, severe dyslexia or a severe speech impairment would clearly be covered by the definition and are not included among the examples below. The purpose of these lists is to provide help in cases where there may be doubt as to whether the effects on normal day-to-day activities are substantial.

C13 The examples below describe the effect which would occur when the various factors described in Parts A and B above have been allowed for. This includes, for

---

[4] Definition Regulations.

example the effects of a person making such modifications of behaviour as might reasonably be expected, or of disregarding the impact of medical or other treatment.

Mobility

C14   This covers moving or changing position in a wide sense. Account should be taken of the extent to which, because of either a physical or a mental condition, a person is inhibited in getting around unaided or using a normal means of transport, in leaving home with or without assistance, in walking a short distance, climbing stairs, travelling in a car or completing a journey on public transport, sitting, standing, bending, or reaching, or getting around in an unfamiliar place.

Examples
It **would be reasonable** to regard as having a substantial adverse effect:
- inability to travel a short journey as a passenger in a vehicle;
- inability to walk other than at a slow pace or with unsteady or jerky movements;
- difficulty in going up or down steps, stairs or gradients;
- inability to use one or more forms of public transport;
- inability to go out of doors unaccompanied.

It **would not be reasonable** to regard as having a substantial adverse effect:
- difficulty walking unaided a distance of about 1.5 kilometres or a mile without discomfort or having to stop—the distance in question would obviously vary according to the age of the person concerned and the type of terrain;
- inability to travel in a car for a journey lasting more than two hours without discomfort.

Manual dexterity

C15   This covers the ability to use hands and fingers with precision. Account should be taken of the extent to which a person can manipulate the fingers on each hand or co-ordinate the use of both hands together to do a task. This includes the ability to do things like pick up or manipulate small objects, operate a range of equipment manually, or communicate through writing or typing on standard machinery. Loss of function in the dominant hand would be expected to have a greater effect than equivalent loss in the non-dominant hand.

Examples
It **would be reasonable** to regard as having a substantial adverse effect:
- loss of function in one or both hands such that the person cannot use the hand or hands;
- inability to handle a knife and fork at the same time;
- ability to press the buttons on keyboards or keypads but only much more slowly than is normal for most people.

It **would not be reasonable** to regard as having a substantial adverse effect:
- inability to undertake activities requiring delicate hand movements, such as threading a small needle;
- inability to reach typing speeds standardised for secretarial work;
- inability to pick up a single small item, such as a pin.

Physical co-ordination

C16 This covers balanced and effective interaction of body movement, including hand and eye co-ordination. In the case of a child, it is necessary to take account of the level of achievement which would be normal for a person of the particular age. In any case, account should be taken of the ability to carry out 'composite' activities such as walking and using hands at the same time.

Examples

It **would be reasonable** to regard as having a substantial adverse effect:
- ability to pour liquid into another vessel only with unusual slowness or concentration;
- inability to place food into one's own mouth with fork/spoon without unusual concentration or assistance.

It **would not be reasonable** to regard as having a substantial adverse effect:
- mere clumsiness;
- inability to catch a tennis ball.

Continence

C17 This covers the ability to control urination and/or defecation. Account should be taken of the frequency and extent of the loss of control and the age of the individual.

Examples

It **would be reasonable** to regard as having a substantial adverse effect:
- even infrequent loss of control of the bowels;
- loss of control of the bladder while asleep at least once a month;
- frequent minor faecal incontinence or frequent minor leakage from the bladder.

It **would not be reasonable** to regard as having a substantial adverse effect:
- infrequent loss of control of the bladder while asleep;
- infrequent minor leakage from the bladder.

Ability to lift, carry or otherwise move everyday objects

C18 Account should be taken of a person's ability to repeat such functions or, for example, to bear weights over a reasonable period of time. Everyday objects might include such items as books, a kettle of water, bags of shopping, a briefcase, an overnight bag, a chair or other piece of light furniture.

Examples

It **would be reasonable** to regard as having a substantial adverse effect:
- inability to pick up objects of moderate weight with one hand;
- inability to carry a moderately loaded tray steadily.

It **would not be reasonable** to regard as having a substantial adverse effect:
- inability to carry heavy luggage without assistance;
- inability to move heavy objects without a mechanical aid.

Speech, hearing or eyesight

C19   This covers the ability to speak, hear or see and includes face-to-face, telephone and written communication.

(i)   Speech

Account should be taken of how far a person is able to speak clearly at a normal pace and rhythm and to understand someone else speaking normally in the person's native language. It is necessary to consider any effects on speech patterns or which impede the acquisition or processing of one's native language, for example by someone who has had a stroke.

Examples
It **would be reasonable** to regard as having a substantial adverse effect:
- inability to give clear basic instructions orally to colleagues or providers of a service;
- inability to ask specific questions to clarify instructions;
- taking significantly longer than average to say things.

It **would not be reasonable** to regard as having a substantial adverse effect:
- inability to articulate fluently due to a minor stutter, lisp or speech impediment;
- inability to speak in front of an audience;
- having a strong regional or foreign accent;
- inability to converse in a language which is not the speaker's native language.

(ii)   Hearing

If a person uses a hearing aid or similar device, what needs to be considered is the effect that would be experienced if the person were not using the hearing aid or device. Account should be taken of effects where the level of background noise is within such a range and of such a type that most people would be able to hear adequately.

Examples
It **would be reasonable** to regard as having a substantial adverse effect:
- inability to hold a conversation with someone talking in a normal voice in a moderately noisy environment;
- inability to hear and understand another person speaking clearly over the voice telephone.

It **would not be reasonable** to regard as having a substantial adverse effect:
- inability to hold a conversation in a very noisy place, such as a factory floor;
- inability to sing in tune.

(iii)   Eyesight

If a person's sight is corrected by spectacles or contact lenses, or could be corrected by them, what needs to be considered is the effect remaining while they are wearing such spectacles or lenses, in light of a level and type normally acceptable to most people for normal day-to-day activities.

Examples
It **would be reasonable** to regard as having a substantial adverse effect:
- inability to see to pass the eyesight test for a standard driving test;
- inability to recognise by sight a known person across a moderately-sized room;
- total inability to distinguish colours;
- inability to read ordinary newsprint;
- inability to walk safely without bumping into things.

It **would not be reasonable** to regard as having a substantial adverse effect:
- inability to read very small or indistinct print without the aid of a magnifying glass;
- inability to distinguish a known person across a substantial distance (eg playing field);
- inability to distinguish between red and green.

Memory or ability to concentrate, learn or understand

C20   Account should be taken of the person's ability to remember, organise his or her thoughts, plan a course of action and carry it out, take in new knowledge, or understand spoken or written instructions. This includes considering whether the person learns to do things significantly more slowly than is normal. Account should be taken of whether the person has persistent and significant difficulty in reading text in standard English or straightforward numbers.

Examples
It **would be reasonable** to regard as having a substantial adverse effect:
- intermittent loss of consciousness and associated confused behaviour;
- persistent inability to remember the names of familiar people such as family or friends;
- inability to adapt after a reasonable period to minor change in work routine;
- inability to write a cheque without assistance;
- considerable difficulty in following a short sequence such as a simple recipe or a brief list of domestic tasks.

It **would not be reasonable** to regard as having a substantial adverse effect:
- occasionally forgetting the name of a familiar person, such as a colleague;
- inability to concentrate on a task requiring application over several hours;
- inability to fill in a long, detailed, technical document without assistance;
- inability to read at faster than normal speed;
- minor problems with writing or spelling.

Perception of the risk of physical danger

C21   This includes both the underestimation and overestimation of physical danger, including danger to well-being. Account should be taken, for example, of whether the person is inclined to neglect basic functions such as eating, drinking, sleeping, keeping warm or personal hygiene; reckless behaviour which puts the person or others at risk; or excessive avoidance behaviour without a good cause.

Examples

It **would be reasonable** to regard as having a substantial adverse effect:
- inability to operate safely properly-maintained equipment;
- persistent inability to cross a road safely;
- inability to nourish oneself (assuming nourishment is available);
- inability to tell by touch that an object is very hot or cold.

It **would not be reasonable** to regard as having a substantial adverse effect:
- fear of significant heights;
- underestimating the risk associated with dangerous hobbies, such as mountain climbing;
- underestimating risks—other than obvious ones—in unfamiliar workplaces.

Code of Practice for the Elimination of Discrimination in the Field of Employment against Disabled Persons or Persons who have had a Disability

The Disability Discrimination Act 1995

The Disability Discrimination Act introduces new laws and measures aimed at ending the discrimination which many disabled people face. Over time, the Act will give disabled people new rights in the areas of:

- employment
- access to goods, facilities and services
- buying or renting land or property.

In addition the Act:

- requires schools, colleges and universities to provide information for disabled people
- allows the Government to set minimum standards so that disabled people can use public transport easily
- sets up the National Disability Council to advise the Government on discrimination against disabled people.

The Act provides for a separate Code of Practice containing guidance on access to goods, facilities and services and the buying and renting of land or property. This can be obtained from HMSO bookshops.

Northern Ireland

The Act (as modified by Schedule 8) also applies in Northern Ireland. A Code of Practice reflecting those modifications is published in Northern Ireland.

1 Introduction

Purpose and status of the Code

1.1 [Pages 3 to 58] are a Code of Practice issued by the Secretary of State for Education and Employment under section 53 (1) (a) of the Disability Discrimination Act 1995 ('the Act'). The Code comes into effect on 2 December 1996.

1.2   The employment provisions of the Act and the Disability Discrimination (Employment) Regulations 1996 protect disabled people, and people who have been disabled, from discrimination in the field of employment. Although the Code is written in terms of 'disabled' people, it also applies to people who no longer have a disability but have had one in the past. The date from which the employment provisions take effect is 2 December 1996 (but see paragraph 7.12). The Code of Practice gives practical guidance to help employers and others—including trade organisations and people who hire staff from employment businesses—in eliminating discrimination and should assist in avoiding complaints to industrial tribunals.

1.3   The Code applies in England, Scotland and Wales. It does not itself impose legal obligations and is not an authoritative statement of the law. Authoritative interpretation of the Act and regulations is for the tribunals and courts. However, the Code is admissible in evidence in any proceedings under the Act before an industrial tribunal or court. If any provision in the Code appears to the tribunal or court to be relevant to a question arising in the proceedings, it must be taken into account in determining that question.

Using the Code

1.4   The Code describes—and gives general guidance on—the main employment provisions of the Act in paragraphs 4.1 to 4.66. More specific guidance on how these provisions operate in different situations is in later paragraphs but it may be necessary to refer back to the general guidance occasionally. For example, someone thinking of recruiting new staff will need to read paragraphs 5.1 to 5.29 and also, unless already familiar with it, the general guidance on the provisions in paragraphs 4.1 to 4.66. Someone dealing with a new or existing employee should read paragraphs 6.1 to 6.23, again with reference to the general guidance as necessary. Examples of how the Act is likely to work in practice are given in boxes (see also paragraph 3.1). Annexes 1–3 are not part of the Code but include information on related subjects. There is a detailed index at the end of the Code.[*]

1.5   References to the legal provisions relevant to the guidance in the Code are generally just on the first, or only, main mention of a provision. For example, 'S5(1)' means Section 5, subsection (1) of the Act. 'Sch 1 Para 1 (1)' means Schedule 1, paragraph 1 subparagraph (1) of the Act.

1.6   References in footnotes to 'Employment Regulations' mean The Disability Discrimination (Employment) Regulations 1996 and to 'Definition Regulations' mean The Disability Discrimination (Meaning of Disability) Regulations 1996.

1.7   In the examples, reference to male and female individual disabled people are given for realism. All other references are masculine for simplicity but could, of course, apply to either sex.

---

* Publisher's note: Annexes 1–3 are not reproduced here.

2   Who is, and who is not, covered by the employment provisions

What is the main purpose of the employment provisions of the Act?

2.1   The Act protects disabled people from discrimination in the field of employment. As part of this protection employers may have to make 'reasonable adjustments' if their employment arrangements or premises place disabled people at a substantial disadvantage compared with non-disabled people. These provisions replace the quota scheme, the designated employment scheme and registration as a disabled person *(S61(7))*.

2.2   The Act does not prohibit an employer from appointing the best person for the job. Nor does it prevent employers from treating disabled people more favourably than those without a disability.

Who has rights or obligations under the Act?

2.3   Disabled people have rights under the Act, as do people who have had disabilities but have fully or largely recovered. The Act defines a disabled person as someone with a physical or mental impairment which has a substantial and long-term adverse effect on his ability to carry out normal day-to-day activities *(S1 and Sch1)*. (See Annex 1)

2.4   The following people and organisations may have obligations under the Act:
*   employers;
*   the Crown (including Government Departments and Agencies) *(S64)*;
*   employees and agents of an employer;
*   landlords of premises occupied by employers;
*   people who hire contract workers;
*   trustees or managers of occupational pension schemes;
*   people who provide group insurance schemes for an employer's employees;
*   trade organisations.

2.5   This Act does not confer rights on people who do not have—and have not had—a disability, with the exception of the provisions covering victimisation (see paragraphs 4.53 and 4.54).

Who does not have obligations or rights under the Act?

2.6   The employment provisions do not apply to employers with fewer than 20 employees *(S7)*. The Act applies when an employer has 20 or more employees in total, regardless of the size of individual workplaces or branches. However, if the number of employees falls below 20 the employer will be exempted for as long as there are fewer than 20 employees. Independent franchise holders are exempt if they employ fewer than 20 people even if the franchise network has 20 or more employees. The Government must carry out a review of the threshold for the exclusion of small firms within 5 years of the employment provisions coming into force.

2.7   The employment provisions do not apply to:
*   members of the Armed Forces *(S64(7))*;
*   prison officers *(S64(5)(b))*;

- firefighters *(S64(5)(c) and (6))*;
- employees who work wholly or mainly outside Great Britain *(S68(2))*;
- employees who work on board ships, aircraft or hovercraft *(S68(3))*;
- members of the Ministry of Defence Police, the British Transport Police, the Royal Parks Constabulary and the United Kingdom Atomic Energy Authority Constabulary *(S68(5)(a))*; and
- other police officers who are in any event not employees as defined in *S68(1)*.

Who counts as an employee under the Act?

2.8   'Employment' means employment under a contract of service or of apprenticeship, or a contract personally to do any work *(S68)*. The last category covers persons who are self-employed and agree to perform the work personally. 'Employee' means anyone whose contract is within that definition of employment, whether or not, for example, he works full-time.

3   General guidance to help avoid discrimination

Be flexible

3.1   There may be several ways to avoid discrimination in any one situation. Examples in this Code are *illustrative only*, to indicate what should or should not be done in those and other broadly similar types of situations. They cannot cover every possibility, so it is important to consider carefully how the guidance applies in any specific circumstances. **Many ways of avoiding discrimination will cost little or nothing**. The Code should not be read narrowly; for instance, its guidance on recruitment might help avoid discrimination when promoting employees.

Do not make assumptions

3.2   It will probably be helpful to talk to each disabled person about what the real effects of the disability might be or what might help. There is less chance of a dispute where the person is involved from the start. Such discussions should not, of course, be conducted in a way which would itself give the disabled person any reason to believe that he was being discriminated against.

Consider whether expert advice is needed

3.3   It is possible to avoid discrimination using personal, or in-house, knowledge and expertise, particularly if the views of the disabled person are sought. The Act does not oblige anyone to get expert advice but it could help in some circumstances to seek independent advice on the extent of a disabled person's capabilities. This might be particularly appropriate where a person is newly disabled or the effects of someone's disability become more marked. It may also help to get advice on what might be done to change premises or working arrangements, especially if discussions with the disabled person do not lead to a satisfactory solution. Annex 2 gives information about getting advice or help.

Plan ahead

3.4   Although the Act does not require an employer to make changes in anticipation of ever having a disabled applicant or employee, nevertheless when planning for change it could be cost-effective to consider the needs of a range of possible future disabled employees and applicants. There may be helpful improvements that could be built into plans. For example, a new telecommunications system might be made accessible to deaf people even if there are currently no deaf employees.

Promote equal opportunities

3.5   If an employer has an equal opportunities policy or is thinking of introducing one, it would probably help to avoid a breach of the Act if that policy covered disability issues. Employers who have, and follow, a good policy—including monitoring its effectiveness—are likely to have that counted in their favour by a tribunal if a complaint is made. But employers should remember that treating people equally will not always avoid a breach of the Act. An employer may be under a duty to make a reasonable adjustment. This could apply at any time in the recruitment process or in the course of a disabled person's employment.

4   The main employment provisions of the Act

Discrimination

What does the Act say about discrimination?

4.1   *The Act makes it unlawful* for an employer to discriminate against a disabled person in the field of employment *(S4)*. **The Act says** 'discrimination occurs in two ways.

4.2   One way in which discrimination occurs is when:
- for a reason which relates to a disabled person's disability, the employer treats that disabled person less favourably than the employer treats or would treat others to whom the reason does not or would not apply; *and*
- the employer cannot show that this treatment is justified *(S5(1))*.

A woman with a disability which requires use of a wheelchair applies for a job. She can do the job but the employer thinks the wheelchair will get in the way in the office. He gives the job to a person who is no more suitable for the job but who does not use a wheelchair. The employer has therefore treated the woman *less favourably* than the other person because he did not give her the job. The treatment was *for a reason related to the disability*—the fact that she used a wheelchair. And the reason for treating her less favourably *did not apply to the other person* because that person did not use a wheelchair.

If the employer could not justify his treatment of the disabled woman then he would have unlawfully discriminated against her.

> An employer decides to close down a factory and makes all the employees redundant, including a disabled person who works there. This is not discrimination as the disabled employee is not being dismissed for a reason which relates to the disability.

4.3   A disabled person may not be able to point to other people who were actually treated more favourably. However, it is still 'less favourable treatment' if the employer would give better treatment to someone else to whom the reason for the treatment of the disabled person did not apply. This comparison can also be made with other disabled people, not just non-disabled people. For example, an employer might be discriminating by treating a person with a mental illness less favourably than he treats or would treat a physically disabled person.

4.4   The other way *the Act says* that discrimination occurs is when:
- an employer fails to comply with a duty of reasonable adjustment imposed on him by section 6 in relation to the disabled person; *and*
- he cannot show that this failure is justified *(S5(2))*.

4.5   The relationship between the duty of reasonable adjustment and the need to justify less favourable treatment is described in paragraphs 4.7–4.9. The duty itself is described from paragraph 4.12 onwards and the need to justify a failure to comply with it is described in paragraph 4.34.

What will, and what will not, be justified treatment?

4.6   *The Act says* that less favourable treatment of a disabled person will be justified only if the reason for it is both material to the circumstances of the particular case *and* substantial *(S5(3))*. This means that the reason has to relate to the individual circumstances in question and not just be trivial or minor.

> Someone who is blind is not shortlisted for a job involving computers because the employer thinks blind people cannot use them. The employer makes no effort to look at the individual circumstances. A general assumption that blind people cannot use computers would not in itself be a material reason—it is not related to the particular circumstances.

> A factory worker with a mental illness is sometimes away from work due to his disability. Because of that he is dismissed. However, the amount of time off is very little more than the employer accepts as sick leave for other employees and so is very unlikely to be a substantial reason.

A clerical worker with a learning disability cannot sort papers quite as quickly as some of his colleagues. There is very little difference in productivity but he is dismissed. That is very unlikely to be a substantial reason.

An employer seeking a clerical worker turns down an applicant with a severe facial disfigurement solely on the ground that other employees would be uncomfortable working alongside him. This will be unlawful because such a reaction by other employees will not in itself justify less favourable treatment of this sort—it is not substantial. The same would apply if it were thought that a customer would feel uncomfortable.

An employer moves someone with a mental illness to a different workplace solely because he mutters to himself while he works. If the employer accepts similar levels of noise from other people, the treatment of the disabled person would probably be unjustified—that level of noise is unlikely to be a substantial reason.

Someone who has psoriasis (a skin condition) is rejected for a job involving modelling cosmetics on a part of the body which in his case is severely disfigured by the condition. That would be lawful if his appearance would be incompatible with the purpose of the work. This is a substantial reason which is clearly related—material—to the individual circumstance.

4.7 *The Act says* that less favourable treatment cannot be justified where the employer is under a duty to make a reasonable adjustment but fails (without justification) to do so, *unless* the treatment would have been justified even after that adjustment *(S5(5))*.

An employee who uses a wheelchair is not promoted, solely because the work station for the higher post is inaccessible to wheelchairs—though it could readily be made so by rearrangement of the furniture. If the furniture had been rearranged, the reason for refusing promotion would not have applied. The refusal of promotion would therefore not be justified.

An applicant for a typing job is not the best person on the face of it, but only because her typing speed is too slow due to arthritis in her hands. If a reasonable adjustment—perhaps an adapted keyboard—would overcome this, her typing speed would not in itself be a substantial reason for not employing her. Therefore the employer would be unlawfully discriminating if on account of her typing speed he did not employ her and provide the adjustment.

An employer refuses a training course for an employee with an illness which is very likely to be terminal within a year because, even with a reasonable adjustment to help in the job after the course, the benefits of the course could not be adequately realised. This is very likely to be a substantial reason. It is clearly material to the circumstances. The refusal of training would therefore very likely be justified.

Someone who is blind applies for a job which requires a significant amount of driving. If it is not reasonable for the employer to adjust the job so that the driving duties are given to someone else, the employer's need for a driver might well be a substantial reason for not employing the blind person. It is clearly material to the particular circumstances. The non-appointment could therefore be justified.

How does an employer avoid unlawful discrimination?

4.8   An employer should not treat a disabled employee or disabled job applicant less favourably, for a reason relating to the disability, than others to whom that reason does not apply, unless that reason is material to the particular circumstances and substantial. If the reason is material and substantial, the employer may have to make a reasonable adjustment to remove it or make it less than substantial *(S5(3) and (5))*.

4.9   Less favourable treatment is therefore justified if the disabled person cannot do the job concerned, and no adjustment which would enable the person to do the job (or other vacant job) is practicable *(S5(3) and (5))*. (See paragraph 4.20 for examples of adjustments which employers may have to make.)

4.10   *The Act says* that some charities (and Government-funded supported employment) are allowed to treat some groups of disabled people more favourably than others. But they can do this only if the group being treated more favourably is one with whom the charitable purposes of the charity are connected and the more favourable treatment is in pursuance of those purposes (or, in the case of supported employment, those treated more favourably are severely disabled people whom the programme aims to help) *(S10)*.

What does the Act say about helping others to discriminate?

4.11   *The Act says* that a person who knowingly helps another to do something made unlawful by the Act will also be treated as having done the same kind of unlawful act *(S57(1))*.

A recruitment consultant engaged by an engineering company refuses to consider a disabled applicant for a vacancy, because the employer has told the consultant that he does not want the post filled by someone who is 'handicapped'. Under the Act the consultant could be liable for aiding the company.

Reasonable adjustment

What does the Act say about the duty of 'reasonable adjustment'?

4.12 *The Act says* that the duty applies where any physical feature of premises occupied by the employer, or any arrangements made by or on behalf of the employer, cause a substantial disadvantage to a disabled person compared with non-disabled people. An employer has to take such steps as it is reasonable for him to have to take in all the circumstances to prevent that disadvantage—in other words the employer has to make a 'reasonable adjustment' *(S6(1))*.

A man who is disabled by dyslexia applies for a job which involves writing letters with fairly long deadlines. The employer gives all applicants a test of their letter-writing ability. The man can generally write letters very well but finds it difficult to do so in stressful situations. The *employer's arrangements* would mean he had to begin his test immediately on arrival and to do it in a short time. He would be *substantially disadvantaged compared to non-disabled people* who would not find such arrangements stressful or, if they did, would not be so affected by them. The employer therefore gives him a little time to settle in and longer to write the letter. These new arrangements do not inconvenience the employer very much and only briefly delay the decision on an appointment. These are *steps that it is reasonable for the employer to have to take in the circumstances to prevent the disadvantage*—a 'reasonable adjustment'.

4.13 If a disabled person cannot point to an existing non-disabled person compared with whom he is at a substantial disadvantage, then the comparison should be made with how the employer would have treated a non-disabled person.

4.14 How to comply with this duty in recruitment and during employment is explained in paragraphs 5.1–5.29 and 6.1–6.21. The following paragraphs explain how to satisfy this duty more generally.

What 'physical features' and 'arrangements' are covered by the duty?

4.15 *Regulations define* the term 'physical features' to include anything on the premises arising from a building's design or construction or from an approach to, exit from or access to such a building; fixtures, fittings, furnishings, furniture, equipment or materials; and any other physical element or quality of land in the premises. All of these are covered whether temporary or permanent.[1]

4.16 *The Act says* that the duty applies to 'arrangements' for determining to whom employment should be offered and any term, condition or arrangement on which employment, promotion, transfer, training or any other benefit is offered or afforded *(S6(2))*. The duty applies in recruitment and during employment; for example, selection and interview procedures and the arrangements for using premises for such procedures as well as job offers, contractual arrangements, and working conditions.

---

[1] Employment Regulations (see paragraph 1.6).

> The design of a particular workplace makes it difficult for someone with a hearing impairment to hear. That is a disadvantage caused by the *physical features*. There may be nothing that can reasonably be done in the circumstances to change these features. However, requiring someone to work in such a workplace is an *arrangement made by the employer* and it might be reasonable to overcome the disadvantage by a transfer to another workplace or by ensuring that the supervisor gives instructions in an office rather than in the working area.

What 'disadvantages' give rise to the duty?

4.17   *The Act says* that only substantial disadvantages give rise to the duty *(S6(1))*. Substantial disadvantages are those which are not minor or trivial.

> An employer is unlikely to be required to widen a particular doorway to enable passage by an employee using a wheelchair if there is an easy alternative route to the same destination.

4.18   An employer cannot be required to prevent a disadvantage caused by premises or by non-pay arrangements by increasing the disabled person's pay. (See paragraph 5.29)

4.19   The duty of reasonable adjustment does not apply in relation to benefits under occupational pension schemes or certain benefits under other employment-related benefit schemes although there is a duty not to discriminate in relation to such benefits (see paragraphs 6.9–6.16).

What adjustments might an employer have to make?

4.20   *The Act gives* a number of examples of 'steps' which employers may have to take, if it is reasonable for them to have to do so in all the circumstances of the case *(S6(3))*. Steps other than those listed here, or a combination of steps, will sometimes have to be taken. The steps in the Act are:

making adjustments to premises

> An employer might have to make structural or other physical changes such as: widening a doorway, providing a ramp or moving furniture for a wheelchair user; relocating light switches, door handles or shelves for someone who has difficulty in reaching; providing appropriate contrast in decor to help the safe mobility of a visually impaired person.

allocating some of the disabled person's duties to another person

Minor or subsidiary duties might be reallocated to another employee if the disabled person has difficulty in doing them because of the disability. For example, if a job occasionally involves going onto the open roof of a building an employer might have to transfer this work away from an employee whose disability involves severe vertigo.

transferring the person to fill an existing vacancy

If an employee becomes disabled, or has a disability which worsens so she cannot work in the same place or under the same arrangements and there is no reasonable adjustment which would enable the employee to continue doing the current job, then she might have to be considered for any suitable alternative posts which are available. (Such a case might also involve reasonable retraining.)

altering the person's working hours

This could include allowing the disabled person to work flexible hours to enable additional breaks to overcome fatigue arising from the disability, or changing the disabled person's hours to fit with the availability of a carer.

assigning the person to a different place of work

This could mean transferring a wheelchair user's work station from an inaccessible third floor office to an accessible one on the ground floor. It could mean moving the person to other premises of the same employer if the first building is inaccessible.

allowing the person to be absent during working hours for rehabilitation, assessment or treatment

For example, if a person were to become disabled, the employer might have to allow the person more time off during work, than would be allowed to non-disabled employees, to receive physiotherapy or psychoanalysis or undertake employment rehabilitation. A similar adjustment might be appropriate if a disability worsens or if a disabled person needs occasional treatment anyway.

giving the person, or arranging for him to be given, training

> This could be training in the use of particular pieces of equipment unique to the disabled person, or training appropriate for all employees but which needs altering for the disabled person because of the disability. For example, all employees might need to be trained in the use of a particular machine but an employer might have to provide slightly different or longer training for an employee with restricted hand or arm movements, or training in additional software for a visually impaired person so that he can use a computer with speech output.

acquiring or modifying equipment

> An employer might have to provide special equipment (such as an adapted keyboard for a visually impaired person or someone with arthritis), or an adapted telephone for someone with a hearing impairment or modified equipment (such as longer handles on a machine). There is no requirement to provide or modify equipment for personal purposes unconnected with work, such as providing a wheelchair if a person needs one in any event but does not have one: the disadvantage in such a case does not flow from the employer's arrangements or premises.

modifying instructions or reference manuals

> The way instruction is normally given to employees might need to be revised when telling a disabled person how to do a task. The format of instructions or manuals may need to be modified (eg produced in braille or on audio tape) and instructions for people with learning disabilities may need to be conveyed orally with individual demonstration.

modifying procedures for testing or assessment

> This could involve ensuring that particular tests do not adversely affect people with particular types of disability. For example, a person with restricted manual dexterity might be disadvantaged by a written test, so an employer might have to give that person an oral test.

providing a reader or interpreter

> This could involve a colleague reading mail to a person with a visual impairment at particular times during the working day or, in appropriate circumstances, the hiring of a reader or sign language interpreter.

providing supervision

> This could involve the provision of a support worker, or help from a colleague, in appropriate circumstances, for someone whose disability leads to uncertainty or lack of confidence.

When is it 'reasonable' for an employer to have to make an adjustment?

4.21 Effective and practicable adjustments for disabled people often involve little or no cost or disruption and are therefore very likely to be reasonable for an employer to have to make. *The Act lists* a number of factors which may, in particular, have a bearing on whether it will be reasonable for the employer to have to make a particular adjustment *(S6(4))*. These factors make a useful checklist, particularly when considering more substantial adjustments. The effectiveness and practicability of a particular adjustment might be considered first. If it is practicable and effective, the financial aspects might be looked at as a whole—cost of the adjustment and resources available to fund it. Other factors might also have a bearing. The factors in the Act are listed below.

The effectiveness of the step in preventing the disadvantage

4.22 It is unlikely to be reasonable for an employer to have to make an adjustment involving little benefit to the disabled employee.

> A disabled person is significantly less productive than his colleagues and so is paid less. A particular adjustment would improve his output and thus his pay. It is more likely to be reasonable for the employer to have to make that adjustment if it would significantly improve his pay, than if the adjustment would make only a relatively small improvement.

The practicability of the step

4.23 It is more likely to be reasonable for an employer to have to take a step which is easy to take than one which is difficult.

> It might be impracticable for an employer who needs to appoint an employee urgently to have to wait for an adjustment to be made to an entrance. How long it might be reasonable for the employer to have to wait would depend on the circumstances. However, it might be possible to make a temporary adjustment in the meantime, such as using another, less convenient entrance.

The financial and other costs of the adjustment and the extent of any disruption caused

4.24   If an adjustment costs little or nothing and is not disruptive, it would be reasonable unless some other factor (such as practicability or effectiveness) made it unreasonable. The costs to be taken into account include staff and other resource costs. The significance of the cost of a step may depend in part on what the employer might otherwise spend in the circumstances.

> It would be reasonable for an employer to have to spend at least as much on an adjustment to enable the retention of a disabled person—including any retraining—as might be spent on recruiting and training a replacement.

4.25   The significance of the cost of a step may also depend in part on the value of the employee's experience and expertise to the employer.

> Examples of the factors that might be considered as relating to the value of an employee would include:
> - the amount of resources (such as training) invested in the individual by the employer;
> - the employee's length of service;
> - the employee's level of skill and knowledge;
> - the employee's quality of relationships with clients;
> - the level of the employee's pay.

4.26   It is more likely to be reasonable for an employer to have to make an adjustment with significant costs for an employee who is likely to be in the job for some time than for a temporary employee.

4.27   An employer is more likely to have to make an adjustment which might cause only minor inconvenience to other employees or the employer than one which might unavoidably prevent other employees from doing their job, or cause other significant disruption.

The extent of the employer's financial or other resources

4.28   It is more likely to be reasonable for an employer with substantial financial resources to have to make an adjustment with a significant cost, than for an employer with fewer resources. The resources in practice available to the employer as a whole should be taken into account as well as other calls on those resources. The reasonableness of an adjustment will depend, however, not only on the resources in practice available for the adjustment but also on all other relevant factors (such as effectiveness and practicability).

4.29   Where the resources of the employer are spread across more than one 'business unit' or 'profit centre' the calls on them should also be taken into account in assessing reasonableness.

A large retailer probably could not show that the limited resources for which an individual shop manager is responsible meant it was not reasonable for the retailer to have to make an adjustment at that shop. Such an employer may, however, have a number—perhaps a large number—of other disabled employees in other shops. The employer's expenditure on other adjustments, or his potential expenditure on similar adjustments for other existing disabled employees, might then be taken into account in assessing the reasonableness of having to make a new adjustment for the disabled employee in question.

4.30   It is more likely to be reasonable for an employer with a substantial number of staff to have to make certain adjustments, than for a smaller employer.

It would generally be reasonable for an employer with many staff to have to make significant efforts to reallocate duties, identify a suitable alternative post or provide supervision from existing staff. It could also be reasonable for a small company covered by the Act to have to make any of these adjustments but not if it involved disproportionate effort.

The availability to the employer of financial or other assistance to help make an adjustment.
4.31   The availability of outside help may well be a relevant factor.

An employer, in recruiting a disabled person, finds that the only feasible adjustment is too costly for him alone. However, if assistance is available eg from a Government programme or voluntary body, it may well be reasonable for him to have to make the adjustment after all.

A disabled person is not required to contribute to the cost of a reasonable adjustment. However, if a disabled person has a particular piece of special or adapted equipment which he is prepared to use for work, this might make it reasonable for the employer to have to take some other step (as well as allowing use of the equipment).

An employer requires his employees to use company cars for all business travel. One employee's disability means she would have to use an adapted car or an alternative form of transport. If she has an adapted car of her own which she is willing to use on business, it might well be reasonable for the employer to have to allow this and pay her an allowance to cover the cost of doing so, even if it would not have been reasonable for him to have to provide an adapted company car, or to pay an allowance to cover alternative travel arrangements in the absence of an adapted car.

Other factors

4.32   Although the Act does not mention any further factors, others might be relevant depending on the circumstances. For example:

- effect on other employees

> Employees' adverse reaction to an adjustment being made for the disabled employee which involves something they too would like (such as a special working arrangement) is unlikely to be significant.

- adjustment made for other disabled employees

> An employer may choose to give a particular disabled employee, or group of disabled employees, an adjustment which goes beyond the duty—that is, which is more than it is reasonable for him to have to do. This would not mean he necessarily had to provide a similar adjustment for other employees with a similar disability.

- the extent to which the disabled person is willing to cooperate

> An employee with a mobility impairment works in a team located on an upper floor, to which there is no access by lift. Getting there is very tiring for the employee, and the employer could easily make a more accessible location available for him (though the whole team could not be relocated). If that was the only adjustment which it would be reasonable for the employer to have to make but the employee refused to work there then the employer would not have to make any adjustment at all.

Could an employer have to make more than one adjustment?

4.33   Yes, if it is reasonable for the employer to have to make more than one.

> A woman who is deafblind is given a new job with her employer in an unfamiliar part of the building. The employer (i) arranges facilities for her guide dog in the new area, (ii) arranges for her new instructions to be in braille and (iii) suggests to visitors ways in which they can communicate with her.

Does an employer have to justify not making an adjustment?

4.34   *The Act says* that it is discrimination if an employer fails to take a step which it is reasonable for him to have to take, and he cannot justify that failure *(S5(2))*. However, if it is unreasonable (under *S6*) for an employer to have to make any, or a particular, adjustment, he would not then also have to justify (under *S5*) not doing so. Failure to comply with the duty of reasonable adjustment can only be justified if the reason for the failure is material to the circumstances of the particular case and substantial *(S5(4))*.

An employer might not make an adjustment which it was reasonable for him to have to make because of ignorance or wrong information about appropriate adjustments or about the availability of help with making an adjustment. He would then need to justify failing in his duty. It is unlikely that he could do so unless he had made a reasonable effort to obtain good information from a reputable source such as contacting the local Placing Assessment and Counselling Team or an appropriate disability organisation.

If either of two possible adjustments would remove a disadvantage, but the employer has cost or operational reasons for preferring one rather than the other, it is unlikely to be reasonable for him to have to make the one that is not preferred. If, however, the employee refuses to cooperate with the proposed adjustment the employer is likely to be justified in not providing it.

A disabled employee refuses to follow specific occupational medical advice provided on behalf of an employer about methods of working or managing his condition at work. If he has no good reason for this and his condition deteriorates as a result, the refusal may justify the employer's subsequent failure to make an adjustment for the worsened condition.

Building regulations, listed buildings, leases

How do building regulations affect reasonable adjustments?

4.35   A building or extension to a building may have been constructed in accordance with Part M of the building regulations (or the Scottish parallel, Part T of the Technical Standards) which is concerned with access and facilities for disabled people. *Regulations provide* in these circumstances that the employer does not have to alter any physical characteristic of the building or extension which still complies with the building regulations in force at the time the building works were carried out.[2]

Where the building regulations in force at the time of a building's construction required that a door should be a particular width, the employer would not have to alter the width of the door later. However, he might have to alter other aspects of the door (eg the type of handle).

---

[2] Employment Regulations (see paragraph 1.6).

4.36   Employers can only rely upon this defence if the feature still satisfies the requirement of the building regulations that applied when the building or extension was constructed.

What about the need to obtain statutory consent for some building changes?

4.37   Employers might have to obtain statutory consent before making adjustments involving changes to premises. Such consents include planning permission, listed building consent, scheduled monument consent and fire regulations approval. The Act does not override the need to obtain such consents *(S59)*. Therefore an employer does not have to make an adjustment if it requires a statutory consent which has not been given.

4.38   The time it would take to obtain consent may make a particular adjustment impracticable and therefore one which it is not reasonable for the employer to have to make. However, the employer would then also need to consider whether it was reasonable to have to make a temporary adjustment—one that does not require consent—in the meantime.

4.39   Employers should explore ways of making reasonable adjustments which either do not require statutory consent or are likely to receive it. They may well find it useful to consult their local planning authority (in England and Wales) or planning authority (in Scotland).

An employer needs statutory consent to widen an internal doorway in a listed building for a woman disabled in an accident who returned to work in a wheelchair. The employer considers using a different office but this is not practicable. In the circumstances the widening would be a reasonable adjustment. The employer knows from the local planning authority that consent is likely to be given in a few weeks. In the meantime the employer arranges for the woman to share an accessible office which is inconvenient for both employees, but does not prevent them doing their jobs and is tolerable for that limited period.

What happens where a lease says that certain changes to premises cannot be made?

4.40   Special provisions apply where a lease would otherwise prevent a reasonable adjustment involving an alteration to premises. *The Act modifies* the effect of the lease so far as necessary to enable the employer to make the alteration if the landlord consents, and to provide that the landlord must not withhold consent unreasonably but may attach reasonable conditions to the consent *(S16)*.

How will arrangements for getting the landlord's consent work?

4.41   *The Act says* that the employer must write to the landlord (called the 'lessor' in the Act) asking for consent to make the alteration. If an employer fails to apply to the landlord for consent, anything in the lease which would prevent that alteration must be ignored in deciding whether it was reasonable for the employer to have to make that alteration *(Sch4 Para 1)*. If the landlord consents, the employer can then carry out the alteration. If the landlord refuses consent the employer must notify the disabled person, but then has no further obligation.[3] Where the landlord fails to reply within 21 days or a reasonable period after that he is deemed to have withheld his consent. In those circumstances the withholding of the consent will be unreasonable (see paragraph 4.44).[4]

4.42   If the landlord attaches a condition to the consent and it is reasonable for the employer to have to carry out the alteration on that basis, the employer must then carry out the alteration. If it would not be reasonable for the employer to have to carry out the alteration on that basis, the employer must notify the disabled person, but then has no further obligation.

When is it unreasonable for a landlord to withhold consent?

4.43   This will depend on the circumstances but a trivial or arbitrary reason would almost certainly be unreasonable. Many reasonable adjustments to premises will not harm a landlord's interests and so it would generally be unreasonable to withhold consent for them.

A particular adjustment helps make a public building more accessible generally and is therefore likely to benefit the landlord. It would very probably be unreasonable for consent to be withheld in these circumstances.

4.44   *Regulations provide* that withholding consent will be unreasonable where:
- a landlord has failed to act within the time limits referred to in paragraph 4.41 above (ie 21 days of receipt of the employer's application or a reasonable period after that); or
- the lease says that consent will be given to alterations of that type or says that such consent will be given if it is sought in a particular way and it has been sought in that way.[5]

When is it reasonable for a landlord to withhold consent?

4.45   This will depend on the particular circumstances.

A particular adjustment is likely to result in a substantial permanent reduction in the value of the landlord's interest in the premises. The landlord would almost certainly be acting reasonably in withholding consent.

---

[3] Employment Regulations (see paragraph 1.6).
[4] Employment Regulations (see paragraph 1.6).
[5] Employment Regulations (see paragraph 1.6).

> A particular adjustment would cause significant disruption or inconvenience to other tenants (for example, where the premises consist of multiple adjoining units). The landlord would be likely to be acting reasonably in withholding consent.

What conditions would it be reasonable for a landlord to make when giving consent?

4.46   This will depend on the particular circumstances. However, *Regulations provide* that it would be reasonable for the landlord to require the employer to meet any of the following conditions:

- obtain planning permission and other statutory consents;
- submit any plans to the landlord for approval (provided that the landlord then confirms that approval will not be withheld unreasonably);
- allow the landlord a reasonable opportunity to inspect the work when completed;
- reimburse the landlord's reasonable costs incurred in connection with the giving of his consent;
- reinstate the altered part of the premises to its former state when the lease expires but only if it would have been reasonable for the landlord to have refused consent in the first place.[6]

What happens if the landlord has a 'superior' landlord?

4.47   The employer's landlord may also hold a lease which prevents him from consenting to the alteration without the consent of the 'superior' landlord. The statutory provisions have been modified by regulations to cover this. The employer's landlord will be acting reasonably by notifying the employer that consent will be given if the superior landlord agrees. The employer's landlord must then apply to the superior landlord to ask for agreement. The provisions in paragraphs 4.41–4.46, including the requirements not to withhold consent unreasonably and not to attach unreasonable conditions, then apply to the superior landlord.[7]

What if some agreement other than a lease prevents the premises being altered?

4.48   An employer or landlord may be bound by the terms of an agreement or other legally binding obligation (for example, a mortgage or charge or restrictive covenant or, in Scotland, a feu disposition) under which the employer or landlord cannot alter the premises without someone else's consent. In these circumstances *Regulations provide* that it is always reasonable for the employer or landlord to have to take steps to obtain the necessary consent so that a reasonable adjustment can be made. Unless or until that consent is obtained the employer or landlord is not required to make the alteration in question. The step of seeking consent which it is always reasonable to have to take does

---

[6] Employment Regulations (see paragraph 1.6).
[7] The Disability Discrimination (Sub-leases and Sub-tenancies) Regulations 1996.

not extend to having to apply to a court or tribunal.[8] Whether it is reasonable for the employer or landlord to have to apply to a court or tribunal would depend on the circumstances of the case.

Agreements which breach the Act's provisions

Can a disabled person waive rights, or an employer's duties, under the Act?

4.49   *The Act says* that any term in a contract of employment or other agreement is 'void (ie not valid) to the extent that it would require a person to do anything that would breach any of the Act's employment provisions, or exclude or limit the operation of those provisions *(S9)*.

4.50   An employer should not include in an agreement any provision intended to avoid obligations under the Act, or to prevent someone from fulfilling obligations. An agreement should not, therefore, be used to try to justify less favourable treatment or deem an adjustment unreasonable. Moreover, even parts of agreements which have such an effect (even though unintended) are made void if they would restrict the working of the employment provisions in the Act. However, special arrangements cover leases and other agreements which might prevent a change to premises which could be an adjustment under the Act but where the possible restrictions to the Act's working were unintentional. These are described in paragraphs 4.40–4.48.

4.51   The Act also says that a contract term is void if it would prevent anyone from making a claim under the employment provisions in an industrial tribunal *(S9)*. Further information is given in Annex 3 about such agreements.

What about permits issued in accordance with the Agricultural Wages Acts?

4.52   Under the Agricultural Wages Act 1948 and the Agricultural Wages (Scotland) Act 1949 minimum wages, and terms and conditions, can be set for agricultural workers. Permits can be issued to individuals who are 'incapacitated' for the purposes of those Acts and they can then be paid such lower minimum rates or be subject to such revised terms and conditions of employment that the permit specifies. *Regulations provide* that the treatment of a disabled person in accordance with such a permit would be taken to be justified.[9] This would not prevent the employer from having to comply with the duty not to discriminate, including the duty of reasonable adjustment, for matters other than those covered by the permit.

Victimisation

What does the Act say about victimisation?

4.53   Victimisation is a special form of discrimination covered by the Act. *The Act makes* it unlawful for one person to treat another (the victim) less favourably than he

---

[8] Employment Regulations (see paragraph 1.6).
[9] Employment Regulations (see paragraph 1.6).

would treat other people in the same circumstances because the 'victim' has:
- brought, or given evidence or information in connection with, proceedings under the Act (whether or not proceedings are later withdrawn);
- done anything else under the Act; or
- alleged someone has contravened the Act (whether or not the allegation is later dropped);

or because the person believes or suspects that the victim has done or intends to do any of these things *(S55)*..

It is unlawful for an employer to victimise either disabled or non-disabled people.

A disabled employee complains of discrimination. It would be unlawful for the employer to subject non-disabled colleagues to any detriment (eg suspension) for telling the truth about the alleged discrimination at an industrial tribunal hearing or in any internal grievance procedures.

4.54   It is not victimisation to treat a person less favourably because that person has made an allegation which was false and not made in good faith *(S55(b))*.

(Harassment is covered in paragraphs 6.22–6.23.)

Setting up management systems to help avoid discrimination

What management systems might be set up to help avoid discrimination?

4.55   *The Act says* that employers are responsible for the actions done by their employees in the course of their employment. In legal proceedings against an employer based on actions of an employee, it is a defence that the employer took such steps as were reasonably practicable to prevent such actions. It is not a defence for the employer simply to show the action took place without his knowledge or approval. Employers who act through agents will also be liable for the actions of their agents done with the employer's express or implied authority *(S58)*.

An employer makes it clear to a recruitment agency that the company will not take kindly to recruits with learning disabilities being put forward by the agency. The agency complies by not putting such candidates forward. Both the employer and the agency will be liable if such treatment cannot be justified in an individual case.

4.56   Employers should communicate to their employees and agents any policy they may have on disability matters, and any other policies which have elements relevant to disabled employees (such as health, absenteeism or equal opportunities). All staff should be made aware that it is unlawful to discriminate against disabled people, and be familiar with the policies and practices adopted by their employer to ensure compliance with the law. Employers should provide guidance on non-discriminatory practices for all employees, so they will be aware what they should do and how to deal with disabled colleagues and disabled applicants for vacancies in the organisation, and should ensure so far as possible that these policies and practices are implemented. Employers should also make it clear to their agents what is required of them with regard to their duties under the Act and the extent of their authority.

4.57 **The Act says** that an employer is not under an obligation to make an adjustment if he does not know, and could not reasonably be expected to know, that a person has a disability which is likely to place the person at a substantial disadvantage *(S6(6))*. An employer must therefore do all he could reasonably be expected to do to find out whether this is the case.

An employee has a disability which sometimes causes him to cry at work although the cause of this behaviour is not known to the employer. The employer's general approach on such matters is to tell staff to leave their personal problems at home and to make no allowance for such problems in the work arrangements. The employer disciplines the employee without giving him any opportunity to explain that the problem in fact arises from a disability. The employer would be unlikely to succeed in a claim that he could not reasonably be expected to have known of the disability or that it led to the behaviour for which the employee was disciplined.

An employer has an annual appraisal system which specifically provides an opportunity to notify the employer in confidence if any employees are disabled and are put at a substantial disadvantage by the work arrangements or premises. This practice enables the employer to show that he could not reasonably be expected to know that an employee was put at such a disadvantage as a result of disability, if this was not obvious and was not brought to the employer's attention through the appraisal system.

4.58 In some cases a reasonable adjustment will not work without the co-operation of other employees. Employees may therefore have an important role in helping to ensure that a reasonable adjustment is carried out in practice.

It is a reasonable adjustment for an employer to communicate in a particular way to an employee with autism (a disability which can make it difficult for someone to understand normal social interaction among people). As part of the reasonable adjustment it is the responsibility of that employer to seek the co-operation of other employees in communicating in that way.

4.59 It may be necessary to tell one or more of a disabled person's colleagues (in confidence) about a disability which is not obvious and/or whether any special assistance is required. This may be limited to the person's supervisor, or it may be necessary to involve other colleagues, depending on the nature of the disability and the reason they need to know about it.

> In order for a person with epilepsy to work safely in a particular factory, it may be necessary to advise fellow workers about the effects of the condition, and the methods for assisting with them.

> An office worker with cancer says that he does not want colleagues to know of his condition. As an adjustment he needs extra time away from work to receive treatment and to rest. Neither his colleagues nor the line manager needs to be told the precise reason for the extra leave but the latter will need to know that the adjustment is required in order to carry it out effectively.

4.60   The extent to which an employer is entitled to let other staff know about an employee's disability will depend at last in part on the terms of employment. An employer could be held to be discriminating in revealing such information about a disabled employee if the employer would not reveal similar information about another person for an equally legitimate management purpose; or if the employer revealed such information without consulting the individual, whereas the employer's usual practice would be to talk to an employee before revealing personal information about him.

4.61   The Act does not prevent a disabled person keeping a disability confidential from an employer. But this is likely to mean that unless the employer could reasonably be expected to know about the person's disability anyway, the employer will not be under a duty to make a reasonable adjustment. If a disabled person expects an employer to make a reasonable adjustment, he will need to provide the employer—or, as the case may be, someone acting on the employer's behalf—with sufficient information to carry out that adjustment.

> An employee has symptomatic HIV. He prefers not to tell his employer of the condition. However, as the condition progresses, he finds it increasingly difficult to work the required number of hours in a week. Until he tells his employer of his condition—or the employer becomes or could reasonably be expected to be aware of it—he cannot require the employer to change his working hours to overcome the difficulty. However, once the employer is informed he may then have to make a reasonable adjustment.

4.62   If an employer's agent or employee (for example, an occupational health officer, a personnel officer or line manager) knows in that capacity of an employee's disability, then the employer cannot claim that he does not know of that person's disability, and that he is therefore excluded from the obligation to make a reasonable adjustment. This will be the case even if the disabled person specifically asked for such information to be kept confidential. Employers will therefore need to ensure that where information about disabled people may come through different channels, there is a means—suitably confidential—for bringing the information together, so the employer's duties under the Act are fulfilled.

In a large company an occupational health officer is engaged by the employer to provide him with information about his employees' health. The officer becomes aware of an employee's disability, which the employee's line manager does not know about. The employer's working arrangements put the employee at a substantial disadvantage because of the effects of her disability and she claims that a reasonable adjustment should have been made. It will not be a defence for the employer to claim that he did not know of her disability. This is because the information gained by the officer on the employer's behalf is imputed to the employer. Even if the person did not want the line manager to know that she had a disability, the occupational health officer's knowledge means that the employer's duty under the Act applies. It might even be necessary for the line manager to implement reasonable adjustments without knowing precisely why he has to do so.

4.63 Information will not be imputed to the employer if it is gained by a person providing services to employees independently of the employer. This is the case even if the employer has arranged for those services to be provided.

An employer contracts with an agency to provide an independent counselling service to employees. The contract says that the counsellors are not acting on the employer's behalf while in the counselling role. Any information about a person's disability obtained by a counsellor during such counselling would not be imputed to the employer and so could not itself place a duty of reasonable adjustment on the employer.

What if someone says they have a disability and the employer is not convinced?

4.64 If a candidate asks for an adjustment to be made because of an impairment whose effects are not obvious, nothing in the Act or Regulations would prohibit the employer from asking for evidence that the impairment is one which gives rise to a disability as defined in the Act.

An applicant says she has a mental illness whose effects require her to take time off work on a frequent, but irregular, basis. If not satisfied that this is true, the employer would be entitled to ask for evidence that the woman has a mental illness which was likely to have the effects claimed and that it is clinically well recognised (as required by the Act).

Effects of other legislation

What about the effects of other legislation?

4.65 An employer is not required to make an adjustment—or do anything under the Act—that would result in a breach of statutory obligations *(S59)*.

> If a particular adjustment would breach health and safety or fire legislation then an employer would not have to make it. However, the employer would still have to consider whether he was required to make any other adjustment which would not breach any legislation. For instance, if someone in a wheelchair could not use emergency evacuation arrangements such as a fire escape on a particular floor, it might be reasonable for the employer to have to relocate that person's job to an office where that problem did not arise.

> An employer shortlisting applicants to fill a junior office post is considering whether to include a blind applicant who the employer believes might present a safety risk moving around the crowded office. A reasonable adjustment might be to provide mobility training to familiarise the applicant with the work area, so removing any risk there might otherwise be.

What about legislation which places restrictions on what employers can do to recruit disabled people?

4.66   The Disability Discrimination Act does not prevent posts being advertised as open only to disabled candidates. However, the requirement, for example, under Section 7 of the Local Government and Housing Act 1989 that every appointment to local authorities must be made on merit means that a post cannot be so advertised. Applications from disabled people can nevertheless be encouraged. However, this requirement to appoint 'on merit' does not exclude the duty under the 1995 Act to make adjustments so a disabled person's 'merit' must be assessed taking into account any such adjustments which would have to be made.

5   Recruitment

Discrimination against applicants

How does the Act affect recruitment?

5.1   *The Act says* that it is unlawful for an employer to discriminate against a disabled person:
- in the arrangements made for determining who should be offered employment;
- in the terms on which the disabled person is offered employment; or
- by refusing to offer, or deliberately not offering, the disabled person employment *(S4(1))*.

5.2   The word 'arrangements' has a wide meaning. Employers should avoid discrimination in, for example, specifying the job, advertising the job, and the processes of selection, including the location and timing of interviews, assessment techniques, interviewing, and selection criteria.

Specifying the job

Does the Act affect how an employer should draw up a job specification?

5.3   Yes. The inclusion of unnecessary or marginal requirements in a job specification can lead to discrimination.

An employer stipulates that employees must be 'energetic', when in fact the job in question is largely sedentary in nature. This requirement could unjustifiably exclude some people whose disabilities result in them getting tired more easily than others.

An employer specifies that a driving licence is required for a job which involves limited travelling. An applicant for the job has no driving licence because of the particular effects in his case of cerebral palsy. He is otherwise the best candidate for that job, he could easily and cheaply do the travelling involved other than by driving and it would be a reasonable adjustment for the employer to let him do so. It would be discriminatory to insist on the specification and reject his application solely because he had no driving licence.

5.4   Blanket exclusions (ie exclusions which do not take account of individual circumstances) may lead to discrimination.

An employer excludes people with epilepsy from all driving jobs. One of the jobs, in practice, only requires a standard licence and normal insurance cover. If, as a result, someone with epilepsy, who has such a licence and can obtain such cover, is turned down for the job then the employer will probably have discriminated unlawfully in excluding her from consideration.

An employer stipulates that candidates for a job must not have a history of mental illness, believing that such candidates will have poor attendance. The employer rejects an applicant solely because he has had a mental illness without checking the individual's probable attendance. Even if good attendance is genuinely essential for the job, this is not likely to be justified and is therefore very likely to be unlawful discrimination.

Can an employer stipulate essential health requirements?

5.5   Yes, but the employer may need to justify doing so, and to show that it would not be reasonable for him to have to waive them, in any individual case.

Can employers simply prefer a certain type of person?

5.6   Stating that a certain personal, medical or health-related characteristic is desirable may also lead to discrimination if the characteristic is not necessary for the performance of the job. Like a requirement, a preference may be decisive against an otherwise well-qualified disabled candidate and may have to be justified in an individual case.

An employer prefers all employees to have a certain level of educational qualification. A woman with a learning disability, which has prevented her from obtaining the preferred qualification, is turned down for a job because she does not have that qualification. If the qualification is not necessary in order to do the job and she is otherwise the best candidate, then the employer will have discriminated unlawfully against her.

Publicising the vacancy

What does the Act say about how an employer can advertise vacancies?

5.7   Where a job is advertised, and a disabled person who applies is refused or deliberately not offered it and complains to an industrial tribunal about disability discrimination, the Act requires the tribunal to assume (unless the employer can prove otherwise) that the reason the person did not get the job was related to his disability if the advertisement could reasonably be taken to indicate:
- that the success of a person's application for the job might depend to any extent on the absence of a disability such as the applicant's; or
- that the employer is unwilling to make an adjustment for a disabled person *(S11)*.

An employer puts in an advertisement for an office worker, 'Sorry, but gaining access to our building can be difficult for some people'. A man, who as a result of an accident some years previously can only walk with the aid of crutches but can do office work, applies for the job and is turned down. He complains to an industrial tribunal. Because of the wording of the advertisement, the tribunal would have to assume that he did not get the job for a reason relating to his disability unless the employer could prove otherwise.

What is an 'advertisement' for the purposes of the Act?

5.8   *According to the Act* 'advertisement' includes every form of advertisement or notice, whether to the public or not *(S11(3))*. This would include advertisements internal to a company or office.

Does an employer have to provide information about jobs in alternative formats?

5.9   In particular cases, this may be a reasonable adjustment.

> A person whom the employer knows to be disabled asks to be given information about a job in a medium that is accessible to her (in large print, in braille, on tape or on computer disc). It is often likely to be a reasonable adjustment for the employer to comply, particularly if the employer's information systems, and the time available before the new employee is needed, mean it can easily be done.

Can an employer say that he would welcome applications from disabled people?

5.10   Yes. *The Act does not prevent* this and it would be a positive and public statement of the employer's policy.

Can an employer include a question on an application form asking whether someone is disabled?

5.11   Yes. *The Act does not prevent* employers including such a question on application forms. Employers can also ask whether the individual might need an adjustment and what it might be.

Selection

Does the duty of reasonable adjustment apply to applicants?

5.12   *The Act says* that the duty to make a reasonable adjustment does not apply where the employer does not know, and could not reasonably be expected to know, that the disabled person in question is or may be an applicant for the post, or, that a particular applicant has a disability which is likely to place him at a disadvantage *(S6(a))*.

Does an employer have to take special care when considering applications?

5.13   Yes. Employers and their staff or agents must not discriminate against disabled people in the way in which they deal with applications. They may also have to make reasonable adjustments.

> Because of his disability, a candidate asks to submit an application in a particular medium, different from that specified for candidates in general (eg typewritten, by telephone, or on tape). It would normally be a reasonable adjustment for the employer to allow this.

Whom can an employer shortlist for interview?

5.14   If an employer knows that an applicant has a disability and is likely to be at a substantial disadvantage because of the employer's arrangements or premises, the employer should consider whether there is any reasonable adjustment which would bring the disabled person within the field of applicants to be considered even though he would not otherwise be within that field because of that disadvantage. If the employer could only make this judgement with more information it would be discriminatory for him not to put the disabled person on the shortlist for interview if that is how he would normally seek additional information about candidates.

What should an employer do when arranging interviews?

5.15   Employers should think ahead for interviews. Giving applicants the opportunity to indicate any relevant effects of a disability and to suggest adjustments to help overcome any disadvantage the disability may cause, could help the employer avoid discrimination in the interview and in considering the applicant, by clarifying whether any reasonable adjustments may be required.

5.16   Nevertheless, if a person, whom the employer previously did not know, and could not have known, to be disabled, arrives for interview and is placed at a substantial disadvantage because of the arrangements, the employer may still be under a duty to make a reasonable adjustment from the time that he first learns of the disability and the disadvantage. However, what the employer has to do in such circumstances might be less extensive than if advance notice had been given.

What changes might an employer have to make to arrangements for interviews?

5.17   There are many possible reasonable adjustments, depending on the circumstances.

A person has difficulty attending at a particular time because of a disability. It will very likely be reasonable for the employer to have to rearrange the time.

A hearing impaired candidate has substantial difficulties with the interview arrangements. The interviewer may simply need to ensure he faces the applicant and speaks clearly or is prepared to repeat questions. The interviewer should make sure that his face is well lit when talking to someone with a hearing or visual impairment. It will almost always be reasonable for an employer to have to provide such help with communication support if the interviewee would otherwise be at a substantial disadvantage.

An employer who pays expenses to candidates who come for interview could well have to pay additional expenses to meet any special requirements of a disabled person arising from any substantial disadvantage to which she would otherwise be put by the interview arrangements. This might include paying travelling expenses for a support worker or reasonable cost of travel by taxi, rather than by bus or train, if this is necessary because of the disability.

A job applicant does not tell an employer (who has no knowledge of her disability) in advance that she uses a wheelchair. On arriving for the interview she discovers that the room is not accessible. The employer did not know of the disability and so could not have been expected to make changes in advance. However, it would still be a reasonable adjustment for the employer to hold the interview in an alternative accessible room, if a suitable one was easily available at the time with no, or only an acceptable level of, disruption or additional cost.

Should an employer consider making changes to the way the interview is carried out?

5.18 Yes, although whether any change is needed—and, if so, what change—will depend on the circumstances.

It would almost always be reasonable to allow an applicant with a learning disability to bring a supportive person such as a friend or relative to assist when answering questions that are not part of tests.

It would normally be reasonable to allow a longer time for an interview to someone with a hearing impairment using a sign language interpreter to communicate.

Does an employer have to make changes to anticipate *any* disabled person applying for a job?

5.19 No. An employer is not required to make changes in anticipation of applications from disabled people in general. It is only if the employer knows or could be reasonably expected to know that a particular disabled person is, or may be, applying and is likely to be substantially disadvantaged by the employer's premises or arrangements, that the employer may have to make changes.

Should an employer ask about a disability?

5.20 The Act does not prohibit an employer from seeking information about a disability but an employer must not use it to discriminate against a disabled person. An employer should ask only about a disability if it is, or may be, relevant to the person's ability to do the job—after a reasonable adjustment, if necessary. Asking about the effects of a disability might be important in deciding what adjustments ought to be made. The employer should avoid discriminatory questions.

> An applicant whose disability has left him using a wheelchair but healthy, is asked by an employer whether any extra leave might be required because of the condition. This is unlikely to be discriminatory because a need for extra time off work may be a substantial factor relevant to the person's ability to do the job. Therefore such a question would normally be justified. Similarly, a reasonable question about whether any changes may need to be made to the workplace to accommodate the use of the wheelchair would probably not be discriminatory.

Does the Act prevent employers carrying out aptitude or other tests in the recruitment process?

5.21   No, but routine testing of all candidates may still discriminate against particular individuals or substantially disadvantage them. If so, the employer would need to revise the tests—or the way the results of such tests are assessed—to take account of specific disabled candidates, except where the nature and form of the test were necessary to assess a matter relevant to the job. It may, for instance, be a reasonable adjustment to accept a lower 'pass rate' for a person whose disability inhibits performance in such a test. The extent to which this is required would depend on how closely the test is related to the job in question and what adjustments the employer might have to make if the applicant were given the job.

> An employer sets a numeracy test for prospective employees. A person with a learning disability takes the test and does not achieve the level the employer normally stipulates. If the job in fact entails very little numerical work and the candidate is otherwise well suited for the job it is likely to be a reasonable adjustment for the employer to waive the requirement.

> An employer sets candidates a short oral test. An applicant is disabled by a bad stammer, but only under stress. It may be a reasonable adjustment to allow her more time to complete the test, or to give the test in written form instead, though not if oral communication is relevant to the job and assessing this was the purpose of the test.

Can an employer specify qualifications?

5.22   An employer is entitled to specify that applicants for a job must have certain qualifications. However, if a disabled person is rejected for the job because he lacks a qualification, the employer will have to justify that rejection if the reason why the person is rejected (ie the lack of a qualification) is connected with his disability. Justification will involve showing that the qualification is relevant and significant in terms of the particular job and the particular applicant, and that there is no reasonable adjustment which would change this. In some circumstances it might be feasible to reassign those duties to which the qualification relates, or to waive the requirement for the qualification if this particular applicant has alternative evidence of the necessary level of competence.

An employer seeking someone to work in an administrative post specifies that candidates must have the relevant NVQ Level 4 qualification. If Level 4 fairly reflects the complex and varied nature and substantial personal responsibility of the work, and these aspects of the job cannot reasonably be altered, the employer will be able to justify rejecting a disabled applicant who has only been able to reach Level 3 because of his disability and who cannot show the relevant level of competence by other means.

An employer specifies that two GCSEs are required for a certain post. This is to show that a candidate has the general level of ability required. No particular subjects are specified. An applicant whose dyslexia prevented her from passing written examinations cannot meet this requirement, but the employer would be unable to justify rejecting her on this account alone if she could show she nevertheless had the skill and intelligence called for in the post.

Can an employer insist on a disabled person having a medical examination?

5.23   Yes. However, if an employer insists on a medical check for a disabled person and not others, without justification, he will probably be discriminating unlawfully. The fact that a person has a disability is unlikely in itself to justify singling out that person to have a health check, although such action might be justified in relation to some jobs.

An employer requires all candidates for employment to have a medical examination. That employer would normally be entitled to include a disabled person.

An applicant for a job has a disabling heart condition. The employer routinely issues a health questionnaire to job applicants, and requires all applicants who state they have a disability to undergo a medical examination. Under the Act, the employer would not be justified in requiring a medical examination whenever an applicant states he has a disability—for example, this would not normally be justified if the disability is clearly relevant neither to the job nor to the environment in which the job is done. However, the employer would probably be justified in asking the applicant with the disabling heart condition to have a medical examination restricted to assessing its implications for the particular job in its context. If, for example, the job required lifting and carrying but these abilities were limited by the condition, the employer would also have to consider whether it would be reasonable for him to have to make a change such as providing a mechanical means of lifting and/or carrying, or arranging for the few items above the person's limit to be dealt with by another person, whilst ensuring that any health and safety provisions were not breached.

How can an employer take account of medical evidence?

5.24   In most cases, having a disability does not adversely affect a person's general health. Medical evidence about a disability can justify an adverse employment decision (such as dismissing or not promoting). It will not generally do so if there is no effect on the person's ability to do the work (or any effect is less than substantial), however great the effects of the disability are in other ways. The condition or effects must be relevant to the employer's decision.

An applicant for a post on a short-term contract has a progressive condition which has some effects, but is likely to have substantial adverse effects only in the long term. The likelihood of these long-term effects would not itself be a justifiable reason for the employer to reject him.

An employer requires all candidates for a certain job to be able to work for at least two years to complete a particular work project. Medical evidence shows that a particular candidate is unlikely to be able to continue working for that long. It would be lawful to reject that candidate if the two-year requirement was justified in terms of the work, and if it would not be reasonable for the employer to have to waive it in the particular circumstances.

Advice from an occupation health expert simply that an employee was 'unfit for work' would not mean that the employer's duty to make a reasonable adjustment was waived.

What will help an employer decide to select a particular disabled person?

5.25   The employer must take into account any adjustments that it is reasonable for him to have to make. Suggestions made by the candidate at any stage may assist in identifying these.

What if a disabled person just isn't the right person for the job?

5.26   An employer must not discriminate against a disabled candidate, but there is no requirement (aside from reasonable adjustment) to treat a disabled person more favourably than he treats or would treat others. An employer will have to assess an applicant's merits as they would be if any reasonable adjustments required under the Act had been made. If, after allowing for those adjustments, a disabled person would not be the best person for the job the employer would not have to recruit that person.

Terms and conditions of service

Are there restrictions on the terms and conditions an employer can offer a disabled person?

5.27 Terms and conditions of service should not discriminate against a disabled person. The employer should consider whether any reasonable adjustments need to be made to the terms and conditions which would otherwise apply.

> An employer's terms and conditions state the hours an employee has to be in work. It might be a reasonable adjustment to change these hours for someone whose disability means that she has difficulty using public transport during rush hours.

Does that mean that an employer can never offer a disabled person a less favourable contract?

5.28 No. Such a contract may be justified if there is a material and substantial reason and there is no reasonable adjustment which can be made to remove that reason.

> A person's disability means she has significantly lower output than other employees doing similar work, even after an adjustment. Her work is of neither lower nor higher quality than theirs. The employer would be justified in paying her less in proportion to the lower output if it affected the value of her work to the business.

Can employers still operate performance-related pay?

5.29 *Regulations provide* that this is justified so long as the scheme applies equally to all employees, or all of a particular class of employees. There would be no requirement to make a reasonable adjustment to an arrangement of this kind to ensure (for example) that a person's pay was topped up if a deteriorating condition happened to lead to lower performance.[10] However, there would still be a duty to make a reasonable adjustment to any aspect of the premises or work arrangements if that would prevent the disability reducing the employee's performance.

6 Employment

Discrimination against employees

Does the Act cover all areas of employment?

6.1 Yes. *The Act* says that it is unlawful for an employer to discriminate against a disabled person whom he employs:

---

[10] Employment Regulations (see paragraph 1.6).

- in the terms of employment which he affords him;
- in the opportunities which he affords him for promotion, a transfer, training or receiving any other benefit;
- by refusing to afford him, or deliberately not affording him, any such opportunity; or
- by dismissing him, or subjecting him to any other detriment *(S4(2))*.

6.2   Therefore, an employer should not discriminate in relation to, for example: terms and conditions of service, arrangements made for induction, arrangements made for employees who become disabled (or who have a disability which worsens), opportunities for promotion, transfer, training or receiving any other benefit, or refusal of such opportunities, pension, dismissal or any detriment.

Induction

What is the effect on induction procedures?

6.3   Employers must not discriminate in their induction procedures. The employer may have to make adjustments to ensure a disabled person is introduced into a new working environment in a clearly structured and supported way with, if necessary, an individually tailored induction programme *(S4(2) and S6(1))*.

> An employer runs a one day induction course for new recruits. A recruit with a learning disability is put at a substantial disadvantage by the way the course is normally run. The employer might have to make an alternative arrangement: for example running a separate, longer course for the person, or permitting someone to sit in on the normal course to provide support, assistance or encouragement.

Promotion and transfer

What are an employer's duties as far as promotion and transfer are concerned?

6.4   Employers must not discriminate in assessing a disabled person's suitability for promotion or transfer, in the practical arrangements necessary to enable the promotion or transfer to take place, in the operation of the appraisal, selection and promotion or transfer process, or in the new job itself—and may have to make a reasonable adjustment *(S4(2)(b) and (c) and S6(1))*.

> A garage owner does not consider for promotion to assistant manager a clerk who has lost the use of her right arm, because he wrongly and unreasonably believes that her disability might prevent her performing competently in a managerial post. The reason used by the employer to deny the clerk promotion has meant that she was discriminated against.

An employer considering a number of people for a job on promotion is aware that one of the candidates for interview has a hearing impairment, but does not find out whether the person needs any special arrangements for the interview, for example a sign language interpreter. If the candidate requires such an adjustment, and it would be reasonable for the employer to have to make it, the employer would fail in his duty if he did not make that adjustment.

A civil engineer whose disability involves kidney dialysis treatment, is based in London and regularly visits hospital for the treatment. She wishes to transfer to a vacant post in her company's Scottish office. She meets all the requirements for the post, but her transfer is turned down on the ground that her need for treatment would mean that, away from the facilities in London, she would be absent from work for longer. The employer had made no attempt to discuss this with her or get medical advice. If the employer had done so, it would have been clear that similar treatment would be equally available in the new locality. In these circumstances, the employer probably could not show that relying on this reason was justified.

Someone disabled by a back injury is seeking promotion to supervisor. A minor duty involves assisting with the unloading of the weekly delivery van, which the person's back injury would prevent. In assessing her suitability for promotion, the employer should consider whether reallocating this duty to another person would be a reasonable adjustment.

What should an employer do to check that promotion and transfer arrangements do not discriminate?

6.5   The employer should review the arrangements to check that qualifications required are justified for the job to be done. He should also check that other arrangements, for example systems which determine other criteria for a particular job, do not exclude disabled people who may have been unable to meet those criteria because of their disability but would be capable of performing well in the job.

Training and other benefits provided by the employer

Does the Act apply to the provision of training?

6.6   Yes. Employers must not discriminate in selection for training and must make any necessary reasonable adjustments *(S4(2)(b) and (c) and S6(1))*.

An employer wrongly assumes that a disabled person will be unwilling or unable to undertake demanding training or attend a residential training course, instead of taking an informed decision. He may well not be able to justify a decision based on that assumption.

An employer may need to alter the time or the location of the training for someone with a mobility problem, make training manuals, slides or other visual media accessible to a visually impaired employee, perhaps by providing braille versions or having them read out, or ensure that an induction loop is available for someone with a hearing impairment.

An employer refuses to allow a disabled employee to be coached for a theory examination relating to practical work which the disability prevented the employee from doing. The employer would almost always be justified in refusing to allow the coaching because it was designed to equip employees for an area of work for which, because of the disability, the person could not be suited even by a reasonable adjustment.

What about other benefits provided by employers?

6.7 An employer must not discriminate in providing disabled people with opportunities for receiving benefits (which include 'facilities' and 'services') which are available to other employees *(S4(2)(b) and (c))*. The employer must make any necessary reasonable adjustment to the way the benefits are provided *(S6(1))* although this does not apply to benefits under occupational pension schemes or certain other employment related benefit schemes (paragraph 6.16).

Benefits might include canteens, meal vouchers, social clubs and other recreational activities, dedicated car parking spaces, discounts on products, bonuses, share options, hairdressing, clothes allowances, financial services, healthcare, medical assistance/insurance, transport to work, company car, education assistance, workplace nurseries, and rights to special leave.

If physical features of a company's social club would inhibit a disabled person's access it might be a reasonable adjustment for the employer to make suitable modifications.

An employer provides dedicated car parking spaces near to the workplace. It is likely to be reasonable for the employer to have to allocate one of these spaces to a disabled employee who has significant difficulty getting from the public car parks further away that he would otherwise have to use.

6.8 If an employer provides benefits to the public, or to a section of the public which includes the disabled employee, provision of those benefits will normally fall outside the duty not to discriminate in employment. Instead, the duty in the Act not to discriminate in providing goods, facilities and services will apply. However, the employment duty will apply if the benefit to employees is materially different (eg at a discount), is governed by the contract of employment, or relates to training *(S4(2) and (3))*.

A disabled employee of a supermarket chain who believes he has been discriminated against when buying goods as a customer at any branch of the supermarket would have no claim under the employment provisions. However, if that employee were using a discount card provided only to employees, then the employment provisions would apply if any less favourable treatment related to his use of the card.

Occupational pension schemes and insurance

What does the Act say about occupational pension schemes?

6.9 *The Act inserts* into every scheme a 'non-discrimination' rule. The trustees or managers of the scheme are prohibited by that rule from doing—or omitting to do—anything to members or non-members of schemes that would be unlawful discrimination if done by an employer *(S17)*. References to employers in paragraphs 6.11–6.15 should therefore be read as if they also apply to trustees or managers when appropriate.

When is less favourable treatment justified?

6.10 Less favourable treatment for a reason relating to a disability can be justified only if the reason is material and substantial.

Trustees of a pension scheme would not be justified in excluding a woman simply because she had a visual impairment. That fact, in itself, would be no reason why she should not receive the same pension benefits as any other employee.

6.11 There are circumstances when a disabled person's health or health prognosis is such that the cost of providing benefits under a pension scheme is substantially greater than it would be for a person without the disability. In these circumstances *Regulations provide* that an employer is regarded as justified in treating a disabled person less favourably in applying the eligibility conditions for receiving the benefit. Employers should satisfy themselves, if necessary with actuarial advice and/or medical evidence, of the likelihood of there being a substantially greater cost.[11]

When could the justification be used?

6.12   The justification would be available whenever the disabled person is considered for admission to the scheme. However, the justification cannot be applied to a disabled member, unless a term was imposed at the time of admission which allowed this.

Which benefits does this justification apply to?

6.13   The justification can apply to the following types of benefits provided by an occupational pension scheme: termination of service, retirement, old age or death, accident, injury, sickness or invalidity.[12]

Would a minor degree of extra cost amount to a justification for less favourable treatment?

6.14   No. Only the likelihood of a substantial additional cost should be taken to be a justification. Substantial means something more than minor or trivial.[13]

An employer receives medical advice that an individual with multiple sclerosis is likely to retire early on health grounds. The employer obtains actuarial advice that the cost of providing that early retirement benefit would be substantially greater than an employee without MS and so the individual is refused access to the scheme. This is justified.

What happens to an employee's rate of contributions if the employer is justified in refusing the employee access to some benefits but not others?

6.15   *Regulations provide* that if the employer sets a uniform rate of contribution the employer would be justified in applying it to a disabled person. A disabled person could therefore be required to pay the same rate of contributions as other employees, even if not eligible for some of the benefits.[14]

Does the duty to make a reasonable adjustment apply?

6.16   No. The duty of reasonable adjustment does not apply to the provision of benefits under an occupational pension scheme or any other benefit payable in money or money's worth under a scheme or arrangement for the benefit of employees in respect of:
- termination of service;
- retirement, old age or death; or

---

[11] Employment Regulations (see paragraph 1.6).
[12] Employment Regulations (see paragraph 1.6).
[13] Employment Regulations (see paragraph 1.6).
[14] Employment Regulations (see paragraph 1.6).

- accident, injury, sickness or invalidity *(S6(11))*. (Although there is power to add other matters to this list by regulations, none have been added at the date of this Code.)

Therefore, neither the employer nor the scheme's trustees or managers need to make any adjustment for a disabled person who, without that adjustment, will be justifiably denied access either to such a scheme or to a benefit under the scheme. Nor will they have to make an adjustment for someone receiving less benefit because they justifiably receive a lower rate of pay.

Does the Act cover the provision of insurance schemes for individual employees?

6.17   The Act also applies to provision of group insurance, such as permanent health insurance or life insurance, by an insurance company for employees under an arrangement with their employer. A disabled person in, or who applies or is considering applying to join, a group of employees covered by such an arrangement is protected from discrimination in the provision of the insurance services in the same way as if he were a member of the public seeking the services of that insurance company under the part of the Act relating to the provision of goods, facilities and services. However the right of redress in this case would be exercised through an industrial tribunal (and not the courts) *(S18)*.

Does the Act cover the provision of insurance to an employer?

6.18   The employer may have to make reasonable adjustments to remove any disadvantage caused to a disabled person which arose from the arrangements made by the employer to provide himself with insurance cover. Such adjustments could include measures which would reduce any risk otherwise posed by the disabled person, so that the insurer would then provide cover, or seeking alternative cover. If cover could not be obtained at all at realistic cost it is most unlikely that the employer would have to bear the risk himself.

It comes to an employer's attention that someone who works for his antiques business has epilepsy. The employer is obliged to notify his insurance company who refuse to cover the employer against damage caused by the disabled person. To avoid dismissing the employee, it might be reasonable for the employer to have to bar the person from contact with valuable items, if this would mean the insurance company then provided cover.

Retention of disabled employees

6.19   An employer must not discriminate against an employee who becomes disabled, or has a disability which worsens *(S4(2))*. The issue of retention might also arise when an employee has a stable impairment but the nature of his employment changes.

6.20   If as a result of the disability an employer's arrangements or a physical feature of the employer's premises place the employee at a substantial disadvantage in doing his existing job, the employer must first consider any reasonable adjustment that would resolve the difficulty. The employer may also need to consult the disabled person at appropriate stages about what his needs are and what effect the disability might have on future employment, for example, where the employee has a progressive condition. The nature of the reasonable adjustments which an employer may have to consider will depend on the circumstances of the case.

> It may be possible to modify a job to accommodate an employee's changed needs. This might be by rearranging working methods or giving another employee certain minor tasks the newly disabled person can no longer do, providing practical aids or adaptations to premises or equipment, or allowing the disabled person to work at different times or places from those with equivalent jobs (for instance, it may be that a change to part-time work might be appropriate for someone who needed to spend some time each week having medical treatment).

> A newly disabled employee is likely to need time to readjust. For example, an employer might allow: a trial period to assess whether the employee is able to cope with the current job, or a new one; the employee initially to work from home; a gradual build-up to full time hours; or additional training for a person with learning disabilities who moves to another workplace.

> It may be a reasonable adjustment for an employer to move a newly disabled person to a different post within the organisation if a suitable vacancy exists or is expected shortly.

> Additional job coaching may be necessary to enable a disabled person to take on a new job.

> In many cases where no reasonable adjustment would overcome a particular disability so as to enable the disabled person to continue with similar terms or conditions, it might be reasonable for the employer to have to offer a disabled employee a lower-paying job, applying the rate of pay that would apply to such a position under his usual pay practices.

> If new technology (for instance a telephone or information technology system) puts a disabled person at a substantial disadvantage compared with non-disabled people, then the employer would be under a duty to make a reasonable adjustment. For example, some telephone systems may interfere with hearing aids for people with hearing impairments and the quality of the inductive coupler may need to be improved.

Termination of employment

6.21   Dismissal—including compulsory early retirement—of a disabled person for a reason relating to the disability would need to be justified and the reason for it would have to be one which could not be removed by any reasonable adjustment.

> It would be justifiable to terminate the employment of an employee whose disability makes it impossible for him any longer to perform the main functions of his job, if an adjustment such as a move to a vacant post elsewhere in the business is not practicable or otherwise not reasonable for the employer to have to make.

> It would be justifiable to terminate the employment of an employee with a worsening progressive condition if the increasing degree of adjustment necessary to accommodate the effects of the condition (shorter hours of work or falling productivity, say) became unreasonable for the employer to have to make.

> An employer who needs to reduce the workforce would have to ensure that any scheme which was introduced for choosing candidates for redundancy did not discriminate against disabled people. Therefore, if a criterion for redundancy would apply to a disabled person for a reason relating to the disability, that criterion would have to be 'material' and 'substantial' and the employer would have to consider whether a reasonable adjustment would prevent the criterion applying to the disabled person after all.

Harassment

What does the Act say about harassment?

6.22   The Act does not refer to harassment as a separate issue. However, harassing a disabled person on account of a disability will almost always amount to a 'detriment' under the Act. (Victimisation is covered in paragraphs 4.53–4.54.)

Are employers liable for harassment by their employees?

6.23   An employer is responsible for acts of harassment by employees in the course of their employment unless the employer took such steps as were reasonably practicable to prevent it. As a minimum first step harassment because of disability should be made a disciplinary matter and staff should be made aware that it will be taken seriously.

7 Particular Provisions

Discrimination against contract workers

7.1   The Act deals specifically with work which is carried out by individuals ('contract workers') for a person (a 'principal') who hires them under contract from their employer (generally an employment business)—referred to below as the 'sending' employer.

What does the Act say about contract workers?

7.2   *The Act says* that it is unlawful for a principal to discriminate against a disabled person:
- in the terms on which the person is allowed to do the contract work;
- by not allowing the person to do, or continue to do, the contract work;
- in the way he affords the person access to, or by failing to afford him access to, benefits in relation to contract work; or
- by subjecting the person to any other detriment in relation to contract work *(S12(1))*.

7.3   *The Act and Regulations apply*, generally speaking, as if the principal were, or would be, the actual employer of the contract worker. Therefore, the same definition of 'discrimination'—including the need to justify less favourable treatment—applies as for employers *(S12(3))*.

The employer of a labourer, who some years ago was disabled by clinical depression but has since recovered, proposes to supply him to a contractor to work on a building site. Although his past disability is covered by the Act, the site manager refuses to accept him because of his medical history. Unless the contractor can show that the manager's action is justified, the contractor would be acting unlawfully.

What will be the effect of the duty to make adjustments for principals?

7.4   The duty to make a reasonable adjustment applies to a principal as to an employer *(S12(3))*.

7.5   In deciding whether any, and if so, what, adjustment would be reasonable for a principal to have to make, the period for which the contract worker will work for the principal is important. It might well be unreasonable for a principal to have to make certain adjustments if the worker will be with the principal for only a short time.

An employment business enters into a contract with a firm of accountants to provide an assistant for two weeks to cover an unexpected absence. The employment business wishes to put forward a person who, because of his disability, finds it difficult to travel during the rush hour and would like his working hours to be modified accordingly. It might not be reasonable for the firm to have to agree given the short time in which to negotiate and implement the new hours.

Will the principal and the 'sending' employer both have duties to make reasonable adjustments?

7.6   Both the 'sending' employer and the principal may separately be under a duty of reasonable adjustment in the case of a contract worker who is disabled. If the 'sending' employer's own premises or arrangements place the contract worker at a substantial disadvantage, then the 'sending' employer may have a duty to make a reasonable adjustment *(S6(1))*. The 'sending' employer may also have a duty to make a reasonable adjustment where a similar substantial disadvantage is likely to affect a contract worker as a result of the arrangements or premises of all or most of the principals to whom he might be supplied. The employer would not have to take separate steps in relation to each principal, but would have to make any reasonable adjustment within his power which would overcome the disadvantage wherever it might arise. The principal would not have to make any adjustment which the employer should make.[15] However, subject to that the principal would be responsible only for any additional reasonable adjustment which is necessary solely because of the principal's own arrangements or premises *(S6(1)* applied by *S12(3))*. It would also usually be reasonable for a principal and a 'sending' employer to have to cooperate with any steps taken by the other to assist a disabled contract worker.

A travel agency hires a clerical worker from an employment business to fulfil a three month contract to file travel invoices during the busy summer holiday period. The contract worker is a wheelchair user, and is quite capable of doing the job if a few minor, temporary changes are made to the arrangement of furniture in the office. It would be reasonable for the travel agency to make this adjustment.

A bank hires a blind word processor operator as a contract worker from an employment business. The employment business provides her with a specially adapted portable computer because she would otherwise be at a similar substantial disadvantage in doing the work wherever she does it. (In such circumstances the bank would not have to provide a specially adapted computer if the employment business did not.) The bank would have to cooperate by letting the contract worker use her computer whilst working for the bank if it is compatible with the bank's systems. If not, it could be a reasonable adjustment for the bank to make the computer compatible and for the employment business to allow that change to be made.

What about contract workers in small firms?

7.7   **The Act** applies to any employment business which has 20 or more employees (including people currently employed by it but hired out to principals). It also applies to any principal who has 20 or more workers (counting both the principal's own employees and any contract workers currently working for the principal). It does not

---

[15] Employment Regulations (see paragraph 1.6).

apply to employment businesses or principals with fewer than 20 employees. Note the extended definition of 'employment' in the Act (see paragraph 2.8).

An employment business has 15 employees (including people currently hired out to others) and enters a contract to provide a worker in a shop. The shop employs 29 people. Neither the duty not to discriminate nor the duty to make a reasonable adjustment applies to the employment business, but both duties apply to the owner of the shop. However, the length of time the worker was contracted to work at the shop would be an important factor in assessing whether the shop-owner had to make any significant adjustment.

A deaf individual is employed by an employment business that has 100 employees (including people currently hired out to others). He is hired regularly to do contract work and, as a reasonable adjustment, the business provides a portable induction loop for assignments. If he works for a principal with, say, 17 workers, (counting both employees and contract workers) that principal would not be required to cooperate with use of the induction loop. However, if the principal has 20 or more such workers the principal would be obliged to cooperate.

What about the Supported Placement Scheme (SPS)?

7.8 These arrangements also apply to the Employment Service's Supported Placement Scheme (SPS) for severely disabled people. The 'contractor' under the scheme (usually a local authority or voluntary body) is the equivalent of the 'sending' employer, and the 'host employer' is the equivalent of the principal. A local authority can even be both the contractor and the host employer at the same time (as can a voluntary body) in which case the duty not to discriminate and the duty of reasonable adjustment would apply to it as to an employer.

Provisions applying to trade organisations

What does the Act say about trade organisations?

7.9   A trade organisation is defined as an organisation of workers or of employers, or any other organisation whose members carry on a particular profession or trade for the purposes of which the organisation exists *(S13(4))*. Therefore trade unions, employers' associations, and similar bodies like the Law Society and chartered professional institutions, for example, must comply with the legislation.

7.10   *The Act says* that it is unlawful for a trade organisation to discriminate against a disabled person:

- in the terms on which it is prepared to admit the person to membership; or
- by refusing to accept, or deliberately not accepting, an application for membership.

It is also unlawful for a trade organisation to discriminate against a disabled member of the organisation:

- in the way it affords the person access to any benefits or by refusing or deliberately omitting to afford access to them;
- by depriving the person of membership, or varying the terms of membership; or
- by subjecting the person to any other detriment *(S13)*.

Trade organisations should therefore check that they do not discriminate as regards, for example, training facilities, welfare or insurance schemes, invitations to attend events, processing of grievances, assistance to members in their employers' disciplinary or dismissal procedures.

7.11 *The Act defines* discrimination by a trade organisation in similar terms to the definition relating to discrimination by an employer. Therefore, the need to justify less favourable treatment for a reason relating to disability applies as in the case of an employer *(S14(3))*.

> A trade organisation is arranging a trip to some of its members' workplaces but it decides to exclude a member in a wheelchair because too many of the sites are inaccessible to make participation worthwhile. This could well be justified. (Note, however, paragraph 7.12)

Do trade organisations have a duty to make adjustments?

7.12 *The Act includes* a requirement on trade organisations to make reasonable adjustments *(S15)*. However, this duty will not be brought into force until after the other employment provisions, at a date which will be subject to consultation.

What about the actions of employees or representatives of trade organisations?

7.13 Individual employees or agents of trade organisations who have dealings with members or applicants are treated in the same way as individual employees or agents of employers who deal with job applicants or employees: the trade organisation is responsible for their actions *(S58)*.

8 Resolving disagreements within the employing organisation

What does the Act say about resolving disagreements?

8.1 The Act does not require employers to resolve disputes within their organisations. However, it is in an employer's interests to resolve problems as they arise where possible. This should be in a non-discriminatory way to comply with the Act's general provisions.

8.2 One method might be the use of a grievance procedure. Grievance procedures provide an open and fair way for employees to make known their concerns and enable grievances to be resolved quickly before they become major difficulties. Use of the procedures can highlight areas where the employer's duty of reasonable adjustment may not have been observed, and can prevent misunderstandings in this area leading to tribunal complaints.

Do existing grievance and disciplinary procedures need changing?

8.3   Where grievance or disciplinary procedures are in place, the employer might wish to review, and where necessary adapt, them to ensure that they are flexible enough to be used by disabled employees. Where a formal grievance (or disciplinary) procedure operates, it must be open, or applied, to disabled employees on the same basis as to others. Employers will have to ensure that grievance (or disciplinary) procedures do not, in themselves, discriminate against disabled employees and may have to make reasonable adjustments to enable some disabled employees to use grievance procedures effectively or to ensure disciplinary procedures have the same impact on disabled employees as on others.

An employee with a learning disability has to attend an interview under the employer's disciplinary procedures. The employee would like his guardian or a friend to be present. The employer agrees to this but refuses to rearrange the interview to a time which is more convenient to the guardian or friend. The employer may be in breach of the duty to make a reasonable adjustment.

(See Annex 3 for information about industrial tribunals.)

Code of Practice: Rights of Access: Goods, Facilities, Services and Premises

1 Introduction

Purpose of Code

1.1 The Disability Discrimination Act 1995 (the Act) brings in new measures to prevent discrimination against disabled people. Part III of the Act is based on the principle that disabled people should not be treated less favourably, simply because of their disability, by those **providing goods, facilities or services to the pubic**, or by those **selling, letting or managing premises**. If you are in either of these categories, you must comply with the duties set out in the Act, which are described and explained in this Code of Practice (the Code).

1.2 The Code gives practical advice on how to comply with the new duties. The Code will also help disabled people to understand the law. The Code is issued by the Secretary of State on the basis of proposals prepared by the National Disability Council. It applies to England, Scotland and Wales and comes into effect on 2 December 1996. A separate Code applies to Northern Ireland.

Status of Code

1.3 The Code does not impose legal obligations. Nor is it an authoritative statement of the law—that is a matter for the courts. However, the Code can be used in evidence in any legal proceedings under the Act. Courts must take into account any part of the Code that appears to them relevant to any question arising. If you follow the advice in the Code, you may avoid an adverse judgement by the court in any proceedings taken against you.

Using the Code

1.4 **Chapter two** describes who is and who is is not affected by the Act, and explains the meaning of discrimination. You will need to read this chapter to have a proper understanding of the Code. Provisions of goods, facilities and services is covered in **chapter three**. If you are selling or letting premises you will need to read **chapter four**. There are some exceptions to the duties set out in chapters three and four—these are covered in **chapter five**. **Chapter six** describes other actions which are unlawful under the access to goods, facilities, services and premises provisions of the Act. **Chapter seven** explains what happens if discrimination is alleged.

1.5   The Code should not be read narrowly. Each section should be viewed as part of an overall explanation of the Act.

1.6   Examples of how the Act is likely to work in practice are given in boxes. The examples are given **for illustrative purposes** only and should not be treated as a complete or authoritative statement of the law. References to the Act are shown in {} (for example {S1(1)} means Section 1(1) of the Act).

General Approach

1.7   Discrimination may stem from lack of awareness about disability. It may also be the result of making assumptions. For example, you might assume that a disabled person would not benefit from a service or that you could not cope with serving him or her. When in doubt, ask the disabled person.

1.8   You will need to think about your **attitude towards disabled people** and the way you and your staff deal with customers. For example, you should consider:
- informing all staff dealing with customers that it is unlawful to discriminate against disabled people;
- establishing a policy towards disabled customers which is communicated to all staff;
- providing disability awareness training for all staff serving customers and monitoring its implementation; and
- having an appropriate complaints mechanism.

Further information

1.9   Copies of the Act, and any regulations made under it, are available from HMSO. A separate code, covering the rights of disabled employees, is also available from the same source. Further information on the Act is available from Disability on the Agenda (telephone 0345 622 633, textphone 0345 622 644). Organisations providing information or advice to business, and advice agencies, may also be able to help.

2   Who is affected by the Act?

What does the Act mean by 'disabled people'?

2.1   An adult or child is disabled if he or she has a physical or mental impairment which has an effect which is:
- substantial (not just trivial or minor);
- adverse; and
- long term (lasting or expected to last for at least a year)

on his or her ability to carry out normal day-to-day activities {S1(1)}. Physical or mental impairment includes a sensory impairment.

2.2   People who have had a disability within the definition are protected from discrimination even if they have since recovered.

2.3   The appendix to the Code gives some more detail about who is covered.

Providing goods, facilities and services—who is affected?

2.4   In the Act the provision of services includes the provision of goods and facilities. Subject to the exclusions set out in paragraph 2.9, the Act affects anyone concerned with the provision of services to the public, whether in the public, private or voluntary sectors. It does not matter if the service in question is provided free (such as access to a public park) or in return for payment (for example, a meal in a restaurant).

2.5   Unlike the Act's employment provisions, there is no exemption for small employers.

2.6   Services not generally available to the public, such as those provided by private clubs, are not covered. Nor does the Act cover the manufacture or design of products. Where clubs or manufacturers do provide services to the public—for example, a company selling the goods it produces by mail order or a private golf club hiring out its facilities for a wedding reception—the Act applies to those services.

2.7   Among the services covered are those provided by local councils, hotels, banks, solicitors, advice agencies, pubs, theatres, hairdressers, any kind of shop, telesales businesses, places of worship, courts and doctors {S19(3)}. All those involved in providing the service are affected—from the most senior person to the most junior employee, whether full or part-time, permanent or temporary.

Premises—who is affected?

2.8   Subject to the exemptions set out in paragraphs 2.10 and 2.11, the Act also covers anyone involved in the sale, letting and management of all types of premises, for example, land, houses, flats and business premises. Local councils, housing associations, private landlords, estate agencies, accommodation agencies, property developers, managing agents and private owner-occupiers could be affected.

What is not affected?

2.9   The only services which are excluded are:
- **education,** and some services which are very closely related to it—such as the youth service (whether provided by a local education authority or the voluntary sector), some examination and assessment services and facilities for research students. Any other services which are provided on school, college or university premises (for example, where a Parent Teachers' Association organises a fund-raising event) are subject to the duties described in the Code. (Part IV of the Act requires schools, colleges and universities to provide information on access).
- **transport vehicles,** although the transport infrastructure, for example, bus stations and airports, is covered (Part V of the Act allows the Government to set access standards for buses, trains, trams and taxis).

2.10   You are exempt from the measures that apply to selling, letting and managing premises if you, or a near relative of yours:
- live on the premises; and

- share accommodation, other than storage accommodation or a means of access, with others who are not members of your household.

This applies only if the premises in question are small which means:

- only you and your household live in the accommodation you occupy, and there is accommodation, let on a separate tenancy or similar agreement, for normally no more than two other households; **or**
- you do not normally let accommodation in your own home to more than six people {S23}.

2.11   In addition, you are exempt from the measures that apply to selling and letting premises if you are an owner-occupier and you do not use an estate agent or advertise publicly {S22(2))}.

What is 'discrimination'?

2.12   It is unlawful for you to discriminate against a disabled person in the circumstances described in chapter 3 and chapter 4 {S19(1) & S21(1)}. The Act says discrimination occurs when:

- for a reason which relates to a disabled person's disability,
- you treat him or her less favourably than you treat or would treat others to whom that reason does not or would not apply, and
- you cannot show this treatment was justified {S20(1) & S24(1)}.

A waiter asks a disabled customer to leave the restaurant because she has difficulty eating as a result of her disability. He serves other customers who have no difficulty eating. The waiter has therefore treated her **less favourably** than other customers. The treatment was for **a reason related to her disability**—her difficulty when eating. And the reason for her less favourable treatment did **not apply to the other customers**.

If the waiter could not justify the less favourable treatment, he would have discriminated unlawfully.

2.13   The disabled person does not have to point to others who **were** treated more favourably than he or she was. It is still 'less favourable' treatment if others **would have been** treated better.

2.14   Less favourable treatment is not necessarily the same as bad treatment. Treatment must be less favourable by comparison with others (including other disabled people). If, for example, all customers were given the same poor standard of service and a disabled customer was treated no worse than others, no less favourable treatment would have occurred.

2.15   Treating a disabled person less favourably cannot be justified on the basis that anyone who behaves in a like manner is treated in the same way. In the above example, the waiter could not justify refusing to serve the disabled customer on the grounds that he would also have refused to serve anyone who was eating messily, for example, a child. Less favourable treatment of a disabled person is unlawful if it is for a reason which relates to his or her disability **and** it cannot be justified in one of the specified circumstances explained in more detail in chapter 5.

2.16   The Act cannot be used as an excuse for disruptive or anti-social behaviour. For example, if a publican refuses to serve a disabled person because he or she is abusive or drunk, the treatment would not be for a reason which related to the disabled person's disability. It would therefore be lawful to treat him or her in the same way as any other customer who was drunk. For such treatment to be caught by the Act, there must be a direct connection between the disabled person's disability and his or her less favourable treatment.

3   Duties under the Act—Goods, Facilities & Services

What does the Act say?

3.1   *The Act says* it is unlawful for you to discriminate against a disabled person:
- in refusing to provide or deliberately not providing any service which you provide, or are prepared to provide, to members of the public (paragraphs 3.3 to 3.5) {S19(1)(a)};
- in the standard of service you provide or the manner in which you provide it (paragraphs 3.6 to 3.7) {S19(1)(c)}; or
- in the terms on which you provide a service (paragraph 3.8) {S19(1)(d)}.

3.2   Discrimination is unlawful if it is for a reason relating to a person's disability (discussed in more detail in paragraphs 2.12 to 2.16) and you cannot justify your actions. There are only limited circumstances in which you may be able to justify treating a disabled person less favourably (see chapter 5). The rest of this chapter should be read in this light.

What is the duty not to refuse service?

3.3   It is unlawful for you to refuse to serve, or deliberately not provide a service to, a disabled person for any reason related to his or her disability {S19(1)(a)}.

> A group of deaf people is refused entry to a night club because the doorman thinks that communication using sign language might be seen as threatening. **This is against the law.**

3.4   Discrimination is unlawful whatever the intention. Even where you think you are helping the disabled person, but are nonetheless refusing to serve them, you may still be breaking the law. For example, you cannot refuse to serve disabled customers on the grounds that another service provider caters better for their needs.

> A sweet shop refuses to serve a deaf child because the owner of a nearby sweet shop can communicate using British Sign Language and is therefore able to offer a better service. **This is against the law.**

3.5   Spurious reasons cannot be used to justify refusing to serve a disabled person.

> A hotel pretends that all rooms are taken in order to refuse a booking from a mentally ill customer. **This is against the law.**

What is the duty not to provide a worse standard or manner of service?

3.6   It is against the law for you to offer a disabled person a lower level of service than the service you offer to other people {S19(1)(c)}. It is also against the law to adopt a worse manner in serving disabled people. Abusive behaviour towards disabled customers, especially the use of insulting language about their disability, is very likely to be used as evidence that they have been provided with a worse standard of service.

> A restaurant tells a severely disfigured person he must sit at a table out of sight of other customers, despite other tables being free. **This is against the law.**

3.7   This duty does not mean that you have to change the service you provide to overcome the effects of the disability. Nor do you have to stock special products for disabled people. In due course, however, the later duties in the Act might require you to make adjustments to the way you provide your services to disabled customers (see inside front cover).

> A shop selling telephones does not stock telephones with keyboards and screens for deaf customers. **This is within the law.**

What is the duty not to provide a service on worse terms?

3.8   It is unlawful for you to provide a service to a disabled person on terms which are worse than the terms offered to other people {S19(1)(d)}. This includes charging more for a service or imposing extra restrictions.

> A travel agent asks a person who is deaf and blind for a larger deposit than she requires from others because she assumes without good reason that the customer will be more likely to cancel his holiday. **This is against the law**.

Can you treat disabled people more favourably?

3.9   The Act does not prohibit positive action in favour of disabled people. You can therefore provide services on more favourable terms to a disabled person.

A theatre manager offers a better seat to a blind person to allow room for her guide dog. **This is within the law.**

4 Duties under the Act—Premises

What does the Act say?

4.1   It is unlawful for you to discriminate against a disabled person:
- in the terms on which you offer to dispose of premises to him or her (paragraph 4.10) {S22(1)(a)};
- by refusing to dispose of premises to him or her (paragraph 4.11) {S22(1)(b)}; or
- in the way you treat him or her in relation to a list of people needing premises (paragraph 4.12) {S22(1)(c)}.

4.2   The Act also says that if you manage premises it is unlawful for you to discriminate against a disabled person:
- in the way that you allow him or her to make use of any benefits or facilities (paragraph 4.13) {S22(3)(a)};
- by refusing or deliberately omitting to allow him or her to make use of any benefits or facilities (paragraph 4.13) {S22(3)(b)}; or
- by evicting him or her or subjecting him or her to any other detriment (paragraph 4.14) {S22(3)(c)}.

4.3   If your consent is required to dispose of premises to a tenant, you must not discriminate against a disabled person by withholding it. This applies to tenancies that were created both before and after the passing of the Act {S22(4)}.

4.4   However, you do not have to make adjustments to the premises to make them more suitable for a disabled person.

4.5   Some landlords and owner-occupiers are exempt from these duties (see paragraphs 2.10–2.11).

4.6   Discrimination is unlawful if it is for a reason relating to a person's disability (discussed in more detail in paragraphs 2.12 to 2.16) and you cannot justify your actions. There are only limited circumstances in which you may be able to justify treating a disabled person less favourably (see chapter 5). The rest of this chapter should be read in this light.

What is 'disposing of premises'?

4.7   Disposing of premises includes selling and letting premises. Premises includes land and buildings, for example, houses, flats and business premises. Disposing of premises does not cover the hire of premises or rooms booked in hotels and guest houses. These are covered by the provisions relating to services (see chapter 3).

What is 'managing premises'?

4.8   The term 'managing premises' could include actions by accommodation agencies, housekeepers and estate agents who, for example, may collect the rent or provide access to particular benefits or facilities.

What are 'benefits and facilities'?

4.9   Examples of benefits and facilities include laundry facilities, access to a garden and parking facilities.

What is the duty not to sell or let premises on worse terms?

4.10   It is unlawful for you to discriminate against a disabled person in the terms on which premises are sold or let {S22(1)(a)}.

> A landlord asks a mentally ill person for a deposit when others have to pay none. **This is against the law.**

What is the duty not to refuse to sell or let premises?

4.11   It is against the law for you to refuse to sell or let premises to a disabled person {S22(1)(b)}.

> Without any supporting evidence a landlord refuses to let a flat to a person who has fully recovered from cancer because he believes her former disability might recur and would prevent her from keeping up the rent payments. **This is against the law.**

Are housing lists affected?

4.12   It is unlawful for you to treat a disabled person less favourably when maintaining housing lists {S22(1)(c)}.

> A housing association keeps all disabled people at the bottom of its waiting list. **This is against the law.**

Using benefits and facilities

4.13   It is against the law for you to discriminate in the way in which a disabled tenant is allowed to make use of the benefits or facilities of premises, such as shared recreational areas {S22(3)(a)}. It is also against the law for you to prevent him or her from using them {S22(3)(b)}.

A landlord prevents a person with a severe facial disfigurement from using the swimming pool in a block of flats. **This is against the law.**

Eviction and other detriments

4.14 It is against the law for you to evict a disabled person simply because of his or her disability or otherwise place him or her at a disadvantage, such as harassment {S22(3)(c)}.

A landlord charges a person with a learning disability more than he charges other tenants for repairs to his flat. **This is against the law.**

Can you treat disabled people more favourably?

4.15 The Act does not prohibit positive action in favour of disabled people. You can therefore offer premises on better terms.

A local authority gives priority to disabled people ahead of other people on their waiting list for housing. **This is within the law.**

5 When less favourable treatment can be justified under the Act

Introduction

5.1 This chapter sets out the limited circumstances in which you may be able to justify less favourable treatment of a disabled person for a reason which relates to his or her disability. No other form of justification is available. You should read this chapter in conjunction with the explanation of the meaning of discrimination (paragraphs 2.12 to 2.16).

5.2 You may be able to justify treating a disabled person less favourably **only if you believed that one or more of the conditions below applied and it was reasonable in all the circumstances of the case for you to have held that opinion.** You do not have to be an expert on disability but you are expected to take account of all the circumstances, including the information available to you, at the time.

A swimming pool attendant refuses to allow a child who uses a wheelchair to use the swimming pool because he believes the child is unable to swim. In the absence of further information, **this may be within the law**

> Despite being told subsequently by the child's mother that the child is a competent swimmer, the attendant persists in refusing him admission. **This is likely to be against the law.**

5.3   If a disabled person can show that he or she has been treated less favourably, you will have to prove that your actions were justified.

5.4   **Some of the conditions specified below (for example, those relating to health or safety) apply both to service providers and to those involved in disposing of premises. Others apply to one group alone. The heading for each section makes clear to whom it applies.**

Health or safety—services and premises

5.5   The Act does not require you to do anything which would endanger the health or safety of any person, including that of the disabled person {S20(4)(a) & S24(3)(a)}.

> A driving instructor refuses to give lessons to a person with such severely impaired vision that he fails the eyesight test, even with glasses. **This is within the law.**

> A landlord refuses to let a third floor flat to a disabled person living alone who is clearly unable to negotiate the stairs in safety or use the fire escape or other escape routes in an emergency. **This is within the law.**

5.6   Spurious health and safety reasons will provide no defence. For example, fire regulations should not be used as an excuse to place **unnecessary** restrictions on disabled people. It is for the management of the establishment concerned, in conjunction with the licensing authority, to make any special provision needed.

> Although there are adequate means of escape, a cinema manager turns away a wheelchair user because he assumes, without checking, that she could be in danger in the event of a fire. **This is against the law.**

> Despite knowing that there is no health risk, a landlord refuses to let a flat to someone with AIDS on the grounds that other tenants might be put at risk. **This is against the law.**

5.7   Every opportunity should be taken, as far as practicable, to enable disabled people to use cinemas, theatres, leisure centres and other entertainment venues. Equally, disabled people should not be prevented from living where they choose through unfounded concerns for safety.

Incapacity to contract—services and premises

5.8   The Act does not require you to contract with a disabled person who is incapable of entering into a legally enforceable agreement or of giving an informed consent {S20(4)(b) & S24(3)(b)}. If a disabled person is unable to understand a particular transaction due to mental incapacity, you may refuse to enter into a contract.

> A landlord refuses to let a flat to a person with a severe learning disability who does not understand that rent would have to be paid. **This is within the law.**

5.9   Your refusal must be reasonable. A person may be able to understand less complicated transactions, but have difficulty with more complex ones. Unless there is clear evidence to the contrary, you should assume that a disabled person is able to enter into any contract.

> Staff in a bakery refuse to sell a loaf of bread to a person with a severe learning disability because they claim she does not understand the nature of the agreement even though her order is clear and she is able to pay. **This is against the law.**

5.10   Regulations will prevent a service provider from justifying less favourable treatment of a disabled person on the grounds of incapacity to contract in a situation where another person is legally acting on his or her behalf (for example, under a power of attorney).

> A salesman refuses to rent a television to someone simply because she is legally acting on behalf of someone who is mentally ill. **This is against the law.**

Providing the service—services

5.11   You may be able to justify refusing to serve a disabled person if this is necessary to serve other customers {S20(4)(c)}.

> A tour guide refuses to allow an unaccompanied wheelchair user on a tour of old city walls because he has well-founded reasons to believe that the extra help he has to give her would prevent the party from completing the tour. **This is within the law.**

5.12   Similarly, you may be able to justify providing a lower standard of service or on worse terms if this is necessary to serve the disabled person or other customers {S20(4)(d)}.

A hotel restricts a wheelchair user to rooms on the ground floor because rooms on other floors are not accessible. This restriction of his choice of rooms is necessary in order to provide the service to him. **This is within the law.**

5.13   These conditions will justify less favourable treatment only where not treating the disabled person less favourably would effectively prevent other customers or the disabled person from using the service. They cannot be used to justify refusal simply because other people would be inconvenienced or delayed. The distinction is between people who have paid for a service and cannot receive it at all and those who are merely being delayed. It is most unlikely, for example, that you could justify asking a disabled person to go to the back of the queue so as not to delay other customers waiting to be served.

A clerk in a post office refuses to serve a deaf person because the extra time taken means that other customers have to queue for longer. **This is against the law.**

Greater expense—services

5.14   In general, it is unlawful for you to charge a disabled person more for a service than you charge anyone else, **except** where **additional costs** are incurred in providing a special service to the disabled person's particular requirements {S20(4)(e)}. Charging more can be justified only where the service is individually tailored to the needs of the customer and the disabled person's particular requirements increase costs due to greater materials or work.

A furniture shop charges more for an orthopaedic bed, made to the disabled person's specification, but does not charge more for a standard bed. **This is within the law.**

Necessary to provide the benefits or facilities—premises

5.15   You may be able to justify restricting access to benefits or facilities associated with premises if this is necessary to allow access to others or to the disabled person {S24(3)(c)}.

A landlord refuses to allow a mentally ill tenant to use the shared laundry facilities because he frequently breaks the washing machine. **This is within the law.**

5.16   Similarly, you may be able to justify denying access to benefits or facilities if this is necessary to allow access to others {S24(3)(d)}.

> A landlord requires a disabled tenant to park her car at the side of the building as otherwise it would block the main entrance for other tenants. **This is within the law.**

5.17 These conditions will justify less favourable treatment only where not treating the disabled tenant less favourably would effectively prevent other tenants, or the disabled person, from using the benefit or facility. They cannot be used to justify less favourable treatment simply because other tenants would be inconvenienced or delayed.

> A landlord refuses to allow a mentally ill tenant to use the shared kitchen because he sometimes takes a little longer and so delays other tenants. **This is against the law.**

What about the effects of other legislation?

5.18 The Act does not:
- make unlawful anything done to comply with other legislation (if you are required to do something under another law this takes precedence over anything required by the Act);
- make unlawful any act done to safeguard national security {S59}.

Special rules for insurance

5.19 Regulations will make special rules for insurance which recognise the need for insurers to be able to distinguish between individuals on the basis of the risks against which they seek to insure. Insurers will be able to justify less favourable treatment only if that treatment is based on actuarial or other statistical data or other information on which it is reasonable to rely. If a disabled person establishes in a court that less favourable treatment has occurred, it will be up to the insurer to prove that there is an additional risk associated with the disabled person which arises from his or her disability.

> An insurance company charges a higher premium to a deaf person for car insurance although it has no evidence of an increased risk. **This is against the law.**

Special rules for guarantees and warranties

5.20 Many retailers go beyond their statutory duties by replacing goods if they wear out or break within a specified period of time. Generally speaking, they do this if the goods have been subjected to only an average amount of wear and tear. However, there are situations in which a person's disability might result in higher than average wear and tear. Regulations will exempt service providers from replacing goods in the latter circumstances.

> A person with mobility problems buys a pair of shoes but wears out the left shoe
> after a few months because his left foot has to bear most of his weight. The
> retailer refuses to provide a new pair of shoes because the old pair has undergone
> abnormal wear and tear. **This is within the law.**

6   Other unlawful actions

Victimisation

6.1   It is unlawful for you to victimise (to pick on or treat less favourably) any person,
whether disabled or not, who has:
- brought legal proceedings under the Act;
- given evidence or information in connection with such proceedings;
- done anything else under the Act; or
- alleged that the Act has been broken;

or because you believe that he or she has done or intends to do any of the above {S55}.

6.2   It is not victimisation to treat a person less favourably because that person has
made an allegation which was false and not made in good faith.

Aiding unlawful actions

6.3   It is unlawful for you to aid anyone to discriminate against a disabled person,
unless you are relying on a statement that the action is allowed under the Act and it is
reasonable for you to rely on that statement. However, anyone who knowingly or
recklessly makes a false statement of this kind is committing an offence {S57}.

> A receptionist in a small hairdresser's, following his employer's instructions,
> refuses to book an appointment for a person with cerebral palsy. His employer
> has told him that small firms are exempt from Part III of the Act, despite knowing
> that this exemption applies only to the employment provisions in Part II. **The
> employee is within the law but the employer is not.**

Liability of employers for their employees' actions

6.4   Each of your employees is individually responsible for complying with the law.
However, if one of your employees breaks the law in the course of his or her
employment, action could also be taken against you even if you were unaware or did
not approve of what he or she had done {S58(1)}. However, in a case where one of your
employees breaks the law, you may have a defence if you can prove that you took such
steps as were reasonably practicable to prevent him or her from discriminating
{S58(5)}. Examples of the type of steps which might be reasonably practicable are set
out in paragraph 1.8.

> A sales assistant refuses to serve a disabled person, despite the employer having provided relevant and recent training, instructing staff to serve disabled people and checking regularly that they are complying. **The employer is likely to be within the law but the employee is not.**

6.5   If someone you authorise to act on your behalf—for example an agent—breaks the law, action could also be taken against you {S58(2)}. This applies whether the authority was expressed or implied and whether it was given before or after the unlawful act. You may, however, have a defence if you can show that your agent was not acting with your authority.

Terms of agreements

6.6   Any term in any agreement, such as a lease, is void if its effect is to:
- require someone to do something which would be unlawful under Part III of the Act (the part relating to services and premises);
- exclude or limit the operation of Part III; or
- prevent someone making a claim under Part III {S26}.

> A landlord's lease includes a term forbidding the tenant from subletting to people with learning disabilities. **This term is not legally binding.**

7   Disputes and penalties

What happens if there is a dispute?

7.1   If you unlawfully discriminate against a disabled person he or she may seek to discuss the problem with you in order to resolve it. He or she may also seek assistance from an organisation representing his or her interests. Similarly, you might wish to seek advice from a business or service providers' organisation.

7.2   The Government will establish a service to provide advice and assistance to the many general or specialist advisers who are already operating. This will ensure that those providing advice on the Act will have access to specialist knowledge of its provisions and a pool of experience in dealing with cases of particular difficulty.

What happens if a dispute cannot be resolved?

7.3   If you cannot resolve a dispute in this way, a disabled person would be able to take you to court and, if successful, could receive compensation for any financial loss or injury to his or her feelings. A disabled person may also be able to seek an injunction or, in Scotland, interdict, against you to prevent the repeat of any discriminatory act {S25}.

Making false statements

7.4   If you are found guilty of making a false statement of the kind described in paragraph 6.3 you will be liable to a fine up to level 5 on the standard scale (£5,000 as of May 1996) {S57(5)}.

Grounds of Application to an Industrial Tribunal

Disability

The Complainant is a disabled person for the purposes of ss 1 or 2 of the DDA 1995. As a result of injuring his left knee whilst at work on 12 December 1988 and suffering a ten per cent loss of function of the left leg from his injury he is restricted permanently from squat-bending or kneeling on that knee with permanent maximum lifting limits of 15–20 pounds (if lifting is frequent) and 30 pounds (otherwise). As a result of a further injury suffered whilst at work on or about [*state date*] the Complainant's right ankle was fused by surgery on 12 May 1996. The Complainant cannot squat, kneel, balance or move everyday objects such as shopping bags. He therefore suffers a substantial and long term adverse effect on a normal day to day activity.

Less favourable treatment and failure to make adjustments

The Complainant complains of less favourable treatment in that he was selected for redundancy for a reason which relates to his disability, namely his absence record, or in the alternative as a result of the restrictions applying to working practices as a result of his disability. The Respondent did not or would not have treated other employees who were not so disabled in the same way.

The Complainant also complains that the Respondent failed to take the steps which it would have been reasonable for him to have to take in all the circumstances of the case to remove the substantial disadvantage suffered by the Complainant in comparison with persons who are not disabled.

The substantial disadvantage suffered by the Complainant was:
(1) being demoted and taken off field inspection work which attracted a better rate of pay and payments package; and
(2) being selected for redundancy by the Respondent's selection procedure.

The arrangements which gave rise to these substantial disadvantages were that the Complainant was demoted from inspector and required to do the less well paid work of a training supervisor, and the redundancy selection procedures employed by the Respondent to select persons for redundancy.

The following measures were reasonable ones for the Respondent to have to take to remove the substantial disadvantage.

Inspector's position

In relation to the demotion of the Complainant on 3 February 1997 the Complainant on numerous occasions, orally and in writing, requested the Respondent to consider or to

make the following adjustments to his working arrangements
  (1) to provide the Complainant with an assistant either full or part time;
  (2) to reallocate field inspection duties which the Complainant was unable to perform among other inspectors;
  (3) to permit the Complainant to consider his own physical limitations in scheduling inspections jobs; and
  (4) to reallocate the duties of the Complainant that involved heavy lifting.

When told that he was to be demoted the Complainant repeated the above requests, but Mr Dennis, his line manager, refused to discuss them with him.

In relation to the redundancy scheme

The Respondent employs a method of selection for redundancy which assesses employees on the basis of several categories. If a person achieves a low score in a category he is more likely to be selected for redundancy than if he achieves a high score. The Respondent failed to adjust the procedure so as to remove the substantial disadvantage suffered by the Complainant in comparison with persons who are not disabled, namely that he would achieve a low score in relation to absence and to flexibility (which was measured by the variation of duties that the employees could perform) in comparison with persons who are not disabled.

The measures taken by the Respondent failed to negate the effects of the arrangements relating to the field inspection post and should not reasonably in the circumstances have been taken because they were themselves discriminatory for a reason relating to the Complainant's disability.

Further the Respondent refused and/or unreasonably failed to take the above or any measures.

As a result of the Respondent's failure to take the measures and/or less favourable treatment the Complainant lost a position which attracted more money than his salary as a training inspector and as a result of the failure of the Respondent to make adjustments to the redundancy selection procedure the complainant was selected for redundancy.

Facts

The Respondent is a national company which conducts non-destructive testing of metals, valves, storage tanks, and vessels (eg the inspection of steel girders before they are installed in a building, pipes as they are laid in the ground, and storage tanks). Inspectors are certified in the methods used in non-destructive testing, and the Applicant was so qualified at all material times. The Applicant was employed by the Swindon branch of the Respondent on 15 November 1986 as an inspector on a part-time basis. He injured his left knee whilst at work on 12 December 1988 suffering a ten per cent loss of function of the left leg from this injury. The Applicant was restricted permanently from squat-bending or kneeling on that knee with permanent maximum lifting limits of 15–20 pounds (if lifting were frequent) and 30 pounds (otherwise).

The Applicant resumed work as an inspector, on 31 January 1989 and performed his job satisfactorily. In July 1990, the Applicant became a full time employee of the Respondent. He was promoted to supervisor of the Swindon Branch on 24 December 1990. The supervisory job required the Applicant to ensure that inspections are performed accurately and on time. In practice the supervisor performs inspections as needed and spent the majority of his time ensuring the accuracy of other inspectors' work. In addition the supervisor was responsible for allocating work among the inspectors.

The Applicant was further injured at work on 23 July 1995, when he fell from a ladder and broke his right leg and right ankle. His recovery from this injury was monitored by the Respondent. The Applicant was absent from work due to these injuries, until December 1995, when he returned to work on light duty.

The Applicant was unable to work more than a few days and went sick again in early January 1996. His right ankle was fused by surgery on 12 May 1996. As a result of his injuries and consequent surgery, the Applicant became a disabled person within the meaning of the Disability Discrimination Act 1995, s 1.

His doctor informed the Respondent that the Applicant could return to work part-time in September 1996, and full time in December 1996.

During the Applicant's absence, Frank Dennis, manager of the Swindon branch of the Respondent, had been performing his own and the Applicant's duties. To reduce his workload, Dennis appointed Michael Craig, a Level II inspector, as acting supervisor on 31 June 1996.

In late June or early July Dennis offered Craig the Swindon supervisor position permanently if he took and passed the appropriate certification tests in early August which he did. The Applicant's doctor had projected his return to part-time light duty work on 15 August 1996. However his doctor suggested a 'functional capacity evaluation' (FCE) which would more fully detail the Applicant's work capabilities. The Respondents therefore postponed the Applicant's return to work until the FCE and a job analysis could be completed. The FCE concluded the Applicant could not squat, kneel or balance. The FCE was completed in November 1996.

On 25 March 1997 the Respondent stated to the Applicant that with the restrictions noted in the FCE, he could not perform field inspections and, so, could not return to the supervisor position. The Respondent then created a training instructor position for the Applicant. However, the new position was part-time, paid less, and did not offer any benefits. The Respondent's personnel department prepared a job description for the new position which the Applicant saw on 3 February 1997. On 20 February 1997 the Applicant issued an originating application to the Industrial Tribunal complaining of the Respondent's failure to make reasonable adjustments and return him to the supervisor position.

On 15 May 1997 Mr Dennis learned that the Applicant had issued a complaint under the Disability Discrimination Act 1995, and informed the Applicant that he could not return to work. Mr Dennis told the Applicant that the company 'couldn't have this shit' and he would either be laid off or fired because of his complaint. However, the next day Mr Dennis telephoned the Applicant telling him he could return to work. The Applicant returned to work at the Respondent in the training instructor position on 30 May 1997.

In June 1997 the Applicant was assigned a field inspection job after Mr Craig reviewed the physical requirements of the job. The job lasted from 21 June to 30 July 1997 for two days per week. It required the Applicant to walk in a field where explosions had been set off and to walk down a rough, eight-foot deep pit without assistance. The Applicant performed the job adequately. On 3 August 1997, the Applicant took sick leave for an operation on his left knee which he had injured in 1989. He returned to work on 30 August 1997.

On or about 15 August 1997, the Respondent announced that it was proposing to make redundancies at the Swindon Branch. The selection was by means of a skills matrix and among the criteria was one of attendance.

The Applicant was selected for redundancy, and was the only person at the Swindon Branch so selected out of a total workforce of 30.

The Complainant was victimised by the Respondents via Mr Dennis, who made the selection for redundancy and who told the Complainant that he could not come to work when he learned that the Complainant had issued proceedings (now consolidated with these proceedings) under the Disability Discrimination Act 1995.

The Respondent discriminated against the Complainant in failing to make the adjustments referred to above.

The Respondent treated the Complainant less favourably (for a reason which relates to his disability) than they treated others to whom that reason did not apply.

Appendix 5

The Disability Discrimination Act 1995, s 56(2) Questionnaire of Complainant

To [*Datchbury Quality Inspections Ltd*] (*name of person to be questioned*) of [*123 Pikestafff Road Swindon*] (*address*)

1(1)   I [*P Jones*] (*name of questioner*) of [*128 Phillips Rd*] (*address*) consider that you have discriminated against me contrary to the Disability Discrimination Act 1995 ('the Act') by unjustifiably

(see Note 1)   (a)   for a reason relating to my disability, treating me less favourably than people to whom that reason does not or would not apply, or

(see Note 2)   (b)   failing to take steps which it was reasonable to have to take to prevent your employment arrangements or premises putting me at a substantial disadvantage compared with people who are not disabled.

1(2)   (*Give details including a factual description of the treatment received or the failure complained of. Describe any relevant circumstances leading up to this and include any relevant dates or approximate dates*).

The Respondent is a national company which conducts non-destructive testing of metals, valves, storage tanks, and vessels (eg the inspection of steel girders before they are installed in a building, pipes as they are laid in the ground, and storage tanks). Inspectors are certified in the methods used in non-destructive testing, and the Complainant was so qualified at all material times. The Complainant was employed by the Swindon branch of the Respondent on 15 November 1986 as an inspector on a part-time basis. He injured his left knee whilst at work on 12 December 1988 suffering a ten per cent loss of function of the left leg from this injury. The Complainant was restricted permanently from squat-bending or kneeling on that knee with permanent maxmium lifting limits of 15–20 pounds (if lifting were frequently) and 30 pounds (otherwise).

The Complainant resumed work as an inspector, on 31 January 1989 and performed his job satisfactorily. In July 1990, the Complainant became a full time employee of the Respondent. He was promoted to supervisor of the Swindon Branch on 24 December 1990. The supervisory job required the Complainant to ensure that inspections are performed accurately and timely. In practice the supervisor performs inspections as needed and spends the majority of his time ensuring the accuracy of other inspectors' work. In addition the supervisor is responsible for allocating work among the inspectors.

The Complainant was further injured at work on 23 July, 1995, when he fell from a ladder and broke his right leg and right ankle. His recovery from this injury was monitored by the Respondents. The Complainant was absent from work due to these injuries, until December 1995, when he returned to work on light duty.

The Complainant was unable to work more than a few days and went sick again in early January 1996. His right ankle was fused by surgery on 12 May 1996. As a result of his injuries and consequent surgery, the Complainant became a disabled person within the meaning of the Disability Discrimination Act 1995, s 1.

His doctor informed the Respondents that the Complainant could return to work part time in September 1996, and full time in December 1996.

During the Complainant's absence, Frank Dennis, manager of the Swindon branch of the Respondent, had been performing his own and the Complainant's duties. To reduce his workload, Dennis appointed Michael Craig, a Level II inspector, as acting supervisor on 31 June 1997.

In late June or early July Dennis offered Craig the Swindon supervisor position permanently if he took and passed the appropriate certification tests in early August which he did. The Complainant's doctor had projected his return to part-time light duty work on 15 August 1996. However his doctor suggested a 'functional capacity evaluation' (FCE) which would more fully detail the Complainant's work capabilities. The Respondents therefore postponed the Complainant's return to work until the FCE and a job analysis could be completed. The FCE concluded the Complainant could not squat, kneel or balance.

On 15 December 1996 the Respondent stated to the Complainant that with the restrictions noted in the FCE, he could not perform field inspections and, so, could not return to the supervisor position. The Respondent then developed a training instructor position for the Complainant. However, the new position was part-time, paid less, and did not offer any benefits. The Respondent's personnel department prepared a job description for the new position which the Complainant saw on 3 February 1997. On 20 February 1997 the Complainant issued an originating application to the Industrial Tribunal complaining of the Respondent's failure to make reasonable adjustments and return him to the supervisor position.

On 15 May 1997 Mr Dennis learned that the Complainant had issued a complaint under the Disability Discrimination Act 1995, he informed the Complainant that he could not return to work. Mr Dennis told the Complainant that the company 'couldn't have this shit' and he would either be laid off or fired because of his complaint. However the next day Mr Dennis telephoned the Complainant telling him he could return to work. The Complainant returned to work at the Respondent in the training instructor position on 30 May 1997.

In June 1997 the Complainant was assigned a field inspection job after Mr Craig reviewed the physical requirements of the job. The job lasted from 21 June to 30 July 1997 for two days per week. It required the Complainant to walk in a field where explosions had been set off and to walk down a rough, eight-foot deep pit without assistance. The Complainant performed the job adequately. On 3 August 1997, the Complainant took sick leave for an operation on his left knee which he had injured in 1989. He returned to work on 30 August 1997.

On or about 15 August 1997, the Respondent announced that it was proposing to make redundancies at the Swindon Branch. The selection was by means of a skills matrix and among the criteria was one of attendance.

The Complainant was selected for redundancy, and was the only person at the Swindon Branch so selected out of a total workforce of 30.

1(3) I consider this treatment or failure on your part may have been unlawful [*because* ————————— *(complete if you wish to give reasons, otherwise delete)*].

[*Normally left blank or deleted.*]

2 Do you agree that the statement in paragraph 1(2) above is an accurate description of what happened? If not, in what respect do you disagree or what is your version of what happened?

3 Do you accept that your treatment of me or any failure complained of was unlawful?

If not—
  (a) why not; and
  (b) do you consider your treatment of me or your failure to act was reasonable in all the circumstances?

4 *(Any other questions you wish to ask.)*

In a case where the respondent has previously disputed disability
4.1 Do you accept that the complainant has a physical impairment, namely a fused right ankle, which results in his being unable to perform certain normal day to day activities, namely those relating to mobility and to lifting and carrying everyday objects over a reasonable distance?

In a case concerning reasonable adjustment
4.2 Do you accept that on 24 February 1997 the Complainant suggested the following matters could be adjusted so as to remove the disadvantage he suffered in performing his duties in comparison with persons who are not disabled. (Set out (1)–(4) on p 331.)

4.3 Do you accept that the following arrangements were made by or on your behalf namely:
  (a) you required the Complainant to do the work of a junior supervisor from 3 April 1997;
  (b) Mr Dennis would not provide an assistant despite a request made in writing on 24 February 1997;
  (c) Mr Dennis refused to consider reallocating duties among the existing inspectors despite a request on 24 February 1997;
  (d) You require your inspectors to conduct inspections on their own without assistance.

4.4 Do you accept that these arrangements placed the Complainant at a substantial disadvantage in comparison with persons who are not disabled?

4.5 Was Mr Dennis aware that the complainant was disabled at any, and if so which time(s)?

4.6 Do you accept that the Complainant required and performed lighter duties on each occasion he returned from a period of sickness due to injury or operation?

4.7   If the answer to 4.6 is 'no' do you accept that the complainant was placed on lighter duties on return from any and if so which period of sickness absence and state any reasons for his being so placed.

4.8   What are Mr Dennis' qualifications in inspection work?

4.9   Is it correct that Mr Dennis holds two certificates in inspection work?

4.10   Why was the Complainant refused an Assistant?

4.11   Is it correct that inspectors are given sites to visit by Mr Dennis?

4.12   Why was the Complainant refused field inspection work of any kind?

4.13   What field inspection work was carried out between 30 May 1997 and 30 August 1997?

4.14   What is the name of each site at which such work was carried out?

4.15   Is it correct, and if it is not why is it not correct, that the majority of the sites named at 4.14 do not require the inspector to walk in rough terrain?

4.16   Is the job description for the supervisor's position an accurate representation of the duties carried out by the Complainant in practice?

4.17   If the answer to 4.16 is 'no', in what respects is the description an inaccurate representation.

4.18   What proportion of the Complainant's duties required him to conduct inspections in the field?

4.19   What proportion of the Complainant's duties consisted in supervisory duties?

4.20   Why was the complainant not allowed to consider his own physical limitations in scheduling jobs?

4.21   Why did the Respondent refuse to require another employee to conduct the field inspections the Complainant is unable to perform while the Complainant took on the other worker's duties?

4.22   Is it correct that after the Complainant returned to work as a training instructor, he adequately performed a field inspection job on one occasion?

4.23   What are the gross sales per year of the Respondent?

4.24   How many branches does the Respondent have nationwide?

4.25   Attached is an occupational therapist's report concerning the supervisor's duties. Do you accept the conclusion that the adjustments set out in the conclusion to that report would have enabled the Complainant to perform the duties of the post? If not what do you reject and why do you reject it?

4.26   Do you accept that the following duties could have been reallocated to another employee:
   (a)   field inspections to be performed on rough terrain?
   (b)   the complainant's duties which involve heavy lifting?
   If not why do you say that the duties could not have have been reallocated in this way?

4.27   Do you accept that it was practicable for you to carry out the steps set out above? If not why do you say that the steps were not practicable?

4.28   Do you accept that it would have been possible for the Complainant to allocate field inspection work so as to accommodate his disability without any cost to the Respondent? If you do not accept this, why do you not accept it?

4.29   Do you accept that such steps would not have disrupted the Respondent's organisation? If not, what disruption do you say would have occurred?

4.30   How much does the Respondent spend in training an inspector to supervisory level?

4.31   How much would it cost the Respondent to recruit and train a replacement for the Complainant?

4.32   Do you accept that the Complainant had 10 years' experience as an inspector?

4.33   Do you accept that the Complainant was fully qualified as a supervisory inspector?

4.34   Do you accept that the Complainant received training on an annual basis?

4.35   In respect of each such course, what was the cost in relation to the Complainant to the Respondent of the course?

4.36   Do you accept that the Complainant had good annual appraisals while he was a supervisor? If not, what problems do you allege there were in respect of his annual appraisals?

4.37   In respect of training and other financial investment in the Complainant, what was the training budget allocated in the years 1993 to 1996 for the Swindon branch of the Respondent?

4.38   Where is the nearest branch to the Swindon branch?

4.39   What assistance or advice was sought from any outside body by the Respondent in respect of the requests by the Complainant for adjustments to be made to the arrangements about which complaint is made?

4.40 What are the names of the organisations/persons from whom advice on the adjustments was sought, and on what dates was advice sought from each such organisation/person?

4.41 Do you accept that the complainant demonstrated on numerous occasions that he was willing to co-operate with any other adjustment the Respondent might suggest?

4.42 Do you state that the treatment of the Complainant was justified? If so what was the reason for that treatment?

4.43 State every criterion applied in deciding who should be selected for redundancy in Swindon in August 1997 explaining:
  (a) how each criterion was weighted;
  (b) the date when the criterion was decided upon;
  (c) who decided the criterion;
  (d) who was consulted concerning the criterion;
  (e) whether the criterion was written down, and if so when it was written down;
  (f) who judged the criterion; and
  (g) the method by which the criterion was assessed.

4.44 State whether there was a decision in advance as to the numbers of employees to be made redundant across the respondent?

4.45 When was the decision made?

4.46 By whom was the decision made?

4.47 Name all branches from which redundancies were to be considered?

4.48 Who made the decision to make the complainant redundant?

4.49 What date was that decision made on?

4.50 Who was consulted, and on what date?

4.51 What views did those consulted express?

4.52 What were the detailed reasons for the selection of the complainant?

4.53 Of all the employees of the Respondent as at 15 August 1997, how many had been registered disabled before the introduction of the Disability Discrimination Act 1995? Did the Respondent keep records? If not, why not? If so where are these records currently?

4.54 How many supervisors were disabled as at that date? In each case what is the person's disability if there are any?

4.55 In respect of each and every person listed in response to questions 4.53 and 4.54, what was the person's position, and if no longer in the employment state the reason for dismissal or termination.

4.56   If the reason for termination given in respect of a person in question 4.55 is redundancy, state the date on which they were made redundant and the reasons for the redundancy.

4.57   How many supervisory inspectors does the Swindon Branch currently employ?

4.58   In the case of each supervisory inspector state the date on which he commenced as a supervisory inspector?

4.59   In each such case is the person disabled or not, and if he is disabled, what is the nature of his disability?

4.60   Does the respondent have an equal opportunities policy? If so please supply a copy.

5   My address for any reply you may wish to give to the questions raised above is [that set out in paragraph 1(1) above] [the following address —————————]

————————————— (*signature of questioner*)

————————————— (*date*)

[Note 1
Section 5(1) of the Act provides 'an employer discriminates against a disabled person if—

    (a)   for a reason which relates to the disabled person's disability, he treats him less favourably than he treats or would treat others to whom that reason does not or would not apply; and
    (b)   he cannot show that the treatment in question is justified.'

Note 2
The first three subsections of s 6 of the Act provide
    (1)   Where—
        (a)   any arrangements made by or on behalf of an employer, or
        (b)   any physical feature of premises occupied by the employer
place the disabled person concerned at a substantial disadvantage in comparison with persons who are not disabled, if is the duty of the employer to take such steps as it is reasonable, in all the circumstances of the case, for him to have to take in order to prevent the arrangements or feature having that effect.
    (2)   Subsection (1)(*a*) applies only in relation to—
        (a)   arrangements for determining to whom employment should be offered;
        (b)   any term, condition or arrangements on which employment, promotion, a transfer, training or any other benefit is offered or afforded.
    (3) The following are examples of steps which an employer may have to take in relation to a disabled person in order to comply with subsection (1)—
        (a)   making adjustments to premises;
        (b)   allocating some of the disabled person's duties to another person;
        (c)   transferring him to fill an existing vacancy;
        (d)   altering his working hours;
        (e)   assigning him to a different place of work;
        (f)   allowing him to be absent during working hours for rehabilitation, assessment or treatment;

(g) giving him, or arranging for him to be given, training;
(h) acquiring or modifying equipment;
(i) modifying instructions or reference manuals;
(j) modifying procedures for testing or assessment;
(k) providing a reader or interpreter;
(l) providing supervision.

NB By virtue of s 56(3) of the Act, this questionnaire and any reply are (subject to the provisions of s 56 and any orders made under that section) admissible in proceedings under Pt II of the Act and a tribunal may draw any inference it considers is just and equitable from a failure without reasonable excuse to reply within a reasonable period, or from an evasive or equivocal reply, including any inference that the person questioned has discriminated unlawfully.

The Disability Discrimination Act 1995 s 56(1)(*b*) Reply to Questionnaire

To [*P Jones*] *(name of questioner)* of

[*address*] *(address)*

1   I [*Valerie Kingholst, Datchbury Quality Inspections*] *(name of person questioned)* of [*address*] *(address)* hereby acknowledge receipt of the questionnaire signed by you and dated ——————— which was served on me on ——————— *(date)*.

2   *I agree that the statement in paragraph 1(2) of the questionnaire is an accurate description of what happened.
     *I disagree with the statement in paragraph 1(2) of the questionnaire in that:

It is admitted that the Complainant is a disabled person. It is denied that the Complainant performed his job satisfactorily, as there were occasional complaints about the quality of his work both as an inspector and a supervisor. It is denied that the supervisor performs inspections as needed. It is in practice part of the supervisor's job which takes up about 45 per cent of his time.

The Respondent took all steps which it was reasonable in all the circumstances of the case for him to take. Such steps included allowing the Complainant to do light duties until he was fully recovered from his operations. The steps demanded by the Complainant were not reasonable in the circumstances for the Respondent to have to take.

It is admitted that during the Complainant's absence the Respondent appointed Mr Craig to the post of supervisory inspector. However this was because he had obtained the qualifications necessary for the post, and the business of the Respondent was undergoing a radical review in an attempt to avoid redundancies.

The Respondent ensured that a functional capacity evaluation took place as recommended by the Complainant's doctor.

A supervisory inspector is required to perform field inspections on a regular basis. These involve lifting heavy objects regularly, such as iron girders, and other objects. A supervisor performs these duties once every two weeks. It was not possible to reallocate these duties as they are part of the essential requirements of the Complainant's job. The job analysis carried out by the Respondents showed that on average such inspections were carried out at Swindon on a more frequent basis than at other branches of the

[* *Delete as appropriate.*]

Respondent. The job analysis showed that at least 50 per cent of the Complainant's post consisted of such inspections.

The steps taken by the Respondent were reasonable. The Respondent ensured that when it became apparent that the Complainant was unable to perform the essential functions of his job a special position was created for him in which he did not have to perform any heavy lifting, or to perform field trips unless an emergency arose. The field inspection mentioned by the Complainant in the questionnaire was carried out in such an emergency.

Mr Dennis did not tell the Complainant that he could not return to work. Mr Dennis did not know of the existence of the proceedings relating to the above matters until September 1997 when the questionnaire was drawn to his attention. However on 15 May 1997 there was a meeting between Mr Dennis and the complainant at which Mr Dennis consulted with the Complainant concerning potential redundancies. During the course of that meeting Mr Dennis stated that it was possible that the Complainant would be selected for redundancy. The Complainant replied that the Respondent 'could not touch' him, and that he would 'get even' with Mr Dennis if he were fired. Mr Dennis told the Complainant that he should go home and calm down. The next day the Complainant failed to attend work and Mr Dennis telephoned him to find out what had happened. During the course of that conversation Mr Dennis told the Complainant to come into work. The Complainant did. It is denied that Mr Dennis said any such words as 'the company can't have this shit'.

It is admitted that the Complainant was sent on a field inspection after Mr Craig had reviewed the physical requirements of the job. As a step of adjustment that was reasonable in all the circumstances of the case Mr Craig would consider the Complainant for field inspection work. However in most cases the Complainant's disability rendered him unable to carry out the essential functions of such inspections, which involve frequent heavy lifting. Mr Craig consulted the Complainant on such field inspections.

As to the redundancy of the Complainant, he was consulted concerning the application of the skills matrix to his case, as were all the staff at the Swindon branch. The Complainant's redundancy was not for a reason which related to his disability which did not apply to others.

3   I accept/dispute that my treatment of you or any failure to act on my part was unlawful.

*My reasons for disputing this are [*The same treatment was given to all*]

*I considered my treatment of you or my failure to take action was justified.

(Include any reason which in your view explains or justifies your treatment of the applicant or any decision not to take action.)

The reasons for the treatment of the Complainant are set out in more detail in reply to the questionnaire and in the Notice of Appearance. However in brief:
  (a)   the Complainant was unable to perform the essential requirements of the position of inspector as regard field inspections;
  (b)   the Respondent requires its inspectors to be able to perform field inspections;
  (c)   however, the Respondent, after taking appropriate medical and occupational health advice considered that although the Complainant could not perform

these inspections regularly, there would be occasions on which he could perform some, and the Respondent instructed Mr Craig to consider these occasions when allocating the work;

(d)   as a result of the above advice the Respondent devised a special position for the Complainant in which the amount of lifting and walking over rough terrain would be minimised;

(e)   as a result of the economic factors referred to in the replies to the questions (set out below) the Respondent rejected the idea put forward (at a later date) by the Complainant that he should have an assistant;

(f)   the Respondent considered the Complainant's suggestion that duties should be reallocated among staff, but rejected this suggestion because it would have entailed removing duties which are valued by other inspectors and giving them to the Complainant—this would have caused too much disruption to the Respondent's business in terms of poor morale.

4   *(Replies to questions in paragraph 4 of the questionnaire.)*

4.1   Yes

4.2   No, on various dates after issuing his first originating application the Complainant made a suggestion that he should have an assistant to enable him to do field inspections and jobs involving heavy lifting. It was pointed out to him by Mr Dennis and Mr Craig that this would not be a viable course.

4.3   The Respondent accepts that the following arrangements were made, but rejects the connotations in the questionnaire that these positions denoted a more junior position for the Complainant:

(a)   from February 1997 the Complainant was relieved of his duties relating to field inspections and other work involving heavy lifting;

(b)   the Respondent has no record of such a request being made in writing on the date stated or at all. Further, Mr Dennis refused the Complainant's request on many occasions. However these were all during 1997 and the Complainant understood that the reason for the refusal was that it would not be economically viable or practicable for the respondent to provide such assistance;

(c)   yes, see above at (b); and

(d)   yes.

4.4   No.

4.5   Yes from the date of the Complainant's injuries.

4.6   Yes

4.7   N/A

4.8   Mr Dennis was an inspector for eight years before becoming manager.

4.9   Mr Dennis currently holds no certificates in inspection work.

4.10 The Complainant was refused an assistant because it would not have been economically feasible for the Respondent to employ such a person specifically for that job, and it would have been too disruptive for the Respondent to have reallocated jobs between existing staff.

4.11 No, Mr Craig gives instructions to inspectors. Mr Dennis is responsible for supervisory inspectors and inspectors alike.

4.12 The Complainant was not refused field inspection work of any kind. He was permitted to go on field inspections which did not involve heavy lifting or travelling over rough terrain.

4.13 The field inspection work carried out by the Respondent from their Swindon branch is as set out in the attached schedule [not included].

4.14 The name of each site is given on the attached schedule.

4.15 It is correct that the majority of such field inspections did not require the inspector to walk in rough terrain. However that was not the reason, as the Complainant knows, why such work was not allocated to him. In the majority of cases the inspection work involved squatting, bending and lifting weights which would not have been possible for the Complainant.

4.16 No.

4.17 The job description is merely a broad description of what the Complainant may have been required to do in his job. However in practice inspectors are required to do field inspections on a regular or frequent basis.

4.18 As a supervisory inspector the Complainant would have been required to perform field inspections roughly 60 per cent of his time.

4.19 The remaining 40 per cent of his post would have consisted of inspection work and other minor duties as set out in the job description.

4.20 Although supervisory inspectors have a discretion in the allocation of jobs, the Respondent requires its senior inspectors to be available for certain of its more important clients. In addition the senior inspector is required to be available if there is an emergency job which requires immediate attention. The inspector in such cases may not be able to allocate the job to anyone else. In those circumstances the Complainant could not perform the essential requirements of the position regarding scheduling.

4.21 The Respondent did not so refuse. In consultation with the Complainant it was agreed that such reallocation would not be feasible. At the same time, the Complainant was told that the Respondent was creating a special post for him, namely that of training inspector.

4.22 Yes.

4.23   The gross sales of the Respondent are £10m. However, the Respondent failed to make a net profit in the accounting year 1996 to 1997, and the Swindon branch of the Respondent made a substantial loss in that year.

4.24   At the time of the Complainant's dismissal the Respondent had 34. However since that time the respondent has had to close five branches.

4.25   In relation to the report of Mr Edmund Campion the Respondent does not accept that the adjustments mentioned in the conclusion of the report would have enabled the Complainant to perform the duties of the post for the following reasons:
  (a)   the report is based on a description of the post which over emphasises the supervisory aspects of the job;
  (b)   the kind of equipment specified in the report as being necessary to overcome the substantial difficulties alleged in the report is prohibitively expensive and therefore would not have been practicable for the Respondent or the Complainant to obtain;
  (c)   the Respondent has dealt with the suggestion that an assistant could have been provided. Further even if an assistant had been provided this would not have prevented the Complainant from having to lift heavy objects on emergency field visits;
  (d)   The Respondent has dealt with the reallocation of duties. The report proceeds on the basis that it would have been possible to reallocate duties. This suggestion is incorrect. In particular the suggestion that Mr Lugg would have been permitted to perform the jobs involving heavy lifting for the Complainant is made by Mr Campion in ignorance of the House Agreement with Mr Lugg's Trade Union, which would have precluded any such reallocation; and
  (e)   Even if all of the adjustments recommended had been made, the Complainant would not have been able to perform the duties as required by the Respondent.

4.26   No. For the reasons given above the Complainant would have been required at short notice to go on field inspections without knowing whether the terrain was too rough for him to be able to walk over to conduct the tests, and in addition it was not practicable to reallocate his duties in these respects among existing staff.

4.27   It was not practicable for the Respondent to have carried out the steps listed in the questionnaire because:
  (a)   the Trade Union agreement referred to above;
  (b)   the effect such reallocation would have had on the morale of the existing staff;
  (c)   the cost of providing the assistance sought by the complainant was prohibitive; and
  (d)   the Complainant did not co-operate with such steps as the Respondent did take to remove any substantial disadvantage he was suffering compared with non-disabled persons

4.28   No. If the Complainant had reallocated work so as to accommodate his disability it would have been necessary, on each occasion of an emergency, for the Respondent to have ensured cover, which would have involved either overtime or additional bonus payments to the person effecting the cover, or to have refused the job. In either case there would have been a cost to the Respondent.

4.29 No. Requiring persons to cover for the Applicant at short notice would have involved extreme disruption of the Respondent's business both in terms of the additional administration and lack of certainty it would have required other staff to undergo. In terms of the suggestion that an additional member of staff should have been employed, the consequent cost to the business of a person who was not fully employed would have caused disruption. The Respondent has made persons redundant at the Swindon branch in any event.

4.30 There are no precise figures available, however an average figure would be about £1000.

4.31 Again there are no precise figures as to how much it costs to recruit and train a replacement for the Complainant as the Respondent has not done so. However recruitment at entry level is by means of advertisement in the local job centre and training thereafter is as in 4.30. Generally recruitment is not carried out at senior inspector level.

4.32 No. The Complainant had five years as a senior inspector and the remainder as an inspector.

4.33 Yes. However the Complainant was not able fully to perform the essential functions of the supervisory inspector role.

4.34 Yes.

4.35 The Respondent does not have any figures for the cost in relation to the Complainant of each such course. The over all training figure is given above.

4.36 No. The Complainant was criticised in his 1996 annual appraisal for the amount of time he was taking off in terms of minor ailments unrelated to his disability.

4.37 The Respondent refuses to answer this question until its relevance to an issue in the case is made clear by the applicant.

4.38 Chippenham.

4.39 The Respondent, by Mr Dennis, made inquiries of the local chamber of commerce, and the occupational health experts who conducted the FCA referred to in the questionnaire.

4.40 The Respondent refuses to answer this question on the grounds that it is not relevant to the subject matter of the proceedings, save insofar as it has been answered in 4.39 above.

4.41 No.

4.42 Yes. The substantial and material reason for the Complainant's treatment was that he could not, with or without an adjustment, perform the essential requirements of the supervisory inspector's post, and therefore could not remain in that post. The post created for the Complainant involved less responsibility and was an easier job. It therefore attracted a lower rate of pay.

4.43 Criteria applied in deciding who should be selected for redundancy included:
    (a) an assessment of each and every person against an objective skills assessment matrix;
    (b) the ability of the candidate to perform the essential requirements of his job with or without adjustment:

Each criterion was weighted equally. The criteria were all decided on at a meeting on 25 June 1997 by Mr Dennis, Mr Craig, and the company director, Ms Rudy Hegel in consultation with the Employers' Federation. The criteria were written down at that meeting. Mr Dennis and Mr Craig applied the criteria first by making a judgement based on their individual knowledge and experience of the candidates, and with reference to the Respondent's personnel record, and then in consultation with one another. After that the candidate was interviewed concerning his prospective redundancy and asked whether there was any objection he had to the score achieved by him.

4.44 The Respondent at the meeting referred to above on 25 June 1997 decided that it was necessary to make 30 persons redundant. It was not decided where the redundancies were to take place.

4.45 The decision as to numbers was made as set out above.

4.46 By the persons referred to above as attending the meeting on 25 June 1997.

4.47 Redundancies were to be considered at all branches.

4.48 Mr Dennis and Mr Craig.

4.49 On 25 June 1997.

4.50 The complainant was consulted on 15 August 1997 and the chairman of the company was consulted on 25 June 1997.

4.51 All those consulted agreed that the Complainant could not perform his duties to the standard required by the Respondent, and that he had achieved a low score relating to sickness absence due to absences unrelated to his disability, such as back pain.

4.52 The Applicant achieved the lowest score at the Swindon branch after an overall consideration of his performance. The other detailed reasons are set out in the letter of dismissal sent to the Complainant on 30 August 1997.

4.53 The Respondent did not keep such records.

4.54 The Respondent employs three persons of whose disability it is currently aware in the supervisor post. Without identifying the individual it is not possible to state the exact nature of the person's disability. However one person suffers a mental disability (depression), another suffers from a musclo-skeletal disorder, and the third is partially sighted.

4.55 The Respondent refuses to answer this question on the basis that to do so would breach the·confidentially of the above persons by effectively identifying them.

4.56 One of the above was made redundant when the whole of his branch was closed.

4.57 Five.

4.58 The inspectors commenced as supervisory inspectors on the following dates: Pietro Salva (25.7.87), Cantona Francis (7.4.96), Franco Highbury (1.3.89), Mo Paul (5.4.90), Sampson Clerk (2.8.91)

4.59 None of the above is disabled to the knowledge of the Respondent.

4.60 Yes. Copy supplied.

*5 I have deleted (in whole or in part) the paragraph(s) numbered [as above] above, since I am unable/unwilling to reply to the relevant questions in the correspondingly numbered paragraphs(s) of the questionnaire for the following reasons
_____

(The reasons given at each number above).

_____(Signature of Respondent)
_____(Date)

Appendix 7

Notice of Appearance: Grounds of Resistance

1   It is denied that the Complainant was discriminated against or that he was unfairly dismissed or victimised.

2   Without prejudice to the above, the allegation of victimisation has been submitted outside the time limit for the presentation of a claim under the Disability Discrimination Act 1995.

3   The description of the duties of inspectors is broadly correct. Common duties include the inspection of steel girders before they are installed in a building, pipes as they are laid in the ground, and storage tanks. All of these jobs require the post holder to lift heavy objects.

4   The Complainant injured his left knee whilst at work on 12 December 1988 and suffered a minor loss of function of the left leg from this injury which did not affect his ability to carry out normal everyday activities as far as the managers of the Respondent were aware or could reasonably have been aware.

5   The Respondents could not have been reasonably aware that the Complainant was a disabled person within the meaning of the Disability Discrimination Act 1995 before the date of his second injury.

6   The Complainant avoided squat-bending or kneeling, and lifting heavy objects.

7   In July 1990, the Applicant became a full time employee of the Respondent, and became a senior inspector at the Swindon Branch in December 1990.

8   In addition to ensuring that inspections were performed accurately and timely, the supervisory inspector ('Senior Inspector') was responsible for attending all short-notice (emergency) field inspections. The senior supervisor performs such inspections as needed. The need for an inspection of this kind may arise at less than 24 hours' notice. It is essential to the nature of the job that the senior inspector be available for such inspections and be fit to perform all types of inspections. It is therefore irrelevant whether the majority of the inspector's time is spent ensuring the accuracy of other inspectors' work.

9   The supervisor is responsible for allocating work among the inspectors.

10 The Applicant was further injured at work on 23 July, 1995, when he broke his right leg and right ankle. For the avoidance of doubt it is not admitted that the injury was suffered while at work or that the Respondent has any responsibility for the injury which is the subject of a separate claim for damages by the Complainant.

11 The Complainant's return to health was monitored by the Respondent. The Respondent instructed independent occupational health advisers to advise them as to the Complainant's return to work, and with the Complainant's permission the Respondent sought advice from the Complainant's general practitioner. The Applicant was absent from work until December 1995.

12 The Complainant was absent from work from January 1996. It is denied that this absence was caused by the injury to his ankle either in part or at all. As a result of surgery to his right ankle the Complainant suffers from a physical impairment which is likely to last for more than 12 months. He was therefore from that point onwards a disabled person within the meaning of s 1 of the Disability Discrimination Act 1995.

13 The Respondent was informed by the Complainant's General Practitioner that he could return to work in September 1996, and offered part-time work to the Complainant at his request until December 1996.

14 It is denied that Frank Dennis appointed Michael Craig in order to reduce his workload. As at 5 February Mr Craig was an inspector with level II certification. He was appointed when it became apparent that the Complainant would be absent for some time, as acting supervisor.

15 Mr Craig was subsequently appointed to the Swindon senior supervisor position after obtaining full certification in early August. The appointment was on the basis of merit and the Complainant's disability played no part in Mr Craig's appointment.

16 The Complainant's General Practitioner in a letter of 28 July recommended that before the Complainant return to work a 'functional capacity evaluation' (FCE) should be carried out. However, the Respondent did not postpone the Complainant's return to work until the FCE and a job analysis could be completed. The FCE was completed in December 1996 and on 25 March 1997 the Respondent wrote to the Complainant stating that because of the restrictions noted in the FCE he would no longer be required to carry out field inspections.

17 In the light of the restrictions noted in the FCE, which were alleged to be permanent, the Complainant could not return to the senior position. This was because the person holding the post is required to lift heavy objects, squat and kneel. All of these the Complainant was said to be unable to perform. As a result of consultation with the experts who carried oiut the FCE, Holmes Personnel Evaluation, the Respondent then specially created a training instructor post for the Complainant. The Respondent consulted with the Complainant before offering the post to him. In order that the position should not be so costly as to be prohibitive a number of changes to the remuneration package and hours of work had to be made. However, these changes were steps of adjustment which in all the circumstances of the case it was reasonable for the Respondent to have to take.

18   A job description for the new post was prepared and presented to the Applicant for his consideration as part of the consultation process.

19   The Respondent, and in particular Mr Dennis, was not aware that on 20 April 1997 the Complainant had issued an originating application to the Industrial Tribunal complaining of the Respondent's alleged failure to make reasonable adjustments and requiring it to return him to the senior supervisor position. The originating application was sent first to the Respondent's personnel department and was not seen by Mr Dennis until September 1997. The Complainant was absent from work due to a further sickness from 15 May until 30 May 1997. The allegation of victimisation as alleged or at all is denied.

20   In accordance with matters discussed in consultation between Mr Dennis and the Complainant, Mr Craig had the duty to assign field inspections to the Complainant after Mr Craig had reviewed the physical requirements of any particular job. Mr Craig determined that the amount of heavy lifting, bending, squatting and walking on rough terrain required for the job was minimal.

21   The Complainant was absent through sickness, unrelated to his disability from 3 August 1997 to 30 August 1997.

22   On 17 August 1997, the Respondent announced that it was proposing to make redundancies at the Swindon Branch. The selection was by means of a skills matrix and among the criteria was one of attendance. The Applicant was selected for redundancy, and was the only person at the Swindon Branch so selected out of a total workforce of 30. The complainant was made redundant with effect from ——————.

23   The Respondent took all the steps that were reasonable in the circumstances for it to take to remove the substantial disadvantage suffered by the Complainant of not being able to carry out field inspections. However given the practical and financial constraints on the Respondent, including the losses made at the Swindon branch of the Respondents, no other steps were reasonable for the Respondent to have to take.

24   The Complainant at various times during the consultation preceding his dismissal made suggestions for adjustments which were either not practicable or were unreasonable, and the Respondent was under no duty to make such adjustments.

25   The Complainant was selected for redundancy having achieved the lowest marks in a skills matrix analysis of any person at the Swindon branch of the Respondent. He was not dismissed for a reason relating to his disability.

Appendix 8

County Court Pleadings

Goods and services, less favourable treatment, aggravated damages

Case No:_____

In the WESTERN COUNTY COURT

BETWEEN

<table>
<tr><td></td><td>JOHN BEDFORD</td><td>Plaintiff</td></tr>
<tr><td></td><td>and</td><td></td></tr>
<tr><td></td><td>(1) JOHN DOE
(2) TOP NOSH LTD</td><td>Defendants</td></tr>
</table>

PARTICULARS OF CLAIM

1 The plaintiff is a disabled person for the purposes of the Disability Discrimination Act 1995.

PARTICULARS

1.1 The plaintiff has had athetoid cerebral palsy since birth. He is unable to walk and uses a wheelchair. He has poor manual dexterity, is unable to lift, carry or move everyday objects and can talk only with the assistance of a voice synthesizer. He has epilepsy. As a result of his cerebral palsy and the medication taken to control his epilepsy, excess saliva sometimes escapes from the plaintiff's mouth.

1.2 The plaintiff was registered as disabled on the register maintained under s 6 of the Disabled Persons (Employment) Act 1944 on 12 January 1995 and on 2 December 1996 and is thereby deemed to be a disabled person.

2 The first defendant is employed by the second defendant to provide goods, facilities and services to the public at the second defendant's bistro known as the Large Lunch.

3   On 25 January 199   the first defendant in the course of his employment
    refused to serve the plaintiff in the bistro and ejected him from the premises for a
    reason related to the plaintiff's disability, contrary to s 19 of the Disability
    Discrimination Act 1995.

4   By reason of the unlawful discrimination, the plaintiff suffered loss and damage,
    including injury to his feelings.

PARTICULARS

4.1   The plaintiff intended to spend the evening at the bistro with his friends to
      celebrate his promotion at work. He was deprived of the opportunity to spend
      the evening at the place of his choosing. His evening was ruined.

4.2   The plaintiff made alternative arrangements and had a meal at the Pricey
      Pudding causing him to incur additional expense.

4.3   The plaintiff was humiliated and distressed by the fact and manner of his
      ejection from the bistro. The first defendant approached the plaintiff and his
      friends at the entrance to the bistro. He did not address the plaintiff but said to
      the plaintiff's friends in a loud voice 'You can't bring him in here dribbling
      like that. This is a quality place. He'd make everyone sick.'

PARTICULARS OF SPECIAL DAMAGES

Taxi fare from the bistro to the Pricey Pudding	£5
Extra costs of meal in the Pricey Pudding (est)	£40
Additional cost of taxi home	£5
Total	**£50**

5   The first defendant's actions were high-handed, malicious, insulting and were
    calculated to and did distress the plaintiff and the plaintiff is entitled to aggravated
    damages.

6   The plaintiff wrote to the second defendant by letter dated 26 January 199
    complaining about the first defendant's actions. The second defendant replied by
    letter dated 13 February 199   from its customer services officer saying that
    it could not comment on the incident but that the right of admission is reserved and
    that the first defendant is entitled to make whatever decisions are necessary for the
    good of the second defendant's customers.

7   The defendants threaten and intend unless restrained by this honourable court to
    continue to deny the plaintiff access to the bistro for a reason relating to his
    disability.

8   The plaintiff claims interest on such damages as may be awarded herein and at such
    rate and for such period as the Court thinks fit pursuant to s 69 of the County Courts
    Act 1984.

AND THE PLAINTIFF CLAIMS:

(1) An injunction restraining the defendants by themselves or by instructing or encouraging any other person from continuing to discriminate against the plaintiff for a reason relating to his disability by denying him access to the bistro known as the Large Lunch;
(2) Damages including aggravated damages;
(3) Interest.

AND THE PLAINTIFF STATES that his claim for damages is limited to £5,000.

DAVID DAVIS

DATED etc,

Goods and services, denying provision of services to the public, denying less favourable treatment

Case No:_____

In the WESTERN COUNTY COURT

BETWEEN

JOHN BEDFORD　　　　　　　　　　Plaintiff

and

(1) JOHN DOE　　　　　　　　　　Defendants
(2) TOP NOSH LTD

DEFENCE

---

1 Paragraph 1 of the Particulars of Claim is not admitted.

2 It is admitted that the first defendant is employed by the second defendant at the second defendant's premises known as the Large Lunch. It is denied that services are provided to the public. The Large Lunch is a private dining club open only to members and their guests. The plaintiff is not a member.

3 It is admitted that the first defendant in the course of his employment refused to serve the plaintiff in the bistro and ejected him from the premises on 25 January 199　　　. It is denied that the first defendant did so for a reason related to the plaintiff's disability. The plaintiff was ejected because he was not a member of the dining club and because the first defendant believed the plaintiff was drunk.

4 Paragraphs 4 and 5 of the Particulars of Claim are denied.

5 It is denied that the second defendant's letter contained any threat or disclosed any

intention to exclude the plaintiff from the bistro for a reason relating to any disability. Save as aforesaid, paragraph 6 of the Particulars of Claim is admitted.

6   Paragraph 7 of the Particulars of Claim is denied.

7   In the premises it is denied that the plaintiff is entitled to relief as sought or at all.

8   Further and alternatively it is averred that the plaintiff's claim for damages has no reasonable prospect of exceeding £3,000 and that the action should be referred to arbitration.

FRANCES TOMMO

DATES etc,

Alternative defence alleging justification

Case No:_____

In the WESTERN COUNTY COURT

BETWEEN

JOHN BEDFORD Plaintiff

and

(1) JOHN DOE Defendants
(2) TOP NOSH LTD

DEFENCE

1   Paragraphs 1 and 2 of the Particulars of Claim are admitted.

2   Paragraph 3 of the Particulars of Claim is admitted, save that it is averred that that treatment was justified.

PARTICULARS

2.1   The dining area of the bistro is reached either by lift or by three flights of narrow stairs. On 25 January 199   the lift had broken down and the only means of access to the dining area was by way of the stairs. The stairs were in constant use by other employees of the second defendant carrying hot food to the dining area from the kitchen.

2.2   The first defendant reasonably believed that it was necessary to refuse to serve the plaintiff to avoid a risk of injury to either the plaintiff or another person, namely:

A   the risk of the plaintiff sustaining injury whilst being carried up the stairs;

B the risk of injury to any person carrying the plaintiff up the stairs;

C the risk presented by the absence of any safe and suitable means by which the plaintiff could quickly leave the dining area in the event of a fire or other emergency.

3 Paragraphs 4 and 5 of the Particulars of Claim are denied.

4 It is denied that the second defendant's letter contained any threat or disclosed any intention to exclude the plaintiff from the bistro for a reason relating to any disability save where that exclusion was reasonably thought necessary in the interests of safety. Save as aforesaid, paragraph 6 of the Particulars of Claim is admitted.

5 Paragraph 7 of the Particulars of Claim is denied.

6 In the premises it is denied that the plaintiff is entitled to relief as sought or at all.

FRANCES TOMMO

DATED etc,

Premises, victimisation, aggravated damages

Case No:_____

In the CENTRAL COUNTY COURT

BETWEEN

<table>
<tr><td></td><td>EDWARD DRAKE</td><td>Plaintiff</td></tr>
<tr><td></td><td>and</td><td></td></tr>
<tr><td></td><td>(1) ROTTENHAM COUNCIL</td><td>Defendant</td></tr>
</table>

PARTICULARS OF CLAIM

1 The defendant is a local housing authority and is the landlord of a number of houses in Adams Street_____.

2 The plaintiff is and has been at all material times the defendant's tenant of premises at No 6, Adams Street, _____ pursuant to a written tenancy agreement between the parties dated 3 May 1993.

3 On 30 March 199   the plaintiff gave evidence on behalf of Charles George in proceedings (under case number _____ in the Central county court) brought by Charles George against the defendant under the Disability Discrimination Act 1995.

4   In May 199   the defendant by its servants or agents was carrying out a programme of improvements to the houses in Adams Street by installing central heating and double glazing.

5   The defendant did not install central heating or double glazing in No 6 Adams Street by reason that the plaintiff gave evidence as aforesaid and thereby unlawfully discriminated against him by victimising him, contrary to s 22(2) of the Disability Discrimination Act 1995.

6   As a result of the matters complained of the plaintiff suffered loss and damage.

PARTICULARS

The plaintiff was denied and continues to be denied the benefit of central heating and double glazing. The premises have continued to be cold, difficult and expensive to heat and noisy. The value of the plaintiff's occupation of the premises has thereby been reduced.

PARTICULARS OF SPECIAL DAMAGES

To extra costs of heating (@£X per week over Y weeks)   £XY

PARTICULARS OF DAMAGES SOUGHT IN LIEU OF AN INJUNCTION

To the cost of installing central heating and double glazing   £ZZ

7   The defendant's actions by its servants or agents were high-handed, malicious, insulting and oppressive and were calculated to distress the plaintiff and the plaintiff is entitled to aggravated damages.

PARTICULARS

7.1   On 15 May 199   the plaintiff asked the defendant's servant or agent and housing officer, Mr Smith, why works were not being carried out to No 6. Mr Smith said 'because we've got better things to do than spend our money on troublemakers. If you're cold, borrow a jumper off your friend Charlie'.

7.2   On 19 May 199   , and in the presence of five contractors carrying out works for the council, the plaintiff asked the defendant's servant or agent and estate officer Mr Miggins to ensure that works were carried out to No 6, Mr Miggins did not reply to the plaintiff but said to the contractors 'Make sure you wear gloves if you go anywhere near No 6. He's probably caught AIDS off his friend'.

7.3   By letter dated 20 May 199   the plaintiff wrote to the defendant's servant or agent and estate manager Mr Cockerall to complain about the failure to install central heating and double glazing to No 6 and about his treatment on 15 and 19 May. Mr Cockerall replied by letter dated 23 May and stated that he did not intend to waste his time or the defendant's money on people like the plaintiff.

8 The plaintiff claims interest on such damages as may be awarded herein and at such rate and for such period as the Court thinks fit pursuant to s 69 of the County Courts Act 1984.

AND THE PLAINTIFF CLAIMS:

(1) an injunction requiring the defendant to install central heating and double glazing to the premises at No 6 Adam Street; alternatively
(2) damages in lieu of an injunction under paragraph 6;
(3) damages, including aggravated damages;
(4) interest

AND THE PLAINTIFF STATES that his claim for damages is worth in excess of £5,000.

PAUL SEAMAN

DATED etc,

Index